ROMANS
and the
PEOPLE OF GOD

Gordon D. Fee

ROMANS
and the
PEOPLE OF GOD

Essays in Honor of Gordon D. Fee
on the Occasion of His 65th Birthday

Edited by

Sven K. Soderlund and N. T. Wright

William B. Eerdmans Publishing Company
Grand Rapids, Michigan / Cambridge, U.K.

255 Jefferson Ave. S.E., Grand Rapids, Michigan 49503 /
P.O. Box 163, Cambridge CB3 9PU U.K.

Printed in the United States of America

04 03 02 01 00 99 7 6 5 4 3 2 1

Library of Congress Cataloging-in-Publication Data

Romans and the people of God: essays in honor of Gordon D. Fee
on the occasion of his 65th birthday / edited by Sven Soderlund and N. T. Wright
p. cm.
Includes bibliographical references.
ISBN 0-8028-3861-8 (alk. paper)
1. Bible. N.T. Romans — Criticism, interpretation, etc.
I. Fee, Gordon D. II. Soderlund, Sven.
III. Wright, N. T. (Nicholas Thomas)
BS2665.2.R63 1999
227'.106 — dc21 99-15035
CIP

Contents

Gordon D. Fee: "Scholar on Fire"

It gives the editors, contributors, and publisher great joy to present this collection of essays to Dr. Gordon D. Fee on the occasion of his 65th birthday, May 23, 1999. For those of us who have had the privilege of knowing him, we are aware of having encountered a personality of unusual vitality and quality.

Raised as a "preacher's kid" in a Pentecostal (Assemblies of God) home in the northwestern states of Oregon and Washington, Gordon attended Seattle Pacific University, where he graduated with a B.A. in 1956 and an M.A. in 1958, both with majors in Biblical Literature. The goal of these studies, as well as four years of pastoral ministry, was to prepare him for missionary service overseas. When this door closed, another one opened up: a part-time faculty appointment at a denominational school that awakened Gordon's love for teaching. In his search for future direction, a letter to the editor of a magazine he was reading at the time crystalized the future for him. The correspondent complained of the magazine's heady intellectualism, adding that he would much prefer to be a "fool on fire" than a "scholar on ice." Gordon felt a divine prompting to pursue another alternative — namely, "a scholar on fire." With his vision clear and his resolve firm, Gordon entered a Ph.D. program at the University of Southern California and graduated in 1966, having submitted a thesis in the area of New Testament textual criticism under the supervision of Professor Eldon J. Epp. As it turned out, this research area would become one of his academic specialties.

In the years that followed, Gordon's name became synonymous with "scholarship on fire," not only a model for many in his own denomination but also an inspiration for generations of students from all backgrounds. Even when lecturing on textual criticism, it was rumored that Gordon engaged the subject with such passion that he could hold an altar call at the end! His competence in both teaching and writing eventually led him to academic appointments at Southern California College, Wheaton College, Gordon-Conwell Theological Seminary, and finally back to the west coast to Regent College in Vancouver, Canada, where for thirteen years he has served with dedication and affection, latterly not only as Professor of New Testament but also as Dean of the Faculty. His worldwide teaching/preaching ministry has taken him from the Philippines to Croatia, from India to Sweden, and many places in between. His writing and editorial work as catalogued in the "Select List of Publications" (pp. 304-11) speak for themselves.

For forty-two years Gordon's faithful companion has been his wife, Maudine, who has developed her own counseling and speaking ministry. They have four children — Mark, Cherith, Craig, and Brian — all married with children of their own. When the extended family meets on alternate years at the summer home on Galiano Island between Vancouver and Victoria, the numbers currently add up to twenty-two. Gordon and Maudine feel that they have their quiver full!

The present collection of essays has been compiled in honor of Gordon's work in New Testament scholarship as well as a contribution to a critical area of biblical research. Of late, a great deal of scholarly energy has been dedicated to the interpretation of Paul's letter to the Romans. While this is an area in which Gordon himself has not published extensively hitherto, it is nonetheless a subject in which he is keenly interested and teaches regularly. One day he plans to publish his own conclusions on the meaning of the text. When that time comes we hope that this collection of essays will help him — and many others — in the process of understanding both the rhetoric and meaning of the *magnum opus* of Paul's letters.

The contributors themselves come from a wide circle of Gordon's friends and colleagues. Several others would have liked to have participated but for one reason or another were unable. All of us, however — editors, contributors, friends from far and near — would like to wish Gordon a very blessed 65th birthday. We thank God for your life, Gordon, and pray that you will find a continual flow of energy and inspiration to complete the tasks that still await you, and that the new phase of life will be even more satisfying and productive than the first sixty-five!

In the production of this symposium special thanks are due to William B. Eerdmans, Jr., President of Eerdmans Publishing Co., for being an enthusiastic supporter of the *Festschrift* idea from the beginning, to Mr. Charles Van Hof, Managing Editor, for his faithful supervision of the entire project, and to Regent College students Jason Carroll, Poul Guttesen, and Paul Lee for their assistance in the task of bibliographic verification and other editorial detective work. The *Festschrift* editors are grateful to all these and others who volunteered their time and skills in helping to achieve this joyful celebration.

Sven K. Soderlund, *Vancouver, B.C., Canada*
N. T. Wright, *Lichfield, Staffordshire*

Contributors

Barbara Aland Director, Institut für Neutestamentliche Textforschung, Münster, Germany

James D. G. Dunn Lightfoot Professor of Divinity, University of Durham

Craig A. Evans Professor of Biblical Studies, Trinity Western University

R. T. France Rector of Wentnor, Shropshire, U.K.

Robert H. Gundry Kathleen Smith Professor of Religious Studies, Westmont College

Michael W. Holmes Professor of Biblical Studies and Early Christianity, Bethel College

Edith M. Humphrey Professor, Augustine College, Ottawa

L. W. Hurtado Professor of New Testament Language, Literature, and Theology, Director of the Centre for the Study of Christian Origins, University of Edinburgh

Richard N. Longenecker Distinguished Professor of New Testament, McMaster Divinity College, McMaster University, and Professor Emeritus of New Testament, Wycliffe College, University of Toronto

I. Howard Marshall Professor of New Testament Exegesis, University of Aberdeen

Ralph P. Martin Distinguished Scholar in Residence, Fuller Theological Seminary, Haggard Graduate School of Theology at Azusa Pacific University, and Logos Evangelical Seminary

J. Ramsey Michaels Professor Emeritus of Religious Studies, Southwest State University

J. I. Packer Board of Governors' Professor of Theology, Regent College

Eugene H. Peterson Emeritus Professor, Regent College

R. Paul Stevens Professor of Applied Theology, Regent College

Marianne Meye Thompson Professor of New Testament Interpretation, Fuller Theological Seminary

Philip H. Towner Translation Consultant, United Bible Societies; Adjunct Professor, Regent College

Rikki E. Watts Associate Professor of New Testament, Regent College

N. T. Wright Dean of Lichfield, Staffordshire, U.K.

EXEGETICAL ESSAYS

"For I Am Not Ashamed of the Gospel": Romans 1:16-17 and Habakkuk 2:4

Rikki E. Watts

I. Introduction

It is a special privilege to contribute to this celebration of Gordon Fee's work in the field of biblical studies. Not only did he introduce me to NT exegesis, but he also inspired me and many others with his passionate commitment to and love for Jesus the Christ whom Paul preached. Over recent years, Gordon has developed a growing interest in both Romans and the phenomenon of intertextuality. It is therefore with pleasure that I offer this essay on Paul's use of Habakkuk 2:4 in Romans 1:16-17.[1]

The problems associated with Romans 1:16-17 are as well known as they are numerous. Our concerns here, however, are only two: (i) Why, at the outset of his letter proper, should Paul declare "I am not ashamed of the gospel," and (ii) why does he appeal to Habakkuk 2:4? A wide variety of explanations have been offered for each, but as yet I know of no instance where these two items have been explicitly connected and their relationship explored.[2]

This essay will suggest, in the light of the larger concerns of both Habakkuk and Romans, that Paul's use of Habakkuk 2:4 goes beyond merely prooftexting his "justification by faith" thesis to the invocation of a larger para-

1. Unfortunately, space limitations preclude a consideration of Paul's other citation of this passage in Gal 3:11.

2. Richard B. Hays, *Echoes of Scripture in the Letters of Paul* (New Haven and London: Yale, 1989), 39-40, comes closest to recognizing this relationship but does not elaborate upon it.

digm and pattern. Paul, it will be argued, had every reason to be ashamed. His gospel, with its apparent displacement of Israel and her traditions in preference for wicked Gentiles, seemed to call God's righteousness into question. But this was not the first time God's mysterious actions required justification. Habakkuk 2:4 is part of Yahweh's response to an earlier question. Lamenting the Law's apparent failure to restrain wickedness, the prophet had appealed for Yahweh's righteous intervention only to face the scandalous prospect of his apparent injustice in seemingly favoring the wicked Chaldeans over his own people. It is thus in response to the question of theodicy that the issue of faith and faithfulness arises. Likewise reflecting on the ineffectiveness of the Law, Paul too is well aware of the problematic implications of his gospel. But as with Habakkuk, and as he outlines in his thesis statement (Rom 1:16-17), salvation is again to be found through faith in the faithfulness of the surprising and now eschatological revelation of righteous Yahweh's saving power.

II. Habakkuk: Themes and Issues

Habakkuk 2:4 is one of the more problematic texts in the OT. Not only are there substantial variations in the ancient versions, but the MT itself is perplexing.[3] Furthermore, in locating the passage in its wider context, a bevy of other difficulties emerge. However, to appreciate fully the potential of Habakkuk 2:4 for Paul in Romans, we will need to work fairly thoroughly through Habakkuk as a whole, noting in particular the various interpretative traditions that might have been available to him as witnessed to by the MT and the versions.

It is universally acknowledged that Habakkuk is wrestling with the problem of theodicy. The first "half" of the book, the pronouncement (or "burden," מַשָּׂא, 1:1–2:20), lays out the matter.[4] Whereas the opening complaint raises some initial concerns (1:2-4), it is Yahweh's surprising response (1:5-11)[5] that introduces the fundamental question of the justice of his deal-

3. See, e.g., the detailed discussions in W. H. Brownlee, "The Placarded Revelation of Habakkuk," *JBL* 82 (1963): 319-25; P. J. M. Southwell, "A Note on Habakkuk ii.4," *JTS* 19 (1968): 614-17; J. A. Emerton, "The Textual and Linguistic Problems of Habakkuk ii.4-5," *JTS* 28 (1977): 1-18. Of more recent commentators, K. Seybold, "Habakuk 2,4b und sein Kontext," in *Zur Aktualität das Alten Testaments: Festschrift für Georg Sauer zum 65. Geburtstag,* hrsg. Siegfried Kreuzer and Kurt Küthi (Frankfurt/New York: Peter Lang, 1992), 99-107, solves the problem by suggesting that 2:4 is the work of a later redactor.

4. See, e.g., Marvin A. Sweeney, "Structure, Genre, and Intent in the Book of Habakkuk," *VT* 41 (1991): 63-83.

5. Robert Haak, *Habakkuk,* VTSupp 44 (Leiden: E. J. Brill, 1992), 14, suggests that only vv. 5-6 are Yahweh's response, with vv. 7ff. being the prophet's own observations.

ings with his people. This occasions a second and longer complaint (1:12–2:1),[6] which leads to Yahweh's second response (2:2-4/5),[7] arguably the heart of this first section, and a concluding series of woes against the wicked (2:5/6-20). The second "half," the prayer (תְּפִלָּה, 3:1-19), is a Psalm-like meditation that celebrates Yahweh's sovereign faithfulness even in the midst of the mystery of his ways.

A. The First Complaint (1:1-4)

Habakkuk begins by lamenting Yahweh's silence in the face of injustice (1:2-3). Not only so, but given that Habakkuk's עַל־כֵּן formulations apparently indicate the climactic element of his complaints (e.g., 1:4, 17),[8] there is a noteworthy emphasis on the ineffectiveness of תּוֹרָה in restraining wickedness. Commentators have customarily understood תּוֹרָה to mean the Book of the Law found in Josiah's reign (2 Kgs 22), with the prophet's protest concerning either Yahweh's (cf. 1:2-3) or his appointees' failure to enforce its sanctions.[9] However, Marshall D. Johnson has argued convincingly that since תָּפוּג ("to be ineffective, weakened") is intransitive (Gen 45:26; Pss 38:9; 77:3),[10] it indicates not a problem with enforcement but instead, as J. Gerald Janzen puts it, "a weakness or failure inherent in the *tôrâ* itself."[11]

But what "weakness" is in view? For Johnson, the issue is the apparent failure of Torah's promises of blessing, in spite of Josiah's (presumably sufficient) reforms, as Judah continues to suffer under foreign domination (1:4). On the other hand, building on Joseph Jensen's proposal that תּוֹרָה in Isaiah means

6. 2:1 is spoken by Habakkuk and should probably not be included with Yahweh's second response, although many commentators do so since it also appears to function as an introduction to 2:2ff.

7. There is some debate as to the relationship between verses 4 and 5; see, e.g., Emerton, and James M. Scott, "A New Approach to Habakkuk II 4-5A," *VT* 35 (1985): 330-40.

8. Haak, *Habakkuk,* 14.

9. As found in, e.g., J. J. M. Roberts, *Nahum, Habakkuk, and Zephaniah,* OTL (Louisville: Westminster/John Knox, 1991), 90; cf. O. Palmer Robertson, *The Books of Nahum, Habakkuk, and Zephaniah,* NICOT (Grand Rapids: Eerdmans, 1990), 140; and Richard D. Patterson, *Nahum, Habakkuk, Zephaniah,* WEC (Chicago: Moody, 1991), 142. Unfortunately none of these works interacts with either Janzen or Johnson (see below).

10. "Habakkuk — Disillusioned Deuteronomist," presented at SBL, Dallas, 1980; see now "The Paralysis of Torah in Habakkuk I 4," *VT* 35 (1985): 257-66, esp. 259-61.

11. "Eschatological Symbol and Existence in Habakkuk," *CBQ* 44 (1982): 394-414, esp. 397; cf. *Tg.* "weakened," פגת; but 1QpHab 1:11, "is rejected." The LXX's διεσκέδασται ("to be scattered, dissipated") probably reflects uncertainty as to the Hebrew since it nowhere else in the LXX renders פוג; see further, Janzen, "Eschatological," 399, n. 8.

the prophet's teaching,[12] Janzen argues on the basis of putative wisdom elements in Habakkuk 2:2-4[13] that תּוֹרָה and its correlative מִשְׁפָּט (cf. Hos 6:5) should be understood in the Isaianic sense. The problem is thus the apparent ineffectiveness of the prophetic word Yahweh has given Habakkuk.

Although attractive, there are difficulties with both Johnson's and Janzen's proposals. Johnson maintains that 1:2-3 describes the absence of Torah's promised blessings, but he is unable to offer any hard evidence. Likewise, Janzen's argument, while possible, fails to demonstrate that the vision of 2:2ff is in fact identical to תּוֹרָה (1:4). Nor is it clear that the similarities with Isaianic language require that Habakkuk use תּוֹרָה to mean only his teaching. On the contrary, given that the "Book-of-the-Law" interpretation conforms to what Janzen himself recognizes as the "standard" use of תּוֹרָה (= Law),[14] it should be given the benefit of the doubt as the intended nuance here, not least in the light of the prominent association of תּוֹרָה and מִשְׁפָּט in Deuteronomy and the latter's apparent influence on Habakkuk (see below).[15] 1QpHab 1:10-11's בתורת אל (". . . the Law of God") also seems to support this view.[16]

The point to be noted is that Habakkuk's opening complaint is predicated on the apparent ineffectiveness of תּוֹרָה in restraining wickedness.[17] If this reading is correct, it suggests the surprising possibility that Habakkuk saw the Law as somehow unable to deal with evil; a possibility that might well have drawn Paul to this prophet since it resonated so well with his own concerns.

12. *The Use of tôrâ by Isaiah: His Debate with the Wisdom Tradition,* CBQMS 3 (Washington: Catholic Biblical Association of America, 1973). On the parallels between Isaiah and Habakkuk, Janzen, "Habakkuk 2:2-4 in the Light of Recent Philological Advances," *HTR* 73 (1980): 53-78; and Walter Dietrich, "Habakuk — ein Jesajaschüler," in *Nachdenken über Israel, Bibel, und Theologie: Festschrift für Klaus-Dieter Schunck zu seinem 65. Geburtstag* (Frankfurt: Peter Lang, 1994), 197-216.

13. Janzen, "Recent," 55-57.

14. Janzen, "Eschatological," 398, n. 6, agrees with Jensen that First Isaiah's use of תּוֹרָה to mean "teaching" is exceptional, but then argues that Second Isaiah and Habakkuk also follow this line.

15. As noted in Johnson, 265-66. Cf. also Haak, 33-34, who sees "law" as some form of legal code.

16. W. H. Brownlee, *The Midrash Pesher of Habakkuk,* SBLMS 24 (Missoula, Mont.: Scholars Press, 1979), 43-44. A second and related difficulty is the identity of "the wicked" (1:4), which depends to some extent on how one interprets "law"; see, e.g., the discussion in Johnson, 257-66, esp. 257-58, and the literature cited therein. On the reading taken here they are the wicked in Judah; see also the comparable use of form and language in Jer 12:1-4; 15:10; 20:7-8; so, e.g., Roberts, 88-90; cf. E. Otto, "Die Stellung der Wehe-Worte in der Verkündigung des Propheten Habakuk," *ZAW* 89 (1977): 73-107.

17. See also Walter E. Rast, "Habakkuk and Justification by Faith," *CurTM* 10 (1983): 169-75, esp. 171, n. 7; and Haak, *Habakkuk,* 34.

B. Yahweh's First Answer (1:5-11) and Habakkuk's Second Complaint (1:12-17[2:1])

But an even greater perplexity awaits. In contrast to the *Law's ineffectiveness,* and ironically taking up the very language of the prophet's earlier appeal, Yahweh replies by instructing the people to look and to gaze (1:5; cf. ראה and נבט in 1:3) at the wonder *he* is about to *effect,* which even if told they will not believe (לֹא תַאֲמִינוּ, the only cognate of which is found in 2:4b). He will indeed intervene, but it will be by raising up the Chaldeans, whom he plainly acknowledges are ruthless, impetuous, a law to themselves,[18] self-seeking, violent, derisive, guilty, and idolatrous; seemingly adding insult to injury by piling up adjectives.

Seeing that 1:2-4 is formally a lament, this response is astonishing.[19] Instead of the expected priestly *Heilsorakel* Habakkuk not only receives a pronouncement of judgment, but a scandalous one at that. Not surprisingly, it sparks a considerably longer complaint (1:12-17): as if it were not enough that the Law is impotent, what word of comfort is this that grants the Chaldeans a limitless ascendancy? Does not this "salvation" constitute an even greater injustice (v. 13; cf. v. 4c)?

C. Yahweh's Second Response (2:2-4[5])

This brings us, as is indicated in both the MT and LXX by the *Stichwörter* מִשְׁפָּט/κρίμα (1:4, 7, 12) and צַדִּיק/δίκαιος (1:4, 13; 2:4),[20] to what is widely held to be the essence of Habakkuk's message: his report of Yahweh's second response. Yahweh declines to answer the complaint directly but instead commands Habakkuk to inscribe "very clearly" (כְּתוֹב . . . בָּאֵר, 2:2) the vision upon "tablets."[21] This is noteworthy in several respects. Whereas other prophets write

18. V. 7, cf. v. 4's יֵצֵא . . . מִשְׁפָּט. Sweeney, 68, takes this to mean that the Babylonians are "the wicked" in 1:4. Against this, 1:5-11 suggests that their coming is yet future, and it misses the significance of the clash of forms generated by the unexpected content of the *Heilsorakel.*

19. Rast, 171; see also B. S. Childs, *Introduction to the Old Testament as Scripture* (Philadelphia: Fortress, 1979), 451.

20. Cf. J. G. Harris, "The Laments in Habakkuk's Prophecy," *EvQ* 45 (1973): 21-29, esp. 24-25.

21. There is considerable debate as to the literary limits of the vision, e.g., Roberts, 149, sees it as 3:1-19; Robertson, *Habakkuk,* 174, as 2:4-5; Sweeney, 64, apparently 1:2–2:20; while Brian Peckham, "The Vision of Habakkuk," *CBQ* 48 (1986): 617-36, includes 1:1-3a[a], 5-7a, 8-9a, 10, 12a, 13a; 2:1-3; 3:2-12, 15-19a.

on a "tablet" or "book" (Isa 8:1, 30:8; Jer 30:2), only Habakkuk has the plural (לֻחוֹת; the LXX, however, reads πυξίον, "tablet"), which elsewhere always refers to the Law (cf. *Tg.* "the book of the Law," ספרא דאוריתא).[22] Likewise, the only other occurrence of writing "very clearly" also refers to how the Law was to be inscribed (Deut 27:2-3, 8; cf. 1:5; and מְפֹרָשׁ in Neh 8:8). Finally, the conjoining of צַדִּיק, אֱמוּנָה, and חָיָה in 2:4 is also found in Deuteronomy 32[23] and especially Psalm 119, both of which have obvious Torah connections (perhaps further evidence that תּוֹרָה in 1:4 refers to Josiah's Book of the Law).

Consequently, it could be that Habakkuk's language reflects something of "the long-established pattern of inscribing a fresh copy of covenant law as an essential step in covenant renewal" (cf. Josh 8:32; 24:25-26).[24] Depending on what one understands as the content of the vision, that one rabbinic tradition saw in Habakkuk 2:4b's aphorism a summation of Torah's 613 commands might also support this interpretation (*b. Makk* 23b-24a). The point seems to be that Yahweh's action, no matter how disturbing, is not only consistent with but renews his covenantal commitment to his people. This is fitting in that at the very time when the Torah appears ineffectual and the covenant cast aside, Yahweh's response evokes images of their original bestowal; regardless of how mysterious his ways, he is faithful still. Interestingly, when Paul in Romans also wrestles with the question of Yahweh's apparent rejection of Israel, his discussion is likewise couched in the images of previous revelation and makes the same point (i.e., Rom 9–11).

Although verse 3 is difficult, the general thrust is that although there would be some delay the vision will surely come to pass.[25] Perhaps here we have another reason for the allusions to covenant renewal: the act of writing in the prescribed way serves to underline the vision's certainty given the likelihood of delay. In any case, as A. Strobel has shown, it was this delay that caught the attention of later Jewish exegetes; as a result this verse figured prominently in the

22. Three of the 37 occurrences refer to construction materials (Ex 27:8, 38:7; 1 Kgs 7:36).

23. Note the references to צוּר in 32: 4 (including יָשָׁר; cf. Hab 1:12, and also Patterson, 219, who notes the presence of three of 2:4's key terms — אֱמוּנָה, צַדִּיק, and יְשָׁרָה/יָשַׁר — in this verse), 20, 31; see also Deut 4.

24. O. Palmer Robertson, "'The Justified (by Faith) Shall Live by His Steadfast Trust' — Habakkuk 2:4," *Presb* 9 (1983): 52-57, esp. 55; cf. David T. Tsumura, "Hab. 2:2 in the Light of Akkadian Legal Practice," *ZAW* 94 (1982): 294-95.

25. Is the vision for *yet* (עוֹד; cf. LXX ἔτι; *Tg.* "ready," עתידא) an appointed time or, if יָפֵחַ is read as a noun "testifier" (cf. יפיח without ו in 1QpHab 7:6, see Brownlee, *Midrash*, 114), is it to be repointed and thus read as *witness* (עֵד) to an appointed time, D. Pardee, "*YPḤ* 'Witness' in Hebrew and Ugaritic," *VT* 28 (1978): 204-13; M. Dahood, *Psalms*, AB (Garden City, N.Y.: Doubleday, 1966), 1:169; S. E. Loewenstamm, "*Yāpîaḥ, yāpiaḥ, yāpēaḥ*," *Leš* 26 (1962-63): 205-8; and Haak, *Habakkuk*, 56?

debates concerning the coming of the messianic age (e.g., 1QpHab 7:7; *b. Sanh* 97b).[26] It is not surprising, then, that Paul might also interpret the adjoining verse 4 from an eschatological perspective (cf. Heb 10:37-38).

In this respect, the LXX is noteworthy in that although ὅρασις ("vision") is feminine, verse 3b continues ἐὰν ὑστερήσῃ ὑπόμεινον αὐτὸν ὅτι ἐρχόμενος ἥξει ("if he tarries, wait for him; he will surely come"), introducing a shift in gender to a masculine pronoun (αὐτόν) and participle (ἐρχόμενος). Citing Hebrews 10:37, these masculine forms are sometimes interpreted as indicating a new subject, the Messiah, with ἐρχόμενος being read as "(the) Coming One" (cf. Ps 117:26 LXX).[27] The suggestion is that Paul picks up on the LXX's messianic rendering.

But there are problems. First, the participle is in fact anarthrous. Second, assuming that 2:4 addresses the same subject as 2:3b, this reading gives rise to the odd notion that the coming deliverer might draw back (2:4a). T. W. Manson adroitly sidesteps the difficulty with some artful rephrasing, "Indeed, if he hangs back, that very fact will be the sign that he is not God's chosen."[28] But this is hardly what the text says. It is not the identity of the Messiah that is open to question; rather, his obedience. But how likely is it that the translator intended such a thing? Third, the appeal to Hebrews is questionable since its addition of the article (ὁ ἐρχόμενος) might be less the removal of "any possible ambiguity" from a messianism already inherent in the LXX[29] than a singularly distinctive application of the book's overriding hermeneutic, namely, that Jesus is the one who fulfills all of Israel's hopes, including Habakkuk's "vision."

26. *Untersuchungen zum eschatologischen Verzögerungsproblem auf Grund der spätjüdisch-urchristlichen Geschichte von Habakuk 2,2ff.*, NovTSupp 2 (Leiden: E. J. Brill, 1961), 8-78.

27. See, e.g., T. W. Manson, "The Argument from Prophecy," *JTS* (o/s) 46 (1945): 129-376, esp. 133-34; Strobel, 47-78, especially 53ff., noted approvingly by D.-A. Koch, "Der Text von Hab 2 4b in der Septuaginta und im Neuen Testament," *ZNTW* 76 (1985): 68-85, esp. 73, n. 25; and more recently championed by A. T. Hanson, *Studies in Paul's Technique and Theology* (London: SPCK, 1974), 42-45; Richard B. Hays, *The Faith of Jesus Christ,* SBLDS 56 (Chico, Calif.: Scholars Press, 1983), 151-54; "'The Righteous One' as Eschatological Deliverer: A Case Study in Paul's Apocalyptic Hermeneutics," in *Apocalyptic and the New Testament: Essays in Honor of J. Louis Martyn,* eds. Joel Marcus and Marion L. Soards, JSNTSupp 24 (Sheffield: JSOT, 1989), 191-215; Carl E. Armerding, "Obadiah, Nahum, Habakkuk," in *EBC,* vol. 7 (Grand Rapids: Zondervan, 1985), 512; cf. F. F. Bruce, *The Epistle to the Hebrews,* NICNT (Grand Rapids: Eerdmans, 1964), 272-74, who quotes Article 18 of the creed of Maimonides, "I believe with perfect faith in the coming of the Messiah, and though he tarry I will wait daily for his coming," and William L. Lane, *Hebrews 9–13,* WBC 47B (Dallas: Word, 1991), 304.

28. "Argument," 134; noted approvingly by Hays, "'Righteous One,'" 202.

29. So Hays, "'Righteous One,'" 202.

So what might the translator mean? Richard Patterson suggests that the LXX could have καιρός in view.[30] This is not as strained as might first appear, since strictly speaking the appointed time is also coming. There is, however, a more mundane possibility. Apparently, the LXX translators characteristically worked line by line, and when confronted with a difficulty resorted to a slavish literalism.[31] Faced with the puzzling Hebrew text of 2:2-3 and the gender incongruities necessarily introduced by the Greek equivalents into what was a consistently masculine Hebrew text, it is not unlikely that the translator, true to form, retreated to a self-contained (i.e., line-by-line) literalism. Thus in moving to the next line, he read לוֹ as masculine and followed suit with the remainder. Allowing the gender incongruities to stand, he apparently left it up to later readers to make of 2:3 what they could. In other words, the entire messianic interpretation is probably based on a mere accident of grammatical gender.[32] In any case, lavish claims that the LXX at 2:3b-4 is of itself "through and through Messianic"[33] are hardly warranted. This is significant since in terms of Paul's reading it at least indicates that the LXX does not require him to interpret 2:3b, and therefore ὁ δίκαιος in 2:4b, messianically (see further below).

This brings us to perhaps the book's most important and most difficult verse, which we will treat in two parts. The major problems in 2:4a are the meaning of עֻפְּלָה, the referents of the third person pronominal suffixes, and what is considered to be the formal imbalance created by the absence of any statement concerning the wicked to parallel the destiny of the righteous in 2:4b.

There is no consensus on the rare form, עֻפְּלָה, and the diversity in the ancient versions suggests that they too were uncertain.[34] However, since its

30. *Habakkuk,* 175. He also notes that gender incongruities between masculine pronouns and participles and their antecedents are not unknown in Greek (e.g., J. H. Moulton, W. F. Howard, and N. Turner, *A Grammar of New Testament Greek,* vol. 3 [Edinburgh: T. & T. Clark, 1963], 312). This might be the case here, especially if the translator has in view the preceding partially synonymous nouns *en toto* (e.g., ὅρασις, καιρός, and αὐτά).

31. I am indebted to Dr. Geoff Jenkins for these and the following observations.

32. As Hays, *Faith,* 152, almost admits. If for later interpreters, the vision, presumably including the restoration of Israel, had not yet been fulfilled (see Rikki E. Watts, *Isaiah's New Exodus and Mark,* WUNT II:88 (Tübingen: Mohr Siebeck, 1997), 73 n. 111, 82ff.), and if its fulfillment was associated with the Messiah, then a subsequent messianic reading of Hab 2:3 would be understandable; see, e.g., the data given in Strobel, 7-78, 192-94.

33. So Manson, "Argument," 134. Ironically, whereas Heb 10:37 is often used to corroborate this reading, the very next verse, 10:38, does not take 2:4 messianically.

34. For details see the excellent surveys in Southwell; Koch, 70; and also J. A. Fitzmyer, "Habakkuk 2:3-4 and the New Testament," in *To Advance the Gospel: New Testament Studies* (New York: Crossroad, 1981), 236-46, esp. 239-41.

interpretation bears on the meaning of אֱמוּנָה in 2:4b, some discussion is necessary. No solution is without problems,[35] but correcting a poetic text on the basis of "expected" forms or balanced phrasing seems precarious.[36] The construction might be unique and even odd, but then it is poetry; provided the sense is tolerable the text should be retained.[37] This being so, עֻפְּלָה appears to mean "to be swollen, puffed up,"[38] and hence anticipates the "greedy one" of verses 5ff. (cf. 1:6-11, 13),[39] with its feminine form agreeing with נֶפֶשׁ. נֶפֶשׁ can mean "desire" or "appetite" (see v. 5, "his desire is [swollen] like Sheol"; cf. Isa 5:14), which would again be consonant with the "greedy one," while יָשַׁר, perhaps taken as "flat, level," would be an antonym of "puffed up."[40] If so, then we read something like "it is bloated, his appetite is not smooth in him."[41] True, the subject of the suffixes needs to be understood from the context, but this is hardly insurmountable. Consequently, 2:4 appears to be an inverted hinge, A-b′-a′-B, where 2:4a (b′) anticipates the fate of the arrogant in 2:5ff. (B) while 2:4b (a′) — and this is the important point — looks back to the vision of 2:2-3 (A).[42]

Before going on to 2:4b, however, there is the problem of the LXX's translation, namely, ὑποστείληται ("to draw back"; cf. Aquila, νωχελευομένου, "to be

35. Some of the many proposals include (a) reading it as a pual ("to swell," cf. Num 14:44), which anticipates 2:5ff. and so points to the arrogant and deceptive man described therein, (b) emending it to various masculine forms (e.g., עַפָּל or עֻפָּל) either in order to balance "the righteous" in 2:4b and/or in the light of the masculine pronominal suffixes on נַפְשׁוֹ and בּוֹ, (c) redividing the consonants (אַף לֹה) again due to the suffixes, (d) reconstructing a supposedly corrupt text to עלף, יעף, or עיף indicating weariness or failure to wait and thus picking up on the sense of 2:3b, or (e) suggesting another similar root on the basis of one of the ancient versions. See, e.g., Emerton, 11-12, who also has a helpful summary of earlier discussions; Janzen, "Recent," 63-68; Roberts, 106; Patterson, 215-16; David T. Tsumura, "An Exegetical Consideration on Hab 2:4a," *Tojō* 15 (1985): 1-26 [OTA, 1986, #578], and the suggestion of Scott, 331-35, which although creative entails too many hypotheticals.

36. 1QpHab's עופלה, reflecting a predilection for *plene* forms, confirms the MT.

37. On the need for a more nuanced understanding of poetic features, particularly in Habakkuk, see, e.g., Haak, "'Poetry' in Habakkuk 1:1–2:4?," *JAOS* 108 (1988): 437-44.

38. Cf. the pun in 1QpHab 7:16, יכפלו, "to be doubled upon"; L. H. Silberman, "Unriddling the Riddle: A Study in the Structure and Language of the Habakkuk Pesher," *RQ* III:11 (1961): 347.

39. Cf. Sweeney, 75-76.

40. Cf. L. Alonso-Schökel, "יָשַׁר," *TDOT* VI:465-67.

41. Alonso-Schökel, 470-71, comes to a similar conclusion, paraphrasing the basic idea "A swollen appetite is not normal [obvious], is not right [ethical judgment], is doomed to failure [result]," as does Haak, *Habakkuk*, 57-59.

42. On inverted hinge structures, see, e.g., H. Parunak, "Transitional Techniques in the Bible," *JBL* 102 (1983): 525-48.

slothful"[43]). At first sight it appears to continue from 2:3, but this results in the contradictory situation of being assured that the coming vision will not tarry and yet there being the possibility that it might draw back. More likely is that ὑποστείληται picks up 2:2b where the right response to the vision is action (διώκῃ, "to hasten, press forward"). Thus we should probably supply "anyone" ("if anyone draws back"; cf. Vulgate's "qui"), and so verse 4a stands in contrast to 4b (the LXX's first person possessive, ἡ ψυχή μου, apparently confuses ו with י). The result is a subtle shift. We are no longer concerned with the "wicked" oppressor but with the one who refuses to trust the vision (Vulgate "qui incredulus est"). Likewise, the *Targum*'s רשיעיא ("the wicked") are those who "think all these things are not so."[44]

The basic difference between these readings is that the MT addresses the arrogance and greed of the Chaldean oppressor so as to introduce the following woes (cf. 1QpHab 7:16-17's denunciation of the wicked), the issue being that Yahweh, having dealt with the wicked in Judah, will eventually deal with the Chaldeans. Verse 4b then provides an encouraging counterpoint. The versions, on the other hand, in their various ways construe 2:4a in more direct contrast to 2:4b, rendering it in terms of one who does not believe (or "draws back" etc.). This places greater weight on 2:4b and has the effect of confronting the reader with the call to believe, something not quite so evident in the MT.

We have spent some time here, but it is worth noting briefly that both of these emphases are present in Romans. Paul too is concerned with the importance of faith (cf. LXX). But at the same time, immediately following his thesis statement, he announces that God's wrath is being revealed against the wicked, both Jew and Gentile (cf. MT).

The second half of the verse is, of course, the part that Paul cites. And once again there are difficulties: What is meant by אֱמוּנָתוֹ, and who or what is the antecedent of its possessive suffix? For אֱמוּנָה, the options are the faith (active) of the righteous person,[45] or the more usual sense of the faithfulness (passive)[46] of ei-

43. 8HevXIIgr reads σκοτία (אֹפֶל), apparently confusing ע and א.

44. Perhaps reflecting a similar understanding of the cognate verb עפל (cf. MT's עפלה) as found in *Tg. Onqelos*'s "to act wickedly" (Num 14:44) and/or simply picking up on 1:4. Kevin J. Cathart and Robert P. Gordon, *The Targum to the Minor Prophets*, ArB 14 (Wilmington, Del.: Michael Glazier, 1989), 151, n. 17.

45. See, e.g., C. F. Keil, *Minor Prophets*, vol. 10 of *Commentary on the Old Testament in Ten Volumes*, by C. F. Keil and F. Delitzsch (Grand Rapids: Eerdmans, 1954), 273; Rast, 173, in the sense of a "steadfast" faith, as also Robertson, "Justified," 60; and Paul Trudinger, "Two Ambiguities in Habakkuk's 'Unambiguous' Oracle," *DownRev* 113 (1995): 282-83.

46. The general sense of the word, though J. Barr, *The Semantics of Biblical Language* (London: Oxford, 1961), 201, 173, n. 1, suggests that "faith" might also be implied in Hab 2:4b.

ther the righteous person[47] or the vision.[48] The suffix is then understood accordingly as "his" or "its." Since the topic at hand is the trustworthiness of the vision (2:2-3), it would seem strange suddenly to shift to either the faith or faithfulness of the righteous. Although one might argue that because 2:4a shifts to the character of the greedy oppressor so 2:4b concerns the character and hence the faith or faithfulness of the righteous, taking 2:4 as an inverted hinge (as noted above) suggests otherwise.

Further, אֱמוּנָה appears to echo 1:5 (תַּאֲמִינוּ). There it was Yahweh's shocking word which if it were told "you would not be able to believe" or, as Wildberger has it, "you would not be able to stand fast" or "you would lose all confidence" (cf. Isa 7:9).[49] Here in 2:4b it is again Yahweh's word, but this time his trustworthy response, which enables the righteous to stand firm and so find life (cf. לֹא נָמוּת, 1:12?; cf. 3:16-19). In view of Genesis 15:6, which shares several key terms with our passage, and if we can assume that the righteous person is by definition one who trusts, then the issue is not his faithfulness or life-giving faith, which would border on being tautologous, but instead and in the usual sense of אֱמוּנָה the trustworthiness of the newly revealed vision.

Having said this, however, a strictly dichotomistic approach is probably mistaken. Undoubtedly the faithfulness of the perplexing vision is affirmed, but surely in order to encourage the righteous to commit themselves to it.[50] The ambiguity here might well be intentional[51] — hardly surprising for poetry — in that it is difficult to think of a better way of putting things if one wanted succinctly and memorably to encapsulate this interrelationship.

The LXX's ὁ δὲ δίκαιος ἐκ πίστεώς μου ζήσεται, if not testifying to an alternative *Vorlage*, seems again to confuse the suffixal ו with י, at least in the majority of MSS (א, B, Q, W*).[52] At the outset, the weakness of the putative messianic reading of 2:3b makes it doubtful that ὁ δίκαιος was intended as a messianic title.[53] In terms of the pronoun, as it is Yahweh who stands behind the integrity of

47. Not in the sense of personal integrity but in relation to the truth (אֱמֶת), e.g., George J. Zemek, Jr., "Interpretive Challenges Relating to Habakkuk 2:4b," *GTJ* 1 (1980): 43-69, esp. 68, who also sees something of the faith of the righteous individual; Scott, 337, but reading the trustworthiness of the *nation;* Sweeney, 76; and Patterson, 221, though the latter appears to see this as implying faith, 177-78.

48. E.g., Janzen, "Recent," 70-71; Ralph L. Smith, *Micah-Malachi,* WBC 32 (Waco, Tex.: Word, 1984), 107; Roberts, 107, 111, but also ultimately of God's faithfulness; and Haak, *Habakkuk,* 59.

49. Cited in A. Jepsen, "אָמַן," *TDOT* I:302-3.

50. Cf. C. F. Keil's still pertinent comments, 2:73-74.

51. So also Haak, *Habakkuk,* 59; Trudinger, 283.

52. Again see the thorough tabulation in Koch and also Fitzmyer, "Habakkuk."

53. On the later use of ὁ δίκαιος as a title, see below.

the vision (just as the prophet earlier appeals to Yahweh over the ineffectiveness of the Law, 1:2-4), μου is not quite so at odds with the MT as might first appear. After all, it is Yahweh's faithfulness that ultimately ensures the reliability of the vision. *A* and group *C*, reading ὁ δὲ δίκαιος μου ἐκ πίστεως ζήσεται (cf. Heb 10:38), if not merely an accidental transposition, stress the close relationship between Yahweh and the righteous one (cf. Gen 15:6).[54] Although the Greek Minor Prophets scroll, 8HevXIIgr, and Aquila resemble more closely the MT with their anarthrous δίκαιος ἐν πίστει αὐτοῦ ζήσεται, in context they appear to have the faithfulness of the righteous in mind, although the antecedent of αὐτοῦ could conceivably be the vision of 2:3.[55] Symmachus's ὁ δίκαιος τῇ ἑαυτοῦ πίστει ζήσεται ("by his own faith") removes any ambiguity.[56]

This verse is missing from 1QpHab, but the interpretation offered also has in view the faithfulness of the righteous, that is, those who observe the Law by being loyal to the Teacher of Righteousness (8:1-3; cf. 4:11; 7:12, 13). The *Targum,* on the other hand, speaks of the "truth of these things" written in the Law.[57]

What can be said of these variations? The MT, the majority of LXX MSS, and probably the *Targum* have the trustworthiness of either the vision (MT, *Tg.* = "the Law") or the God who stands behind it (majority of LXX MSS) as their locus. The other Greek versions and 1QpHab in various ways emphasize the faithfulness of the righteous. Without minimizing the differences, there is a sense in which all these variations comport with Habakkuk as a whole. The certainty of the vision, undergirded by Yahweh's own faithfulness, is clearly vital. But unless the message is believed there will be no conviction for the righteous to be faithful in the midst of bewildering times which look anything but just. In this respect, the other Greek versions and 1QpHab, far from excluding the trustworthiness of the vision, assume it. Again, as we shall see, both perspectives resonate with Paul's concerns in Romans and might have informed his own, unique rendering. Finally, it should be noted that although the delay mentioned in 2:3 was related by later interpreters to the last days, there is very little to suggest that 2:4, even with the LXX's ὁ δίκαιος, played a role in messianic speculation.[58]

54. Cf. Fitzmyer, "Habakkuk," 240.

55. On the question of lack of agreement in gender, see n. 30 above.

56. Koch, 70, also lists the variant ὁ δὲ δίκαιος ἐκ πίστεώς ζήσεται, citing 763* and a few texts (cf. Rom 1:17 and Gal 3:11), but this looks like an assimilation to Paul.

57. Manson, 133, takes קושטהון to mean the uprightness of the righteous, but the suffix seems instead to refer back to כל אלין in 2:4a which goes back to the prophecy written in the book of the Law in 2:2; see also Cathart and Gordon, 151, n. 18.

58. See, e.g., the meager and to my mind unconvincing data in Strobel, 192-94, and the discussion in Schrenk, "δίκαιος," *TDNT* II:186-87, where Hab 2:4 is not listed among the

D. The Final Prayer (3:1-19)

Habakkuk concludes with his response to Yahweh's answer (cf. 2:1d). In contrast to the previous two complaints, he offers a prayer recalling Yahweh's awesome deeds (3:1-19). It is universally agreed that the prayer is replete with imagery recalling Israel's epic past, notably the Exodus and Conquest, and for F. M. Cross belongs in the same category as the "Blessing of Moses" in Deuteronomy 33[59] (further indicating, perhaps, that the referent of תּוֹרָה in 1:4 and 2:2-3 is the Deuteronomic Law). At the same time, since both תְּפִלָּה ("prayer") and שִׁגְיֹנוֹת ("Shiggaion") have lament connotations (cf., e.g., Pss 17:7; 56:1; 90:1; etc.; and Ps 7:1),[60] their use here is apt given not only the preceding materials but also the recognition that hard times are yet to be endured (Hab 3:16-18).

However, just as Habakkuk earlier offered a *Heilsorakel* of judgment, in yet another surprising turnabout this "lament" becomes something of a victory song (cf. Ex 15:1-18; Judg 5; Deut 33:2-5, 26-29; and Ps 68).[61] Having been convinced of Yahweh's justice and wisdom, even in the face of circumstances apparently to the contrary, he concludes with confident praise: "I will rejoice in God my Savior (יִשְׁעִי/σωτῆρί μου); the Sovereign Lord is my strength (חֵילִי/δύναμίς μου)" (3:18b-19a; cf. LXX Pss 20:2; 117:15; 139:8; Jer 3:23) — language, as we shall see, not dissimilar to that in Paul's thesis statement (Rom 1:16-17).

To recapitulate: Habakkuk's primary concern is with theodicy. If he at first complains about Yahweh's silence, particularly in the face of the apparent inability of Torah to restrain wickedness, then his second and longer complaint rises ironically from Yahweh's utterly perplexing answer: granted that wicked Judah deserves judgment, how can Yahweh favor the supremely wicked Chaldeans over his own people? Yahweh's response is to assure the prophet that this vision is entirely in keeping with his Torah-covenant — hence the allusions to Deuteronomy. The outcomes are three. First, even though the vision might delay, it will come. Second, Habakkuk need not worry since Yahweh's judgment of the wicked (cf. 1:2-4) will also eventually extend to the Chaldean oppressor

---

texts "specifically related to the righteous Messiah," but instead is used in discussions concerning the heart of the Law; see further Str-B, I:651, 907; III:199-200, 542-44; and D. Moody Smith, "ΗΟ ΔΕ ΔΙΚΑΙΟΣ ΕΚ ΠΙΣΤΕΩΣ ΖΗΣΕΤΑΙ," in *Studies in the History and Text of the New Testament in Honor of K. W. Clark*, ed. B. L. Daniels and M. J. Suggs (Salt Lake City: University of Utah, 1967), 13-15.

59. *Canaanite Myth and Hebrew Epic: Essays in the History of the Religion of Israel* (Cambridge, Mass.: Harvard, 1973), 70-71, 99-105, cited in Johnson, 263-64, who notes further parallels.

60. Sweeney, 78.

61. Theodore Hiebert, *God of My Victory*, HSM 38 (Atlanta: Scholars Press, 1986), 118-24.

(2:5ff.). Third, the righteous will not be abandoned (2:4b). They will find life through the faithfulness of Yahweh's word (MT, LXX most MSS, *Tg.*), assuming of course they remain faithful to it (some LXX MSS, 8HevXIIgr, Aquila, Symmachus, cf. 1QpHab). Hence the final prayer of praise. As Walter Rast says, "In the end what Habakkuk was coming to grips with was the often inscrutable ways of God's workings."[62]

III. Habakkuk 2:4 in Romans 1:17

It is generally agreed that Romans 1:16-17 outlines the thesis of the letter[63] and that Habakkuk 2:4b, at least as Paul quotes it, is particularly appropriate since it provides the requisite scriptural justification for what is commonly held to be his central concern, namely, justification by faith.[64] It has also been maintained that Habakkuk 2:4 had contemporary messianic connotations and that these too are in view (cf. 1:3).[65] But, as argued earlier, the evidence for a messianic reading is quite thin. Granted, this does not preclude a Pauline innovation — Richard Hays declares that the LXX form "would have appeared to Paul as unmistakably messianic."[66] But it must be remembered that whereas ὁ δίκαιος can be a messianic title (e.g., *1 Enoch* 38:2, 3; 39:6 [noting Hab 2:4]; cf. 53:6) and is sometimes applied to Jesus (e.g., Acts 3:13-15; 7:51-53; 1 Pet 3:18), it is the context that signals the messianic connection. The lack of contextual indicators in Romans 1:17 (1:3 notwithstanding) makes it unlikely that ὁ δίκαιος is messianic,[67] and that Paul no-

62. Rast, 175.

63. Opinions vary as to how this might be so. See the discussions and literature cited in Glenn D. Davies, *Faith and Obedience in Romans,* JSNTSupp 39 (Sheffield: JSOT, 1990), 40-46, and Douglas Moo, *The Epistle to the Romans,* NICNT (Grand Rapids: Eerdmans, 1996), 64-65. This naturally raises the much larger question of the purpose of Romans, which is impossible to treat here.

64. For A. Feuillet, "La citation d'Habaccuc II.4 et les huit premiers chapitres de l'Epître aux Romains," *NTS* 6 (1959-60): 52-80, Hab 2:4 even provides the key to the literary structure of Rom 1–8; cf. A. Nygren, *Commentary on Romans* (London: SCM, 1952), 82-83; and D.-A. Koch, *Die Schrift als Zeuge des Evangeliums,* BZHT 69 (Tübingen: Mohr Siebeck, 1986), 275-77. Surprisingly, the latter work does not even consider the Habakkuk context.

65. See earlier, e.g., C. H. Dodd, *According to the Scriptures* (London: Nisbet, 1952), 51; E. Earle Ellis, *Paul's Use of the Old Testament* (Edinburgh/London: Oliver and Boyd, 1957), 121; Strobel, 173-202; Hanson, 42-45; and more recently Hays, *Jesus,* "'Righteous One'"; and Douglas Campbell, "Romans 1:17 — A *Crux Interpretum* for the ΠΙΣΤΙΣ ΧΡΙΣΤΟΥ Debate," *JBL* 113 (1994): 265-85, esp. 281-85.

66. *Jesus,* 151.

67. In spite of Dodd's hopeful suggestion that Hab 2:4 was already a *testimonium* to the coming of Christ (*According to the Scriptures,* 51), for which as yet there is no evidence.

where else uses it in this way only increases the odds against its being so intended here. Significantly, in the one NT passage where part of Habakkuk 2:3-4 is interpreted messianically (Heb 10:37-38), it is "the coming one" who is so understood, not ὁ δίκαιος, who is instead simply the person who has faith in the interim. Add to this that Jesus' messianic status does not appear to be of major concern in Romans, and it looks very much as if Paul's choice of Habakkuk is motivated by other reasons.

Although Paul gives no explicit indication that he has in view Habakkuk's opening complaint about the Law's ineffectiveness, it is noteworthy that he is especially concerned with this issue.[68] True, the emphasis is different — Habakkuk laments the weakness of the Law to restrain sin, while Paul focuses more on human inability to keep the Law — but Paul nevertheless makes it clear that the Law cannot solve the problem of wickedness. Much of his argument proceeds on precisely this premise. Granted the wickedness of pagan idolaters (1:18-32), Paul spends considerably more time arguing that the Jew is no better off, in spite of having Torah (2:1–3:20). All are under God's righteous judgment (1:18; 3:9). Not only so, but he concludes his first section by declaring that "no one will be acknowledged righteous through the works of the Law" (3:20; cf. 6:14). It is intriguing that just as Habakkuk, on my reading of the all-important 2:4 and **עֻפְּלָה**, contrasts the puffed up and arrogant Chaldean (2:4a), who steals and is an idolater, with the righteous (2:4b), so too Paul is concerned to undercut those who "boast" in the Law (Rom 2:1-3, 5, 12-16, 17-24; 3:19, 27) and yet steal and rob temples (2:17-24), which "boasting" is excluded by the law of faith (3:27) that leads to righteousness.[69]

The extended discourse in 7:5–8:4, in which Paul sums up his perspective on the Law, goes even further: not only is the Law unable to restrain sin but because of sin brings death (cf. 5:20; 4:15). Throughout this section, although again and again affirming the Law as good, holy, and spiritual (7:7, 10a, 12, 13, 14, 16, 22), he presses home its inability to deal with sin (7:10b, 11, 14-24), concluding finally on a note of pathos, "How wretched I am! Who will deliver me from this body of sin?" (7:24). This sounds surprisingly close to Habakkuk's first lament where, distressed at the ineffectiveness of the Law (1:3b-4), he too cries out for help (1:2-3b).

But whereas Habakkuk complained of Yahweh's silence, Paul argues that

68. It is doubtful that the rabbinic traditions in *b. Makk* 23b-24a are in mind since its formulation might well have been in response to the Christian use of this text; see Str-B III: 543-44, and John T. Townsend, "How Can Late Rabbinic Texts Inform Biblical and Early Christian Studies?," *Shofar* 6 (1987): 26-30, esp. 29-30.

69. Cf. Jan Lambrecht, "Why Is Boasting Excluded? A Note on Rom 3,27 and 4,2," *ETL* 61 (1985): 365-69.

God has now acted. Echoing his thesis statement, "For, in it [the gospel] the righteousness of God has been revealed," Paul triumphantly declares in 8:3, "For what the Law was ineffective to do through the weakness of human nature, God did by sending his own Son." And herein lies the rub. As R. M. Moody and Richard Hays have observed,[70] Paul's "revelation" concerning God's intervention clearly raises the problem of theodicy, just as did Habakkuk's vision in his day. In both cases, God's covenantally faithful action seems tantamount to the rejection of his people in favor of even more wicked Gentiles. Given, as Hays has noted, the eschatological overtones of Paul's language in 1:16-17 (see the various collocations of σωτήριον, ἐθνῶν, ἀπεκάλυψεν, and δικαιοσύνην in (e.g.) LXX Ps 97:2-3; Isa 51:4-5; and 52:10)[71] and particularly their implications for the Gentiles, the dilemma can only be heightened. The question must inevitably arise: Has the word of God fallen (9:1-5; cf. 3:1-4)?

This tension becomes even more clear when one recalls that introductory thematic statements in literary antiquity were intended to provide a brief sketch of the work's major themes.[72] If Habakkuk 2:4b is interpreted solely in terms of "instrumental means" whereby the righteous live by their faith or God's faithfulness, or, having been made righteous by faith, find life,[73] this tends to marginalize Romans 9–11. But when one analyzes the distribution of the language of 1:16-17 throughout the major sections, 1:1–3:20, 3:21–5:21, 6:1–8:39, 9:1–11:36, and 12:1–15:13, even granted the crude nature of the method, we find that the only chapters in which nearly all of the key word groups are present are 9–11.[74] On the reading of Habakkuk proposed here, Romans 9–11 falls into place, neither as postscript nor as center, but vital nevertheless.[75] Having argued consistently for (a) the ineffectiveness of the Law both

70. Respectively, "The Habakkuk Quotation in Romans 1:17," *ExpT* 92 (1981): 205-8, esp. 208; and "'Righteous One,'" 207, with *Echoes*, 39-41.

71. *Echoes*, 36-37.

72. See, e.g., D. Earl, "Prologue-form in Ancient Historiography," in *ANRW* I:22, 842-56.

73. On this question, e.g., Feuillet, "La citation," 52-80; H. C. C. Cavallin, "'The Righteous Shall Live by Faith': A Decisive Argument for the Traditional Interpretation," *ST* 32 (1978): 33-43; Campbell, "Debate," 279-81; and Brian Dodd, "Romans 1:17 — A *Crux Interpretum* for the ΠΙΣΤΙΣ ΧΡΙΣΤΟΥ Debate," *JBL* 114 (1995): 470-73.

74. The data are far too extensive to document here but are based on the various cognate forms of εὐαγγέλιον, δύναμις, σωτηρία, πιστεύω, Ἰουδαῖος, Ἕλλην, δικαιοσύνη, and ζάω, all of which are represented in chs. 9–11. Although neither ἀποκαλύπτω nor its nominal cognate appears in 9–11 (but see 1:18; 2:5; 8:18, 19; and 16:25), the clearly related term μυστήριον (κατὰ ἀποκάλυψιν μυστηρίου, 16:25) is found in 11:25, which introduces Paul's crucial explanation of the problem's resolution.

75. On the importance of Rom 9–11, if perhaps sometimes overstated, see, e.g., F. C. Baur, *Paul, the Apostle of Jesus Christ: His Life and Work, His Epistles and His Doctrine*, trans.

at the beginning (2:1–3:20) and the end (7:5–8:4) of the first eight chapters and (b) the priority of faith in this new era (3:21–4:25), Paul finally addresses the theodicy question in chapters 9–11; an issue which had been on the agenda since 3:1-4.[76] No matter how it looks, Paul reasons, God is still faithful to his word, and, as in Habakkuk, life is to be found on the basis of faith (cf. 11:30-32). One notes here in passing that if, as we have suggested, Habakkuk alludes to the foundational giving of the Law (2:2) to underscore that his vision affirms God's covenant faithfulness, then Paul even more so links his gospel with earlier revelation.[77] No other chapters in Paul come close to the density of scriptural citations found in Romans 9–11.[78] Both prophet and apostle endeavor to show that Yahweh's strange and mysterious work (Hab 1:5; Rom 3:31; 9:6, 14; 11:1, 11, 25) is consistent with his previous dealings with his people.

This too, I suggest, explains Paul's use of ἀποκαλύπτω.[79] It is not merely the revelation of God's righteousness and wrath in "impending eschatological judgment" (cf. 2:1-11);[80] although just as Habakkuk envisages judgment first on the

---

E. Zeller, 2nd ed. and rev. by A. Menzies (London: Williams and Northgate, 1876), 1:338; Anthony J. Guerra, "Romans: Paul's Purpose and Audience with Special Attention to Romans 9–11," *RB* 97 (1990): 219-37; J. C. Beker, "The Faithfulness of God and the Priority of Israel in Paul's Letter to the Romans," in *The Romans Debate*, ed. Karl P. Donfried (rev., Peabody, Mass.: Hendrickson, 1991), 329-32; *pace* David Aune, "Romans as a *Logos Protreptikos*," in ed. Donfried, 278-96, esp. 295, who finds 9–11's placement after 5:1–8:39 difficult to explain and thus regards it as an excursus or digression.

76. See Hays, "Psalms 143 and the Logic of Romans 3," *JBL* 99 (1980): 107-15, esp. 109.

77. On the role of scripture in apologetic, see Guerra, *Romans and the Apologetic Tradition: The Purpose, Genre and Audience of Paul's Letter*, SNTSMS 81 (Cambridge: Cambridge University Press, 1995), 15-16, 65-66.

78. See, e.g., Bruce Chilton, "Romans 9–11 as Scriptural Interpretation and Dialogue with Judaism," *Ex Auditu* 4 (1988): 27-37, esp. 28; Guerra, "Romans," 226; see Christopher D. Stanley, *Paul and the Language of Scripture: Citation Technique in the Pauline Epistles and Contemporary Literature*, SNTSMS 74 (Cambridge: Cambridge University Press, 1992), 103-71.

79. On the use of this and related terms, see, e.g., R. E. Brown, *The Semitic Background of the Term 'Mystery' in the New Testament* (Philadelphia: Fortress, 1968); M. N. A. Bockmuehl, *Revelation and Mystery in Ancient Judaism and Pauline Christianity*, WUNT II:36 (Tübingen: Mohr Siebeck, 1990), 140-41; and J. Coppens, "'Mystery' in the Theology of Saint Paul and Its Parallels at Qumran," in *Paul and Qumran*, ed. J. Murphy-O'Conner (Chicago: Priory, 1968), 132-58.

80. For Davies, 44-45, the working out of God's wrath in v. 18 derives from the division between the proud and the righteous in Hab 2:4; see also Bockmuehl, 138-41, who concentrates on explaining the link between vv. 17 and 18 such that the revelation of God's righteousness also includes divine judgment; and particularly G. Herold, *Zorn und Gerechtigkeit Gottes bei Paulus: Ein Untersuchung zu Röm. 1,16-18*, EuHoch XIII:14 (Frankfurt/Bern: Lang, 1973), 275-329; cf. Hays, "'Righteous One,'" 206.

wicked in Judah (1:12; cf. v. 4) and then the Chaldeans (2:5-20), Paul too speaks of "trouble and distress for every evil-doer . . . for the Jew first, then for the Gentile"[81] (Rom 2:9; cf. 1:16, and Hab 1:5 in Acts 13:41[82]). It is also, like Habakkuk's "wonderful" work (Hab 1:5), a μυστήριον κατὰ ἀποκάλυψιν (16:25).[83] This is exactly the language (רז) used by 1QpHab when it speaks of the unforeseen length of the delay of Habakkuk's vision concerning the final generation (7:8, 14; cf. 7:5; and 1:2-3).[84] Marcus Bockmuehl has already noticed that in Paul the language of revelation and mystery is linked with his reading of the scripture in the light of Christ.[85] But Greg Beale has further argued that Paul's use of mystery language in such settings usually signals not only that the fulfillment has already begun but that it is happening in a particularly unexpected manner (as, e.g., in 1QpHab).[86] This is again the issue in Romans. The fulfillment has indeed begun, and as in Qumran there is an element of the unexpected. But on the other hand, unlike Qumran but like Habakkuk, the issue for Paul is not so much the delay as it is God's righteousness in his dealings with Israel.[87]

81. On the importance of this motif in Romans see James D. G. Dunn, "The Formal and Theological Coherence of Romans," in ed. Donfried, 245-50, esp. 249-50. Douglas A. Campbell, "Determining the Gospel through Rhetorical Analysis in Paul's Letter to the Roman Christians," in *Gospel in Paul: Studies on Corinthians, Galatians and Romans for Richard N. Longenecker,* eds. L. Ann Jervis and Peter Richardson, JSNTSupp 108 (Sheffield: JSOT, 1994), 315-36, esp. 333-35, questions Paul's adherence to this principle since he constantly overturns Jewish priority in his reiteration of Jew-Gentile equality. But this seems to confuse the priority of God's historical intervention both to save and to judge, as in the prophets and Jesus, with the fact that God's dealings with both Jew and Gentile are, without distinction, on the basis of faith.

82. Note the language of vv. 38-39, which presupposes the ineffectiveness of the Law (cf. also Hab 2:4b), and the warning that if they do not repent God might well "turn to" the Gentiles (vv. 41, 46, 51). This after all is the "wonder" for Habakkuk, not merely the threat of military destruction, *pace* Hays, *Echoes,* 40n.19.

83. See, e.g., S. Kim, "The 'Mystery' of Rom 11.25-26 Once More," *NTS* 43 (1997): 412-29.

84. The text is fragmented here, but see the discussion and literature in Brownlee, *Pesher,* 10.

85. 133-56; see also Strobel, 177.

86. In a chapter to be published in *John's Use of the Old Testament in Revelation,* JSNTSupp (Sheffield: JSOT) in 1999; noting also G. Bornkamm, "μυστήριον," *TDNT* IV:822; cf. Bruce W. Longenecker, *Eschatology and the Covenant: A Comparison of 4 Ezra and Romans 1–11,* JSNTSupp 57 (Sheffield: JSOT, 1991), 169-71, who notes both the problem of the apparent denial of "the effectiveness of God's election of . . . Israel" and the eschatological novelty inherent in ἀποκαλύπτεται.

87. Strobel, 173-202, sees the delay/fulfillment schema (Hab 2:3) as underlying Paul's use of Hab 2:4. While Paul's νυνὶ δέ might suggest something along these lines, I am not convinced that the issue in Romans is as much the timing as it is the questionable nature of this fulfillment.

But what about the precise form of Paul's citation, which follows neither the MT nor the versions?[88] It is likely that Paul, adhering to the citational practice of his day which accepted modifications of this kind to help readers/hearers understand what an author saw as the point of the passage,[89] deliberately omitted the pronouns precisely with the resultant ambiguity in mind.[90] First, in keeping with Habakkuk's fundamental concerns, Paul's version allows for both the MT and what we have argued are the valid interpretative perspectives evident in the versions. Paul maintains the trustworthiness of his revelation (cf. Habakkuk's "vision") of the gospel (cf. MT, *Tg.*) because it is the expression of God's faithfulness (cf. majority of LXX MSS). But at the same time, there is clearly a call to be faithful, to live in keeping with this revelation (cf. 8HevXIIgr, Aquila, Symmachus, cf. 1QpHab, and implicit in Hab).[91] From this perspective, God has mysteriously and unexpectedly revealed his righteousness ἐκ πίστεως εἰς πίστιν, that is, arising out of his faithfulness, with the goal being life through the obedience of faith for the Jew first, but also for the Gentile. Second, its language is ideally suited to allow Paul simultaneously to pursue his argument, via Abraham, of justification by faith.

This brings us finally to Paul's "I am not ashamed." Numerous interpretative options have been proposed. The older psychological approach, often buttressed by an appeal to 1 Corinthians 1:18-25, saw this as a reference to the perception that Paul was an unknown provincial bearing an outrageous message.[92] One of the more recent expositions along these lines is that of Gregory M. Corrigan, who examines Romans from the sociological perspective of honor and shame.[93] While offering helpful insights, the problem (as with all versions of this view) is that there is, in Romans, no comparable evidence of the cross-rejecting Corinthian fixation with wisdom and power. C. K. Barrett takes a slightly different tack and, although not reading Paul's declaration merely as a litotes as does Ernst Käsemann,[94] he locates the language in the Son of Man tra-

88. See the discussions in Fitzmyer, "Habakkuk," and Stanley, 83-84.

89. See Stanley, 342-50.

90. Cf., e.g., Peter Stuhlmacher, *Paul's Letter to the Romans,* trans. Scott J. Hafemann (Louisville: Westminster/John Knox, 1989), 29; Dunn, *Romans 1–8,* WBC 38A (Dallas: Word, 1988), 45; Hays, *Echoes,* 40-41. Interpretations which force the reader to relate ἐκ πίστεως with either ὁ δίκαιος or ζήσεται rarely appreciate the reciprocity inherent both in the MT and in the versions of Hab 2:4.

91. *Pace* Barnabas Lindars, *New Testament Apologetic* (London: SCM, 1961), 230, whose declaration that 1QpHab's use "is the exact opposite" of Paul's proceeds from dichotomizing salvation-life as goal and manner of life as means.

92. So, e.g., Moo, 65; Fitzmyer, *Romans,* AB 33 (New York *et al.:* Doubleday, 1993), 225, who sees this as an option.

93. "Paul's Shame for the Gospel," *BTB* 16 (1986): 23-27.

94. *Commentary on Romans,* trans. G. W. Bromiley (Grand Rapids: Eerdmans, 1980), 22.

dition (Mk 8:38//Lk 9:26) and so sees Paul explicitly identifying himself with Jesus.[95] But why say this to Roman believers? They might have trouble with Paul's gospel, but there seems no intimation that they are questioning his loyalty to Jesus.

Another alternative is that taken by Gerhart Herold, who, noting that "shame" language occurs in numerous OT laments, proposes that Paul is not ashamed because God's eschatological lawsuit against his enemies (1:18ff.) had now resulted in his people's vindication.[96] Hays argues for something similar, citing ἐπαισχύνομαι-related terms in, for example, LXX Psalms 43:10; 24:2; Isaiah 50:7-8; and 28:16 (quoted in Rom 9:33).[97] Given Paul's eschatological orientation, this is more persuasive. But again, why should Paul say this to the Romans in particular? And in his thesis statement? And especially when he does so to no other group? Hays, correctly in my view, goes on to discuss Habakkuk 2:4 and the problem of theodicy in the light of uncircumcised Gentiles apparently usurping Israel's privileged position, but he only briefly links them with Paul's declaration in verse 16a.

I want to suggest that this connection is in fact the way forward. Steve Mason has recently proposed that the reason for Paul's profession lies in criticism he is facing from within the Roman church.[98] Paul ought to be ashamed because in the minds of the recipients of Romans he had, among other things, "corrupted the apostles' teaching in order 'to please men' (Gal 1:10-12), and . . . effectively written off Israel and its traditions (Acts 21:21, 28)."[99] Our reading of Habakkuk 2:4, Paul's critique of the Law, and the significance of Romans 9–11, certainly coheres with this view.

From this perspective, the reason Paul might be expected to be ashamed is precisely because of the theodicy question: How could he make the claims he did when his gospel seemed to mean the setting aside not only of Israel's tradi-

95. "I Am Not Ashamed of the Gospel," in *Foi et Salut Selon S. Paul,* AnBib 42 (Rome: Institut Biblique Pontifical, 1970), 19-50, esp. 19-41; O. Michel, "Zum Sprachgebrauch von *epaischynomai* in Rom 1:16," in *Glaube und Ethos, Festschrift für Professor D. Dr. G. Wehrung,* ed. R. Paulus (Stuttgart: Kohlhammer, 1940), 36-53; C. E. B. Cranfield, *The Epistle to the Romans,* ICC (Edinburgh: T. & T. Clark, 1975), 1:86; Dunn, 39; Stuhlmacher, 28; Fitzmyer, *Romans,* 255; cf. Moo, 65.

96. *Zorn,* 138-41, 331-36.

97. *Echoes,* 38-39, observing with respect to Isa 50:7-8, "Paul transforms Isaiah's emphatic future negation . . . into a present negation."

98. "'For I Am Not Ashamed of the Gospel' (Rom. 1.16): The Gospel and the First Readers of Romans," in eds. Jervis and Richardson, 254-87.

99. 280; citing G. Lüdemann, *Opposition to Paul in Jewish Christianity,* trans. M. E. Boring (Minneapolis: Fortress, 1989), 35-115. Cf. Stuhlmacher, "The Purpose of Romans," in ed. Donfried, 231-42; Campbell, "Determining," in eds. Jervis and Richardson: 315-36, and the literature cited therein.

tions but also of the nation itself? And, if anything, his track record made matters even worse since he antagonized Jews wherever he went. It could well be that these criticisms provoked Paul's prodigious efforts to demonstrate his gospel's continuity with Israel's tradition. This could also explain why Romans, uniquely among Paul's letters, contains such positive theological statements on circumcision, on being Jewish, on the Law, and on Israel's priority (e.g., 2:25a; 3:1-2, 30-31; 7:7, 12-14, 22; 8:4; 9:1-5; 10:2a; 11:1-5, 11-12, 15, 26-29; cf. 11:17-24). And is not this exactly the point of Paul's thesis statement? In spite of how things look and even though traumatic for him (Rom 9:1-5; just as it was for Habakkuk), his gospel (cf. Hab 2:2-3's "vision") is in fact the revelation (ἀποκάλυψις) of the mysterious fulfillment of Yahweh's promise.

In Robert Jewett's "Ambassadorial Letter" model, the question is "whether the sovereign [that] an ambassador represents is capable of achieving the purposes of an embassy," namely to restore God's "righteous control over a disobedient creation."[100] Paul is not ashamed because his gospel is God's *power* (cf. Hab 3's celebration of the same). And quite so in that according to the approach taken here — although Jewett does not describe God's power in this way — Paul argues that not only is his gospel the revelation of God's judgment against πᾶσαν ἀσέβειαν καὶ ἀδικίαν (Rom 1:18; cf. Hab 1:3, 4, 9, 13; 2:8, 12, 17), it can moreover do what the ineffectual Law could not (3:20-22). But it is equally clear that Paul is very much concerned to show that this is *God's* power, particularly in the face of questions about its vexing modus operandi: by faith and not by Law, and largely for the benefit of Gentiles while Israel seems to be sidelined.

The gospel, then, is the revelation of Yahweh's faithful exercise of his power in effecting salvation (Hab 3:18-19; Rom 1:16), but it is a salvation on the basis of faith in the revealed gospel (Rom 1:17b; cf. the vision of Hab 2:1-4). This was Israel's problem, even though the gospel came first to her. She boasted in the Law (Rom 2:17; 9:30-33; cf. Hab 2:4a, MT), but in failing to recognize its ineffectiveness had cut herself off from the "faithful" vision (Rom 9:30-32). And as the scripture had spoken, "See, I have set in Zion a Stone that causes stumbling and a Rock that causes offence; but the one who believes in him will not be ashamed" (Isa 28:16 and 8:14, quoted in Rom 9:33). Paul had believed in the faithfulness of this One; and, consequently, in the eschatological time-between-the-times he was not ashamed. Nevertheless, it is not as if Israel has been cast off. She too would be included but only on the grounds of faith, not of Law, for in the end both Israel and the Gentiles have been bound under dis-

100. "Romans as an Ambassadorial Letter," *Interp* 36 (1982): 5-20, esp. 15, citing O. Glombitza, "Von der Scham der Glaubigen: Erwägungen zu Röm i 14-17," *NovT* 4 (1960): 74-80.

obedience so that Yahweh might have mercy on all (Rom 11:31). Paul finally exults in the unsearchable wisdom and glory of the God who works out all things according to his purpose (Rom 11:33-36).

This leads to a final point of comparison. Just as Habakkuk both recognizes the need for perseverance (3:16-17) and concludes with a song of praise (3:2-15), so too does Paul. He both stresses the need to endure (4:18-21; 5:1-5; 8:18-27) and concludes all three of his central major sections with praise (5:6-11; 8:28-39;[101] 11:33-36). Not only so, but whereas Habakkuk ends his resolution of the mystery by proclaiming "I will rejoice in the God of my salvation (σωτῆρί μου). The Lord God is my strength (δύναμίς μου)" (3:18-19), Paul echoes this language as he outlines his thesis "for it [the gospel] is the power [δύναμις] of God for salvation [σωτηρίαν] to everyone who believes [πιστεύοντι, cf. Hab 2:4]" (Rom 1:16). This might also explain why Romans alone of Paul's letters concludes with a doxology (16:25-27):[102] "Now to the one who is able to strengthen you [δύναμαι, cf. Hab 3:19; Rom 1:16] . . . according to my gospel . . . and the revelation of the mystery . . . to bring about the obedience of faith" (cf. 1:5). Just as God had dealt mysteriously with Israel in the past, so also now. The right response is to believe.

IV. Conclusion

When the larger purposes of Habakkuk are taken into account, Paul's innovative citation of Habakkuk 2:4 functions particularly well in introducing the fundamental themes of Romans. This happens at several levels. By evoking the question of theodicy, and especially in the context of the ineffectiveness of Torah to restrain sin, it introduces the matter of the mystery of God's ways vis-à-vis Israel, and as such provides a scriptural matrix in which Paul can justify his gospel. In the face of this mystery revealed, his version of Habakkuk 2:4, by allowing room for the interpretative traditions of the MT and the versions, also draws attention both to God's covenantal faithfulness and to the reciprocal need for the obedience of faith and perseverance on the part of the hearer as the path to life. Here too it provides Paul an opportunity to establish that his gospel and its problematic outworkings are in fundamental continuity with the earlier

101. R. M. Moody, "The Habakkuk Quotation in Romans 1[17]," *ExpT* 92 (1981): 206, mentions R. M. Spurin, but without bibliographic data, as noting the "intense" similarity between Rom 8:28ff. and Hab 3. I was unable to locate Spurin's work.

102. Klyne Snodgrass, "The Gospel in Romans: A Theology of Revelation," in eds. Jervis and Richardson, 288-314, esp. 294-95, argues for its authenticity, observing that it "encapsulates the wording and concerns of the letter."

"mysterious" revelation of God's promised salvation. At the same time, Habakkuk 2:4's syntax and terminology provide a basis on which Paul can develop the link between justification and faith. All in all, it is hard to imagine a text better suited to his concerns.

New Exodus, New Inheritance: The Narrative Substructure of Romans 3–8

N. T. Wright

An essay presented to a colleague is a poor substitute for a face-to-face discussion, much in the way that a Pauline letter was a poor substitute (though sometimes an effective one) for the apostolic presence. My only regret about offering this essay to Gordon Fee in this setting is that I shall be bound not to mention it to him until its publication. One of the joys of our friendship has been the fact that at any moment of sudden meeting, at a conference, over a meal, or in a coffee break between classes at a summer school, we have been able to pick up complex and intricate discussions of Paul where we left them a day or a year before, and to offer new suggestions to one another in the knowledge that one will receive instant understanding, sharp and well-informed critique, and further insights or modifications that one had not thought of for oneself. I can only hope that when Gordon has had a chance to digest this essay we will be able to build it into our future friendship as one further element among many.

The topic that I propose has to do with the large-scale question of Paul's argument in a central and lengthy section of Romans. There is no chance, of course, of interacting with all the scholarly literature on even some parts of the topic, let alone (though Gordon will regret this) considering the textual variants that might make crucial little differences along the way. In line with some recent studies, I want to explore the way in which Paul makes implicit and explicit use of the story of the Exodus throughout Romans 3–8, and to draw some conclusions from this for our understanding of the letter and of the theological issues it raises, as a whole.[1]

My starting point for this train of thought — the actual point that set me thinking, not the point I choose for rhetorical advantage in this presentation — is the question of the place of baptism, and hence of Romans 6 as a whole, within the argument of the letter. This question has often been expressed in terms of an antithesis between two types of theological thought supposed to underlie the different sections of the letter: "juristic" in Romans 1–4, "participationist" in 5–8, and so on — a distinction which, as is well known, goes back in the present century to Albert Schweitzer, and has been reinforced by the work of E. P. Sanders and others.[2] Has Paul in fact changed gears from one style or theology to another, and, if so, which is more central both to his thought and to this letter? Or, to sharpen it up another way, what has baptism to do with justification by faith, the promises to Abraham, and the revelation of God's righteousness, as set out in 3:21–4:25? And, to complete the set of initial questions, how does the entire argument of Romans 5–8, in which (obviously) chapter 6 plays such a vital role, relate to that of 1–4?

My overall proposal is that throughout this section of the letter Paul has not just the story of Israel, but more specifically the redeeming story of the Exodus, in mind, and that both in the large-scale shape of his presentation and in many details of actual arguments this emerges into the light of day, making fresh sense of passages which otherwise remain opaque, and holding together the different sections of the argument in a way that transcends the distinctions just mentioned. This proposal has on the one hand some analogies to Frank Thielman's very suggestive paper about the story of Israel in Romans 5–8, though he does not make anything like the specific suggestion I am offering. It also draws on Sylvia Keesmaat's fascinating work on the Exodus-language of Romans 8, though she, too, is not responsible for this particular flight of fancy — though I perhaps would not have been nudged to think in this direction without the stimulus of her work.[3] Standing behind all of this is of course the

1. I have published a very brief preliminary statement of the same point under the title "The New Inheritance according to Paul," in *Bible Review* 14.3 (June 1998): 16, 47.

2. Albert Schweitzer, *Paul and His Interpreters: A Critical History*, trans. William Montgomery (London: A. & C. Black, 1912); idem, *The Mysticism of Paul the Apostle*, trans. William Montgomery, with a preface by F. C. Burkitt (London, New York: A. & C. Black, Seabury Press, 1968 [1930]); E. P. Sanders, *Paul and Palestinian Judaism: A Comparison of Patterns of Religion* (Philadelphia/London: Fortress/SCM, 1977).

3. Sylvia C. Keesmaat, "Paul's Use of the Exodus Tradition in Romans and Galatians," D. Phil. dissertation, Oxford University (1994) (to be published by Sheffield Academic Press in the *JSNT* monograph series); Frank Thielman, "The Story of Israel and the Theology of

major pioneering work of Richard Hays on Paul's echoing of scriptural passages and themes.[4]

I am well aware, of course, that there is enormous resistance within some branches of the New Testament studies guild to any proposal of this sort. This is partly due, I think, to a proper caution about grand overarching patterns, and a preference for small-scale exegesis — a caution which, though laudable and necessary, often owes more to personality than to scholarship, and in any case always runs the risk of not seeing the forest but only the trees, and hence of not understanding the trees either. It is also partly due to an unwillingness to countenance the possibility that Paul might well have been alluding all over the place to the story of Israel, on the theological grounds that he was doing something new, leaving covenantal categories behind, expounding the new life in Christ in antithesis to Judaism. What I have to offer will not convince those who on other grounds are never prepared to recognize the existence of such themes and patterns. But the fact that some people cannot see certain objects does not mean they do not exist. The case for the reading I propose is cumulative. As often with such readings, individual parts can be controverted in isolation, but when the proposal is seen as a whole its strength should be apparent.

My initial specific proposal is to explore the possibility that when Paul speaks of baptism in Romans 6 he has in mind the crossing of the Red Sea at the Exodus. He makes exactly this connection, of course, in 1 Corinthians 10:2, where it forms an important part of his exhortation to the Corinthian church that they should see themselves as the heirs of the scriptural narrative, as God's true-Exodus people now engaged in their homeward-bound wilderness journey. "Our fathers were all under the cloud, and all passed through the sea, and all were baptized into Moses in the cloud and in the sea. . . . Now these things were examples to us, that we might not desire evil as they did."[5]

The primary strength of this proposal lies in the sense it makes of Romans 6 as a whole. Baptism, and that which it embodies and symbolizes (the death of the "old man" and the new life in Christ), is here expounded specifically in terms of the liberation of the slave:

Romans 5–8," in *Romans,* vol. 3 of *Pauline Theology,* eds. David M. Hay and E. Elizabeth Johnson (Minneapolis: Fortress, 1995), 169-95.

4. Richard B. Hays, *Echoes of Scripture in the Letters of Paul* (New Haven and London: Yale University Press, 1989).

5. 1 Cor 10:1-2, 6. See Richard B. Hays, *First Corinthians,* Interpretation Commentaries (Louisville: John Knox Press, 1997), 159-73. See also Hays's paper "The Conversion of the Imagination: Scripture and Eschatology in 1 Corinthians," delivered at the 1998 Society of New Testament Studies meeting in Copenhagen, and to be published in *New Testament Studies.*

> Thanks be to God that you who once were slaves of sin have become obedient from the heart to the pattern of teaching to which you were committed, and, being set free from sin, have become enslaved to righteousness. (6:17-18)

There is no question that in Judaism in general any story about slaves and how they come to be free must be seen at once as an allusion to the events of the Exodus. When, in that context, we discover that the critical event in the story of the great liberation, the new exodus, is when the Christian passes through the water of baptism, we have (I suggest) a prima facie reason for making the same connection. "Sin," conceived here as an independent power, takes of course the role of Egypt and/or Pharaoh; "righteousness," suggestively, seems to be almost a periphrasis for God. To this we shall return.

What effect does this reading of chapter 6 have on 6–8 as a whole? If 6 tells the story of the Exodus, or at least the crossing of the Red Sea, the next thing we should expect is the arrival at Sinai and the giving of the Torah. This is, of course, exactly the topic of Romans 7:1–8:11, with all its attendant puzzles. Paul is not, of course, operating a slavish typology in which he merely reproduces the earlier story point by point in its new guise; and in the present case particularly this could not be so, precisely because the Torah given to the freed slaves in the first Exodus has now become, paradoxically, part of the enslavement from which the second Exodus frees the people of God (though one of Paul's main tasks in Romans 7 is to show how the law is not at fault in this, being an unwilling accomplice of sin and the flesh).

We could summarize the narrative sequence as follows: those who were enslaved in the "Egypt" of sin, an enslavement the law only exacerbated, have been set free by the "Red Sea" event of baptism, since in baptism they are joined to the Messiah, whose death and resurrection are accounted as theirs. They are now given as their guide, not indeed the law, which, although given by God, is unable to do more than condemn them for their sin, but the Spirit, so that the Mosaic covenant is replaced, as Jeremiah and Ezekiel said it would be, with the covenant written on the hearts of God's people by God's own Spirit. At this point 7:4-6 and 8:1-11 look back, within the larger logic of the letter, to 2:25-29.

This brings us to the place within the whole section where, as Keesmaat has shown, Exodus-language is most obvious on the surface of the text. In 8:12-17, Paul treats the Christians as precisely God's new-Exodus people. They are led by God through their present wilderness (compare again 1 Cor 10:6-13). Their guide is the Spirit, who here takes up the role of the pillar of cloud and fire in the wilderness; were there world enough and time, this would be worth exploring in terms of its implications for Paul's overall view of the Spirit within a Christian vision of God. They are "the sons of God," echoing the language used by God, through Moses, to Pharaoh (Ex 4:22). They must not slide back into the state of slavery; they must not, that is, go back to Egypt. And if they are God's children, currently being led through the wilderness, they are assured that they are also God's heirs: the concept of "heir," and the correlated concept of "inheritance," are of course repeated over and over in the Pentateuch in reference to Israel's promised inheritance of the land, the land to which their wilderness wanderings were leading them.

The Christian inheritance, however, is not a matter of one piece of geographical countryside. It is nothing less than the renewed, restored creation. Paul's spectacular picture of creation groaning in birth-pangs, longing to share the freedom of the glory of God's people (8:16-27), owes a great deal on the one hand to the image of the "Messianic woes," but on the other hand to the scriptural sense in which the fate of the land is bound up with the fate, and the covenant behavior, of Israel.[6] When Christians are finally redeemed, Paul is saying, then the land — only now, in this case, the whole cosmos — will be redeemed. The specific argument of chapter 8 then winds to its glorious close, held in place and given coherence and theological power by the Exodus story, now rethought in and through Jesus and the Spirit.

How does this reading of Romans 6–8 help with the wider question of the relationship between Paul's argument in these chapters and that in 1–4? The answer is found in two sometimes neglected features of Romans 4.

First, Paul is working throughout the chapter with Genesis 15 as his base. He brings in other Abrahamic passages as well, of course, not least Genesis 17 and 22, but it is to chapter 15 that he returns time and again. I propose that he had in mind, in using this chapter, not simply the text about Abraham believing God, and this being "reckoned to him as righteousness" (Gen 15:6, quoted in 4:3 and frequently), but also the conclusion of the chapter, in which God establishes his covenant with Abraham. Here (Gen 15:13-14) there is a specific prediction of the slavery in Egypt, God's rescue of Israel after four hundred years, and the gift of the promised land. Within the narrative structure of the Pentateuch, this complex prediction and promise looks ahead to the events described in the remainder of the Five Books, indicating that these events are to be understood as the fulfillment of God's covenanted promises to Abraham. Paul is very much aware of this aspect of the chapter, as Galatians 3:15-18 reminds us.[7] And he believes, and in Romans 4 he emphasizes, that in Christ God has fulfilled his

6. For the positive side, see, e.g., Isa 35; for the negative, compare the suggestive Lev 26:24, 43; 2 Chron 36:21.

7. Admittedly, when Paul tells the same story in Gal 3, he follows the chronology of Ex 12:40, in which the period in question is 430 years (Gal 3:17). The Genesis figure of 400 years is quoted in Acts 7:6.

covenant promises to Abraham. We should not therefore be surprised to find in Romans 6–8 an exposition of the Christian's status, hope, and vocation (it is more than that, but not less), which not only employs terms which evoke the story of Israel but which follows in its structure the path of the people of God from slavery in Egypt to inheritance in the land of promise.

Second, Paul gives an indication within chapter 4 that his thought is going to move in exactly this direction. In verse 13 he says "the promise to Abraham and his seed, *that they should inherit the world,* did not come through the law, but through the righteousness of faith." His point in context is that the promises belong to all Abraham's family, not merely to those who are defined by possessing the Torah, i.e., Jews (4:13-17). But the revealing explanation of what God promised to Abraham, included here almost as a throwaway line, is a clear indication that he already has in view the way in which God's fulfillment of his promises in Christ and by the Spirit will result in God's renewed people receiving as their inheritance not merely one piece of territory but the whole restored cosmos. Paul was not the first Jew to suggest that God promised Abraham more than just the holy land.[8] But within his argument it is more than just a pious hope or expression of nationalist territorial expansionism. It goes with his whole theology, to which we shall turn presently, of how God's intention in the beginning of creation itself is now fulfilled through Christ and the Spirit, and how this was likewise God's intention when he called Abraham.

We can trace the Exodus story in Romans, then, not only through Romans 6, 7, and 8 but back to chapter 4. What about the earlier part of the argument of which Romans 4 is an integral part, namely 3:21-31? And what about chapter 5, the bridge between the promise in chapter 4 and the fulfillment in 6–8?

3:21-31 forms Paul's majestic statement of the revelation of God's righteousness. Every verse is of course controversial, often for several reasons simultaneously. I have elsewhere argued at length that "the righteousness of God" must here be understood as *God's faithfulness to the covenant,* specifically the covenant with Abraham; this is why chapter 4 is to be seen as the full exposition of what Paul announces as his theme in 3:21, not simply a miscellaneous, or politically advantageous, "proof from scripture" of some other more detached doctrinal point.[9]

8. Cf., e.g., Sir 44:21 and Jub 19:21, looking back to, e.g., Gen 15:18, Ex 23:31, Ps 72:8, and Zech 9:10; cf. 2 Bar 14:13; 51:3.

9. Cf. N. T. Wright, "On Becoming the Righteousness of God: 2 Corinthians 5:21," in *Pauline Theology Volume II: 1 & 2 Corinthians,* ed. David M. Hay (Minneapolis: Fortress, 1993), 200-208; idem, "Romans and the Theology of Paul," in *Romans,* vol. 3 of *Pauline Theology,* eds. David M. Hay and E. Elizabeth Johnson (Minneapolis: Fortress, 1995), 38-39; idem, *What St. Paul Really Said* (Oxford/Grand Rapids: Lion/ Eerdmans, 1997), ch. 6.

To explain more fully, we must glance for a moment even further back in the letter. In 1:18–3:20 Paul has analyzed the problem of the world and of Israel in terms not only of universal sin, and the wrath of God which it incurs, but more specifically of the way in which the people called to provide God's solution, namely Israel, have themselves become part of the problem. God remains faithful to the covenant, which always envisaged blessing for the world; but the people through whom this blessing was intended to reach the world have been unfaithful. That is the point of the dense little argument at 3:1-4. Precisely because God remains faithful, and does not change his mind about his call to Israel to be the light of the world, what is required at this point, if a solution is to be found, is precisely a faithful Israelite. This, declares Paul, is what we have in Jesus: as Messiah, he brings Israel's intended covenant obedience, covenant faithfulness, to birth at last, not just being an example of a faithful Jew, but the climactic and decisive faithful Jew. "God's righteousness is revealed, *through the faithfulness of the Messiah,* for the benefit of all who believe."[10]

But in what does this covenant faithfulness consist? In Romans 5, Paul summarizes what he has said about the death of Jesus in terms of his "obedience." This, to be sure, is partly in order to contrast Jesus with Adam in his disobedience. But it is also a concept which, already in the letter, is closely aligned with faithfulness: when Paul speaks of "the obedience of faith" in Romans 1:5, he brings together two ideas often separated in Christian theology but often held closely together in Judaism. I propose, not least with Philippians 2:5-8 in the background, that Paul can speak of Jesus' death (and his life insofar as it led to his death) as his "faithfulness" and/or his "obedience" — his faithful obedience, that is, to the whole saving plan and purpose of God, to that plan which Israel was called to implement but in which she failed.

The details of how this works out in 3:21-31, though extremely interesting in themselves, need not concern us, except for one particular. In 3:24 Paul introduces his dense statement of the meaning of Jesus' death by saying that justification has come about through the "redemption" that is in the Messiah, Jesus. "Redemption," to a Jew, again means one thing principally: the act whereby God went down to the slave market called Egypt and bought there his

10. I regard this as the most compelling reason for reading some if not all of Paul's linguistically ambiguous references to *pistis Christou* as denoting "the faithfulness of the Messiah." It would take us too far afield to develop this further; on the whole debate, see recently B. W. Longenecker, *The Triumph of Abraham's God: The Transformation of Identity in Galatians* (Edinburgh: T. &. T. Clark, 1998), ch. 5, with references to copious other secondary literature. I am in broad agreement with Longenecker, though in what follows there are implicit differences of emphasis as well.

enslaved people in order to set them free.[11] Paul is here putting down a marker, as in 4:13 and indeed many other passages in the early parts of Romans, for the theme he is subsequently going to explore in more detail.

All of this forces us to abandon any idea that Romans 3–4 embodies or expresses a different sort of theology from that which we find in 6–8. We can go further. It has often been remarked as odd that, despite this supposed change in theological substance, Paul still uses the language of "righteousness" in 6–8. We can now give a satisfying explanation of what is going on. As a result of 3:21–4:25, "righteousness" can stand as a synecdoche for God himself, the God who in Jesus Christ has revealed his covenant faithfulness. The new Exodus is the result precisely of this God being faithful to what he promised to Abraham. Thus in 6:13-20, where the word *dikaiosynē* occurs no fewer than five times, all its overtones of covenant faithfulness (that of God, and that of God's people) are still to be heard; an older flattening out of these nuances into the either/or of "forensic" and "ethical" meanings simply fails to catch what Paul is talking about. When, in 6:18, Paul writes that "having been liberated from sin, you have become slaves to righteousness," "righteousness" stands once more for the covenant God himself, whose demands of absolute covenant loyalty from his people include but far transcend what we mean by "ethics." The proof of this point comes in verse 22, where, after speaking for the previous several verses of "righteousness" as the new master of the freed slaves, Paul finally abandons the trope and declares that now, "having been set free from sin, you have been enslaved to God."

A reflection is therefore in order about the different categories with which Paul's thought has been analyzed. Schweitzer's distinction of "mystical/eschatological" and "forensic," Sanders's similar one of "participationist" and "juristic," and the more recent distinction between "covenant" and "apocalyptic," are all ultimately beside the point. The story of the Exodus, as Paul uses it, overlaps and enfolds all these categories. The Exodus is the fulfillment of the covenant with Abraham; it is that which constitutes those "in Christ" as the people of God; it is that which declares that those who share Christ's faithfulness are the true, sin-forgiven people of God; it is that through which God has broken in to the world and to the sorry history of Israel, unveiling his faithfulness in a radically new way in the death and resurrection of the Messiah and the outpouring of the Spirit.

What then about the place and role of chapter 5 within this structure of thought? As is well known, 5:1-11, and within that 5:1-5, anticipates in many respects the thought of chapter 8. Paul is once again putting down a marker for where his argument is going. In these paragraphs he is summing up where the

11. The fact that the primary metaphorical overtone is the Exodus, not some hypothetical slave market, shows that the older systematic discussion concerning the ransom-price, and the question to whom such a price was paid, is beside the point.

argument has so far taken him: now that, by faith, we are declared to be in the right, the inheritance of glory is in view, and the present life is characterized by hope in the midst of suffering — the theme which will be expanded in chapter 8 in terms reminiscent of the wilderness wanderings of Israel. And whereas in Deuteronomy the astonishing love of God for Israel was evidenced by the events of the original Exodus, the same point is now made with overwhelming power through the death of Jesus, which has not simply rescued those to whom God was already bound in a familial covenant but has reconciled to him those who were "enemies" (5:6-11).[12]

5:12-21 can then take its place as the overarching narrative through which the whole of 1:18–8:39 is comprehended, summing up what has gone before and laying foundations for what is to come. By means of the faithful obedience of Israel's representative, the Messiah, not only has all the glory, all the inheritance, of Adam accrued to the people of God, as the Qumran sect already claimed for themselves;[13] all the evils that accrued from Adam's disobedience are undone. Within this large-scale historical story, the arrival of the Torah strikes a negative, not a positive, note (5:20, pointing ahead to 7:7-12); the new Exodus is not simply to be a repeat performance of the old, but must itself undo the extra problems that arose through Israel's being "under the law." Through his faithful obedience, the Messiah has brought with him out of the Egypt of sin and death a great multitude who now live under the rule, and in the hope, of grace, righteousness, and life (5:21). This then sets the context for the question of 6:1, bringing the argument of this paper back where it started.

There are several further lines of inquiry that cry out to be pursued, but must be patient for another occasion. Three brief concluding remarks must suffice.

First, it is obvious that if Paul is retelling the story of Israel in this way in Romans 3–8, this simply intensifies the anguish of 9:1-5. The list of Israel's privileges in 9:4-5, in any case, has a strong "Exodus" ring to it: sonship, glory, covenants, lawgiving, worship, promise, and "the fathers" all evoke the story of the Exodus.[14] The opening of chapter 9 thus confirms the reading I have offered, and is itself given added poignancy by the connection.

12. Cf. Deut 4:37; 7:7-8; 10:15.

13. Cf., e.g., 1QS 4.23 (glory); 4QpPs37 (= 4Q171) 3.1f. (inheritance [despite the translation "glory" in Geza Vermes, *The Dead Sea Scrolls in English,* 4th ed. (Harmondsworth: Penguin, 1995), 488; the word *nhlth,* "inheritance," is clearly visible in Plate XVI of John M. Allegro, *Discoveries in the Judaean Desert of Jordan V: Qumran Cave 4, I (4Q158-4Q186)* (Oxford: Clarendon, 1968)]).

14. In 1 Cor 10:1 Paul speaks of "our fathers" in reference not to Abraham, Isaac, and Jacob, or even Jacob's twelve sons (as the RSV, NRSV, NEB, REB, etc. translation "patriarchs" in Rom 9:5 might suggest), but to the Exodus generation.

Second, when discussing the future hope of Christians it is important that Romans 8, seen as Paul's reworking of the Exodus-shaped "inheritance" theme, is given full weight. It is not sufficient, that is, to speak of "eternal life," on the basis of, e.g., Romans 5:21 and 6:23, and to assume that this refers to a generalized "heaven" such as characterizes much common Christian tradition. Paul's expectation was more specific: "the life of the coming age" (an expanded translation of *zōē aiōnios*) was to be enjoyed, not in "heaven" as opposed to "earth," but in the renewed, redeemed creation, the creation that has itself shared the Exodus-experience of the people of God.

Third, we may reflect that this reading joins together that which Paul's interpreters have often put asunder. It was always dubious, in view of the combination of the same themes in Galatians 3–4, especially 3:23–4:7, to set apart faith and justification on the one hand, and baptism and the Spirit on the other, and to suppose that they belonged, in Paul's mind, to distinct universes of discourse. As John the Baptist would no doubt have agreed, baptism and Spirit speak of new covenant, new Exodus, and thereby of the renewal, however unexpected, of the people of Abraham.[15] And the Exodus is itself the action whereby God justifies as well as liberates. It is the action, bursting in upon the world ruled by the principalities and powers (in the one case, Pharaoh and Egypt; in the other, sin and death), which declares: these are my people. And that declaration, constituting the liberated ones as God's true people, sets before them the inheritance to which they must now make their way, and promises them the presence of God, in the person of the Spirit, to guide and strengthen them on the journey.

15. Cf. Mt 3:9/Lk 3:8, on which see N. T. Wright, *Jesus and the Victory of God*, in *Christian Origins and the Question of God*, vol. 2 (London/Minneapolis: SPCK/Fortress, 1996), 248.

Reconciliation: Romans 5:1-11

Ralph P. Martin

In accepting the invitation to contribute to this well-deserved tribute to Gordon Fee, I am minded to offer a set of theological and exegetical reflections on a passage in Romans that both falls within my continuing interest and, I believe, will make its appeal to preachers and Bible class teachers in a churchly setting. Guidance and encouragement for this enterprise have come from a precedent set by a former teacher, T. W. Manson, who years ago was asked to contribute to the Bultmann Festschrift, and with characteristic aplomb chose to offer ruminations, in homiletical style, on the command to love in John's Gospel.[1]

I. The Text: Romans 5:1-11 (omitting vv. 3-4)

1 Since then we have been justified through faith,
Let us enjoy the peace we have with God
through our Lord Jesus Christ:
2 Through him moreover we have secured access [by faith]
To this grace in which we abide,
And we exult in our hope of the [coming] divine glory. . .
5 [That] hope does not put us to shame,

1. In the chapter headed "Preaching and Exegesis," contribution to *Neutestamentliche Studien für Rudolf Bultmann*, ed. W. Eltester (BZNTW 21; Berlin: Töpelmann, 1954), pp. 10-14, Manson draws on a sermon of F. W. Robertson to illumine John 13:34 and to reflect on the relation of the scientific study of the scriptures, practiced in University and Colleges, and the homiletic tradition of the church.

For God's love has been poured out in our hearts
through the Holy Spirit who was given to us.
6 For when we were still powerless, at the appointed time,
Christ died for ungodly people.
7 For it would be difficult [to find] someone
to die for a righteous person;
For a good person perhaps someone may even bring
himself to die;
8 But God proves his love for us by the
fact that, while we were still sinners,
Christ died for us.
9 Since then we have now been justified
At the cost of his blood,
We shall be saved with greater certainty
from [God's] wrath through him.
10 For if when we were enemies we were reconciled to
God through his son's death,
now that we are reconciled, we shall with greater certainty
be saved by his life.
11 Not only do we have this as our hope, but
we also exult in God through our Lord Jesus Christ,
through whom we have now already received reconciliation.

II. The Apostle's Teaching

By common consent, the exploration of the theme of reconciliation in the Pauline corpus is found in 2 Corinthians 5:18-21, Colossians 1:15-22, and Romans 5:1-11, with a glance at Romans 3:24-26 as providing material for his atonement teaching, and with a forward look to Ephesians 2:11-22 for the shape of development within the Pauline school.

According to Paul, reconciliation postulates an estrangement. A rift in relation between God and humankind makes the repair of the breach and restoration of amity a prime necessity if ever God's purposes are to be realized and humans are to be "saved" from their plight and peril.

A. Background: The Human Condition

Paul is under no illusion as to the serious and hopeless state of humanity's condition. Subjectively considered, human beings are "helpless," i.e., powerless to aid themselves, "ungodly," blighted with a malaise that recalls the exposé of Romans 1:18-32, and "sinners," which is Paul's favorite term for humans' lostness and sorry state. Romans 3:23 expresses the meaning of ἁμαρτία (sin) as both a missing the target of divine righteousness and a coming short of the divine δόξα, God's splendor, seen in the first Adam and restored in the "second man," Jesus Christ.

On the objective side, humans stand under God's judgment, his "wrath" (5:9). This term (ὀργή) is not an affective or emotionally charged disposition of God, as though God bore personal malice or exhibited pique against offending rebels. Indeed, Ephesians 4:26, 31 (drawing on Ps 4:4; cf. Jas 1:19-20) warns against precisely these outbursts of temper and bad feeling as well as indicting a settled attitude of hatred of our fellows. And God's love is the center of Paul's thought (5:5, 8). Yet God's ὀργή is real in terms of his moral resistance to evil and his judicial indignation in its presence. Evil invites his judgment by calling down his condemnation and his edict of banishment.

Two other parts of our passage fit into this whole picture. (i) If men and women find "access" through Christ's reconciling work, it follows that outside of Christ, there is only alienation and separation from God; and this, we may suppose from the consistent Old Testament tradition (e.g., Gen 3:24; Isa 59:2), is the essence of humanity's sinful state. They are distanced from God because God has declared them outlaws and exiles.

(ii) Yet the obverse side of the picture is seen in Romans 5:10: "when we were enemies. . . ." Interpreters are hopelessly divided over the question: Does "being enemies" mean "while we were hating God" (active) as in Romans 1:30; 8:7, or "while God was opposed to us" (passive)? Two arguments tip the scales on the side of the latter. In the total context of Romans 1:18–3:20 where God's righteous wrath is directed to the ungodly world and in consequence the world stands under his sentence, it must be an offense to God to view such a scene, Paul infers, and can only be met with a stern face of disapproval and opposition. Then, as Wolter has noted,[2] since the reconciliation spoken of in verse 10 is said to be "to God," it is logical to assume that Paul meant: once we were hostile *to God*, now we are reconciled *to him*. That sad state of being God's enemies is the lot of Israel according to Romans 11:28 (where, incidentally, no anti-Semitism can be justifiably traced; the writer is himself a Jew, passionately involved in his nation's fate [Rom 9:1-5; 10:1]).

Divine displeasure and human alienation sum up the state of men and women who are the objects of reconciliation. Earlier in the letter, Paul has concluded that as sinners such persons were placed "in the wrong" forensically and

2. M. Wolter, *Rechtfertigung und zukünftiges Heil. Untersuchungen zu Röm. 5.1-11* (Berlin: de Gruyter, 1978), p. 86.

eschatologically[3] and needed to be cleared and "set right." That is the language of justification. At this point in his statement of the message, Paul moves to another dimension of the human state. The gift of "peace" (5:1) makes sense only as it is understood as coming to those formerly estranged and at enmity. On God's side that barrier is denoted by his "wrath."

"Wrath" combines both forensic and eschatological ideas corresponding to humankind's state as "unrighteous" (ἄδικος) and "ungodly" (ἀσεβής): both terms are found in Romans 1:18 and both call down the divine ὀργή as a present reality. Evidently, Paul has taken this term (ὀργή) from the thought world of Jewish apocalypticism, where it connotes the "day of judgment," and has brought it into the present, where its effects are already at work (1 Thess 2:16; Rom 9:22). But the future aspect is not overlooked, as verse 9 reminds us ("how much more shall we be saved from God's wrath"). "Wrath" is replaced by "eternal life" in Romans 2:5-8; therefore "peace" in 5:1 has to be understood as a synonym in Jewish expectation for the new age of messianic bliss and favor. The term "peace" (שָׁלוֹם/εἰρήνη) is the relationship of acceptance with God based on eschatological salvation, not human feelings of inner harmony or tranquillity. But here Paul has personalized it by relating it to human experience of "access to God" and knowledge of his "grace" (5:2; there may be an anticipation of this in Job 22:21; Isa 27:5; 57:19; cf. 57:21). If, as E. Schweizer has said,[4] Romans 1:18–3:20 "deal with the eschatological outburst of God's wrath," the turning point comes at 5:1 with a celebration of the new age of God's salvation when "peace with God" is both heralded and enjoyed by his people.

B. Theological Motifs: God's Action

(i) At the heart of this passage is the revelation of divine love. The phrase "the love of God" (ἡ ἀγάπη τοῦ θεοῦ) is, perhaps contrary to popular expectation, used by Paul only rarely. In fact, there are but two other references (Rom 8:39; 2 Cor 13:13). Nor does Paul use the verb "to love" of the Christian's response to God very frequently (Rom 8:28; 1 Cor 8:3; note that 1 Cor 2:9 is a borrowing from some Jewish source). It is just possible that verse 5 may be translated: "our love for God has been poured into our hearts by the Holy Spirit," but the context is decisively against this rendering which Augustine promoted (*Spiritu lit.* 32:56). The following verse clearly emphasizes how Christ's dying for the ungodly is related to

3. For what this term implies in Paul's justification language, see N. T. Wright, *What Saint Paul Really Said* (Oxford: Lion, 1997), ch. 7.

4. E. Schweizer, "The Church as the Missionary Body of Christ," in *Neotestamentica* (Zürich: Zwingli Verlag, 1963), p. 319; reprinted from *NTS* 8 (1961-62): 1-11 (p. 2).

this love; and in verse 8 Paul writes unmistakably of God's own love for us (τὴν ἑαυτοῦ ἀγάπην) as demonstrated in Christ's death for sinners.

So here is one clear datum in Paul's soteriology: he can bring himself to express the love of God in this way because he found the focus of that love in the cross of Christ. God's love was no axiom or postulate he could take for granted. The believer's own experience, while it confirmed the reality of that love, did not prove it. Rather, its convincing proof was seen in what God did in the past event of the cross ("Christ died," vv. 6, 8), though the demonstration continues — Paul's verb συνίστησιν ("shows," "proves" NRSV) is present tense — because that one historical event of the cross has given for all time the paradigm of what is always true of God, namely that he is love. Yet his eternal nature once — and once for all — came into focus at Christ's cross, and its power remains.

The love of God is set in contrast to several other items in the discussion. First, its remarkable character is brought out in the somewhat tortuous syntax of verse 7. Paul starts out from the premise of Christ's death for the ungodly (v. 6). He proceeds: to contemplate a person dying even for a righteous person is wonderful, for it hardly ever happens. The inference would be drawn, that to imagine anyone dying on behalf of an unrighteous person is quite unthinkable, as it never occurs. Then the second half-verse seems to lessen the dramatic thrust of the arguments by introducing a qualification: perhaps for a good person a voluntary death is thinkable, whereas the opening of verse 8 invites us to consider, as a climax, that the totally unthinkable has taken place. Christ died for us wretched sinners to manifest God's distinct love, greater even than human love, which conceivably could lead him to surrender his life for a good person or perhaps a good cause (taking ὑπὲρ τοῦ ἀγαθοῦ as neuter). The point of Paul's argument, if the text is not corrupt or has been left unrevised by its author as has been suggested, is that a signal display of human love should be seen in a person's dying for a good cause (e.g., patriotism); on the contrary, God's love shines out in that he gives his son to death for the most undeserving of causes, since those for whom he died were rebels and enemies. That kind of love is "scarcely conceivable among human beings,"[5] and "without analogy" (Eichholz),[6] but it actually did once take place.

5. W. G. Kümmel, "Interpretation of Romans 5:1-11," in his *Exegetical Method: A Student's Handbook,* ed. O. Kaiser and W. G. Kümmel (New York: The Seabury Press, 1981), pp. 57-65 (63).

6. G. Eichholz, *Die Theologie des Paulus im Umriss* (Neukirchen: Neukirchener Verlag, 1972), p. 168; referred to in J. D. G. Dunn, *Romans 1–8,* WBC 38a (Dallas: Word, 1988), p. 256. The expedient that the Pauline text has suffered in transmission is appealed to by L. E. Keck, "The Post-Pauline Interpretation of Jesus' Death in Rom. 5:6-7," in *Theologia Crucis — Signum Crucis,* FS. E. Dinkler, ed. C. Anderson and G. Klein (Tübingen: Mohr, 1979), pp. 237-48.

Secondly, Paul sees the divine ἀγάπη coming to expression in a concrete event — "at the right time," "at the appointed hour" (καιρός) of prophetic destiny and eschatological hope when God's promises came to realization (see Mk 1:15; 12:2; Ps Sol 17:21: "Look, O Lord, and raise up for them their king, the son of David, at the appointed time [καιρός] which, O God, you did choose"). That "decisive moment" reflects the divine initiative in so choosing the time and place for his love to be made known (Gal 4:4); it also speaks to the desperate human condition, for it was when human beings were "helpless," "ungodly," and "enemies" that the drama was enacted. No more compelling indication of God's taking the first step in human recovery could be given, a fact reinforced by the twice-repeated adverb "still (ἔτι) powerless," "still (ἔτι) sinners" in verses 6 and 8.

Thirdly, references to Christ's "death" (v. 10) and "blood" (v. 9) seem to be there in the text as shorthand expressions or code words for his self-sacrifice on behalf of human sins. Unsuccessful attempts have been made to draw a distinction between the words "death" and "blood," and we note how rarely Paul uses the description, "the blood" of Christ (Rom 3:25; Col 1:20; cf. Eph 1:7; 2:13). The language is cultic-sacrificial, denoting the life laid down in death and as an atonement (i.e., a covering) for sins. The "death" in verse 10 picks up the earlier references to the verbal form, "he died" (vv. 6, 8), and expresses the self-offering of Jesus in obedience to God's holy design in love (Rom 8:32, with its reminiscence of Gen 22 and the rabbinic ideas of the sacrifice made in the "binding of Isaac").[7] The "death" of Christ takes on deeper poignancy and saving value when it is viewed as the death of the son whom God loves (Col 1:13; cf. Eph 1:6).

(ii) Reconciliation stands in some degree of tension with both "justification" and "wrath," two important words represented in our passage. We have seen how Paul begins with the judicial idiom (v. 1), picks it up later (v. 9), but does not explore its significance at any depth. Instead, the immediate consequence of being set right with God is "peace," a term synonymous with "reconciliation," which then takes over in the discussion and which is used to denote both restored relationship with God (so reversing and nullifying the baneful effects of sin) and a real participation in the life of the risen Christ, a theme which is later worked out in chapters 6–8.

"Wrath" naturally is that which sets up the hiatus between God and humans, and is given here its eschatological meaning, as in 1 Thessalonians 1:10;

7. For negative assessment of the concept of the *aqedah,* see P. R. Davies and B. D. Chilton, "The Aqedah: A Revised Tradition History," *CBQ* 40 (1978): 514-46. More positive are J. Swetnam, *Jesus and Isaac: A Study of the Epistle to the Hebrews in the Light of the Aqedah,* AB 94 (Rome: Biblical Institute, 1981), and A. F. Segal, "'He who did not spare his own son': Jesus, Paul and the Aqedah," in *From Jesus to Paul,* FS F. W. Beare, ed. P. Richardson and J. C. Hurd (Waterloo, Ont.: Wilfred Laurier University Press, 1984), pp. 169-84.

5:9; and Romans 2:5, 8; 12:19. If the verbs "saved" in verses 9 and 10 are of equal weight, the hoped-for deliverance from God's final judgment is secured by Christ's "life." The latter term would mean in context his advocacy of his people's cause at the last day and their preservation from divine retribution. Nothing is said about Christ's assuming their sin or enduring God's wrath on the cross, even if the term "enemies" does carry the thought of being "hostile to God." Paul again has left unexplained "how" the reconciliation is effected except to make certain reportorial statements. These are:

(a) God's hostility to sinners is the essential background of Paul's doctrine. On the human side the sorry condition of alienation is seen in humanity's unrighteousness and inability to save itself.

(b) God's unconstrained initiative gives proof of his love, for which Paul can find no parallel since God is not dealing with "righteous" or "good" people but his "enemies."

(c) Man's part is to "receive the reconciliation" or "enjoy peace with God" as a present possession. On either reading, it is the gift of God which no one can merit or earn. Paul's antinomistic strain is evident in the language he uses. "Let us have peace" (reading ἔχωμεν in v. 1) is therefore inappropriate as an unqualified translation in this context, whatever the merits of its textual pedigree. On the other hand, while Paul certainly wished to stress the present availability of God's grace in reconciliation, it still remains true that men and women must "receive" it, and for that to happen human responsibility is called into play. E. Dinkler therefore puts his finger on a real concern when he suggests that the gift of God's peace is to be matched by our seeking to live in that relationship (Rom 14:19; Col 3:15; Phil 4:7).[8] The concurrence of the indicative ("We have peace") and the imperative ("Let us have peace") is typically Pauline in manner, and there is therefore no real need to choose between the disputed readings.[9] Rather we should combine them: "let us enjoy the peace we have" (Moffatt's rendering).

(d) A person's "exulting" (RSV "rejoice"; other versions like NRSV give "boast" for καυχᾶσθαι) is a significant feature in this paragraph. Paul's pre-Christian life as a pious Jew was characterized by this outlook and attitude: he boasted of his compliance with the minutiae of Torah religion. By what happened in his "conversion" he came to a reevaluation of this "boasting," and saw it as a species of sinful pride. Henceforth he will "boast in the Lord" (1 Cor 1:31) now that he has been set right with God by his grace in Christ crucified

8. E. Dinkler, *Eirēnē: Der urchristliche Friedensgedanke* (Heidelberg: Winter, 1973), pp. 34-35, n. 108, citing Ps 34:15.

9. N. Elliott, *The Rhetoric of Romans: Argumentative Constraint and Strategy and Paul's Dialogue with Judaism* JSNTSS 45 (Sheffield: Academic Press, 1990), p. 228.

and through meritless faith. All other boasting is excluded (Rom 3:27), and even his missionary service is not suitable for this exercise (2 Cor 11:12-30). He may only truly "boast" of his weaknesses (2 Cor 12:5).

Yet here we find him "boasting" not only in his trials (5:3) but in God from whom, in Jesus Christ the Lord, he has received the restored relationship (v. 11). It is a concluding tribute to his full reliance on God's free grace and strength (χάρις means both) that has met and answered his deepest needs as a sinner: as an ungodly person he has been forgiven, as a powerless individual he has been reinforced by divine energy for his life as a Christian. And the gift of reconciliation is thus none other than the Spirit in his life (v. 5) bringing the privilege of filial adoption and joy.

III. Romans 5:1-11: In the Setting of a Developing Pauline Tradition

Our attention will now be directed to the question of how far Romans 5:1-11, which marks "the pivot on which the letter's argument turns,"[10] carries forward, confirms, or modifies Paul's earlier teaching on reconciliation as seen in the other places where he has commented on the tradition. First of all, we may note certain definite features that serve to crystallize his earlier thinking.

(i) In the Romans passage, Paul has given a sharper profile to the love of God in providing the means of reconciliation in the person of Jesus Christ. In 2 Corinthians 5:19, the statement "in Christ, God was reconciling the world" runs parallel with the previous verse, "God . . . through Christ reconciled us to himself" (v. 18); but it says no more than that Christ was the agent of the divine enterprise, even if it does stress God's personal presence in what happened. The passage in Romans 5 leaves us in no doubt that God's personal involvement was one in which his love focused in a single deed: "Christ died for us." In Colossians 1:20, "making peace (εἰρηνοποιήσας) by the blood of his cross" is certainly a strong statement of God's activity in securing cosmic harmony by the cross, but what that "peace" entailed is left undefined, and so has been the source of much diverse interpretation.[11] Romans 5:1 rephrases the term in an unmistakable way: reconciliation is none other than "peace with God through our Lord Jesus Christ," who unites us to the Father and is not (in this context) described as the unifying center of the cosmos.

(ii) Our present passage firmly and clearly anchors the reconciliation in

10. Elliott, *Rhetoric of Romans,* pp. 226, 233.

11. J. D. G. Dunn, *The Epistles to the Colossians and to Philemon,* NIGTC (Grand Rapids: Eerdmans, 1996), pp. 102-4.

the historical event of the cross. Paul had prefaced the citation of 2 Corinthians 5:18-21 with reminders of Christ's love (v. 14) seen in his death "for all," but a clearer focus is given by asserting that he "died for us" (Rom 5:8) and that we are "reconciled to God by the death of his Son" (Rom 5:10). Moreover, the Father and the Son are more closely brought together here; and this collocation gives added weight to what the death of Christ involved. Moreover, the beneficiaries of his reconciling work are made more personal: it was not only "the world" or "those who live" (2 Cor 5:15) that are mentioned as the ones for whom Christ died. Instead, in Romans Paul writes warmly of Christ's dying "for us" and "our being reconciled."

It is true that in Paul's redaction of Colossians 1:22 the death of Christ is prominent and an emphasis on his real bodily suffering serves to oppose any gnostic or docetic tendency to turn redemption into a divine charade. In 1:20, the reconciliation of "all things" is qualified by the insertion of "the blood of his cross"; this more vivid idiom, however, is not repeated at verse 22, whereas Romans 5:9 relates "his blood" more precisely to what Christ did in securing our pardon and amnesty. Both Paul's editorial supplements in Colossians 1 and his teaching in Romans 5 emphasize by the use of past (aorist) tenses of the verbs that reconciliation is a historical event, complete in its "having-happenedness." The phrases "he has now reconciled" in Colossians 1:22 and "we were reconciled" and "now that we are reconciled" in Romans 5:10 (both aorist passive in verb formation) leave no room for misunderstanding as to the completeness and certainty of what God has done. Admittedly, 2 Corinthians 5:18 has the aorist participle as well, yet verse 19 with its periphrastic tense leaves the reconciliation more as the state of an ongoing process than a final deed.

(iii) The "world" of 2 Corinthians 5:19 may well have been understood in a cosmic sense, and it is clear that the scope of reconciliation in Colossians 1:18-20 embraces all of creation, only to be applied concretely to human beings at 1:21-22. Romans 5 rules out any misunderstanding and possible confusion. Paul is talking throughout of the lives of men and women who are in need as sinners. The background is not so much one of "trespassers" (2 Cor 5:19; Col 1:21) and "estranged persons" in an alien universe (Col 1:21), as "enemies of God" who stand in need of being delivered from their exposure to "the wrath of God." And human impotence to secure deliverance is accepted here, since men and women are both "powerless" and "ungodly," an analytical judgment on the human situation which is deeper than that given in the other passages.

(iv) Paul's language of justification (in Rom 3:24-26; 2 Cor 5:18-21) and deliverance from the dark domain of evil powers (Col 1:13) leading to the assurance of forgiveness (Col 1:14) is essentially negative. The stress is on the removal of all impediments to reconciliation. But in Paul's teaching, by using the language of "reconciliation," he stresses that the positive side of man's restoration to God is really the goal of the salvific drama. Romans 5:1-11 therefore is not content to leave human beings as "justified" individuals or members of a new community, "the kingdom of his beloved Son"; rather, this passage ushers them into God's presence (v. 2) and assures them of a welcome in the family of God, where the Spirit is the Spirit of adoption (v. 5; Rom 8:14-16).

These distinctive features obviously may be offset by a body of common elements that unite Paul's teachings which we have so far considered. We want freely to grant that this commonality is what counts in the long run. Paul's exposition of reconciliation reveals the following clear-cut statements:

(i) God is the provider of the new relationship he freely offers. The author of reconciliation is referred to consistently as God himself, who initiates and carries through the process. And he does so in love. This feature is characteristic of both Jesus' recorded teaching on God as Father (e.g., Lk 15) and the way he saw his mission as God's messenger to the world. In each instance the picture of a seeking, caring, and forgiving God who meets sinners before they repent is one that has no parallel in Second Temple Judaism, though there are evidences in the Old Testament (e.g., Hos; Isa 65:1-2).[12]

(ii) At great cost, epitomized in Christ's blood or death on the cross, God has moved to deal with a situation that only he could resolve. Here is a knot only God could untie, said Luther quaintly.[13] The "dilemma" is that reconciliation is not cheaply secured, since God both "justifies" (i.e., vindicates) himself and offers "justification" (Rom 3:26) as a ground on which he extends that grace of reconciliation. God's love and "righteousness" — in some mysterious way never quite explained by Paul — come together in the cross of Jesus. That death is the focal point of the divine love; but it is also needful that sin should be exposed, though Paul draws back from saying that Christ bore the divine wrath. He was "appointed" (2 Cor 5:21) a sacrifice for sin and took humanity's part over against God in a representative way. Since "blood" and "death" are words in the vocabulary of atonement, we may infer that his death was the vicarious sacrifice because of which barriers to reconciliation are now overcome; moreover, it is the saving love of God seen in Christ's death, by God's appointing, that has power to reconcile.

12. J. D. G. Dunn, *Romans 1–8*, pp. 259-60, Dunn citing Martin.

13. As quoted in D. M. Baillie, *God Was in Christ* (New York: Scribner's, 1948), p. 171. Referring to Horace's rule of dramatic art, that a god must never be introduced *(deus ex machina)* into the action unless the plot has got so tangled that only a god could unravel it — *nec deus intersit nisi dignus vindice nodus inciderit* (*Ars Poetica*, 191-92) — Luther concedes that sin is such a problem.

We now conclude that in the two places where Paul has expressions that give a rationale for "reconciliation" (in the terms ἱλαστήριον,[14] expiation/propitiation, in Rom 3:25 and "Christ made sin" in 2 Cor 5:21), he has drawn upon traditional teaching which he has not stopped to explain further. We assume that this use certifies his agreement with what he quotes and that therefore some atonement teaching probably had a wide currency before Paul pressed it into service. It would equally be true that Paul's acceptance of the tradition *as far as it went* has to be seen in the context of his concern to draw out some matters that were not sufficiently prominent in the original formulation. In specific terms, "expiation" has to be lifted out of its cultic setting and related to divine salvific righteousness for the whole world. The sacrifice of Christ as a sin offering has to be reinterpreted in terms of justification and the new age of reconciliation that the cross and resurrection (2 Cor 5:14-17) ushered in. The same principle of "tradition" and Paul's "redaction," which gave the old forms a new depth, is seen in one other place, where Paul quotes an interpretative text to answer the question: How did Christ save his people? We refer to Galatians 3:13, where the "curse" that came on Christ is a prelude to the conclusion Paul is seeking to establish, "that in Christ Jesus the blessing of Abraham might come upon the Gentiles" (Gal 3:14, 22). That "blessing" is the promised Spirit of the new age, available to all.

(iii) Human need is the dark canvas against which the divine love shines brightly. Alienation and positive wickedness make men and women unable to save themselves, and lead to their being dependent on the free forgiveness of God. While Paul says that we are "justified by faith," he does not say "we are reconciled by faith." The attitude to reconciliation is, on believers' part, one of grateful acceptance (Rom 5:11), not, we may contend, answering the call, "Be reconciled to God" (2 Cor 5:20), though that is the usual interpretation. Reconciliation is the concomitant of justification, but it is a larger term. Reconciliation is "peace with God" and ensures a place not only in the new world now "rectified" but in the new fellowship of the Spirit (Rom 5:5).

(iv) Above all, reconciliation moves always on the plane of personal relationships. It expresses both the privilege of being in a happy relationship of friendship with God and the demand of so living in grace (Rom 5:2) as not to frustrate that grace (2 Cor 6:1). The relationship is, we may say, more fragile than the new standing suggested by justification. Paul never contemplates a reversal of justification or an overturning of either legal acquittal or royal amnesty (Rom 8:33-34; Gal 5:5). But the Corinthians, or some of them at least, can turn their

14. See Judith M. Gundry-Volf, "Expiation, Propitiation, Mercy Seat," in *Dictionary of Paul and His Letters,* eds. G. F. Hawthorne, R. P. Martin, D. G. Reid (Downers Grove, Ill.: InterVarsity Press, 1993), pp. 279-84 for discussion and literature.

backs on God's offer which they once received in the gospel preached by Paul. They can and in fact did range themselves with the "unbelievers" (ἄπιστοι, 2 Cor 4:4; 6:14-15; 2 Cor 11:4, 13-15) who must be reconciled to God by the message of the kerygma. Their failure to abide in "righteousness" is seen in their acceptance of those whom Paul branded as "servants of [counterfeit] righteousness" (2 Cor 11:15) who are Satan's emissaries. They have put themselves back under the devil's jurisdiction by opposing his gospel.[15] And they need to see once again the outstretched hand of Paul as he appeals to them, "Be reconciled to God." The Colossians also are warned to abide in their new relationship with God by adherence to the apostolic teaching (Col 1:22-23). So the category of reconciliation shares an existential quality, thus making it admirably suited to express the tension in Paul's theology between "already justified . . . not yet finally saved," as it is formulated *(die Spannung zwischen dem Schon und Noch-Nicht).*

(v) If it is true that justification and reconciliation are partners in being associated yet each having a distinct nuance, we may ask why Paul moved from justification (in chapters 1–4 of Romans) to the new vocabulary beginning in chapter 5. Part of the reason may be seen in the consideration of Romans 3:24-26. There Paul, we suggest,[16] expressed dissatisfaction with the forensic-cultic idiom that limited soteriology to covenant-renewal for the Jewish nation and sought to universalize the scope of Christ's saving deed to include the Gentiles on the basis of faith, not covenantal nomism.

The prominence given to reconciliation from Romans 5 onwards, together with the language of 2 Corinthians 5 (where justification terms in v. 19 are added to correct a possible wrongheaded idea) and Colossians 1:21-22, suggests yet another reason for the movement from justification to reconciliation at this point of Romans 5:1. "Reconciliation" is (or perhaps became)[17] the way Paul formulated his gospel in communicating it to the Gentiles. The terminology is not restricted to the Old Testament–Judaic tradition; it has little if any cultic-forensic association; it relates to a universal human need, namely forgiveness and personal relationship; and it can take within its scope both personal and cosmic dimensions. For pagans newly won over to Christ there was this pressing need: to receive assurance that the Lord who had granted them pardon and had broken the entail of their sinful past was indeed the ruler of the spirit forces that held their erstwhile lives in the bondage of fear and cosmic dread.

15. Susan R. Garrett, "Paul's Thorn and Cultural Models of Affliction," in *The Social World of the First Christians: Essays in Honor of Wayne A. Meeks,* eds. L. M. White and O. L. Yarborough (Minneapolis: Augsburg Fortress, 1995), p. 98.

16. On Romans 3:24-26, see my discussion in *Reconciliation: A Study of Paul's Theology,* rev. ed. (Eugene, Ore.: Wipf & Stock, 1997), pp. 83-89.

17. William S. Campbell, review, *Theology* 86 (July 1983): 300-302.

With this submission before us, it may be appropriate to draw out an ancillary conclusion. Paul employed the "reconciliation" imagery as a tool of communication to the Gentile world, but from all we have seen he was not the first to invent or use the term. "Reconciliation" was already part of the Christian vocabulary before he adopted it.[18] But in his hands it took on a new meaning. Its earlier setting was the cosmos; Christ was viewed as lord of all worlds and the central principle by which all the disparate elements of the universe were held together. That is clearly the sense of "reconcile" in Colossians 1:15-20 in its first "version" (if we may so isolate it); similarly 2 Corinthians 5:18-21 may have taught a cosmic salvation by divine fiat. Paul seized upon the term as altogether suited to express what the Christian kerygma meant to those unversed in Jewish thought-forms and whose "needs" were not those of the world of justification/guilt/acquittal, represented by the Jewish-Christian credo of 1 Corinthians 15:3-5.

Paul's use of the hymn in Philippians 2:6-11 shows how he could adapt a pre-Pauline composition, edit it by the insertion of "even the death of the cross" (v. 8) and possibly widen its scope by enriching verse 10, to make it express more clearly the kerygma for Hellenistic society.[19] We submit as a hypothesis that exactly this procedure has been applied to early Gentile-Christian hymnic celebrations of "Christ the cosmocrat, ruler of creation," and that in Paul's creative hands the teaching is more securely anchored in the cross with the emphasis on a removal of all barriers that obstruct reconciliation with God, whether innate fear of demons or personal insecurity caused by alienation or human distress, all of which the offer of forgiveness and new life was designed to overcome.

In Ephesians we are faced with the use of reconciliation terminology in reference to Jew-Gentile relations, and we can test this hypothesis and see whether, in fact, in the mind of Paul and his later school, "Christ our peace" met the needs of Gentiles who were wrestling with the conundrum of Israel's role in salvation history (Rom 9–11) and seeking to find in a now multiracial church a rationale for Christ's reconciling work as it affected ancient society (Eph 2:11-22). But that, on any showing, is a later story[20] — or rather, a later part of the same story.

18. On the background of the term, traced to Paul's conversion experience, see now Seyoon Kim, "2 Cor. 5:11-21 and the Origin of Paul's Concept of 'Reconciliation,'" *NovT* 39.4 (1997): 360-84.

19. Gordon Fee has, of course, sustained a number of objections to my understanding of Phil 2:5-11, notably in his commentary *Paul's Letter to the Philippians,* NICNT (Grand Rapids: Eerdmans, 1995). My responses are found in *A Hymn of Christ: Philippians 2:5-11* etc. (Downers Grove, Ill.: InterVarsity Press, 1997), preface.

20. See R. P. Martin, *Reconciliation,* ch. 9.

The Focus of Romans: The Central Role of 5:1–8:39 in the Argument of the Letter

Richard N. Longenecker

In his highly significant *magnum opus* on "the Holy Spirit in the letters of Paul,"[1] Gordon Fee, in dealing with Romans 1:11, observes (1) that a letter in antiquity (as also today) was meant to serve as "a second-best substitute for a personal visit," (2) that the opening Thanksgiving sections of Paul's letters reveal the apostle's central concerns and purposes in writing, and (3) that in Romans 1:11-15, which continues the Thanksgiving section begun at 1:8, Paul states his reasons for writing believers at Rome and wanting to be with them — somewhat generally in verse 13b ("in order that I might have fruit also among you") and verse 15 ("so that I might preach the gospel also to you who are in Rome"), but expressly in verse 11: "In order that I might share with you *some spiritual gift* so that you might be strengthened." In fact, as Fee rightly asserts, it is the expression "spiritual gift" (χάρισμα πνευματικόν) that Paul uses to characterize what he writes in the letter.

But the question arises: How, then, should Romans be understood in the light of that expression? More specifically, Was Paul referring by that expression to his whole letter generally, or did he have in mind a particular focus or central thrust? Fee points out that the combination of the noun χάρισμα ("gift") and the adjective πνευματικόν ("spiritual") is a "unique col-

1. G. D. Fee, *God's Empowering Presence: The Holy Spirit in the Letters of Paul* (Peabody, Mass.: Hendrickson, 1994).

location" of terms in Paul's letters, which requires both linguistic and contextual explication.[2] Investigating the expression linguistically, he concludes that Paul is not here talking about some "gifting" by the Spirit, as in 1 Corinthians 12:8-10 and Romans 12:6-8, but about the present letter as a "Spirit gift" sent to believers at Rome in order to strengthen them in lieu of a personal visit from him (v. 11) — and so, as more generally stated (v. 13), to bring about some "fruit" among them as well as to proclaim the gospel to them as he had done throughout the eastern Roman empire (vv. 14-15). With approval he cites James Denney: "No doubt, in substance, Paul imparts his spiritual gift through this epistle."[3]

Then referring to the immediate and extended contexts of the expression, Fee suggests:

> In its present context, and especially in light of the letter as a whole, the "Spirit gift" that he most likely wishes to share with them is his understanding of the gospel that in Christ Jesus God has created from among Jews and Gentiles one people for himself, apart from Torah. This is the way they are to be "strengthened" by Paul's coming, and this surely is the "fruit" he wants to have among them when he comes (v. 13). If so, then in effect our present letter functions as his "Spirit gifting" for them. This is what he would impart if he were there in person: this is what he now "shares" since he cannot presently come to Rome.[4]

I am in complete agreement with Fee's general introductory observations and his linguistic analysis of the expression "spiritual gift" in 1:11, and so will not reconsider here the points he has already made. In particular, I am sure Fee is right in understanding χάρισμα πνευματικόν as having reference to the letter itself, either in its entirety or with particular reference to its central thrust. Likewise, I agree that what Paul "most likely wishes to share with them [his readers] is his understanding of the gospel." I would, however, argue that the focus or central thrust of Romans is not to be found — as has been traditionally argued — in 1:16–4:25, which can be epitomized by the statement "in Christ Jesus God has created from among Jews and Gentiles one people for himself, apart from Torah." Rather, I propose that the focus of the letter — which Paul refers to as "my gospel" in 16:25 of the doxology — is to be found in 5:1–8:39, which highlights the themes of "peace" and "reconciliation" with God, the antithesis of "death" and "life," and the relationships of being "in Christ" and "in the Spirit."

2. Fee, *God's Empowering Presence,* 486-89.

3. Fee, *God's Empowering Presence,* 488, n. 48.

4. Fee, *God's Empowering Presence,* 488-89.

In support of such a thesis it is necessary to scan Romans contextually. In particular, it is necessary to deal critically with certain features regarding the structures and arguments of the letter.

For our present purposes, the discussion will be limited to the first eight chapters of Romans. More detailed explication of these chapters, as well as comments on how they relate to the rest of Romans, will be reserved for a forthcoming commentary.

I. The Structures and Arguments of Romans 1:18–3:20

A number of perplexing issues arise in any critical reading of Romans. Many of these reflect what has been called the "dual character" of the letter. And most of them come to the fore when comparing the materials set out in 1:16–4:25 vis-à-vis the presentation of 5:1–8:39. We will begin the analysis by highlighting first the structures and arguments of 1:18–3:20, with special attention to chapter 2.

A. Some Important Issues

The interpretation of 1:18–3:20 has been notoriously difficult for almost every commentator. Problems begin to take form when one attempts to identify exactly who is being talked about or addressed in the passage. Is it Gentiles in 1:18-32, Jews in 2:1-5, Gentiles in 2:6-16, then Jews again in 2:17–3:19, with a conclusion in 3:20? Or is it Gentiles in 1:18-32 and Jews in 2:1–3:19, with a conclusion pertaining to both in 3:20? Or is it humanity generally in 1:18–2:16 and Jews (or a particular type of Jew) in 2:17–3:19, with a conclusion in 3:20? Earlier interpreters such as Origen, Jerome, Augustine, and Erasmus wrestled with this issue, and it continues to plague commentators today.

Likewise, problems arise when one tries to evaluate the structures incorporated within 1:18–3:20. In the first part of that section, in 1:18-32, there appears a denunciation of the idolatry and immorality of the Gentile world that parallels quite closely the denunciation of Gentile idolatry and immorality in *Wisdom of Solomon* 13:1–14:31, with scholars generally agreed that Paul must have drawn on this work for his portrayal in 1:18-32 (perhaps also in 2:1-15) or that he and the writer of *Wisdom* drew from similar traditions. Furthermore, the second part of the section, 2:1–3:8, abounds with characteristic features and stylistic traits that correspond to what was practiced in the Greek diatribal dialogues. And 3:10-18, which is the longest catena of biblical passages in the Pauline corpus, has been seen by many to be a collection of passages that was originally brought together within Judaism and/or Jewish Christianity and then used by Paul in support of his thesis (and theirs?) that "Jews and Gentiles alike are all under sin" (3:9; cf. 3:19, 23).

More importantly, however, problems of interpretation multiply when one asks: How does what Paul says about Gentiles and Jews in chapter 2 correspond to what he says about humanity generally and Jews in particular in the rest of his letter? For while his conclusions regarding God's impartiality (2:11), Jews and Gentiles being alike under sin (3:9-19, 23), and no one being able to be declared righteous by observing the law (3:20) are clear, there are four texts in Romans 2 that seem to espouse a theology of salvation by works or by obedience to the Mosaic law. And only once in this chapter, in verse 16, does explicit Christian language come to the fore.

The first problem text appears in 2:7, 10, where it is said that God will give "eternal life" — or, "glory, honor, and peace" — to those who persistently do good works, which seems to conflict with what is said about being justified solely by faith in 3:21-30, 4:1-25, and throughout 9:1–11:36. The second is 2:13, where it is said that "those who obey the law [are the ones] who will be declared righteous," which seems to be in conflict with Paul's statement about no one being declared righteous by observing the law in 3:20, his references to humans being unable to obey the law in 7:14-25, and his denunciation of Israel for attempting to gain righteousness by means of the Mosaic law in 9:30–11:12. The third is 2:14-15, where there is the parenthetical statement that some Gentiles do by nature "the things of the law" and "show the work of the law written in their hearts," with the inference being that in so doing they are justified before God. But assuming that Paul is using "law" throughout this passage in a consistent way, such an inference seems to contradict his earlier picture of the Gentiles in 1:18-32 and his conclusion in 3:20 about the impossibility of righteousness before God being obtained by observing the law. The fourth problem text is 2:25-27, which appears to be built on the assumption that righteousness is associated with the practice of the Mosaic law. But, again, this seems to fly in the face of Paul's express conclusion to this section in 3:19-20, his thesis statement regarding the "righteousness of God" being "apart from the law" in 3:21-23, his use of Abraham as the exemplar of faith in 4:1-25, and his entire depiction of the relation of the gospel to the hope of Israel in 9:1–11:36 — as well as, of course, his arguments in Galatians 2:15-16; 3:6-14 and exhortations in Galatians 4:12–5:12, arguments repeated here and there in his other letters.

B. Some Preliminary Observations

What has been made of these seemingly non-Pauline statements in Romans 2? One popular way of reconciling them with Paul's thought elsewhere in Romans and his other letters is to propose that the apostle is here speaking of *Christian* Gentiles, not pagan Gentiles — that is, of Gentiles who obey the Jewish law through faith in Christ and life in the Spirit.[5] Another way is to posit that Romans 2 is speaking primarily about *pre-Christian* Gentiles who had faith in God or about godly Jews *before* the coming of the gospel — or perhaps, in some blended manner, about pre-Christian Gentiles who possessed a God-given faith, faithful Jews who before the coming of Christ expressed their trust in God through the forms of the Mosaic law, *and* Christian believers.[6] And still other ways of viewing these statements have been proposed, mostly by means of some combination of the above two approaches.[7] Ernst Käsemann, for example, interprets Romans 2 in terms of "three distinct moments in the chapter":[8] pagan Gentiles in 2:12-16; a "purely fictional" Gentile soteriology in 2:24-27; and the "true Jew" as a Gentile Christian in 2:28-29.[9] Joseph Fitzmyer argues that in 2:7, 10, Paul is referring to Christians "whose conduct (good deeds) is to be understood as the fruit of their faith,"[10] but that in 2:14-15 and 2:26 he is referring to pagan Gentiles and not Christian Gentiles.[11] And James Dunn believes that in 2:7, 10 and 2:26-29 Paul is

5. Cf., e.g., R. Bultmann, *Theology of the New Testament,* trans. K. Grobel (New York: Scribner's, 1951), 261; K. Barth, *A Shorter Commentary on Romans* (Richmond: John Knox, 1959), 36-39; M. Black, *Romans* (London: Marshall, Morgan & Scott, 1973), 55-56; C. E. B. Cranfield, *Romans,* 2 vols. (Edinburgh: T. & T. Clark, 1975), 1.152-62, 173-76; A. König, "Gentiles or Gentile Christians? On the Meaning of Romans 2:12-16," *Journal of Theology for South Africa* 15 (1976): 53-60; A. Ito, "Romans 2: A Deuteronomist Reading," *Journal for the Study of the New Testament* 59 (1995): 33-34.

6. E.g., A. Schlatter, *Gottes Gerechtigkeit. Ein Kommentar zum Römerbrief* (Stuttgart: Calwer, 1935), 74-112; idem, *Der Glaube im Neuen Testament,* 5th Aufl. (Stuttgart: Calwer, 1963), 323-28, 380-81; P. P. Bläser, *Das Gesetz bei Paulus* (Münster: Aschendorff, 1941), 195-97; C. K. Barrett, *A Commentary on the Epistle to the Romans* (New York: Harper & Row, 1957), 42-51; J.-M. Cambier, "Le jugement de tous les hommes par Dieu seul, selon la vérité, dans Rom 2:1–3:20," *Zeitschrift für die Neutestamentliche Wissenschaft* 67 (1976): 187-213, esp. 210; K. R. Snodgrass, "Justification by Grace — To the Doers: An Analysis of the Place of Romans 2 in the Theology of Paul," *New Testament Studies* 32 (1986): 72-93; G. Theissen, *Psychological Aspects of Pauline Theology,* trans. J. P. Galvin (Edinburgh: T. & T. Clark; Philadelphia: Fortress, 1987), 70-71; and G. N. Davies, *Faith and Obedience in Romans* (Sheffield: JSOT, 1990), 53-71, esp. 55-56 (both OT and NT believers). Snodgrass epitomizes this position in saying: "Those people who have seen Romans 2 as a description of circumstances prior to the coming of the gospel are correct" ("Justification by Grace — To the Doers," 81).

7. C. E. B. Cranfield cites and evaluates ten such ways (*Romans,* 1.151-53).

8. To use E. P. Sanders's expression in characterizing Käsemann's understanding, which Sanders calls an example of "tortured exegesis" (*Paul, the Law, and the Jewish People* [Philadelphia: Fortress, 1983], 127).

9. E. Käsemann, *Commentary on Romans,* trans. G. W. Bromiley (Grand Rapids: Eerdmans, 1980), 59, 65, 73.

10. J. A. Fitzmyer, *Romans* (New York-London-Toronto: Doubleday, 1993), 297, cf. 302.

11. Fitzmyer, *Romans,* 310, 322.

thinking of Christian Gentiles, whereas in 2:14-15 he is referring to pagan Gentiles.[12]

Quite another approach has been to understand Romans 2 as referring to the *hypothetical* possibility of being justified by good works or obedience to the law, but then to deny that possibility in order to highlight the reality of righteousness before God as being only by faith — that is, arguing that *if* people *could* obey the law they would be justified, but no one can. This is basically an Augustinian approach, which was reiterated by Martin Luther in his insistence that "All the Scriptures of God are divided into two parts: commands and promises" — the former being "God's strange work" to bring us down; the latter "God's proper work" to raise us up.[13] This position was established in modern critical scholarship by Hans Lietzmann, who argued that Paul is here viewing matters "from a pre-gospel standpoint" and setting out what would have been the case "if (1) there were no gospel, and (2) it were possible to fulfill the Law."[14] Essentially the same position has been espoused by many scholars both before and after Lietzmann.[15] Earlier, in 1964, I also adopted this approach, arguing in my *Paul, Apostle of Liberty:* "The contrast we see between Romans 2:6ff. and 3:21ff. is the same as that between Law and Gospel. In Romans 2:6ff. the Apostle cites the Law, which promises life and would bring life *if* the factors of human sin and inability were not present."[16]

12. J. D. G. Dunn, *Romans,* 2 vols. (Dallas: Word, 1988), 1.86, 98, 100, 106-7, 122-25. Cf. also T. R. Schreiner, "Did Paul Believe in Justification by Works? Another Look at Romans 2," *Bulletin for Biblical Research* 3 (1993): 131-55. Somewhat similarly, H. Schlier held that pagan Gentiles are designated in 2:14-15, while in 2:27 Paul passes unconsciously into describing Christian Gentiles (*Der Römerbrief* [Freiberg: Herder, 1977], 77-79, 88).

13. M. Luther, "A Treatise on Christian Liberty," in *Works of Martin Luther,* vol. 2, trans. W. A. Lambert (Philadelphia: Holman, 1916), 317.

14. H. Lietzmann, *An die Römer,* 5 Aufl. (Tübingen: Mohr-Siebeck, 1971), 39-40 (my translation). Cf. also 44.

15. E.g., M. Kähler, "Auslegung von Kap. 2,14-16 in Römerbrief," *Theologische Studien und Kritiken* 47 (1974): 274, 277; A. Friedrichsen, "Der wahre Jude und sein Lob: Röm. 2.28f.," *Symbolae Arctoae* I (1922): 43-44; J. Knox, *The Epistle to the Romans* (New York: Abingdon, 1954), 409, 418-19; O. Kuss, *Der Römerbrief* (Regensburg: Pustet, 1957), 1.64-68, 70-71, 90-92; G. Bornkamm, "Gesetz und Natur (Röm. 2,14-15)," in *Studien zu Antike und Urchristentum* II (Munich: Kaiser, 1959), 110; U. Wilckens, *Der Brief an der Römer* (Neukirchen-Vluyn: Neukirchener Verlag, 1978), 1.132-33, 145; F. F. Bruce, *The Letter of Paul to the Romans* (Grand Rapids: Eerdmans, 1985), 90; R. A. Harrisville, *Romans* (Minneapolis: Augsburg, 1980), 43-50; B. L. Martin, *Christ and the Law in Paul* (Leiden: Brill, 1989), 40-41, 92-93; F. Thielman, *From Plight to Solution: A Jewish Framework for Understanding Paul's View of the Law in Galatians and Romans* (Leiden: Brill, 1989), 94-96; D. Moo, *The Epistle to the Romans* (Grand Rapids: Eerdmans, 1996), 155-57, 171-72.

16. R. N. Longenecker, *Paul, Apostle of Liberty* (New York: Harper & Row, 1964), 121-22.

On the other hand, there are scholars today who assert that some or all of the above-listed problem passages of Romans 2 are flatly contradictory to Paul's thought elsewhere in Romans, though they offer diverse explanations for the texts in question. John O'Neill, as might be expected from his treatment of Galatians, sees all of 1:18–2:29 to be contradictory to Paul's teaching and irrelevant to his purpose, and so declares this section to be an interpolation by a later glossator who drew on material from a Hellenistic Jewish missionary tractate.[17] Heikki Räisänen, rejecting an interpolation theory, argues that 2:14-15 and 26-27 are flatly contradictory to Paul's main thesis in 1:18–3:20 that all are under sin, and so evidence quite clearly that "Paul's mind is divided" with respect to humanity's ability to keep the Mosaic law.[18] For his part, Ed Sanders believes that in 1:18–2:29 "Paul takes over to an unusual degree homiletical material from Diaspora Judaism, that he alters it in only insubstantial ways, and that consequently the treatment of the law in chapter 2 cannot be harmonized with any of the diverse things which Paul says about the law elsewhere."[19]

Most of the attempts to understand Romans 2 sketched out above — apart from those of O'Neill, Räisänen, and Sanders — start on the assumption that everything that is said in the chapter represents Paul's teaching directly, however derived, and that therefore everything said needs to be reconciled in some way with what is said elsewhere in Romans and Paul's other letters. Yet for most of these same scholars, it has seemed incredible that Paul would speak about justification without also having the idea of faith in mind. So they have found it necessary either (1) to clarify the nature of the referents beyond what the apostle himself has done, or (2) to interpret Romans 2 as a hypothetical presentation that functions rhetorically to prepare the way for a later discussion.

C. Some Proposals

How, then, can the issues that arise in 1:18–3:20 be understood? Personally, while I am prepared to relinquish the designation "hypothetical," I still believe that 1:18–3:20 was written in order to prepare for the discussion of 3:21–4:25 — with 1:16-17 being the thesis for the entire section, 3:21-23 the repetition

17. J. C. O'Neill, *Paul's Letter to the Romans* (Harmondsworth: Penguin Books, 1975), 41-42, 49, 53-54, 264-65.

18. H. Räisänen, *Paul and the Law* (Tübingen: Mohr-Siebeck, 1983), 100-107. For a critique of Räisänen, see C. E. B. Cranfield, "Giving a Dog a Bad Name: A Note on H. Räisänen's *Paul and the Law*," *Journal for the Study of the New Testament* 38 (1990): 77-85.

19. E. P. Sanders, *Paul, the Law, and the Jewish People* (Philadelphia: Fortress, 1983), 123.

and expansion of that thesis, and 9:1–11:36 the climactic resumption of the issues raised in 2:17–3:20 regarding a Jewish response (or lack of response) to the gospel. But 1:18–3:20 is not properly understood only when seen as containing declarations about God's impartiality (2:11),[20] Jews and Gentiles being alike under sin (3:9-19, 23), and no one being able to be declared righteous by observing the law (3:20). What also needs to be recognized is (1) that 2:1–3:8 is structured along the lines of two diatribal dialogues,[21] and (2) that 2:17–3:8 is entirely, both in the objections raised and the answers given, set out in terms of an intramural Jewish debate.[22]

The first of the diatribal dialogues is introduced at 2:1 by the sudden address to an imaginary interlocutor in the second person singular, "O man!" It follows on the heels of the depiction of humanity's idolatry and immorality presented in 1:18-32 — which, as noted above, has often been seen to parallel the depiction of the Gentile world given in *Wisdom of Solomon* 13:1–14:31. It begins in 2:1 with an indicting statement addressed to a censorious person; it continues with a series of questions addressed to that imaginary interlocutor in 2:2-5; and it concludes in 2:6-11 with a quotation from Psalm 62:12 (MT 62:13) and an explication of the significance of that passage — such quotations from ancient sources being not uncommon in Greek diatribal dialogues. Its theme is God's impartiality in dealing with humanity. And its referent is humanity in general, both Gentiles and Jews. For while 1:18-32 seems to have Gentiles primarily in mind, the diatribe of 2:1-11 and the further comments of 2:12-16 broaden out to include both Gentiles and Jews.

A second diatribal dialogue is introduced at 2:17, not by a vocative but by the second person singular pronominal phrase, "You a Jew!" — a form of address that was also common in ancient diatribes. It too begins with a number of questions addressed to an imaginary interlocutor in 2:17-23, with an appended quotation from Isaiah 52:5 in 2:24. As it continues, it poses another set of questions in 3:1-8. And it comes to a close with a conclusion in 3:9-19, which contains what was probably a traditional catena of biblical passages (vv. 10-18) stitched together by a sixfold repetition of the phrase "there is no one" (οὐκ ἔστιν) and an enumeration of various parts of the body ("throats," "tongues,"

20. While J. M. Bassler's structural analysis of 1:18–3:20 can be questioned, she is certainly correct in positing that "divine impartiality" is the central axiom of the passage (*Divine Impartiality: Paul and a Theological Axiom* [Chico, Calif.: Scholars, 1982], esp. 121-23, 137).

21. Cf. S. K. Stowers, *The Diatribe and Paul's Letter to the Romans* (Chico, Calif.: Scholars, 1981), esp. 93-98, 110-13; idem, "Paul's Dialogue with a Fellow Jew in Romans 3:1-9," *Catholic Biblical Quarterly* 46 (1984): 707-22; idem, *A Rereading of Romans* (New Haven: Yale University Press, 1994), 83-193.

22. In addition to S. K. Stowers cited above, see G. P. Carras, "Romans 2,1-29: A Dialogue on Jewish Ideals," *Biblica* 73 (1992): 183-207.

"lips," "mouths," "feet," and "eyes") to make the point that all human beings in their totality are sinful. The referent throughout this whole latter section of 2:17–3:19 is certainly Jewish — probably, however, not Jews generally or Judaism *per se,* but rather some type of proud and inconsistent Jew who viewed himself as a moral teacher of Gentiles, but who caused the name of God to be dishonored among the Gentiles because he failed to live up to the standards of the Mosaic law.

More important to note with regard to 1:18–3:20, however, is the fact that in both its structures and its arguments the passage is exceedingly Jewish. In fact, as George P. Carras observes (particularly with regard to chapter 2), the entire passage reflects an "inner Jewish debate" and "is best understood as a diatribe whereby two Jewish attitudes on the nature of Jewish religion are being debated."[23] The thesis statement of 1:16, "first for the Jew, then for the Gentile," alerts readers to expect that what follows will deal with relationships between Jews and Gentiles before God. And that is what is spelled out throughout all of 1:18–4:25 — first in 1:18–3:20 in depicting God's impartiality in judging all people, both Gentiles and Jews; then in 3:21–4:25 in proclaiming God's impartiality in bestowing his righteousness on all people, whether Jews or Gentiles.

So I propose that here in 1:18–3:20 we see Paul beginning his argument in Romans by agreeing with both Judaism generally and Jewish believers in Jesus in particular about (1) the impartiality of divine judgment (2:11), (2) Jews and Gentiles being alike under sin (3:9-19, 23), and (3) no one being able to be declared righteous by observing the law (3:20). Furthermore, I propose that in arguing these points Paul used what he considered to have been rather standard Jewish and Jewish Christian sources and arguments, believing that such materials were used in similar ways in those same circles. And if all this be true, then it cannot be said that the focus of Paul's teaching in Romans — and therefore what he specifically had in mind in speaking about imparting "some spiritual gift" to his addressees in 1:11 — is to be found in 1:18–3:20.[24] Rather, it seems that what he sets out in 1:18–3:20 is something he believed he held in common with his addressees and that he used in preparation for what appears later in his letter.

II. The Structures and Arguments of Romans 3:21–4:25

Coupled with 1:18–3:20 is 3:21–4:25, which presents the counterbalance to what has just been depicted. And though this second part of the first section of

23. Carras, "Romans 2,1-29," 185 and 206.

24. As, e.g., H. P. Liddon, *St. Paul's Epistle to the Romans* (London: Longmans, Green, 1893), 43; C. Gore, *St. Paul's Epistle to the Romans,* 2 vols. (London: Murray, 1900), 1.106.

Romans is similar in tone and language to the first, a critical reading of this latter part highlights certain distinctive issues that need to be observed and evaluated as well.

A. Some Important Issues

The passage begins in 3:21-23 with what appears to be a thesis paragraph that repeats and expands on the opening thesis statement of 1:17. Immediately readers are faced with an issue of some significance for interpretation. For while the emphatic "but now" (νυνὶ δέ) marks a shift to a new level in Paul's argument, commentators vary as to whether the expression is to be understood as having a purely logical function (i.e., signaling a further stage in the argument, without necessarily contrasting the two parts of the section) or as having a temporal force (i.e., contrasting the two parts). Likewise, interpreters have varied widely with respect to the meaning of "the righteousness of God," principally as to whether it signifies an attribute of God that determines his actions on behalf of humanity or a quality of existence that he bestows on those who respond to him — and, if the latter, whether it should be viewed in a forensic or an ethical manner. Furthermore, interpreters vary widely in their treatment of the two sets of statements that are used ascriptively with regard to "the righteousness of God," a righteousness which has been manifested in the gospel: (1) "apart from the law," yet "witnessed to by the Law and the Prophets" (v. 21); and (2) "through faith in [or, 'by the faithfulness of'] Jesus Christ" and "to all who believe" (v. 22).

A shift in style certainly occurs in 3:21-26, set as it is between the question-and-answer styles of 3:1-8 and 3:27-31. And repeating, as it does, the declarative tone and content of 1:16-17, the passage not only ties together the two halves of the first section of Romans, but also looks to be kerygmatic in nature. For by its emphatic repetition of the phrase "the righteousness of God" in verses 22-23, its ascriptive statements regarding that righteousness in those same verses, its emphasis on divine impartiality in verse 23, and its weighty soteriological affirmations in verses 24-26, the passage highlights the central thrust of Paul's argument at least in 1:16–4:25.

The question, however, must be asked: Is 3:21-26 (in conjunction with 1:16-17) the structural center and argumentative focus of all of Romans, which provides "the key to the structure and thought of the letter"[25] — as has traditionally been argued, at least since the Protestant Reformation? Does it, in fact,

25. Quoting W. S. Campbell, "Romans 3 as the Key to the Structure and Thought of the Letter," *Novum Testamentum* 23 (1981) esp. 24, 32-35.

embody the heart of the Christian gospel in miniature?[26] Or, stated more prosaically: Does 3:21-26 (in conjunction with 1:16-17) set out the controlling thesis of the whole of Romans? Alternatively, could it be the thesis of the first eight chapters of the letter, or, more narrowly still, the thesis of only the first four chapters?

Also at issue in any discussion of 3:21–4:25 are questions regarding (1) the provenance of what appears to be early Christian confessional material in 3:24-26 (or 3:25-26a), (2) the nature of the argument about the oneness of God and God's impartial treatment of all people in 3:27-31, (3) the use of Abraham as the exemplar of faith in 4:1-24, and (4) the inclusion of an early Christian confessional portion at the end of this section in 4:25. For 3:24-31 has been seen, particularly of late, to incorporate many fundamentally Jewish ideas about justification, justice, redemption, repentance, and atonement; 4:1-24 to highlight the chief Jewish exemplar of relationship with God; and 4:25 to epitomize the essence of the earliest Christian proclamation. Furthermore, the two key terms of the thesis statements of 1:17 and 3:21-23, δικαιοσύνη and πίστις, which appeared also in 1:18–3:20, come to dominant expression in 3:24–4:25, so that this "word chain" appears to tie together these two parts of the first section of Romans.

B. Some Preliminary Observations

How has this important section of Romans been treated by commentators? The subject is too vast for any brief, comprehensive answer. Suffice it here to say that, since at least the Protestant Reformation, 3:21–4:25 has been seen by most interpreters to be the heart of Paul's teaching in the letter. Reading Romans as a compendium of Christian theology, ignoring Paul's own religious background and possible literary sources, and caricaturing the Judaism of the apostle's day as a religion of "works-righteousness," Christians have felt fairly secure in understanding 3:21–4:25 as the focus of what Paul writes in the letter. So the central thrust of Romans has been seen as consisting of (1) a polemic against any form of acceptance before God by human endeavor, and (2) a proclamation of righteousness through faith alone — with these two emphases taken to be the central features of the Christian religion vis-à-vis Judaism and all other religions.

But quite a revolution has taken place among Christian scholars during the past few decades in understanding the Judaism of Paul's day and that of the early

26. So A. Hultgren, who expresses the view of many, in *Paul's Gospel and Mission: The Outlook from His Letter to the Romans* (Philadelphia: Trinity Press International, 1985), 47.

(tannaitic) rabbis whose teachings are codified in the Talmud.[27] It may be that scholarship has swung, in pendulum-like fashion, too far in the other direction, exchanging blind condemnation for an almost equally blind approbation, which at times goes beyond the evaluations of the better Jewish teachers themselves. Nonetheless, no longer can the Judaism of Paul's day be simply written off as a legalistic religion of human works-righteousness. And interpreters of Paul have today been alerted to the fact that there is much in the apostle's writings that he took over from Judaism. Though all of his earlier thought and piety were "rebaptized" into Christ, the basic structures of his Jewish thought and the basic ethos of his Jewish piety continued to play a large part in his life as a Christian.

Scholars, of late, have demonstrated that much of what Paul says in 3:21–4:25 about "the righteousness of God," "justification," "redemption," "expiation-propitiation," "divine impartiality," and "faith" rests solidly on Jewish foundations, and have argued that much of what he affirms with respect to these matters was voiced by Jewish and Jewish Christian teachers of the day as well.[28] Likewise, scholars have shown that pre-Pauline Christian confessional material is used in 3:24-26 in support of the thesis paragraph in 3:12-23 — material which Bultmann, Käsemann, and others have seen as contained in verses 24-26a, starting with the participle δικαιούμενοι ("being justified"), but which Lohse and others view as contained in verses 25-26, starting with the relative personal pronoun ὅν ("who").[29] Yet, however we evaluate the specific details of the materials in 3:24-26 — or, for that matter, the presence and use of tradi-

27. Rightly credited, in large part, to E. P. Sanders, *Paul and Palestinian Judaism: A Comparison of Patterns of Religion* (Philadelphia: Fortress, 1977). But just for the record, I quote T. L. Donaldson's comment in his recent *Paul and the Gentiles: Remapping the Apostle's Convictional World* (Minneapolis: Fortress, 1997), 311: "Aspects of Sanders's analysis, including the use of 'nomism' itself, were anticipated in significant ways by Richard N. Longenecker, *Paul, Apostle of Liberty* (New York: Harper & Row, 1964)." See particularly ch. 3, "The Piety of Hebraic Judaism," in my *Paul, Apostle of Liberty*, 65-85.

28. Note particularly J. D. G. Dunn, "Paul and Justification by Faith," in *The Road from Damascus: The Impact of Paul's Conversion on His Life, Thought, and Ministry*, ed. R. N. Longenecker (Grand Rapids: Eerdmans, 1997), 85-101. Among Dunn's many other writings on the subject, see also his "The New Perspective on Paul," *Bulletin of the John Rylands Library* 65 (1983) 95-122 (reprinted in *Jesus, Paul and the Law: Studies in Mark and Galatians* [London: SPCK; Louisville: Westminster, 1990], 183-214); *Romans*, 2 vols. (Dallas: Word, 1988), 1.161-241; *The Partings of the Ways between Christianity and Judaism* (London: SCM; Philadelphia: Trinity Press International, 1991), 117-39; "How New Was Paul's Gospel? The Problem of Continuity and Discontinuity," in *Gospel in Paul*, ed. L. A. Jervis and P. Richardson (Sheffield: Sheffield Academic Press, 1994), 367-88.

29. On the history of the interpretation of 3:24-26 as a pre-Pauline tradition, see the published dissertation of Herbert Koch, *Römer 3,21-31 in der Paulusinterpretation der letzten 150 Jahre* (Göttingen: Andreas Funke, 1971), 107-34.

tional structures and language elsewhere in Paul's letters — the suggestion seems irresistible that what Paul writes in 3:21–4:25 was part and parcel of the shared faith of his addressees, with what he writes being based immediately on the confessions of the earliest Jewish believers in Jesus and ultimately on the fundamental structures and thought of Early Judaism.

C. A Proposal

What needs here to be noted from our contextual scanning above is that 3:21–4:25 is extensively Jewish and/or Jewish Christian in both its structures and its expressions, as we found also to be true for 1:18–3:20. On the basis of such observations, therefore, I propose that Paul begins his letter to believers at Rome in 1:16–4:25 in quite a traditional manner — not only praising them for their faith in Christ Jesus, but also using materials and arguments that they and he held in common. He believes, as he said in the first part of the *Propositio* of Galatians 2:15-21, that all true believers in Jesus — particularly Jewish believers, but also, by extension, Gentile believers who have been influenced by Jewish thought in some way — know that a person is not justified "by the works of the law" (ἐξ ἔργων νόμου) but by what Christ has effected (διὰ/ἐκ πίστεως Ἰησοῦ Χριστοῦ, which I understand as a subject genitive) and one's faith in him (ἐπιστεύσαμεν εἰς Χριστὸν Ἰησοῦν, vv. 15-16). So he writes with confidence to Christians at Rome, setting out in the two parts of 1:16–4:25 what he believes they and he held in common, before then going on in 5:1–8:39 to speak of matters that pertain to the distinctive nature of his preaching (i.e., "my gospel") within the Gentile mission.

If our proposal be true, then, of course, it cannot be said that the focus of Paul's teaching in Romans — and therefore what he had in mind in speaking about imparting "some spiritual gift" to his addressees in 1:11 — is to be found primarily in 3:21–4:25, as has been traditionally held. Rather, it may be argued that what he sets out in his thesis paragraph of 3:21-23, in the early Christian confessional material of 3:24-26, in the highlighting of God's oneness and impartiality in 3:27-31, in the illustration of Abraham as the exemplar of faith in 4:1-24, and in the traditional portion incorporated in 4:25 are all matters that he believed he held in common with his addressees and that he used in preparation for what he would write later in his letter, particularly in 5:1–8:39.

III. The Structures and Arguments of Romans 5:1–8:39

The relation of 5:1–8:39 to 1:16–4:25 has been a perennial problem for interpreters. One common way has been to understand 1:16–4:25 as being about sin in the first part and justification in the second, whereas 5:1–8:39 deals with sanctification. Another way is to view these two sections as setting forth somewhat parallel lines of thought: first by the use of judicial and forensic language in 1:16–4:25; then in language more mystical and participatory in 5:1–8:39. The issues are complex, but they call for some evaluation here.

A. Some Important Issues

When moving from 1:16–4:25 to 5:1–8:39, the reader is immediately confronted with the problem of how the two forms of "therefore" in 5:1 and 5:12 function to set up the material of these chapters. For 5:1 begins with the statement, "Therefore being justified by faith," with the postpositive transitional conjunction οὖν ("therefore") connecting "being justified by faith" with what was argued in 1:16–4:25; while in 5:12 there appears the prepositional phrase διὰ τοῦτο ("therefore"), which seems not to be a transition from 5:1-11 but to signal some type of logical break and (perhaps) to reach back to 1:16–4:25. Likewise, one must determine whether 5:1a should be read as "let us have (ἔχωμεν, a hortatory subjunctive) peace with God," which is the better-supported reading in the manuscript tradition, or "we have (ἔχομεν, an indicative) peace with God," which most scholars prefer for internal reasons. In effect, what one concludes regarding these seemingly minor linguistic points has a profound effect on how one relates 5:1-11 (also, perhaps, 5:12-21) to the flow of the argument from chapters 1–4 to chapters 5–8 — that is, whether it is the conclusion to what precedes in 1:16–4:25, whether it serves as transitional material between 1:16–4:25 and 5:12–8:39, or whether it functions as an introduction to what follows in 5:1–8:39.

There are, of course, a number of similarities between these first and second sections of Romans, however the sections are precisely delineated — with the similarities often continuing on throughout the rest of the letter. For example, the theme of righteousness, which was prominent in 1:16–4:25, appears also in 5:1–8:39 (i.e., in 5:17, 21; 6:13, 16, 18, 19, 20; 8:10) and throughout 9:30–10:21. Likewise, issues concerning the Mosaic law, which were raised in 3:20, 21, 31 and 4:13-15, receive further treatment in 5:13-14, 20; 7:1-6, 7-25; and 8:1-4 — with the conclusions reached in these passages underlying the whole presentation of 9:1–11:36. And convictions about Jesus Christ that were implicit in the thesis statement of 1:16-17, interjected almost parenthetically into the discussion at 2:16, and further expressed in the thesis paragraph of 3:21-26, are elaborated in 5:1–8:39; in turn, these convictions are then presupposed throughout the discussion of 9:1–11:36 and the exhortations of 12:1–15:13.

On the other hand, there are a number of striking differences between these two sections. Most obvious is their difference in the use of Scripture.[30] For while there are about 18 quotations of Scripture in eight or nine places in 1:16–4:25 — with about 30 quotations in 25 to 26 places in 9:1–11:36, an additional ten in the exhortations of 12:1–15:13, and one more in the Apostolic Parousia of 15:14-32 — only two biblical quotations appear in 5:1–8:39, and then somewhat tangentially: once in 7:7, citing in illustrative fashion the tenth commandment "Do not covet" of Exodus 20:17 and Deuteronomy 5:21; and once in 8:36, in what appears to be an early Christian confessional portion that makes use of Psalm 44:22. Likewise, the word chain shifts from δικαιοσύνη and πίστις/πιστεύω in 1:16–4:25 to ζωή/ζάω and dominance of ἁμαρτία and θάνατος in 5:1–8:39 (though also, of course, with the appearance of δικαιοσύνη in eight verses of this section, as noted above).

Furthermore, the form of address varies in these two sections. For whereas imaginary interlocutors are addressed in 2:1 ("O man!") and 2:17 ("You a Jew!"), with a rhetorical "we" appearing in 4:1 ("What then shall we say?"), Paul — for the first time since the Salutation of 1:1-7 and the Thanksgiving of 1:8-15 — speaks directly to his addressees in 5:1–8:39. He sets up his direct address in this latter section by the pronoun "us" in 4:24, which concludes his illustration of Abraham in 4:24, and the pronoun "our" in the incorporated traditional portion of 4:25, which closes off the first section. In 5:1–8:39, however, he speaks directly and consistently to his readers by the use of the pronouns and verbal suffixes "we," "you," "yourselves," and "us" — addressing them also as "brothers" in 7:1, 4, and using, as well, a type of rhetorical προσωποποιια or "speech-in-character" in 7:7-25 as he expresses in the first person singular "I" the tragic soliloquy of humanity in its attempts to live by its own insights and strength. In addition, the style in these two sections shifts from being argumentative, particularly in the diatribes of 2:2-11 and 2:17–3:8 and the rhetorically structured presentation of God's oneness and impartiality in 3:17-31, to being more "confessional," cast as it is in 5:1–8:39 in the first person plural.

Also significant are the differences in content between these two sections of Romans. Two matters, in particular, call for mention here. The first has to do with the differing diagnoses of the "human predicament." For in depicting humanity's situation apart from God, the narrative of 1:18-32 unfolds in terms of humanity's *decline* into idolatry and immorality *during the course of history* — without any reference to Adam's sin; whereas in 5:12-21 (probably also in 7:7-13) the focus is on the disobedience of the "one man" and how his transgres-

30. Cf. my "Prolegomena to Paul's Use of Scripture in Romans," *Bulletin for Biblical Research* 7 (1997): 145-68, esp. 146-47, 158-67. See also ch. 4, "Paul and the Old Testament," in the second edition of my *Biblical Exegesis in the Apostolic Period* (Grand Rapids: Eerdmans, 1999).

sion has affected all human beings. The diagnosis of 1:18-32, of course, may be built on *Wisdom of Solomon* 13:1–14:31 and/or similar Jewish traditions (as postulated above), and so conditioned by the materials used. Nonetheless, while the story of Adam's sin in Genesis 2–3 was certainly retained within the Jewish Scriptures, it seems not to have been widely used as an explanation for humanity's predicament in Early Judaism (except in *4 Ezra* 3:7-8, 21-22; 7:116-26 and *2 Baruch* 23:4; 48:42-43; 54:15; 56:5-6). Certainly it was not used by the tannaitic rabbis whose teachings were codified in the Talmud.

Likewise, 7:7-25 poses numerous problems with respect to both its content and its possible parallels. Commentators have traditionally been concerned with the identity of the speaker and the type of experience described. Questions, however, have also been raised regarding the rhetoric of the passage, with parallels pointed out between 7:14-24 and the tragic soliloquies of the Greek world.[31] In particular, Paul's use of the first person singular and his laments throughout verses 14-24 have been compared to those of Euripides' Medea, who, driven by rage and thoughts of revenge, determined to murder her own children, and in reflecting on such a heinous act cries out: "I am being overcome by evils. I know that what I am about to do is evil, but passion is stronger than my reasoned reflection; and this is the cause of the worst evils for humans" (*Medea* 1077-80).[32] This "famous Medean saying," as Stanley Stowers points out, was widely known in Paul's day, occurring "not only in drama and philosophers' debates, but also in such contexts as letters and public orations."[33]

B. Some Preliminary Observations

What can be said with respect to such issues? Though many have taken Paul's discussion in 1:16–4:25 to continue on through 5:11,[34] or on through 5:21,[35] most scholars today view 5:1–8:39 as a distinguishable unit of material.[36] That

31. Cf. H. Hommel, "Das 7. Kapitel des Römerbriefs im Licht Antiker Überlieferung," *Theologia viatorum* 8 (1961): 90-116; G. Theissen, *Psychological Aspects of Pauline Theology* (Philadelphia: Fortress, 1987), 211-19; S. K. Stowers, *A Rereading of Romans,* 260-64.

32. Among the many parallel Greek texts that could be cited, note also Ovid, *Metamorphoses* vii.19-20: "Desire persuades me one way, reason another. I see the better and approve it, but I follow the worse."

33. S. K. Stowers, *A Rereading of Romans,* 263.

34. E.g., Luther (with 5:12-21 considered an excursus), Melanchthon, T. Zahn, F. Leenhardt, M. Black, J. A. T. Robinson.

35. E.g., Calvin, U. Wilckens, O. Kuss, F. F. Bruce, J. D. G. Dunn.

36. E.g., H. Schlier, A. Nygren, O. Michel, C. H. Dodd, N. Dahl, C. E. B. Cranfield, E. Käsemann, J. A. Fitzmyer, D. Moo.

is not only because the example of Abraham as a "proof from Scripture" is a fitting conclusion to what precedes, but also because 5:1-11 appears to serve as something of a thesis section for what follows — with most of the themes and many of the terms of 5:1-11 reappearing in 8:18-39, thereby setting up an *inclusio* or type of "ring composition." Furthermore, as noted above, (1) 5:1 seems to function as a literary hinge, first summarizing the argument of 1:16–4:25 — particularly that of 3:21–4:25 ("Since, therefore, we have been justified through faith") — and then preparing for what follows in 5:2–8:39 ("we have peace [or, 'let us have peace'] with God through our Lord Jesus Christ"); (2) the word chain shifts from πίστις/πιστεύω and the dominance of δικαιοσύνη in 1:16–4:25 to ζωή/ζάω and the dominance of ἁμαρτία and θάνατος in 5:1–8:39; (3) the tone shifts from being argumentative in 1:16–4:25 to more confessional in 5:1–8:39; and (4) there appears throughout the section the repeated refrain διὰ/ἐν τοῦ(ῷ) κυρίου(ῷ) ἡμῶν 'Ιησοῦ Χριστοῦ, not only as an *inclusio* at 5:1 and 8:39 but also at the end of each separate unit at 5:11, 5:21, 6:23, and 7:25.

Interpreters have usually not been too concerned about the differences identified above between these two sections of Romans, 1:16–4:25 and 5:1–8:39 — that is, about differences in their use of Scripture, their respective word chains, their forms of address, or their tones or styles. Usually these matters are viewed as being purely circumstantial in nature, without any inferences drawn as to their significance. On the other hand, where such differences are recognized, they have often been seen as evidencing either later interpolations by some undiscerning Paulinist or outright contradictions in Paul's own thought. One scholar has even proposed that Romans 1–11 should be viewed as two distinctly different Pauline sermons: one to a Jewish audience, which is now found in chapters 1–4 and 9–11, but whose parts have somehow become separated; the other to a Gentile audience, which is preserved in chapters 5–8.[37]

Likewise, though the analysis of humanity's condition is set out differently in 1:18-32 and 5:12-21, most interpreters have been content to read 1:18-32 as "the obviously deliberate echo of the Adam narratives,"[38] and so have denied or minimized any difference between them. And though scholars have frequently noted parallels between 7:14-24 and the tragic soliloquies of the Greek world, most have dismissed them as being somewhat trivial in comparison to the seemingly more significant parallels between 7:7-13 (also, of course, 3:21–

37. So R. Scroggs, "Paul as Rhetorician: Two Homilies in Romans 1–11," in *Jews, Greeks, and Christians* (*Festschrift* for W. D. Davies), ed. R. Hamerton-Kelly and R. Scroggs (Leiden: Brill, 1976), 271-98.

38. J. D. G. Dunn, *Romans,* 1.53; cf. M. D. Hooker, "Adam in Romans 1," *New Testament Studies* 6 (1960): 297-306; idem, "A Further Note on Romans 1," *New Testament Studies* 13 (1966): 181-83; A. J. M. Wedderburn, "Adam in Paul's Letter to the Romans," in *Studia Biblica* 3, ed. E. A. Livingstone (Sheffield: JSOT, 1980), 413-30; and many others.

4:25) and the Jewish world.[39] But it may be doubted whether the differences between 1:16–4:25 and 5:1–8:39 and the parallels between 7:14-24 and the tragic soliloquies of the Greeks can be treated so summarily.

C. A Proposal

I have not dealt here directly with matters pertaining to the identity and circumstances of Paul's Roman addressees. That is not because I consider such questions unimportant. On the contrary, I consider them to be highly significant. But I have discussed Paul's Roman addressees and Roman Christianity in a recent article,[40] and I have space here only to refer to that article and repeat its conclusions.

My argument, in agreement with Raymond Brown,[41] is that the important question to ask regarding Christians at Rome is not the ethnic question, "Were they Jews or Gentiles, or, if ethnically mixed, dominantly one or the other?" — with the implications being that if Jewish believers, then they should be viewed as non-Pauline in outlook, but if Gentile believers, then adherents to Paul's teaching. Probably the addressees constituted both Jewish and Gentile believers in Jesus. And most likely the Gentile believers were in the majority, for Paul considered the Roman church to be within the orbit of his Gentile ministry.

Rather than trying to determine the addressees' character on the basis of their ethnicity, "the crucial issue," as Brown points out, "is the theological outlook of this mixed Jewish/Gentile Christianity."[42] In analyzing the factors to be considered for any judgment regarding the theological outlook of the Roman Christians, Brown concludes (1) that for both Jews and Christians "the Jerusalem-Rome axis was strong," (2) "that Roman Christianity came from Jerusalem, and indeed represented the Jewish/Gentile Christianity associated with such Jerusalem figures as Peter and James," and (3) that both in the earliest days of the Roman church and at the time when Paul wrote them, believers at Rome

39. Cf. E. Käsemann, *Commentary on Romans,* trans. G. W. Bromiley (Grand Rapids: Eerdmans, 1980), 198-211; and many others.

40. See my "Prolegomena to Paul's Use of Scripture in Romans," esp. 148-52.

41. Cf. R. E. Brown, "The Beginnings of Christianity at Rome" and "The Roman Church near the End of the First Christian Generation (A.D. 58 — Paul to the Romans)," in *Antioch and Rome: New Testament Cradles of Catholic Christianity,* ed. R. E. Brown and J. P. Meier (New York: Paulist, 1983), 92-127; idem, "Further Reflections on the Origins of the Church of Rome," in *The Conversation Continues: Studies in Paul and John in Honor of J. L. Martyn,* ed. R. T. Fortna and B. R. Gaventa (Nashville: Abingdon, 1990), 98-115.

42. R. E. Brown, "The Beginnings of Christianity at Rome," 109, n. 227.

could be characterized as "Christians who kept up some Jewish observances and remained faithful to part of the heritage of the Jewish Law and cult, without insisting on circumcision."[43] And it is this understanding that I bring to the discussion here, believing it to be the position best supported by all the available data — and believing that it casts Paul's argument in Romans in an entirely new light.

My proposal, then, is that in 5:1–8:39 is to be found the focus of what Paul writes in Romans, and so the section that contains, in a special way, the "spiritual gift" to which he refers in 1:11 and what he qualifies later as being "my gospel" in 16:25. This is not to discredit what he writes in 1:16–4:25, for that is what he held in common with his addressees. Indeed, it is on the basis of their acceptance of the message of 1:16–4:25 that both he and they originally became believers in Jesus. Undoubtedly he often proclaimed that message, particularly when addressing Jews or those who had been influenced by Jewish thought for the better (as the Christians at Rome) — or in addressing those who had been influenced by Jewish thought for the worse (as the Christians at Galatia). But what he wanted believers at Rome also to know was the gospel that he had been preaching to purely Gentile audiences. For believers at Rome, too, were predominantly Gentiles, and he wanted to include them within his Gentile proclamation and so to strengthen them. Furthermore, he wanted them to become partners in his Gentile mission as the sending church to the western regions of the Roman empire, just as the church at Antioch of Syria functioned as the sending church to the eastern regions.

So Paul addresses his readers as Gentiles within his Gentile mission (cf. 1:5-6, 13-15; 11:13; 15:15-18), distinguishing between them and his "own people" (e.g., 11:14). He also, however, speaks of Abraham as "our forefather" (4:1), refers to his addressees as "those who know the law" (7:1), presupposes that they have lived under the law (7:4-6; 8:3-4), and lays stress on the messianic tradition in this letter more than anywhere else in his extant writings (cf. 1:3-4; 9:5; 15:12, quoting Isa 11:10). More particularly, in 1:16–4:25 he argues in a thoroughly Jewish and Jewish Christian manner. And he continues that type of argumentation in relating the gospel to the hope of Israel in 9:1–11:36 and in his exhortations of 12:1–15:13.

In 5:1–8:39, however, he sets out the essence of what he proclaims in his Gentile mission — that is, to Gentiles who had not been prepared for the gospel

43. Brown, "The Beginnings of Christianity at Rome," 104. For a different attempt to deal with the same data, arguing that the addressees were "a group of Judean Christians" at Rome, see S. Mason, "'For I Am Not Ashamed of the Gospel' (Rom. 1.16): The Gospel and the First Readers of Romans," in *Gospel in Paul,* ed. L. A. Jervis and P. Richardson (Sheffield: Sheffield Academic Press, 1994), 254-87.

by Jewish or Jewish Christian teaching, and so did not think in Jewish categories. That message, he acknowledges in 5:1a, is based on being "justified by faith." Its thrust, however, consists of (1) a proclamation of "peace" and "reconciliation" with God "through our Lord Jesus Christ," which is unfolded in the theme or thesis section of 5:1-11; (2) the telling of the universal, foundational story of sin, death, and condemnation having entered the world by "one man," but grace, life, and righteousness brought about "through Jesus Christ our Lord" in 5:12-21; (3) the spelling out of the relations of sin, death, and the law, on the one hand, and grace, life, and righteousness, on the other, through the use of three rhetorical questions at 6:1, 6:15, and 7:7 — with a particularly tragic soliloquy, which had many parallels in the Greek world, coming to voice in 7:14-24; (4) the highlighting of relationships "in Christ" and "in the Spirit" in 8:1-30; and (5) a triumphal declaration, which verges on being a defiant assertion, of God's love and care for his own "in Christ Jesus our Lord" in 8:31-39, with that final portion probably incorporating a number of early Christian confessional statements.

It is in this section that the three basic features of classical rhetoric — that is, *logos* (content or argument), *ethos* (the personal character of the speaker or writer), and *pathos* (the power to stir the emotions) — come most fully to expression in Paul's letter to the Romans. It is in this section that themes most distinctly Pauline are clustered: "peace" and "reconciliation" with God,[44] and the believer being "in Christ" and "in the Spirit." And it is in Romans 8, using J. A. T. Robinson's analogy of "a journey by canal across an isthmus" with its "series of locks" rising to and then falling away from "a central ridge," that "the heights of the epistle are reached" and there occurs "a sustained climax which takes the argument across the watershed."[45]

IV. Conclusion

The *Propositio* or proposition statement of Galatians 2:15-21 has alerted us to the fact that one way that Paul argued was, first, to set out matters of basic agreement with his addressees (vv. 15-16), then to deal with matters of disagreement (vv. 17-20), and finally to draw a conclusion (v. 21) — with matters

44. This is, in particular, the insight of S. Kim, "God Reconciled His Enemy to Himself: The Origin of Paul's Concept of Reconciliation," in *The Road from Damascus: The Impact of Paul's Conversion on His Life, Thought, and Ministry*, ed. R. N. Longenecker (Grand Rapids: Eerdmans, 1997), 102-24; idem, "2 Cor. 5:11-21 and the Origin of Paul's Concept of 'Reconciliation,'" *Novum Testamentum* 39 (1997): 360-84.

45. J. A. T. Robinson, *Wrestling with Romans* (London: SCM, 1979), 9.

of agreement explicated in his Galatian letter in 3:1-18, matters of disagreement dealt with in 3:19–4:7, and expressions of concern for the believers appended in 4:8-11.[46] Most commentators have taken the central thrust of Galatians to be Paul's argument against "legalism" in 3:1-18. I have argued, however, on the basis of his *Propositio* ("proposition") in 2:15-21 and his *Probatio* ("arguments") in 3:1–4:11, that Paul's principal message in Galatians is against "nomism" in 3:19–4:11 — and that his experiential and biblical arguments in 3:1-18, while valid and meaningful, are primarily given to prepare for his major arguments in 3:19–4:11.[47]

Likewise, in his pastoral counsel set out in 1 Corinthians, Paul often begins with statements that he and his addressees agreed on — though, in this case, they seem to have interpreted the statements in one way and he in another. The most obvious of these statements are "Everything is permissible" (6:12; 10:23), "It is good for a man not to touch a woman" (7:1), "We all possess knowledge" (8:1), "An idol is nothing at all in the world" (8:4), and "There is no God but one" (8:4). In all of these instances Paul began by seeking common ground and then moved on to explicate his own understanding.

Something similar, I suggest, is taking place in Paul's letter to believers at Rome, though with the parallels closer to the pattern in Galatians than to that in 1 Corinthians. Thus while the presentations of God's impartiality, Jews and Gentiles being alike under sin, no one being able to be declared righteous by observing the law, and justification by faith in 1:16–4:25 are vitally important, these seem to have been matters of agreement between Paul and his addressees. What Paul wanted to give his readers as a "spiritual gift," which he refers to in the doxology of the letter as "my gospel," is to be found, I suggest, in 5:1–8:39: a gospel that focuses on "peace" and "reconciliation" with God, that deals with humanity's essential tension of "death" and "life," and that highlights the personal relationships of being "in Christ" and "in the Spirit."

Understanding Romans in this fashion, of course, has rather revolutionary implications for New Testament criticism and Christian theology. Most of all, however, it has great significance for our living as Christians, our proclamation of the gospel, and our contextualization of the essential Christian tradition.

46. Cf. my *Galatians* (Dallas: Word, 1990), esp. 80-96.

47. Longenecker, *Galatians*, 97-178.

The "Wretched Man" Revisited: Another Look at Romans 7:14-25

J. I. Packer

That the term *dogmatician* has nothing to do with dogs does not, I trust, need saying. But when exegetes and dogmaticians get together it is noticeable that they tend to sniff suspiciously at each other, as dogs do, uncertain whether they can be friends. There is reason for this: too often, since the time when the biblical and dogmatic disciplines were formally separated, exponents of both have found themselves out of step with each other, and have been made to feel that their opposite numbers are obstructing what they themselves are doing. For me, therefore, who if anything am a sort of dogmatician, to get into an exegetical symposium on Romans might seem to be an act of both bad judgment and bad taste. But the purpose of the present symposium is to honor my colleague Gordon Fee, which is something I want to do; and it so happens that in Dr. Fee's massive monograph on Paul's pneumatology, a landmark study if ever there was one, a matter comes up regarding Romans that I would like to review, namely the identity and condition of the "wretched man" of Romans 7:24 — that is, the "I" of verses 14-25.[1] So I worm my way in among the exegetes for this purpose; and should my discussion merely make Gordon feel that my slip

1. Gordon D. Fee, *God's Empowering Presence* (Peabody, Mass.: Hendrickson, 1994), pp. 510-11. I have written on this topic before: see J. I. Packer, *Keep in Step with the Spirit* (Old Tappan, N.J.: Revell, 1984), pp. 263-70, reprinted from *Studia Evangelica* (Berlin: Akademie-Verlag, 1964), pp. 621-27.

Unless otherwise identified, all biblical quotations are from the New International Version (NIV).

is showing, then I ask his pardon in advance for intruding into things that may be too high for me, after all.

The identity of the "wretched man" has been a main question in at least three major historical debates, over and above the intramural contentions of commentators in more recent times. The three are these:

In the fifth century, facing the Pelagian claim that power to keep God's law remains universal, despite sin, Augustine came to think that the "wretched man" is Paul as he writes Romans, showing by means of his self-assessment that we must rely every moment on God's mercy and grace for salvation, inasmuch as our attempted obedience always fall short.[2] By contrast, Pelagians then and since have taken the "wretched man" to be someone other than a Christian. But for Augustine, Romans 7:14-25 stood as a bulwark against any idea of salvation by one's own effort, and a proof that apart from God's sovereign grace all are lost.

In the sixteenth century, confronted by theologies that referred this whole passage to preconversion existence and denied that desires to sin are sinful when not yielded to, Luther, Calvin, and all the magisterial Reformers except Bucer and Musculus invoked the passage as exegeted by Augustine to show that there is sin in the best Christians' best works: all that we do, however good by comparison with what we once did and others do still, falls short of perfection, both motivational and substantive, and so cannot gain merit in God's sight.[3] So for the Reformers this passage was a bulwark against any thought of salvation by works, or by the merit of works added to the merit of Christ, and a proof that God's own gift of justification here and now — by grace only, through faith only, because of Christ only — is our only ground of hope as we prepare to stand before Christ on the day of judgment.

2. Augustine, *Retractions (Retractationes),* I.xxiii.1, II.i.1; *Against Two Letters of the Pelagians,* I.x.22; tr., *A Select Library of the Nicene and Post-Nicene Fathers* (Grand Rapids: Eerdmans, 1971), V.384.

3. Calvin, for one, is emphatic on this, including flawed motivation in the category of polluted thoughts issuing from an unclean heart. "The Lord . . . declares that all the works that come forth from sinners are contaminated with impurity of heart. Take, then, the name of righteousness from those works which are condemned as works of pollution by the Lord's mouth!" John Calvin, *Institutes of the Christian Religion,* tr. F. L. Battles (Philadelphia: Westminster Press, 1960), III.xiv.7, I.775. Richard Hooker waxes rhetorical for emphasis: "If God should make us an offer thus large: 'Search all the generations of men since the fall of your father Adam, find one man that hath done any one action which hath passed from him pure, without any stain or blemish at all, and for that one man's one only action neither man nor angel shall feel the torments which are prepared for both' — do you think that this ransom, to deliver men and angels, would be found among the sons of men? The best things we do have somewhat in them to be pardoned" (cited from Philip Edgcumbe Hughes, *Faith and Works: Cranmer and Hooker on Justification* [Wilton, Conn.: Morehouse-Barlow, 1982], p. 68).

In the nineteenth century the mainline heirs of the Great Awakening and its British counterpart faced both the Wesleyan heart-perfectionism of pure love out of a cleansed inner being and the Higher Life act-perfectionism of unflawed, Spirit-empowered performance despite the continuance of indwelling sin in the saint's spiritual system.[4] For these evangelical mainliners, Romans 7:14-25 stood as a bulwark against all forms of Christian perfectionism, and a proof that any claim to sinlessness would be self-deceived and spiritually dangerous.

Moral and spiritual inability in consequence of the fall, free justification as of now through faith in Christ, and the incompleteness of sanctification in this life can be established with certainty from the New Testament even without endorsing Augustine's identification of the "wretched man." To identify that man, however, as the healthy Christian in honest and realistic self-assessment, at once rules out alternatives to these three positions in a quite decisive way, and this very decisiveness naturally stirs interest in seeing how strong are the arguments in favor of Augustine's view. To do this is one aim of the present essay.

Our starting point is recognition of the thrust of Romans 7:7-25, which is Paul's paragraph unit. Having in previous paragraphs linked together the states of being "under law" and "under sin" (6:14; 7:5), and having spoken of the rule of sin as being exercised and made effective through the law (5:20; 7:5), he now sees that the relation between the law and sin must be clarified, or the conclusion may be drawn that the law itself is somehow sinful and evil. So he raises the question: "Is the law sin?" (v. 7), answers it with an emphatic negative, and then justifies his answer by analyzing what the relation between God's law and human sin really is. In this analysis there are three main points:

1. The effect of the law is to give knowledge of sin — not merely of the abstract notion of sin, but of the quasi-personal reality of sin as a driving force within us all, a spirit of rebellion and self-assertion against God, of pride and unwillingness to be dominated by anything or anybody from outside, and specifically of dislike and disobedience in relation to God's commands (7:7, 13, cf. 3:20).
2. The law gives this knowledge by setting God's commands and prohibitions before us; for these first goad sin into active rebellion and

4. On this see *The Works of Benjamin B. Warfield,* vols. VII and VIII, *Perfectionism* (Grand Rapids: Baker, 1981; reprint of original volumes, New York: Oxford University Press, 1931-32), esp. VII.vi and vii and VIII.iv and v, and note VIII.583-84 on Rom 7. See also J. C. Ryle, *Holiness,* centenary edition (Welwyn, U.K.: Evangelical Press, 1979), pp. xxi-xxii, and J. I. Packer, *Keep in Step with the Spirit,* pp. 127-29, 143-45, 161-63, 263-70.

then enable us to see the specific shortcomings of motive and behavior into which sin has led us (7:8, 19, 23).

3. The law gives no ability to perform the good it prescribes, nor can it in any way diminish or deliver from the power of sin (7:9-11, 22-24).

In making these points, Paul speaks throughout in the first person singular. In verses 7-13 he elaborates the thesis: "I would not have known what sin was except through the law," depicting this discovery as a move from life to death. Then in verses 14-25 he moves from the aorist to the present tense and describes the experience of a person who sees himself constantly failing to do the good that the law commands, and that he himself actually wants to do, and who through reflecting on this fact has come to see the bitter truth stated at the outset as the thesis of the section — "I am unspiritual [carnal, KJV; of the flesh, NRSV], sold as a slave to sin" (7:14).[5] It is this perception that prompts the cry: "What a wretched man I am! Who will rescue me from this body of death?" — which is followed by the verbless shout, "Thanks be to God — through Jesus Christ our Lord!" and the final summary statement: "So then, I myself in my mind am a slave to God's law, but in the sinful nature [flesh, KJV, NRSV] a slave to the law of sin" (7:25).[6]

Who, now, is the "I," the "wretched man" living the life of recognized and agonized imperfection in relation to God's holy, just, good, "spiritual" (i.e., God-given, divinely originating) law?[7] That Paul in verses 14-25 is describing an experience that was, or once had been, his own, as he is certainly doing in verses 7-13, is surely beyond dispute. The suggestion that this pas-

5. "Sold as a slave to sin" is pictorial rather than theological language (as is "sprang to life" and "died" in v. 9), expressing how the condition being described feels rather than categorizing it directly in explicit and intentional theological terms. The argument that no regenerate person could say he was sold as a slave to sin, because this would be tantamount to saying he was back in the condition from which 6:18, 22, proclaimed him freed, misses this point.

6. "Sinful nature" is not a happy rendering of "flesh," though it is hard to find a better. "Nature" suggests that sin is the "real me," which in a regenerate believer is not the case. "Flesh" in Paul has to do with the person, not just that person's body, and points to the reality of desire misdirected toward earthly and self-serving objectives rather than the service of God. Sin, personified as a tyrant in 3:9; 5:21; 6:12, 14, 23, is the chameleon energy that thus misdirects. "Sinful streak" and "corrupt and deviant conation" would hardly do in a general-purposes translation of the Bible, but both phrases have a semantic field nearer to what Paul means by "flesh."

7. "Spiritual" declares that the law "derives from the Spirit (given by inspiration), embodies the Spirit, manifests the Spirit, was intended to address at the level of the Spirit" (James D. G. Dunn, *Romans 1–8* [Dallas: Word Books, 1988], p. 387). The old exegesis, "heart-searching," though stating a truth, is not linguistically correct.

sage "does not represent a personal experience at all, but is no more than a secondhand account of the experience of others, or even an imaginative picture of a condition of mind into which men might fall were it not for the grace of God" is, says Kirk, "difficult to believe."[8] The idea that the emphatic "I" (ἐγώ, vv. 14, 17, 24; αὐτὸς ἐγώ, v. 25) means "not I, you understand, but you, or somebody else," and that the spontaneous "wretched man" outcry was one that Paul had never had to utter on his own behalf, out of his own heart, seems so artificial and theatrical as to be incredible.[9] It may then be taken as certain that this is Paul sharing out of his own pilgrimage, both in 7-13 and in 14-25. Paul never hesitates to share himself in his letters when he believes that by doing so he will help others in their life with God, and it is entirely in character for him to be invoking his experience here in order to help his readers see how sin and the law relate to each other, which is what he wants them to know.

But how exactly is he doing it? Look first at verses 7-13. Should we understand Paul as speaking here in a directly autobiographical way, narrating his personal experience the way it was because he thinks it paradigmatic of the relation between the law and sin in everyone's life? (That everyone without exception knows something of God's law, through general revelation if not via the Jewish Torah, has already been stated; see 1:32; 2:14-15.) Or should we suppose he is speaking representatively against the background of his own remembered experience, directly personating a mainstream Jew,[10] or Adam,[11] or a human being in Adam as such, and purposefully shaping his speech as he does so for maximum universality and didactic force? (Preachers of a certain type do this regularly, and Paul was a dyed-in-the-wool preacher whose apostolic letters are, before they close, invariably

8. Kenneth E. Kirk, *Romans* (Oxford: Clarendon Press, 1937), p. 206.

9. Douglas J. Moo, in *The Epistle to the Romans* (Grand Rapids: Eerdmans, 1996), pp. 427-28 and note 12, observes that the rhetorical use of "I" without a specific personal reference, which W. G. Kümmel highlighted as a reality in Greek and specifically in Paul in his *Romer 7 und die Bekehrung des Paulus* (Leipzig: J. G. Hinrichs, 1929), appears only when the sense is hypothetical and the "I" is, to use his term, "fictive" (e.g., Rom 3:7). He concludes, with recent scholarship generally, that in the factual first-person-singular account in Rom 7 "some reference to Paul must be included."

10. In *Theology of the New Testament,* vol. 1 (London: SCM, 1952) the late Rudolf Bultmann described Rom 7:7-25 as "a passage in which Paul depicts the situation of a man under the Torah as it had become clear to a backward look from the standpoint of the Christian faith." Dr. Fee agrees with Dunn that this is probably the majority view among scholars today (*op. cit.*, p. 511, note 113).

11. Modern commentators generally agree that the story of Adam in Gen 2–3 has had some influence at least on the wording of 7:7-13, though there is no agreement as to the relation between Adam and Paul's first person singular.

pastoral sermons on paper, however informal and chatty their beginnings.) It is hard to decide, and perhaps not important to do so, for whichever it is, Paul's point is the same — that in all human lives God's law first stirs up sin and then shows it up without offering any remedy against its invasive perverting force. Thus the Christless person's life is lived on the treadmill of moral and spiritual failure, so that for sensitive souls it becomes increasingly a nightmare of consciously not pleasing God (which is what Paul is evidently talking about when he says that after the law came into his heart "sin sprang to life and I died" [7:9]). Paul's point, as illustrated by his narrative, is summarized in verse 13: "Did what is good, then, bring death to me? By no means! It was sin, working death in me through what is good, in order that sin might be shown to be sin, and through the commandment might become sinful beyond measure" (NRSV). Law is one thing, sin is another, and their interaction in each human life brings out the goodness of the former and the badness of the latter.

And now a further question arises. How do verses 14-25 relate to verses 7-13? Is the speaker here still Paul remembering himself as a Pharisee or personating a pagan moralist and so speaking for unregenerates who, whatever their idealism and moralism, fall short behaviorally and have not yet learned to thank God for Jesus Christ and to receive through him the free gift of pardon and acceptance? If so, the rescue from "this body of death" for which the "wretched man" cries out is deliverance from the final, judicial, eternal death of 1:32; 6:16, 21, 23, for which his sin-dominated life qualifies him afresh every day;[12] and his thanksgiving is precisely for the present gift of righteousness (justification, 5:17) and new life in Christ, with power for godly living (6:4, 11-14; 7:4-6).

Or does Paul's shift from the past to the present tense in verse 14 mean that now he is augmenting his account of the law as detecting sin in the unregenerate by testimony to the law as also detecting the reach-exceeds-grasp dimension of the moral life of justified sinners? Does the rest of this paragraph thus extend Paul's point, rather than merely reinforcing his appeal to unregenerate experience as showing how law and sin relate? And if it does, is this an aspect of Christian experience that shows the believer to be in bad shape, laboring in self-reliance and pride to keep God's law by his own willpower and strength instead of drawing on the help of the Holy Spirit, who is not men-

12. Cf. the following note by Joseph A. Fitzmyer, *Romans* (New York: Doubleday, 1993), on the body of sin being rendered powerless in Rom 6:6: "The 'body of sin' is not merely the material part of a mortal human being, as opposed to the soul, but the whole person considered as earth-oriented, not open to God or his Spirit, and prone to sin. In 7:24 he will call it the 'body of death'" (p. 436).

tioned in this paragraph?[13] Were this the case (and some have argued that it is), then the moral impotence complained of would be a pathological condition that would cease once the saint learned to live in the Spirit's power, and the cry of thanks in verse 25b would be specifically for this enabling (supplying a verb in the present tense: "Thanks be to God that he *does,* here and now, rescue me through Jesus Christ our Lord").

The alternative is that the reach-exceeds-grasp aspect of the Christian's moral life, which the law detects and which prompts the "wretched man" outburst, is the mark of a healthy believer who loves God's law and aims to keep it perfectly, but finds that something within him whose presence is known only by its effects, namely indwelling sin, obstructs and thwarts his purpose; for it betrays him time and again into doing things which at the moment of action seem good but in hindsight appear bad — meaning unwise, unprincipled, unjust, unloving, thoughtless, faithless, cowardly, self-serving, disobedient, irreverent, and so on (see vv. 21-23). The wretchedness of the "wretched man" then springs from thus discovering his continued sinfulness, and from knowing that he cannot hope to be rid of indwelling sin, his unwelcome and troubling inmate, as long as he is in the body — that is, while his present life lasts. On this view, the verb to supply in verse 25a will be the same tense (future) as is the "wretched man" outcry, which is what in any case the ordinary rules of Greek grammar require: "Who *will* rescue me . . . ? Thanks be to God that he *will* rescue me (in the coming aeon, when bodily resurrection and transformation will be mine: see 8:23) through Jesus Christ our Lord." The thanksgiving proclaims, not present justification or present enabling, as the other views would require, but personal Christian hope, the theme of chapters 5 and 6, soon to be taken up again in chapter 8. Both the outcry and the thanksgiving are parenthetical, however, and so there is nothing surprising, awkward, or unnatural in the fact that Paul goes straight on to summarize what he was saying from verses 14 to 23 about the way things are now: "So then, with my mind I am a slave to the law of God, but with my flesh I am a slave to the law of sin" (7:25b, NRSV). Such a statement would be an anticlimactic jolt on either of the other two views, but on this understanding it is just a clinching crystalization of what God's law, which has been fomenting sin in us all along, finally tells the Christian about himself, and so is an entirely appropriate conclusion to the paragraph.

From the fullness of my statement of it the reader will already have di-

13. This view, characteristic of the holiness movements on both sides of the Atlantic that stemmed from the ministry of W. E. Boardman and Robert Pearsall Smith and his wife in the 1870s, was given its best exegetical expression in H. C. G. Moule, *Romans* (London: Hodder & Stoughton, 1994). What Moule there says about Rom 7 and 8 marks a shift from his 1879 commentary in the Cambridge Bible series.

vined that this seems to me the superior and indeed only natural view of the passage, and the reader is right. But before I argue its superiority in a direct way, I must counter three common misconceptions of what it implies.

First, Paul is not describing a struggle, as is sometimes supposed, but a discernment.[14] "I know," "I find," "I see" (7:18, 21, 23), as seems plain from the context, refer to what Paul becomes aware of after acting, with much or little or no conscious struggling against evil urges as the case may have been: he looks back and realizes that what he has done is not precisely the unqualified good he intended, so that he has not fulfilled the law as he meant to do. Paul's text delineates a state of frustration at this repeated discovery, rather than of unavailing struggle remembered as such. In exegeting these verses we must not forget what Paul told us in verse 11 — that sin *deceives* to secure its effect.

Second, Paul is not describing total moral failure, as if behaviorally the "wretched man" never gets anything right in any sense at all. The bewildered and distressed consciousness that Paul analyzes is simply of a very much desired perfection not being attained. If the "wretched man" is indeed a Christian, then he is one who here and now serves God "in the new way of the Spirit" (7:6), who lives not according to the flesh but according to the Spirit, and who actually does to death sinful habits through the Spirit as he goes along (8:4-14). Paul is not telling us that the life of the "wretched man" is as bad as it could be, only that it is not as good as it should be, and that because the man delights in the law and longs to keep it perfectly his continued inability to do so troubles him acutely. On the view we are exploring, the "wretched man" is Paul himself, spontaneously voicing his distress at not being a better Christian than he is, and all we know of Paul personally fits in with this supposition.

All the thinking of all the New Testament writers, Paul's as much as any, moves within the frame of "inaugurated eschatology" — that is, it involves recognition that through the Spirit Christians enjoy the firstfruits, foretaste, initial installment, and dawning enjoyment of the life of the new aeon, the kingdom era of redeemed existence, while the old aeon, the era of existence spoiled by sin, continues, and the fullness of new aeon life remains future. The two ages overlap, and Christians are anchored in both, so that language proper to both is appropriate, indeed necessary, for describing their condition theologically. Justified by faith and "alive to God in Christ Jesus" (6:11), believers serve God "in the new life of the Spirit" (7:6, NRSV), as those who belong to the new aeon; but sin, the anti-God driving force whose dominion has marked and marred the old aeon from the start, still indwells them, holding them back and leading them away from the full-scale righteousness at which they now aim. Living simultaneously in both aeons and finding in themselves both dynamics, that of

14. NIV is thus wrong to head 7:7-25 "Struggling with Sin."

their own law-loving, new-aeon "inner being" (7:22; "inmost self," NRSV) and that of the law-opposing, old-aeon "sin living in me . . . within my members" (7:20, 23), Christians have a two-sided experience: the uplifting of the Spirit and the downdrag of sin both operate, and bewilderment results. Christians know themselves as people who, living as new creatures in Christ and under grace, have yet failed to do what they wanted to do and done instead things they wanted to avoid doing. Each is thus aware of himself or herself as what James Dunn calls a "split self," the "split 'I.'"[15] It is the humbling pain of this frustration that is expressed, as was said above, in the "wretched man" outburst (literally, "I am a miserable human being," a hapless, helpless, hopeless creature as it seems). Who, now, is going to say that Paul would never have felt like that? or that healthy Christians today never do?

Third, Paul, though transcribing a dimension of experience that he clearly thinks is characteristic, has in this passage and its context no purpose of assessing the quality of his own or anyone else's Christian condition, whether healthy or sickening, mature or unformed, balanced or unbalanced, strong or weak, nor any interest in indicating the technique of living a holier life. Evangelical culture, with its Reformational and pietist roots, has in the past prompted the reading of these interests into the passage, but they cannot be read out of it. In Romans 6–8 Paul is delineating and celebrating the reality of the believer's new life in and with the risen Christ, the life of temptation, trouble, and felt weakness that is lived under grace, through the Spirit, in hope of the final glory of full redemption "through the eternal love."[16] This excursus on the link between the law and sin belongs to that celebration, and is there to ensure that no one hears Paul's good news as reflecting badly on the holiness of God's law. Whatever can be learned from Romans 6–8 by way of pastoral therapy for ailing and disobedient Christians, Paul's purpose in these chapters is, only and precisely, to expound life in Christ and to minister theological therapy to any who had not before grasped the greatness of the grace of God or who suspected that Paul's own grasp of it was leading him to undervalue the law in some way. In 7:7-25 Paul moves to counter this suspicion by showing that the goodness of the law as setting forth God's commands for human living is in no way diminished by the fact that it stirs up the sin it condemns, and thereby causes distress and desperation, both in those who do not yet have faith in Christ and in those who now do. The rationale, and consequently the meaning, of Paul's style and phraseology in these verses become fully clear as soon as this is seen.

15. Dunn, *op. cit.*, p. 388. "The 'I' is split and the law is split in complementary fashion because each belongs to both epochs at the same time in this period of overlap . . . between the era of the flesh and the era of the Spirit."

16. I echo here Thomas Binney's hymn "Eternal Light!" which ends thus: "The sons of ignorance and night/May dwell in the eternal light/Through the eternal love."

I conclude by listing the lines of argument which favor the view of the passage that has been taken, and which count against any other.

First: the above view gives the only natural explanation of Paul's shift from past to present in verse 14 as he continues his first-person-singular analysis of how sin in one's system reacts to the law. To shrug off the shift as a rhetorical device for giving extra vividness to what, essentially, he has said already would be exegetically evasive and grammatically hazardous. The use of the historic present in the Gospels and other Greek literature to add vividness to narrative does not provide any parallel to putting the narrative in the aorist (7:7-13) and the explanatory comment (which is what, on this view, 7:14-25 would be) in the present. The supposed rhetorical device of using the present tense for lively comment on what is past and gone does not exist in Greek, and so the shift of tense would be gratuitously misleading to Paul's readers if it did not mark a narrative advance from past to present. Was Paul so crass and inept as a writer of Greek as to commit such a solecism? Surely that question answers itself. And, furthermore, was Paul not bright enough to see that if he did not deal with sin and law in the Christian's present experience there would be a gap in his treatment of the problem he raised in 7:7? Surely this question too answers itself.

Second: the above view gives the only natural explanation of verse 25b's following verses 24 and 25a. "So then" (ἄρα οὖν) is a connective drawing a conclusion from what has been said so far. If verse 25a, Paul's thanksgiving, is held to proclaim present deliverance from whatever bondage to sin is described in verses 14-24, then the second part of the conclusion ("with my flesh I am a slave to the law of sin," NRSV) is a *non sequitur,* as well as being a shattering anticlimax that actually goes back on what has just been said. Commentators who reject the view for which I am arguing either assume, without the least manuscript support, that verse 25b is misplaced and should follow verse 23,[17] which is, to say the least, a high-handed *tour de force,* or they read the emphatic "I" (αὐτὸς ἐγώ, I the selfsame person) in verse 25b as meaning "I by myself; I alone, without Christ; I thrown on my own resources,"[18] which lays a weight of theological meaning on αὐτός which it can hardly bear and once more accuses Paul of being less than clear in his language, using words in a way that would more naturally signify something other than what he means. Wise exegetes must shy away from such theories.

17. James Moffatt, C. H. Dodd, and Kenneth E. Kirk are among those who have taken this line. Equally high-handed is the view of Julicher and Bultmann, that 7:25b is a gloss and no part of Paul's authentic text.

18. Meyer, Denney, R. St. J. Parry, and C. L. Mitton are among those who have taken this view, and BAGD seems to be in agreement. See J. I. Packer, *Keep in Step with the Spirit,* pp. 267, 284-85.

Third: the above view preserves Paul's consistency with regard to the human condition. The "wretched man" approves God's law (7:16), delights in it (7:22), wants to fulfill it (7:15, 18-21), and serves it with his mind (νοῦς) in his "inner being." But in the next paragraph Paul says that while "those who live in accordance with the Spirit have their minds set on what the Spirit desires . . . the sinful mind (*mg.*, the mind set on the flesh) is hostile to God. It does not submit to God's law, nor can it do so" (8:5, 7). So unless we are to suppose that Paul has reversed his anthropology within less than ten verses we must conclude that in 7:14-25 Paul is describing, not a man in Adam, writhing under the condemnation of a law that he resents even as he acknowledges its authority, but a man in Christ, whose heart is now tuned to love the law and to bewail only his inability to keep it perfectly.

Fourth: only the above view does justice to the preposition *ek* (ἐκ) in the utterance of the "wretched man." What he cries out for, explicitly, is deliverance "*out of* (ἐκ) this body of death" — meaning, either this mortal body which is at present sin's place of residence, or this state of selfhood in which the death-dealing, death-inducing operation of sin is so painfully obtrusive, or both together. But such deliverance will only come with "the redemption of our bodies" (8:23), when the whole of our being is finally transformed into Christ's likeness (1 Cor 15:52-56; Phil 3:21): a consummation for which those who have "the firstfruits of the Spirit" wait, groaning. It is surely this groaning, in exact terms, that 7:24 voices, and this prospect for which verse 25a gives thanks. What the "wretched man" says he seeks is not a changed relationship with God in this present aeon, but the fullness of transformed personal life in the aeon to come, in which his present condition is entirely left behind.

Fifth: counter-arguments to the view stated are not cogent. Two might seem to have substance: let us look at them.

It is said that were Paul dealing with the Christian's life in 7:14-25 he would be writing, not about the law, which believers are no longer "under" as a way of salvation, but about the Spirit who now controls them (see 7:6 and 8:2-4). But, first, Christians are still tied to God's law, now the law of Christ, as a standard of conduct; this appears from Paul's early insistence that his gospel upholds (literally, "sets up") the law (3:31) and from his teaching in 13:8-10 on how the law is to be fulfilled. And, second, the lack of reference to the Spirit in 7:14-25 proves nothing; not only because arguments from silence are intrinsically inconclusive, but because Paul's theme here, focused by his own question in verse 7, is sin's antipathy to God's law, and as a man of strong and orderly mind he stays with that theme till he has finished with it, after which he moves on to develop the further theme of life in the Spirit, which he had reached the point of announcing in 7:6.

Again, it is said that 7:14-25 cannot be Paul speaking personally because

7:7-13 was not that: 7-13 show a sinner very much tormented by knowing he had not kept the law, whereas Philippians 3:6 states that before Paul's conversion he was "faultless" (literally, not exposed to blame) with regard to the righteousness of the law; nor in any case was it likely that conversion had led Paul to lapse from this law-keeping way of life. But in the context of Philippians 3:6 Paul is looking at his past from the outside, as it were, in terms of how he was valued and told to value himself as a member of the Pharisaic community, and, as pastors know, meticulous outward performance by strong and brilliant men may be a sign that they are being driven by a sense of failure, inadequacy, and guiltiness inside. It would be natural, and not in the least surprising, if this were Paul's story.

Pace my honored colleague Gordon Fee, then, I remain a convinced and unrepentant Augustinian with regard to the "wretched man."

Spirit Speech: Reflections on Romans 8:12-27

James D. G. Dunn

I

It is a familiar fact that the biblical Spirit is generally understood as the Spirit that speaks. The Spirit of the Jewish scriptures (the OT) is classically remembered as the Spirit of prophecy, the Spirit that inspired the sacred writings. The Spirit anointed Jesus "to preach good news to the poor" (Lk 4:18). The Spirit was poured out at Pentecost "upon all flesh, . . . and they shall prophesy" (Acts 2:17-18). And Paul evidently prized the charisms of speech most highly of all the charisms, and above all prophecy (1 Cor 12:8-10; 14:1, 39).

In the light of this fact it is interesting to compare Paul's treatment of the Spirit in Romans 8. For that chapter is not only Paul's most sustained exposition of the work of the Spirit; it also forms the climax to Paul's exposition of the gospel in Romans 1–8. That is to say, the work of the Spirit as described in Romans 8 is Paul's climactic account of the way the grace of God comes to clearest and fullest effect in believers. It is not surprising, then, that this climactic function of the Spirit is thought of in terms of speaking — the Spirit continues to be the Spirit that speaks. What is striking and at least a little surprising is the way in which Paul characterizes that speech.

The chapter begins by describing the fundamental role of the Spirit as the Spirit of life in liberating from the power of sin and death (8:2). This fundamental function of the Spirit in enabling the conduct which is pleasing to God (8:4-6, 13), in defining who belongs to Christ (8:9), and as the life-giver (8:10-11), is the starting point of Paul's exposition. Nothing is said at this point about the Spirit as the inspirer of speech, except to the extent that the idea is implied in the phrase "thinking the things of the Spirit = maintaining the attitude of the Spirit" and "the Spirit's way of thinking" (8:5-6).[1]

All the more striking is the fact, therefore, that the next three functions of the Spirit all have to do with inspired speech. Still more to the point is the observation that these are the last functions that Paul attributes to the Spirit in this climactic account of the Spirit's work in individuals. Most striking of all is the nature of the speech this Spirit inspires — the cry "Abba, Father" (8:15), the groans of incomplete sonship (8:23), and the inarticulate intercession of and for the saints (8:26-27). Given the importance of the character of the Spirit as the Spirit that speaks, it is worth reflecting more fully on this diversity of speech which is thus attributed to the Spirit by Paul in this great "Spirit chapter."

II

Romans 8:14-17

There are several features of these verses which call for attention.

a) The Spirit is being characterized as the Spirit of sonship: "as many as are led by the Spirit of God, they are sons of God" (8:14); "you received not a spirit of slavery . . . but the Spirit of adoption" (8:15).[2] In the former clause we should note that Paul's thought is still on the defining role of the Spirit: as in 8:9, so here the status of "sons of God" is defined in terms of the Spirit; in this case it is attributed to "those[3] who are led by the Spirit" (8:14). In the latter (i.e., 8:15), the sonship is more precisely defined as "adoption," that is, either the Spirit which effects adoption, or the Spirit which expresses adoption. The metaphor is a reminder that the relation of sonship to God is not a "natural" one but a status achieved for humankind by divine choice.[4]

1. It will hardly be accidental that the term *phronēma* ("way of thinking") occurs in Paul's letters only in 8:6-7 and 8:27.

2. In the NT only the Pauline corpus makes use of the metaphor of "adoption" (Rom 8:15, 23; 9:4; Gal 4:5; Eph 1:5). "The use of 'adoption' rather than 'son' at this point actually increases the contrast with 'slavery' since it emphasizes the double gulf between the two: the believer's status has been transformed not only from slave to freedman, but also from freedman to adopted son" (J. D. G. Dunn, *Romans 1–8* [WBC 38A; Dallas: Word, 1988], p. 452).

3. "As many as" can have a restrictive force ("only those who") or an inclusive force ("all those who").

4. The idea of divine sonship links back into Israel's sense of election as God's son (see Dunn, *Romans 1–8*, p. 526, on Rom 9:4). It is true that the language is drawn from Graeco-Roman law and custom, since adoption *per se* was not a characteristically Jewish practice; but

b) It is fundamental to this role of the Spirit as the Spirit of sonship that the Spirit is also the Spirit of the Son. Indeed, the Spirit is the Spirit of sonship precisely because it is the Spirit of the Son.[5] That is to say, the Spirit for Paul links the believer directly to Jesus; the Spirit defines the person as Christian precisely by establishing this link. And it makes this plain by reproducing the prayer relation of Jesus himself with God[6] in believers: like Jesus, believers cry "Abba! Father!" and thus attest that they are children of God and joint heirs with Christ (8:16-17). This clarification of the character of the Spirit, beyond the older more animistic or dynamistic talk of the Spirit as an inspiring or empowering presence, is one of Paul's most important contributions to Christian thought and spirituality.[7] In one brief clause it provides a critical test of what may be and what should not be attributed to (or blamed on) the Spirit; only that is to be welcomed which affirms and nurtures a true sense of sonship, that is, of responsibility before God and of care by God.[8]

c) It is worth noting, then, that Paul does not hesitate to express this defining relationship in forceful — we might almost say dangerous — language. He defines as sons those who are "led by the Spirit," where the verb could invite the sense of the Spirit as a compelling force, what some would regard as an "enthusiastic" understanding of the Spirit.[9] And he describes the address to God as "Father" using the strong verb "cry" (8:15), where an intense or loud cry is most likely in mind (as usually in its use elsewhere in the NT).[10] We need/should not assume that Paul has in mind what today might be called "charismatic prayer"

see J. M. Scott, *Adoption as Sons of God: An Exegetical Investigation into the Background of HUIOTHESIA in the Pauline Corpus* (WUNT 2.48; Tübingen: Mohr, 1992), pp. 61-88.

5. This is more clearly indicated in the parallel passage Gal 4:6: "God sent the Spirit of his Son into our hearts, crying, 'Abba! Father!'"

6. That "Abba" was a distinctive feature of Jesus' own prayer to God has been generally accepted since the main statement of the case by J. Jeremias, *The Prayers of Jesus* (London: SCM, 1967), ch. 1, despite a certain amount of overstatement by Jeremias; see further my *Romans*, pp. 453-54; J. A. Fitzmyer, *Romans* (AB 33; New York: Doubleday, 1993), p. 498.

7. More than any other NT writer Paul redefines the Spirit as the "Spirit of Christ" (Rom 8:9), "the Spirit of his [God's] Son" (Gal 4:6), "the Spirit of Jesus Christ" (Phil 1:19). See also, e.g., 1 Cor 12:3; 15:45; 2 Cor 3:18.

8. The image of "father" should not be sentimentalized. In a society where the paterfamilias had all legal power the image spoke as much if not more of authority.

9. E. Käsemann, *Commentary on Romans* (Grand Rapids: Eerdmans/London: SCM, 1980), p. 226; but see further G. Fee, *God's Empowering Presence: The Holy Spirit in the Letters of Paul* (Peabody, Mass.: Hendrickson, 1994), p. 563, and others mentioned in my *Theology of Paul the Apostle* (Grand Rapids: Eerdmans, 1998), p. 435n.119.

10. See, e.g., Mk 3:11; 5:5, 7; 9:24, 26; 10:47-48; 11:9; 15:13-14, 39. Fitzmyer notes that the same verb is used of various situations in the OT where one "cries out" to God (e.g., Ex 22:23; Pss 3:4; 17:6; 18:6; 30:2; 34:17; 88:1, 9; 107:13) (*Romans*, p. 501); but most of these speak specifically of cries of distress or for help.

in these references. It is a relationship he is describing, not just an experience. But Paul's language does not permit us to forget that the relationship in view is one which for Paul was expressed in intensity of feeling as well as intimacy of expression. That this Spirit is expressly contrasted with "a spirit of slavery" (8:15), having already been described as "the Spirit of life" which liberates (8:2), confirms the sense of up-welling delight and trust expressed in the Abba prayer.

d) Not least of interest here is the way Paul sees this Spirit speech as correlated with human speech. In so speaking, "the Spirit bears witness with our spirit" (8:16). The one who actually says the words "Abba! Father!" is the human voice, but the human voice as inspired and enabled by the Spirit — "by whom, we cry."[11] In other words, the Spirit that speaks here speaks to and from the human spirit. Through speech it links us with the sonship of Jesus and with our innermost selves at one and the same time. It provides a means of expression for deep-felt emotion. And in all these ways it defines and brings to the reality of existential experience the sonship of God which believers share with Christ.

III

Romans 8:18-25

Here the key passage is v. 23 — "we ourselves who have the firstfruits of the Spirit, we also ourselves groan within ourselves, eagerly awaiting adoption, the redemption of the body." Again several features call for comment.

a) Whereas in the preceding paragraph the Spirit defined the status of believers, here the Spirit defines the process of salvation. The character of the process is well caught by the repetition of the imagery of "adoption" (8:15, 23):[12] salvation is a process which moves believers from one "adoption" to another. The first adoption establishes the status of sonship (8:15). But the second adoption is "the redemption of the body," by which Paul clearly understands the resurrection of the body (8:11). That is to say, the process of salvation lasts from the reception of the Spirit of adoption to the final transformation or resurrec-

11. The implication of Mk 14:36 and Gal 4:6 is that the Greek translation quickly became established together with the Aramaic as a double (Aramaic/Greek) address to God characteristic and distinctive of those who named the name of Jesus. Whether the Aramaic-speaking churches of the land of Israel used only the Aramaic "Abba" by itself (cf. Lk 11:2), it was the double cry which would most typically echo within the gatherings of the Greek-speaking churches.

12. Some manuscripts omit the second occurrence, but Fee, who argues that the omission is secondary (*Empowering Presence*, p. 572n.295), has the better of the argument over Fitzmyer, who argues that the omission was original (*Romans*, p. 510).

tion of the body. The process is lifelong and will not be complete until the end of normal, physical life. The process is in some sense an ongoing transformation, elsewhere described as a transformation of the person into the image of Christ (2 Cor 3:18), or as a renewal of the inner person even while the outward person is in decay (2 Cor 4:16–5:5).[13]

The role of the Spirit in this process is also clear. It is nicely summed up in the metaphor of the "firstfruits." The dominant image in this metaphor is that of the harvest, the firstfruits of winepress and threshing floor.[14] The emphasis is on *first*fruits, since the reference is to the first bunches of grapes plucked or the wine made from them, the first sheaves reaped or the loaves made from them: by dedicating the firstlings to God the rest could be used by Israel. The fact that the Spirit is particularly in view might well have evoked or be intended to evoke the thought of Pentecost, the Feast of Weeks (Pentecost) being the principal celebration of the firstfruits of the harvest.[15] To be noted is the fact that the Spirit is identified as the firstfruits — "the firstfruits of the Spirit" = the firstfruits consisting of the Spirit, the firstfruits which are the Spirit. In other words, the Spirit is the firstling of God's harvest; the one who has received the Spirit has been thus dedicated to God.[16] The process of the divine harvest of salvation begins with the gift of the Spirit itself.

Moreover, the firstfruits as the beginning of the harvest are of a piece with the rest of the harvest, for the complete harvest simply consists of the rest of the grapes or grain. In Paul's adaptation of the metaphor, since the harvest is the harvest of resurrection, of resurrection bodies, that means that the end of the process of salvation (resurrection) is of a piece with its beginning. That is to say, the gift of the Spirit and the transformation begun by the Spirit in and through believers is of a piece with that final resurrection.[17] No wonder, then, that Paul both attributes the final resurrection to the Spirit (God "will give life to your mortal bodies through his Spirit which dwells in you" — 8:11) and describes the resurrection body itself as a "spiritual body," by which he presumably means a bodily existence made possible, vivified, and characterized by the Spirit, just as this present existence is made possible, vivified, and characterized by the soul (1 Cor 15:44-49).[18]

13. Hence the character of salvation as hope (8:24-25).

14. Full references can be found in my *Romans*, p. 473.

15. Ex 22:29; 34:22; Deut 16:9-12; Philo, *Spec. Leg.* 2.179.

16. The fact that the Spirit is given *by* God rather than *to* God does not affect the point, which has to do with the set-apartness of the "firstfruits" ensuring the sanctification of the whole (cf. Rom 11:16).

17. Note the complementary use of the "firstfruits" imagery in 1 Cor 15:20, 23.

18. The metaphor of "first instalment, guarantee" *(arrabōn)* as used by Paul is also complementary (2 Cor 1:22; 5:5; cf. Eph 1:14).

b) In this case the utterance mentioned is not attributed to the Spirit as such. But the groaning in view is that of the Spirit-gifted person. And the groaning is occasioned by the gift of the Spirit: it is precisely "we ourselves who have the firstfruits of the Spirit" who "groan within ourselves." Not only so, but the same term is used a few verses later to describe the prayer of the Spirit (8:26). It is important, then, to grasp the fact that this groaning is itself the result and expression of the process of salvation.[19] The image of "groaning" implies thought of discomfort, irritation, frustration, even pain. This is what is involved in the process of salvation. The gift of the Spirit disturbs and disrupts what was previously a settled pattern, introducing the irritation at the heart of the oyster which will produce the pearl. The gift of the Spirit reclaims the believer for God and begins or heightens the tension between human belonging to God and human entrancement with the world of human control and success, the warfare between Spirit and flesh. Believers caught in this tension and warfare cannot simply look on the process of salvation spectator-like or dispassionately, as though it was an intellectual exercise; they are themselves caught within the tension and warfare — "we also ourselves groan within ourselves, eagerly awaiting adoption, the redemption of the body."[20] In other words, the process of salvation is no primrose path; rather, it is more like the experience of "cold turkey," as believers are weaned from the drugs that kept reality at arm's length from them.

This groaning, then, is also Spirit speech. This Spirit speech reminds us that the process of salvation is not all smooth, not all sweetness and light. Nor is all Spirit speech the experience of being taken out of oneself, lifted to heights of inspiration. This Spirit speech comes from the heart of the believer still knowing the deadness of the body because of sin (8:10), still having to resist the blandishments of the flesh (8:12-13),[21] still very much *in via,* still very much in process of being saved and not yet saved or saved only "in hope" (8:24). But it is as much an expression of the Spirit, of the life and presence of the Spirit in and through the individual believer, as any charismatic speech.

c) It is also important to note the correlation between verses 22 and 23: "we know that the whole creation groans and suffers the pains of childbirth together up till now" (8:22). Clearly Paul understood the two groanings as of a piece.[22] The point is that creation itself is caught up in the same process of salvation, the same process of being "liberated from the bondage to decay" to share the freedom of

19. The line of thought is similar to that which includes Rom 7:24 and 2 Cor 5:2. Cf. D. Moo, *Romans* (NICNT; Grand Rapids: Eerdmans, 1996), p. 520.

20. See further my *Theology of Paul,* §18.

21. It is at this point that I part company with Gordon Fee in his exposition of Paul's understanding of the process of salvation and of the Spirit's role in it (see my *Theology of Paul,* p. 480 and n. 86).

22. 8:22 — *systenazei;* 8:23 — *stenazomen.*

the glory of the children of God (8:21). Creation, too, is caught in the same tension and frustration. Believers are being saved not *from* creation but *with* creation. Here too we are reminded that the Spirit in biblical thought is also the Spirit of creation — "the *ruach* of God hovering over the deep" (Gen 1:2), the Spirit which is the presence of God in all creation (Ps 139:7). Having the Spirit does not distance believers from creation but increases the solidarity of believers with creation. The sonship they are privileged to share in some sense with Christ, they in turn share in some sense with creation. So too, as Spirit speech confirms their status as God's children, Spirit speech also confirms their belongingness within creation, and expresses that shared experience of frustration. Again it is worth noting, then, that the Spirit speech which relates believers to their created environment — their ecological Spirit speech, we might say — is not a speech which transcends human limitation but a speech which recalls the extent to which believers continue to be thoroughly bound up with creation, and that precisely as part of and not despite the process of salvation.

IV

Romans 8:26-27

This third and last example of Spirit speech is the most striking of all.

a) We should note, first of all, the continuity of thought with the preceding context. When Paul speaks of "our weakness" he no doubt had in mind the weakness of the human condition and the futility of creation of which he had just been speaking (8:18-23); the "groans" *(stenagmois)* of 8:26 undoubtedly link back to the "groaning" *(stenazomen)* of 8:23. But where in the previous paragraph the Spirit had constituted the beginning of the process (but still only the beginning, and so initiated or strengthened the resultant sense of dis-ease), here the role of the Spirit is depicted as much more supportive: "the Spirit helps *(synantilambanetai)* us in our weakness" — the image being that of shouldering a burden too heavy for the weakness of the human condition to support.[23] Paul does not pretend the life of discipleship is easy: human weakness continues to be all too evident;[24] groaning is also and continues to be an expression of spiritual life. The Spirit helps precisely in that weakness.

23. Two of the three (or four) LXX occurrences of the verb *synantilambanetai* refer to the support given to Moses through the appointment of 70 elders (Ex 18:22; Num 11:17); cf. the only other NT reference (Lk 10:40).

24. For Paul's understanding of human weakness see also Rom 8:3; 1 Cor 2:3; 15:43; 2 Cor 11:30; 12:5, 9-10; 13:4; Gal 4:13; Phil 2:26-27.

b) The weakness comes to its most poignant expression in prayer: "what we are to pray for as we should[25] we do not know" (8:26). Here the believer is in an even worse state than the "I" of 7:14-24. The "I" knew what to do, knew what the law of God stipulated, and wanted to do it; but failed. Here the problem is different: not that believers know all along what to pray for and simply cannot turn their desires into words. The measure of their confusion and frustration is that they just do not know what God's will is for them; they do not know what to want.[26] Here too is a reminder that salvation is not a matter of knowledge, of being informed as to the nature of reality. Nor is there a liberation or illumination of mind which renders unnecessary the redemption of the body or the liberation of the cosmos. Even within the process of salvation, for those already being saved, a marked degree of spiritual ignorance and of darkened mind remains an all too present reality.

c) So, what is the Spirit's help in this case? Once again Paul does not cherish the hope of being removed from this weakness during this life or of a speech which nullifies that weakness and leaves it behind. On the contrary, the Spirit speech is itself an expression of that weakness: "the Spirit intercedes[27] on our behalf with inarticulate groans *(stenagmois alalētois)*" (8:26). The key word, *alalētos*, occurs only here in biblical Greek. But its meaning is clear — literally "lacking speech," lacking that which distinguishes humans from animals. This indicates the depth of human weakness — in the last resort no more able than brute beasts to speak to God in articulate speech.[28] In the event, this groaning is little different from that shared between creation and those in process of being saved in 8:22-23.

In this case, however, it functions as effective prayer. Why? Because God is at both ends of the process. The Spirit is in tune with God. That is, the Spirit working deep at the root of human inarticulateness, the Spirit working deep at the root of creation's futility and the believer's frustration, is working with God, as part of and in accordance with God's will (8:27). Because the heart is where

25. The phrase presumably expresses the traditional sense that what matters is God's will, and that prayer is or should be a process of seeking to align human will with divine will, rather than of trying to bend divine will to human will.

26. Cf. Fee, *Empowering Presence,* pp. 578-79; Moo, *Romans,* p. 523. The point can be cloaked, but the NRSV has retained RSV's rendering — "we do not know how to pray as we ought," as though it was a matter of finding the right words.

27. The thought draws on the Jewish tradition of angelic intercessors; see further my *Romans,* p. 478.

28. Fee earlier argued for the sense "words not generated by or understandable to the mind," that is, glossolalia (*Empowering Presence,* pp. 581-83), despite the fact that Paul thought of glossolalia as speech (e.g., 1 Cor 14:2, 16). But he has since changed his mind — "Toward a Pauline Theology of Glossolalia," in W. M. and R. P. Menzies (eds.), *Pentecostalism in Context: W. W. Menzies FS* (Sheffield: Sheffield Academic, 1997), pp. 24-37 (here pp. 29-30).

the inner reality of the person is,[29] the openness and opening of the heart to God is an effective communication with God and succeeds in keeping open the channels of grace between believers and God. At this point Spirit speech and heart language are one. Here as elsewhere Paul had found that recognition of human weakness is an unavoidable, even necessary complement to divine strength and power (2 Cor 12:9-10).[30]

d) What a surprise! Here again, it is not the speech of high spiritual rapture or profoundest prophetic inspiration which achieves effective communication with God, but the speech which expresses human inability, human solidarity with nonhuman creation in its futility. It is not the heavenly journey to hear "unutterable words" (2 Cor 12:4) which puts the believer in tune with the will of God. It is the Spirit speaking with primal speech, putting believers in touch with their deepest being where language fails, expressing the instinctive recognition of the creature that its existence depends solely and ultimately on God alone. It is the Spirit stripping the human creature of all the pride and pretense which human ability with words brings, of all the power to persuade and charm, to manipulate and deceive which human speech makes possible. This is the cry of the creature both acknowledging its creatureliness and confessing God as its God. That is why it constitutes effective prayer.

V

Here then in this great Spirit chapter, surely the climax of Paul's exposition of how salvation works out in this life, and so also the climax of his pneumatology, we have some of his clearest and profoundest thoughts on Spirit speech.

a) It is important that the contribution of Romans 8 on this subject be adequately recognized. Paul says a great deal about Spirit speech elsewhere, particularly as inspired speech in evangelism (e.g., 1 Cor 2:4-5) and in worship (e.g., 1 Cor 14). But it would be a mistake to see these categories as definitive of the character of inspired speech for Paul. He had already warned about misevaluations and false priorities on this subject in 1 Corinthians 13 and 2 Corinthians 12. And it would be as much a mis-evaluation and misunderstanding of Paul's thought here to limit discussion to whether the "Abba" prayer or the "in-

29. The "heart" which God "searches" — an OT formulation (1 Sam 16:7; 1 Kings 8:39; Pss 44:21; 139:1-2, 23; Prov 15:11) — is the seat of the inner life, the center of the human person hidden from onlookers' eyes.

30. Cf. the thesis of Fee, "Pauline Theology of Glossolalia": "that Paul's understanding of glossolalia is to be found in the paradox of 2 Cor. 12:9 . . . and that speaking in tongues therefore reflects a position of weakness, not of strength," p. 25.

articulate groans" were to be understood simply as inspired or charismatic speech like glossolalia,[31] as though these were the only categories of Spirit speech with which Paul was concerned. There are other kinds and more profound kinds of Spirit speech than these.

b) Notable is the interaction of divine Spirit and human spirit, divine voice and human voice: the Spirit "by whom we cry 'Abba! Father!' [and thereby] the same Spirit bears witness with our spirit that we are God's children" (8:15-16); "having the firstfruits of the Spirit we ourselves groan within ourselves" (8:23); "the Spirit itself intercedes on our behalf with inarticulate groans, and he who searches the hearts knows that is the Spirit's way of thinking" (8:26-27). In the intensity of prayer and abandonment to God in what would otherwise be total human despair, Spirit speech and heart language become as one.

c) The Spirit speech in Romans 8 is all speech to God or before God; two of the three instances are specifically designated as prayer (8:15, 27). A fundamental role of the Spirit for Paul, then, is in maintaining a line of communication open with God. The one expresses the sense of sonship to God, of trust in God's paternal care, of submission before God's paternal authority. The others express the sense of human weakness and incompleteness without God, the groaning of creatureliness experienced as such.

d) The Spirit speech bonds the believer with Christ. Whereas the groaning is that of creation, shared with creation, the cry "Abba! Father!" expresses that sense of intimate belonging to God inherited from Christ, both the prayer itself and the status expressed. Thanks to Christ, then, those identified with him have a more profound relation with God — as Father and not just as Creator. And to that extent humans are in advance in the process of salvation and redemption in relation to the rest of creation.

e) At the same time, the "Abba" prayer does not mean that believers are able to dispense with the prayer of inarticulate groaning. They have not left behind creation or their own creatureliness. Indeed, Paul's double emphasis on the groaning Spirit speech should probably be seen as a warning for humans not to act like spoiled children but always to remember their solidarity with nonhuman creation. At the end of the day, human inarticulateness before God is the greatest gift of Spirit speech because it helps prevent that pride and striving to manipulate both God and others which has always been the primary cause of human downfall and evil.

This small offering is dedicated to Gordon Fee as a token of appreciation for his contributions as commentator on the Spirit.

31. In particular, Fee, *Empowering Presence*, pp. 580-85; see above n. 28.

The Redemption of Our Body: The Riddle of Romans 8:19-22

J. Ramsey Michaels

In a lifetime given to teaching, a handful of colleagues stand out. They are those whose friendship and whose respect and enthusiasm for the biblical text are such that together we can pick up the thread of a detailed discussion of a passage or a verse of Scripture after an interruption of a day or a week — or a decade — without missing a beat. Gordon Fee is such a colleague. It is a privilege to have him as a friend, and a delight to have a part in honoring him with a *Festschrift*.

My contribution builds on a bit of personal history. My first exposure to serious exegesis came in 1955 at Grace Theological Seminary in Winona Lake, Indiana, where every senior had to submit, as a requirement for graduation, something called a "critical monograph," usually on a single verse of Scripture. I chose Romans 8:21, in the context of Paul's comments about the κτίσις, "creature" or "creation," in 8:19-22.[1] The sources I used were mostly older commentaries (old even in 1955!), and I discovered an extraordinary variety of interpretations. To some extent I have kept track of the literature on the passage since then, and I now find hardly any variety at all. There is almost universal agreement that the κτίσις is, as Douglas Moo puts it, "the subhuman creation"[2] —

1. J. R. Michaels, "A Critical Examination of Romans 8:21," submitted in partial fulfillment of the requirements for the degree of Bachelor of Divinity in Grace Theological Seminary, May, 1955.

2. *The Epistle to the Romans* (Grand Rapids: Eerdmans, 1996), p. 514; cf. J. A. Fitzmyer, *Romans*, Anchor Bible 33 (New York: Doubleday, 1993), p. 506: "Paul is affirming a solidarity of the nonhuman world with the human world in the redemption that Christ has wrought."

that is, the whole created universe except for human beings and angels. What happened to produce such unanimity? Nothing that I know of, unless it is the simple fact that the English Revision of 1885 changed the translation of κτίσις in 8:19, 20, and 21 from "creature" (as in the KJV) to "creation,"[3] and that virtually all translations since have followed its example.

My own researches as a beginner in 1955 led me to a different conclusion. I argued that κτίσις should be translated "creature," not "creation," that Paul used it simply as a metaphor for the body, and that Romans 8:21 is an affirmation of the bodily resurrection of believers, no more and no less.[4] This essay gives me the opportunity to go back for a second look. There is no denying that the resurrection of the body is a conspicuous theme in the context. "If the Spirit of him who raised Jesus from the dead dwells in you," Paul writes, "he who raised Christ from the dead will also give life to your mortal bodies through his Spirit dwelling in you" (8:11). Just after mentioning the "groaning" of the κτίσις, he adds, "Not only so, but even those who have the firstfruits of the Spirit, even we ourselves, groan within ourselves as we wait eagerly for adoption, the redemption of our body" (8:23). Paul's interest here, whatever it may have been in the four preceding verses, is in the body, and the hope of resurrection. In this essay, after a brief survey of the resurrection hope in Paul's earlier letters (1 Thessalonians and 1 and 2 Corinthians), I propose to focus on what he calls "the redemption of our body" in relation to his theology of the resurrection, Romans as a whole, and 8:19-22 in particular.

I. The Resurrection of the Dead: 1 Thessalonians and 1 Corinthians

According to the book of Acts, Paul the Pharisee claimed to have found his Pharisaism confirmed in the Christian gospel of the resurrection of Jesus of Nazareth (Acts 23:6-8; cf. 24:14-15, 20-21, 26:6-8). Paul's letters, beginning with 1 Thes-

3. The KJV rendered ἡ κτίσις in vv. 19, 20, and 21 as "the creature," and πᾶσα ἡ κτίσις in v. 22 as "the whole creation." Earlier versions, including Tyndale, Cranmer, Geneva, and Rheims, used "creature" in vv. 19-21 and "every creature" in v. 22. See *The English Hexapla* (London: Bagster, n.d.).

4. The assignment required a paraphrase of Rom 8:21, and I paraphrased the verse as follows: "The content of the creature's hope is this: that the creature itself, that is, this human creature, this very body which we Christians possess and in which we suffer, shall be set free from that slavery which consists of subjection to those physical laws which inevitably issue in death and decay, and shall be brought into that freedom which consists of the glory of the children of God, that glory which shall be unveiled when their legal adoption as sons is consummated, and their true inner nature as children of God by the new birth is revealed" (Michaels, 88).

salonians and 1 Corinthians, give evidence that the inseparable link he forged between the resurrection of Jesus and his personal "hope in the resurrection of the dead" (Acts 23:6) was more than a shrewd tactic called forth by an immediate need to defend himself before Jewish authorities. It went to the very heart of his theology. Almost from the start, he found it necessary to argue from the bodily resurrection of Jesus to a future resurrection of Christian believers. Paul first addresses the issue in 1 Thessalonians 4:13-18. His introductory words to that section, "we do not want you to be ignorant about those who fall asleep" (4:13), stand in contrast to other matters in the same letter about which he says, "you know what instructions we gave you" (4:2) or "we do not need to write to you" (4:9, 5:1). The fate of "those who fall asleep" was something the Thessalonian Christians did *not* know. They were in fact "ignorant" because they had not been taught. In 4:13-18 Paul supplies what is lacking, and in doing so makes his first programmatic statement on future resurrection. He argues on two grounds that Christians who have died will live again. First, Jesus himself had done exactly that; he died, and yet rose again (4:14). Second, the Thessalonians themselves believed in a future "coming," or παρουσία, when Jesus would return and deliver them "from the wrath to come" (1:10; cf. 2:19, 3:13, 5:23). Paul insisted that there would be equality among believers on that day. Those who had the good fortune to be still alive when the Lord returned would have no advantage over those who had died (4:15-17), for as the Lord had said, the last would be first and the first last. It was a matter of simple fairness.[5]

The issue in 1 Corinthians 15 is similar, but not identical. It was not that the Corinthian congregation was ignorant of the resurrection, but that "some" were denying it altogether (15:12). Paul's argument is far more complex and lengthy here than in 1 Thessalonians, but its two basic elements are the same. Just as in 1 Thessalonians, Paul again argues from Jesus' resurrection to the resurrection of the dead: "If there is no resurrection of the dead, then Christ is not risen, and if Christ is not risen, then our proclamation is vain, and your faith is also vain" (15:13-14) — this after a careful review of the evidence that Jesus did in fact rise from the dead (vv. 1-11). He also argues, as in 1 Thessalonians, from the παρουσία, a time when *all* "shall be made alive," both the dead and the living. Paul relativizes the distinction between living and dead on the grounds that *both* groups are in some sense "dead." He claims that "as in Adam *all* died, even so in Christ shall *all* be made alive" (my italics), adding, "But each in its own order: Christ the firstfruits, then those who belong to Christ at his coming"

5. For further development of this proposal, see J. R. Michaels, "Everything That Rises Must Converge: Paul's Word from the Lord," in *To Tell the Mystery: Essays on New Testament Eschatology in Honor of Robert H. Gundry* (Sheffield: Sheffield Academic Press, 1994), pp. 182-95.

(παρουσία, 15:22-23). Later he announces, "Look, I tell you a mystery: We shall not all sleep, but we shall all be changed, in a moment, in the twinkling of an eye, at the last trumpet; for the trumpet will sound, and the dead will be raised incorruptible, and we shall be changed" (15:51-52). Living or dead makes no difference according to Paul. Both are subject to corruption and both will be raised to life (15:53).

II. 2 Corinthians: The Dying Apostle

The hope of resurrection becomes crucial to Paul personally in 2 Corinthians. He speaks in the first chapter of his severe hardships in Ephesus: "We were under great pressure, far beyond our power to endure, so that we even gave up hope of life. We had within us the sentence of death, so that we might not rely on ourselves, but on God, who raises the dead. And he rescued us from that terrible death, and he will rescue us" (2 Cor 1:8-10). Three chapters later he continues, "We are hard pressed everywhere, but not crushed; perplexed, but not in despair; persecuted, but not abandoned; struck down, but not destroyed. We always carry around *in the body* [ἐν τῷ σώματι] the dying of Jesus, so that Jesus' life may also be revealed *in our body* [ἐν τῷ σώματι ἡμῶν]. For we the living are always being given over to death for Jesus' sake, so that Jesus' life may be revealed *in our mortal flesh* [ἐν τῇ θνητῇ σαρκὶ ἡμῶν]" (2 Cor 4:8-11, my emphasis).

Resurrection here is no longer a hope centering on those who are in the grave, or those who will be alive at the Lord's coming. Because of his confidence "that the one who raised the Lord Jesus from the dead will also raise us with Jesus" (2 Cor 4:14), Paul embraces resurrection as the metaphor for the power of God already within him, overcoming weariness and death. "Even though our outer person [ὁ ἔξω ἡμῶν ἄνθρωπος] is wasting away," he says, "our inner one [ὁ ἔσω ἡμῶν] is being renewed day by day. For the lightness of our temporary affliction is producing for us a far more overwhelming, eternal weight of glory" (4:16-17). The much-discussed tension in Paul's theology between the "already" and the "not yet" is here firmly rooted in his personal experience as an apostle and minister of the "new covenant" (see 2 Cor 3:6). The pronoun "we" is largely an apostolic "we" both here and in chapter 5,[6] where he reflects more

6. See V. P. Furnish, *II Corinthians*, Anchor Bible 32A (Garden City, N.Y.: Doubleday, 1985): "Paul is referring specifically to apostles as participants in and bearers of the death and life of Jesus, because his subject here is the meaning and character of the apostolic ministry" (p. 283), and "Paul's comments here continue to be directed to the subject of the apostolic ministry, and specifically the question of how the hardships he and his associates experience are serving that ministry rather than invalidating it" (p. 288).

explicitly on his resurrection hope: "Now we know that if the earthly tent we live in is destroyed, we have a building from God, an eternal house in heaven, not built by human hands. Meanwhile we groan, longing to be clothed with our heavenly dwelling, because when we are clothed, we will not be found naked. For while we are in this tent, we groan and are burdened, because we do not wish to be unclothed but to be clothed with our heavenly dwelling, so that what is mortal may be swallowed up by life. Now it is God who has made us for this very purpose and has given us the Spirit as a deposit, guaranteeing what is to come" (2 Cor 5:1-5 NIV).

Paul is uncomfortable with his physical body because it is "mortal" (τὸ θνητόν, 5:4), the same "mortal flesh" in which he "carried around" the death and the life of Jesus (4:10-11). He longs for a new body, which he describes metaphorically as a "building" or "house" or "dwelling" (vv. 1-2), yet at the same time as something in which he will be "clothed" (vv. 2-4). The old body is a "house" too, but a temporary one like a "tent" (vv. 1, 4), destined to be "destroyed" (v. 1). He feels as if the new body is already his. He can say "we have" (ἔχομεν) this body even now (v. 1), just as surely as "we have" (ἔχομεν, 4:7) the "treasure" defined as "the light of the knowledge of God's glory in the face of Christ" (4:6; cf. 3:18). When he spoke of that "treasure," Paul knew it was contained "in jars of clay" (4:7), and when he speaks here of "a building from God, an eternal house in heaven, not built by human hands" (v. 1), he knows he still lives in "the earthly tent" that is his present body. But because the new body is also his, Paul is confident of being "clothed" at death, not "found naked" (v. 3).[7] His language abounds with metaphors. The resurrection body is never called a "body" in 2 Corinthians, but always a dwelling of some kind or, implicitly, a piece of clothing. The only "body" in 2 Corinthians is the present body (4:10), which Paul calls his "mortal flesh" (4:11).[8] This is the body Paul means when he contrasts being "at home in the body" and "away from the Lord" (2 Cor 5:6), with being "away from the body and at home with the Lord" (5:8). The "body" in 2 Corinthians is by definition part of *earthly,* not heavenly, existence. This was not the case in 1 Corinthians, where Paul spoke of "the body that will be" (τὸ σῶμα τὸ γενησόμενον) in 15:37, and the "spiritual body" (σῶμα πνευματικόν) in 15:44. When Paul wants to refer to this "spiritual body" in 2 Corinthians, he uses other imagery. His expression, "away from the body and at home with the Lord" (5:8), does not necessarily imply a disembodied "intermediate

7. With P^{46}, ℵ, and B, I am reading ἐνδυσάμενοι, "clothed," rather than ἐκδυσάμενοι, "unclothed," in v. 3. Yet the point is not appreciably different if the other reading is adopted. Paul would then be saying, "Assuming, of course, that having put off [the present body], we will not be found naked."

8. Every other use of "body" in 2 Corinthians bears this out: see 5:10, 10:10, and 12:2-3.

state," but is simply Paul's claim that "the earthly tent" in which we now live will give way to a more substantial and more permanent dwelling.

Whatever the terminology, 1 and 2 Corinthians agree in accenting *discontinuity* between the present and the future body. Paul sharply differentiates the "natural" from the "spiritual" body (1 Cor 15:44), the "outer" from the "inner" person (2 Cor 4:16), and the "body" as earthly tent from something he does not call a body at all, but a heavenly dwelling or garment (2 Cor 5:1-10). Where the two letters differ is that the "spiritual body" in 1 Corinthians is essentially future, a "body that will be" (15:37), while in 2 Corinthians Paul has a heightened sense of the "already" in contrast to the "not yet." The new body, or person, or dwelling is even now at work in Paul's ministry alongside the old. He carries within himself both the "dying" and the "life" of Jesus at the same time (4:10-11). His "inner person" is being renewed even as the "outer person" wastes away (4:16). He is poised to receive a "heavenly dwelling" even as he "groans" (στενάζομεν, 5:2, 4) in his poor earthly "tent." The power of the future resurrection is at work in the present, to the point that Paul can say, "anyone in Christ is a new creature [καινὴ κτίσις]: the old things are gone; see, new things have come" (5:17).

III. Romans: The Body of Sin and Death

Although the hope of resurrection does not appear to be Paul's primary theme in Romans, he begins the letter with a reference to Jesus having been "appointed Son of God with power according to the Spirit of holiness by the resurrection of the dead" (ἐξ ἀναστάσεως νεκρῶν, Rom 1:4). The latter phrase is widely translated "resurrection *from* the dead" (NIV, NRSV),[9] but ἀναστάσις νεκρῶν is the same phrase used in Acts (17:32; 23:6; 24:21; 26:23), and in 1 Corinthians (15:12, 13, 21, 42) for the hope of a general resurrection, whether of all the dead or of believers. Here as in 1 Corinthians 15, Paul sees the resurrection of Jesus and the future resurrection of the dead as inseparable. Jesus' resurrection is the first step in the resurrection process (1 Cor 15:20; also Acts 26:23: πρῶτος ἐξ ἀναστάσεως νεκρῶν).[10] Five chapters later, in his only other use of the term "resurrection" in Romans, Paul writes: "For

9. The argument is that it is a case of "the preposition being omitted so as to avoid repeating ἐκ" (C. E. B. Cranfield, *The Epistle to the Romans* [ICC; Edinburgh: T. & T. Clark, 1980], 1.62). But Cranfield's own view is that νεκρῶν is "a generalizing or allusive plural."

10. See James Dunn, *Romans 1–8*, Word Biblical Commentary 38A (Dallas: Word, 1988), pp. 15-16; also J. A. Bengel, *Gnomon Novi Testamenti* 3 (Edinburgh: T. & T. Clark, 1895), who concluded from this text "that the resurrection of all is intimately connected with the resurrection of Christ" (pp. 6-7).

if we have been united with him in the likeness of his death, so too will we be in that of his resurrection" (τῆς ἀναστάσεως, Rom 6:5). Two chapters beyond that he mentions the body explicitly: "If the Spirit of him who raised Jesus from the dead [ἐκ νεκρῶν] dwells in you, he who raised Christ from the dead [ἐκ νεκρῶν] will make even your mortal bodies [καὶ τὰ θνητὰ σώματα ὑμῶν] come alive through his Spirit that dwells in you" (Rom 8:11). In Romans, no less than in Acts, 1 Thessalonians, or 1 and 2 Corinthians, Paul awaits a "resurrection of the dead," understood (on the analogy of the raising of Jesus) as a bodily resurrection.

The turning point in Paul's view of the body (σῶμα) within Romans is 8:23: "And not only so, but even ourselves, having the firstfruits of the Spirit, even we ourselves, groan within ourselves waiting for adoption, the redemption of our body." Every mention of σῶμα to that point in Romans associates the body in some way with sin or death (note the italicized words):

1:24: God gave humans up in the lusts of their hearts to impurity, so as to "*dishonor their bodies* [τοῦ ἀτιμάζεσθαι τὰ σώματα][11] among them."

4:19: Abraham considered "his own *body as good as dead* [τὸ ἑαυτοῦ σῶμα νενεκρωμένον]."

6:6: "Our old self [ὁ παλαιὸς ἡμῶν ἄνθρωπος] was crucified with him, so that *the body of sin* might be put away [ἵνα καταργηθῇ τὸ σῶμα τῆς ἁμαρτίας]."

6:12: "Do not let sin, therefore, reign in *your mortal body* [ἐν τῷ θνητῷ ὑμῶν σώματι], so as to obey its lusts."

7:4: "You have been *put to death* [ἐθανατώθητε] to the law through *the body of Christ* [διὰ τοῦ σώματος τοῦ Χριστοῦ]."[12]

7:24: "Wretched man that I am, who will deliver me from *this body of death* [ἐκ τοῦ σώματος τοῦ θανάτου τούτου]?"

8:10: "If Christ is in you, *the body is dead because of sin* [τὸ μὲν σῶμα νεκρὸν διὰ ἁμαρτίαν], but the Spirit is life because of righteousness."

11. Cf. 1 Cor 15:43, "It is sown in dishonor" (ἐν ἀτιμίᾳ).

12. Here "the body of Christ" is used to mean "the death of Christ," in much the same way that "the blood of Christ" is frequently used (Dunn, p. 362; Fitzmyer, p. 458). Cf. Col 1:22; also Eph 2:13-14, where "in the blood of Christ" and "in his flesh" are almost interchangeable terms for Christ's reconciling death.

8:11: If the Spirit of him who raised Jesus from the dead dwells in you, he who raised Christ from the dead will make even *your mortal bodies* [καὶ τὰ θνητὰ σώματα ὑμῶν] come alive through his Spirit that dwells in you."

8:13: "If you live *according to the flesh* [κατὰ σάρκα], you will die; but if by the Spirit you *put to death the deeds of the body* [τὰς πράξεις τοῦ σώματος θανατοῦτε], you will live."

By contrast, the three remaining occurrences of σῶμα *after* 8:23 carry no such negative connotations, but refer either to the body as a potential instrument for good, or (as in 1 Corinthians 12) to the Christian community corporately:

12:1: "I appeal to you . . . by the mercies of God, to present *your bodies* [τὰ σώματα ὑμῶν] a living sacrifice, holy, acceptable to God, your spiritual worship."

12:4: "For just as *in one body* [ἐν ἑνὶ σώματι] we have many members. . . ."

12:5: "So we the many are *one body* [ἓν σῶμα] in Christ, and members of one another."

Admittedly, the distinction between the uses of σῶμα before and after Rom 8:23 is arbitrary, and to some degree coincidental. Already in 6:13, without the specific word σῶμα, Paul could write, "Do not present your members [τὰ μέλη ὑμῶν] as instruments of unrighteousness for sin, but present yourselves [ἑαυτοὺς] to God as alive from the dead, and your members instruments of righteousness for God." Similarly, in 6:19: "For as you presented your members [τὰ μέλη ὑμῶν] as slaves to impurity, and to lawlessness for the purpose of lawlessness, so now present your members as slaves to righteousness for the purpose of holiness." Paul could have said "your body" instead of "your members" or "yourselves" and the point would have been much the same. Still, the dominant image of the body in Romans 1–8 is as an instrument of wrongdoing subject to corruption — in short, a body of sin and death.

The same tension is evident in 1 and 2 Corinthians, where σῶμα has for the most part a neutral or even positive meaning (see 1 Corinthians 6: "the body is not for sexual immorality but for the Lord, and the Lord for the body," v. 13; "your bodies are members of Christ," v. 15; "every sin that a person commits is apart from the body," v. 18; "your body is a temple of the Holy Spirit which you have from God," v. 19; "glorify God in your body," v. 20). Yet when Paul speaks of resurrection in 1 Corinthians 15, he accents the body's weakness, even corruption. "It is sown in corruption; it is raised in incorruption," he writes; "It is sown in dishonor; it is raised in glory. It is sown in weakness; it is raised in power" (15:42-43). In part, his language is shaped by the fact that he is speaking explicitly of "the resurrection of the dead" (v. 42a), that is, of corpses "sown" or "planted" in the grave. And even here he sees the body as simply "natural," not as an instrument of sin or death. "It is sown a natural body [σῶμα ψυχικόν], he concludes; "it is raised a spiritual body [σῶμα πνευματικόν]" (v. 44). Like Adam at creation, the body is "of the dust" (vv. 47-49). Paul goes on to insist that "flesh and blood [σὰρξ καὶ αἷμα] cannot inherit the kingdom of God, nor can corruption [φθορά] inherit incorruption" (v. 50). At the resurrection, whether of the living or the dead (vv. 51-52), Paul continues, "This corruptible [τὸ φθαρτὸν τοῦτο] must put on incorruption, and this mortal [τὸ θνητὸν τοῦτο] must put on immortality" (v. 53). Then and only then are the promises fulfilled, "Death is swallowed up in victory. Where, O Death, is your victory? Where, O Death, is your sting?" (vv. 54b-55; cf. Isa 25:8, Hos 13:14). The Paul of 1 Corinthians is sounding more and more like the Paul of Romans as chapter 15 draws to a close: "The sting of death is sin, and the power of sin is the law. But thanks be to God, who gives us the victory through our Lord Jesus Christ" (vv. 56-57).[13]

Romans takes up where 1 Corinthians 15 leaves off, not only on the issues of sin, death, and the law, but on that of the body and its resurrection. While the phrase "the resurrection of the body" never occurs in the New Testament, Paul's reference to "the redemption of our body" in Rom 8:23 is a close — perhaps his closest — approximation. Paul's choice of words reflects his view of the body throughout Romans 1–8. The "redemption," or release of the body from sin and death, is also an "adoption" (υἱοθεσία). Both words, "redemption" and "adoption," occur twice in Romans, first as a present experience in relation to the person, and second as a future hope in relation to the body. All who believe are already "justified freely by [God's] grace through the redemption [διὰ τῆς ἀπολυτρώσεως] that is in Christ Jesus" (3:24), yet they still wait for "the redemption of our body" (ἡ ἀπολύτρωσις τοῦ σώματος ἡμῶν, 8:23).[14] Paul tells them that, as God's "sons" or "children" (υἱοὶ θεοῦ, 8:14), "You have not received the spirit of slavery [πνεύμα δουλείας] again so as to fear, but you have received the Spirit of adoption [πνεῦμα υἱοθεσίας], by which we cry, 'Abba, Father'" (8:15). Yet only eight verses later he admits that

13. Gordon Fee comments, "The full explication of this sentence will emerge in the Epistle to the Romans" (*The First Epistle to the Corinthians* [Grand Rapids: Eerdmans, 1987], p. 806).

14. The same tension is evident in Ephesians: "In him we have the redemption through his blood" (1:7; cf. Col 1:14), yet the Spirit is "the pledge of our inheritance until the redemption of the purchased possession" (1:14; cf. 4:30, "until the day of redemption"). The future aspect of ἀπολύτρωσις is rooted in Jewish notions about the redemption of Israel or Jerusalem (see Lk 21:28, and cf. Lk 1:68, 2:38).

we still "groan within ourselves waiting for adoption" (υἱοθεσίαν ἀπεκδεχόμενοι, 8:23). Both "redemption" and "adoption" are caught up in the classic Pauline tension between the "already" and the "not yet." We who were once slaves are now redeemed and adopted as "children," yet we await "the redemption of our body" to make our "adoption" complete. This expectant "waiting," accompanied by inward "groaning" (στενάζομεν), is what Paul calls "this hope" (τῇ . . . ἐλπίδι, 8:24), defining at last "the hope of the glory of God" which he said earlier "does not disappoint us" (5:2, 5). By this hope, he says, "we are saved" (8:24).

The passage leaves no doubt that the future resurrection or redemption of the body is as crucial to Paul's argument in Romans as in 1 Thessalonians or 1 or 2 Corinthians. But while the accent in both 1 and 2 Corinthians was on discontinuity between the present and the future body (to the point that in 2 Corinthians the future body was not called σῶμα at all!), the accent in Romans is on continuity — this in spite of Paul's consistently negative characterization of the body in Romans 1–8. Paul in Romans is moving, in thought if not in terminology, in the direction of the later creedal notion of "resurrection of the flesh" (σαρκὸς ἀνάστασις).[15]

At certain points in Paul's argument, this appears not to be the case. He can express an intention (6:6) that "the body of sin" (τὸ σῶμα τῆς ἁμαρτίας) be "put away" (ἵνα καταργηθῇ), and he can cry out to God (7:24), "Who will deliver me from this body of death [ἐκ τοῦ σώματος τοῦ θανάτου τούτου]?" Yet when he comes to 8:23, it is not a matter of the body being "put away," or the believer being delivered *from* the body, but rather an intense longing for the redemption *of* the body. Joseph Fitzmyer (p. 510) resolves the problem by viewing 8:23 through the lens of 7:24, as "the liberation from 'this doomed body' or 'this body of death' [7:24] in which they presently live." In so doing he harmonizes Romans 8 with 1 Corinthians 15: "That body of death has to give way to the 'spiritual body' of risen life: 'when the perishable puts on the imperishable, and the mortal puts on immortality' (1 Cor 15:54)." Dunn (p. 475) is on better ground in acknowledging "that the σῶμα here is not to be sharply distinguished from the σῶμα of 6:6 and 7:24. . . . it is the same embodiment in this age, with all that that involves (including 'the slavery of corruption' — v. 21; but also 'the deeds of the body' — v. 13), which can only be transformed when this age itself is transformed with the whole of creation into a new environment in which a different embodiment (σῶμα πνευμάτικον — 1 Cor 15:44; Phil 3:21) is possible." Dunn, in a rather different way from Fitzmyer, is harmonizing Romans 8 and 1 Corinthians 15, but his comment also underscores the close relationship

15. For the term, see P. Schaff, *Creeds of Christendom* (New York: Harper & Brothers, 1877), 2.45, 48.

of Romans 8:23 to verses 19-22, and with it the distinctive contribution of Romans to the Christian hope of bodily resurrection.

So which is it? Are we redeemed *from* the body of sin and death, or is the body of sin and death *itself* redeemed? A couple of observations come to mind. First, the reference in Romans 6:6 to the "body of sin" being "put away" has to do with the possibility of victory over sin *in the present life* ("so that we may no longer be slaves to sin," v. 6b), not with the question of whether or not there will be a future resurrection body. It is much the same here as in 6:4, where Paul builds up to a possible reference to future resurrection ("that as Christ was raised from the dead through the glory of the Father . . ."), but concludes with a statement having to do simply with ethical conduct in the present ("so we too will walk in newness of life"). Second, is the interlocutor in chapter 7 who cries out to be delivered *from* "this body of death" (7:24) to be accepted as a "reliable narrator" (to borrow a term from narrative criticism)? Does his anguished perspective accurately represent Paul, or is it subject to correction by what follows in chapter 8? Certainly, the answer to his cry, "Thanks be to God through Jesus Christ our Lord" (v. 25a), is Paul's answer, but does the positive answer validate the question? The interlocutor continues, "So then I myself with the mind serve the law of God, but with the flesh the law of sin" (v. 25b), and the same issue arises there. Whether or not this sentence is to be punctuated as a question,[16] or whether it carries with it an implied question ("Is that the way it has to be?"), it does appear to be answered, even corrected, by the whole of chapter 8 and by its opening verses in particular: "No, there is no condemnation to those in Christ Jesus, for the law of the Spirit of life in Christ Jesus has set you free [ἠλευθέρωσέν σε] from the law of sin and death" (8:1-2). The singular "you" (σε)[17] signals Paul's response to the tormented "I" (ἐγώ) of chapter 7.[18] The truth is *not* that "I myself with the mind serve the law of God, but with the flesh the law of sin" (7:25b), but that "You [ὑμεῖς, plural] are not in the flesh but in the Spirit, assuming the Spirit of God dwells in you. Anyone who does not have the Spirit of Christ is not one of his" (8:9). Although Paul's readers are described as not "in the flesh" (ἐν σαρκί) in this chapter (vv. 8, 9), and do not live "according to

16. Dunn (p. 399) rejects as "unfounded" the suggestion of W. Keuck ("Dienst des Geistes und des Fleisches: Zur Auslegungsgeschichte und Auslegung von Römer 7:25b," *Theologische Quartalschrift* 141 [1961]: 279) that the sentence be read "as a question (to be answered by an implied 'No longer!')." Yet clearly 7:25b is not Paul's final word on the subject. Whether read as a question or not, it is in some sense "answered" by the argument of ch. 8.

17. "You" (σε), besides being supported by the best manuscripts, including א and B, is the most difficult reading, plausibly explaining the alternatives "me" (με) or "us" (ἡμᾶς).

18. Cf. Fee, *God's Empowering Presence* (Peabody, Mass.: Hendrickson, 1994), p. 527, n. 158.

the flesh" (κατὰ σάρκα, vv. 4, 5), they are quite emphatically in the *body*, and their bodies are still seen as mortal — as the same "body of sin and death" that dominated chapters 1 through 7.

Paul continues, "If Christ is in you, the body is dead because of sin [τὸ μὲν σῶμα νεκρὸν διὰ ἁμαρτίαν], but the Spirit is life because of righteousness" [τὸ δὲ πνεῦμα ζωὴ διὰ δικαιοσύνην, 8:10]." His language recalls 2 Cor 4:10-11: "We always carry around in the body the dying of Jesus, so that the life of Jesus may also be revealed in our body. For we the living are always being given over to death for Jesus' sake, so that Jesus' life may be revealed in our mortal flesh." But there are two differences. First, Paul in Romans seems to have generalized from his own apostolic experience to the experience of all believers. Second, "the life" (ἡ ζωή) of Jesus which Paul saw at work in his own "body" or "mortal flesh" is now identified specifically as "the Spirit" (τὸ δὲ πνεῦμα ζωή, 8:10).[19] He elaborates the thought in the next verse: "If the Spirit of him who raised Jesus from the dead dwells in you, he who raised Christ from the dead will make even your mortal bodies come alive [ζῳοποιήσει καὶ τὰ θνητὰ σώματα ὑμῶν], through his Spirit dwelling in you" (8:11). The significant point of reference is still 2 Corinthians, where Paul expressed confidence that God "who raised the Lord Jesus from the dead will also raise us with Jesus" (2 Cor 4:14). In Romans as in 2 Corinthians we have the "already but not yet," only now in relation not simply to Paul the dying apostle but to all who, like him, live in "mortal bodies" and "in the Spirit" at the same time. The substance of Paul's hope is much the same, but his terminology now centers on the Spirit, and therefore, as the next few verses show, on adoption, and sonship in contrast to slavery:

> For as many as are led by the Spirit of God are the sons of God; for you have not received the spirit of slavery [πνεῦμα δουλείας] again so as to fear, but you have received the Spirit of adoption [πνεῦμα υἱοθεσίας], by which we cry, "Abba," or "Father." The Spirit himself testifies, along with our spirit, that we are children of God [τέκνα θεοῦ], and if children then heirs [κληρονόμοι], heirs of God and co-heirs with Christ, if indeed we suffer with him so that we may also be glorified with him. (8:14-17)

The link between the Spirit and sonship may rest in part on stories of the baptism of Jesus, in which the Spirit designates Jesus as God's "beloved Son" (see Mk 1:11), but within Paul's letters it recalls more directly a passage in Galatians:

> When the fullness of the time came, God sent his Son, made of a woman, made under the law, to redeem those who were under the law, so that we

19. Cf. 8:6, "The mind of the Spirit is life and peace" (ζωὴ καὶ εἰρήνη).

> might receive the adoption [τὴν υἱοθεσίαν]. And because you are sons [υἱοί], God sent the Spirit of his Son into your hearts, crying 'Abba,' or 'Father.' So then, you are no longer a slave [δοῦλος], but a son [υἱός], and if a son then an heir [κληρονόμος] through God. (Gal 4:4-7)

Quite clearly, the language of Galatians 4 has found its way into Paul's argument in Romans 8. Yet the argument itself centers on the hope of bodily resurrection, an issue raised not in Galatians[20] but in 1 and 2 Corinthians. Resurrection is what Paul means by being "glorified" with Christ (συνδοξασθῶμεν), a hope conditioned on "suffering" (συμπάσχομεν) with him (8:17). Again Paul echoes the thought of 2 Corinthians 4:10-11, and in the following verse weighs present sufferings against future glory: "For I consider the sufferings of the present time [τὰ παθήματα τοῦ νῦν καιροῦ] unworthy to be compared to the glory [τὴν μέλλουσαν δόξαν] that will be revealed to us" (8:18). Here he repeats in different words what he had said in 2 Corinthians 4:17: "For the lightness of our temporary affliction is producing for us a far more overwhelming, eternal weight of glory [δόξης]." Again Paul generalizes from his personal experience as an apostle to the experience of all the "children of God" everywhere, poised between the "already" and the "not yet." The question yet to be answered is whether or not Paul widens the generalization still further to embrace the whole created order.

IV. Creation or Creature? The Riddle of Romans 8:19-22

Paul introduces ἡ κτίσις, "the creature" or "the creation," abruptly in 8:19, as if he has used it before, or as if his readers are familiar with it. In fact he has used the term once before in Romans (1:25), where he introduced it in the same abrupt manner: "They exchanged the truth of God for a lie, and worshiped and served the creature rather than the Creator [τῇ κτίσει παρὰ τὸν κτίσαντα]." There the meaning was "creature" or "created thing," perhaps *any* created person or thing, but probably not the whole creation.[21] The same is true further on in chapter 8 itself, where Paul lists the things that "cannot separate us from the love of God" (8:39): "neither death nor life, nor angels nor rulers, nor things

20. Moisés Silva ("Eschatological Structures in Galatians," *To Tell the Mystery* [Sheffield: JSOT Press, 1994], p. 143) admits that apart from its opening greeting "the letter contains no explicit references to the resurrection." The opening greeting mentions Jesus' resurrection, not that of believers.

21. Κτίσις in 1:25 is best defined by v. 23, "They exchanged the glory of the incorruptible God for an image resembling a corruptible human being, or birds, animals, and reptiles."

present or to come, nor powers, nor height nor depth, nor any other created thing [οὔτε τις κτίσις ἑτέρα]."[22]

Paul makes four pronouncements in 8:19-22 about this "created thing": it waits eagerly for "the revelation of the sons of God" (v. 19); it was subjected to "vanity" against its will (v. 20); its hope is to be set free from "slavery to corruption" into "the freedom of the glory of the children of God" (v. 21); and at present it "groans" like a woman in labor (v. 22). While Cranfield catalogues eight different options for ἡ κτίσις (*not* including the one featured in this article!),[23] the overwhelming majority of interpreters agree in identifying it as the whole created order except for humanity. The near consensus rests on three main arguments. First, Paul in 8:23 seems to go to some length to distinguish the κτίσις (vv. 19-22) from Christian believers (vv. 23-25). Second, the κτίσις cannot include humankind because it was "subjected to vanity" οὐχ ἑκοῦσα, "not of its own will" (NRSV), or "not by its own choice" (NIV), while humans became subject to sin and death precisely by their own willful transgression.[24] Third, the κτίσις cannot include humankind because Paul is no universalist, and would not have held out an expectation for the whole human race to be "set free from slavery to corruption into the freedom of the glory of the children of God" (v. 21).[25] Moreover, the four uses of κτίσις in *Wisdom of Solomon*, a document rich in parallels to Romans, tend to support this conclusion: *Wisdom* 2:6: "Come, let us enjoy the good things that exist, and make use of the creation [τῇ

22. The rendering of 8:39 in both the NIV and NRSV, "nor anything else in all creation," obscures the point that κτίσις *by itself* here means a single created thing, not the whole creation. While death and life, present and future, height and depth are not normally thought of as specific "creatures," all are instituted by God and under God's sovereignty. It is also possible that by "any other creature" Paul means simply "any human being," i.e., any human creature other than ourselves. His point would then be, "If none of the supernatural powers in the universe can separate us from God's love, how much less can our human enemies do so?"

23. Cranfield's list includes "mankind both believing and unbelieving and also the angels; all mankind; unbelieving mankind only; believers only; the angels only; sub-human nature together with the angels; sub-human nature together with mankind in general; sub-human nature only" (1.411). He omits at least two other options: the Gentile world in distinction from the Jews (the view of Adam Clarke and John Gill), and the body, whether of humans generally or believers in particular.

24. So John Murray, *The Epistle to the Romans* (Grand Rapids: Eerdmans, 1973), p. 302; also Fitzmyer (pp. 507-8), and Cranfield (1.411, 14), who adds (citing Augustine) that if κτίσις *is* taken to refer to humanity, then οὐχ ἑκοῦσα must refer "to the involuntariness of the creation's submission to the penalty imposed on it" (414).

25. Murray comments: "The *unbelieving* of mankind cannot be included because the earnest expectation does not characterize them. Even those who are at present unbelieving but will be converted are excluded because they will be comprised in the children of God" (p. 302).

κτίσει] to the full as in youth"; 5:17, "The Lord will take his zeal as his whole armor, and will arm all creation [τὴν κτίσιν] to repel his enemies"; 16:24, "For creation [ἡ γὰρ κτίσις], serving you who made it, exerts itself to punish the unrighteous, and in kindness relaxes on behalf of those who trust in you"; 19:6, "For the whole creation [ὅλη γὰρ ἡ κτίσις] in its nature was fashioned anew, complying with your commands, so that your children might be kept unharmed" (translations are from the NRSV).

Another point in favor of κτίσις as the whole created order is the appropriateness of the reference to its being "subjected" (ὑπετάγη, v. 20). The language vaguely recalls Psalm 8:6 LXX, where God is said to have "subjected all things" (πάντα ὑπέταξας) under the feet of humankind. The psalmist's utterance is cited three times in the NT, once in relation to humanity (and implicitly to Jesus as its representative, Heb 2:6), and twice in relation to Jesus as exalted Lord (1 Cor 15:27, Eph 1:22; cf. also Phil 3:21). But in Romans 8:20, by a strange twist, the subjection is neither to humanity in general nor to Jesus in particular, but to "vanity" (τῇ γὰρ ματαιότητι). Another text seems to have been at work alongside Psalm 8. The LXX of Psalm 143[144]:3-4, in what sounds like a parody of Psalm 8, asks, "Lord, what is man, that you are made known to him, or the son of man, that you take account of him? Man is like to vanity [ἄνθρωπος ματαιότητι ὡμοιώθη]: his days pass as a shadow." Quite possibly, both the later Psalm and Romans share a rather skeptical view of Psalm 8's assertion that God subjected "all things" (πάντα) to human beings (cf. Heb 2:8, "But now we do not yet see all things subjected"). What Paul sees instead is the continuing subjection of the created order to "vanity" and its "slavery to corruption" (Rom 8:21).[26] In such a state it yearns for "the revelation of the sons of God," and for redemption into "the freedom of the glory of the children of God" (vv. 19, 21).

All of this seems to confirm the conventional wisdom as to the identity of the "creature" or "creation." So why did I, as a young seminarian years ago, flout conventional wisdom in favor of a "minimalist" interpretation of κτίσις as simply the body of sin and death, awaiting resurrection? Two books influenced me decisively:

William Fitzhugh Whitehouse, *The Redemption of the Body* (London: Eliot Stock, 1892).

William G. Williams, *An Exposition of the Epistle of Paul to the Romans* (Cincinnati: Jennings and Pye, 1902).

26. Dunn comes to a similar conclusion by a slightly different route: "The difficulty is probably that Paul was attempting to convey too briefly a quite complicated point: that God subjected all things to Adam, and that included subjecting creation to fallen Adam, to share in his fallenness" (p. 471).

Their title pages identified Whitehouse as "Layman of the Diocese of New York,"[27] and Williams as "Late Professor of Greek in the Ohio Wesleyan University"; the two seemed to have come to their conclusions quite independently.[28] Williams's commentary is of interest in its own right because of his insistence (anticipating later trends in Pauline studies) that what Romans is all about is not justification by faith, but "the one practical issue which runs through the whole discussion; namely, that, in God's plans, the Gentiles stand on a perfect equality with the Jews" (p. 21).[29]

Williams's view of Romans 8:19-22 is not necessarily linked to his view of Romans as a whole. He argues from Paul's immediate context, a context centering on the hope of bodily resurrection:

> But clearly "the glory that will be revealed," or manifested, at the last day is here declared to be, specifically, "to *us*-ward," "in regard to *us*," a "revelation" of glory, in which neither the "creation" at large nor any assignable part of creation outside of ourselves has a share, — nothing but "*us*." This thought runs through the paragraph to the final word in the twenty-third verse, "the redemption of our *body*"; and this explicit word, which the apostle has held in suspense until he has reached the climax, — this word "body" gives explicitly the lucid and sufficient, and only possible, explanation of the word "creature." If this explanation is correct, "the creature" is simply the human body; and by this phrase, "the redemption of our body," the apostle shows in what respect this consummate glory is to be manifested "to us-ward." (p. 253)

Whitehouse, in a similar vein (p. 42), comments:

> This living body, the κτίσις, waits with longing, intense and painful, for the revealing of the sons of God, for *then* this mortal body shall be delivered from its subjection to the law of decay into the liberty of the glory of the *children* of God. The body waits for this revealing of sonship to secure its own release, and this deliverance must be into the freedom of the glory of

27. Whitehouse in his preface acknowledges a debt to "my father, the late Bishop of Illinois," and to "the Rev. Walter Lock of Keble College [Oxford], for valuable suggestions and critical revision."

28. I have since traced their interpretation to F. F. Zyro, "Neue Erklärung von Röm. 8,18-25," *Theologische Studien und Kritiken* 18.1 (1845): 403-16; and "Neue Erörterung der Stelle Röm. 8,18-25," *TSK* 24.2 (1851): 645-66. Joseph Fitzmyer (alone among major commentators) lists Whitehouse, Williams, and Zyro in his bibliography (pp. 214, 514), but does not interact in any way with their arguments.

29. Williams was far ahead of his time, but his work is unfortunately marred by a strident polemic against Calvinism, which may help explain (though not excuse) its neglect by later scholarship.

the *children* of God, for the body must attain its glory and perfection, and then, and then only, will sonship be fully realized.

What Williams and Whitehouse were both getting at is that Romans 8:21, no less than 8:23, seems to refer to an act involving "adoption" (υἱοθεσία) and "redemption" (ἀπολύτρωσις).[30] The κτίσις waits expectantly for "the revelation of the sons of God" (v. 19), not simply out of curiosity (like the angels of 1 Pet 1:12 who desire to look into the plan of salvation), but with the hope of sonship *for itself.* Like Christian believers, it "awaits" adoption and redemption (ἀπεκδέχεται, v. 19; cf. ἀπεκδεχόμενοι, v. 23), and its expectation, like that of Christian believers, is called "hope" (ἐφ' ἑλπίδι, v. 20; cf. τῇ γὰρ ἐλπίδι, v. 24), a hope made explicit in verse 21: "that the creature itself [αὐτὴ ἡ κτίσις][31] will be set free from slavery to corruption into the freedom of the glory of the children of God."[32] The κτίσις, whatever it might be, is destined to share with believers in redemption, the experience of being "set free" from sin and death (ἐλευθερωθήσεται, v. 21; cf. 6:18, 20, 22), and adoption, the experience of entering into "the glory of the children of God" — that is, in some sense *becoming* God's son or child (cf. also 8:29, "conformed to the image of his Son"). This hope is consistent with the identification of the κτίσις as the body (for both things are predicated of the body in verse 23), but presents a problem for those who view it as the material creation.

Not surprisingly, a number of those who make the latter identification are quick to add a qualification or disclaimer of some kind. Frederick Godet, for example, commented, "Paul does not say that nature will participate in *the glory,* but only in *the liberty* of the glory of the children of God. Liberty is one of the elements of their glorious state, and it is the only one to which nature can lay claim."[33] According to Murray (p. 304), "The creation . . . can only partici-

30. Zyro argues more from the preceding context: ". . . und wenn es nun zweifellos ist, dass v. 18 von den Gläubigen redet, so kann v. 19 nur von diesen reden. . . . Was heisst denn κτίσις, wenn es auf die Gläubigen zu beziehen ist und doch nicht diese selbst bezeichnen darf? Es bedeutet einen Theil des Gläubigen, nämlich das Irdische und Vergängliche am Menschen, das schlechthin Creatürliche, was der Gläubige mit jedem Menschen ohne Unterschied gemein hat, und was dem κόσμος angehört. . . . Der Apostel hätte also statt κτίσις ganz gut σάρξ setzen kann" (*TSK* 18.1 [1845]: 407-8).

31. With a different breathing and accent, αὐτὴ ἡ κτίσις, "the creature itself," could be read as αὕτη ἡ κτίσις, "this creature," with a rather natural reference to the body, as in "this corruptible" or "this mortal" (1 Cor 15:53-54), "in this" (2 Cor 5:2), "in this tent" (some mss. of 2 Cor 5:4), and "these hands" (Acts 20:34).

32. "Sons" (υἱοί) and "children" (τέκνα) are used interchangeably throughout this passage. Note the alternation from "sons of God" (v. 14), to "children of God" (vv. 16-17), to "sons of God" (v. 19), to "children of God" (v. 21).

33. *Commentary on St. Paul's Epistle to the Romans* (New York: Funk & Wagnalls, 1883), p. 315.

pate in that glory in a way that is compatible with its nature as non-rational." To Cranfield (1.416), "Paul's meaning is hardly that the creation will share the same liberty-resulting-from-glory as the children of God will enjoy, but that it will have its own proper liberty as a result of the glorification of the children of God." Fitzmyer (p. 509) sees this freedom as "an attendant aftermath" of that glorification. Each comment in its own way sets limits to the full participation of the κτίσις in the "glory of the children of God," but no such limitations are found in the text itself. The tendency of commentators is to make up their minds as to the identification of the κτίσις when it first appears in Romans 8:19, and then adjust their interpretations of verses 20-22 to fit a predetermined conclusion. James Dunn (p. 469) is on better ground in admitting from the outset, "It is unlikely that Paul intended a precise definition (cf. v. 39)" even while judging it "more than likely that his thought focused primarily on nonhuman creation."

Dunn's caution reminds us that in testing any interpretation, each of Paul's four pronouncements about the κτίσις in verses 19-22 must be examined carefully. How well does the interpretation of κτίσις as "the body of sin and death" stand up under such a test? If verse 21 is, as we have seen, a rather apt description of the resurrection or redemption of the body, what of verses 19, 20, and 22? All sides will readily admit that 8:19-22 is metaphorical from beginning to end, but surely the metaphor of "eager expectation" (ἀποκαραδοκία) in verse 19 is at least as appropriate when applied to the body as when applied to the whole animate (much less inanimate!) creation. Paul's only other use of the term (Phil 1:20) links it with "hope" as a characteristically *human* quality. As for verse 20, Paul's language bristles with difficulties[34] no matter how the κτίσις is identified, but the difficulties are no greater with the view of Williams and Whitehouse than with any other. If the whole creation was "subjected to vanity," so too was the human body as part of that creation. If the ground was cursed for Adam's sin so that "thorns and thistles it shall bring forth for you" (Gen 3:18), so too was Eve told, "I will greatly increase your pangs in childbearing; in pain you shall bring forth children" (Gen 3:16), while Adam was reminded, "out of [the ground] you were taken; you are dust, and to dust you shall return" (Gen 3:19, all from the NRSV).

To Paul the human body, no less than the ground from which it was taken, is a created thing, part and parcel of the created order: "then the Lord God formed man from the dust of the ground, and breathed into his nostrils

34. On the last phrase, "not willingly, but on account of him who did the subjecting, in hope," Dunn comments: "The phrasing is awkward and suggests a dictation where Paul's thought became slightly tangled but where he decided to press on" (p. 470; see also n. 25 above).

the breath of life; and the man became a living being" (Gen 2:7, NRSV). The body, like the rest of creation, was subjected to vanity through no fault of its own (οὐχ ἑκοῦσα), but as a consequence of Adam and Eve's willful disobedience. The much-despised "body of sin and death" in Romans is *not* the source of sin. It is the victim, not the perpetrator of sin. As Paul put it in an earlier discussion of sin's origin, "God gave them up[35] in the lusts of their hearts to impurity, so as to dishonor *their bodies* [τὰ σώματα αὐτῶν] among them" (1:24, my emphasis). The parallel leaves open the long-debated question whether "the one who subjected" (τὸν ὑποτάξαντα) the κτίσις to vanity was God or Adam. As we have seen, God was the One who according to Psalm 8:6 LXX "subjected all things" (πάντα ὑπέταξας) to humankind, and God is likely the One doing the subjecting here. But just as "God gave them up" (παρέδωκεν) to all kinds of evil according to the refrain of 1:24, 26, and 28, so here God's sovereignty does not exclude human involvement and responsibility in the subjection of the body (or the natural order, as the case may be) to "vanity" and "slavery to corruption."

Verse 20 ends on a positive note, justifying the "eager expectation" of the κτίσις with the affirmation that even its subjection to vanity took place "in hope" (ἐφ' ἐλπίδι), not necessarily a hope subjectively felt (whether literally by humans or metaphorically by the created order), but a hope objectively grounded in the plan of God. The content[36] of the hope is given in verse 21, where, as we have argued, it sounds remarkably like the characteristic hope of bodily resurrection. As for verse 22, Williams and Whitehouse try to maintain their interpretation here as well, but less convincingly than in the three previous verses.[37] A better course is to recognize a certain merit in the decision of the King James translators in favor of "creature" in verses 19, 20, and 21, but "the whole creation" in verse 22. Certainly it is natural to suppose that a shift from ἡ κτίσις to πᾶσα ἡ κτίσις marks a change of focus from a single created thing to

35. Ernst Käsemann (*Commentary on Romans* [Grand Rapids: Eerdmans, 1980]) sees in 8:20 "a backward glance at the παρέδωκεν of 1:24." He also (rightly) connects the language of 1:21 ("they became vain [ἐματαιώθησαν] in their imaginations, and their foolish heart was darkened") with the "vanity" (τῇ . . . ματαιότητι) of which Paul speaks here (p. 235; cf. p. 44).

36. This assumes ὅτι, "that," at the beginning of verse 21 (with P^{46}, A, B, and C). If διότι is read (with ℵ, D, and F; see Cranfield, 1.415), then Paul is giving not the content of hope, but God's purpose in subjecting the κτίσις to vanity in the first place. The practical difference is negligible.

37. Whitehouse claims, "The reference is to man, and man alone, who in all his members groans and travails in agony, and feels the weakness and imperfections, pains and sorrows, of this mortal body" (p. 49). To Williams, "The words *all the creature* mean that our entire being is absorbed in the 'agonizing' for deliverance. This verse declares that the body groans with the spirit, and the next verse declares that the spirit answers back with responsive woe" (p. 260).

the whole created order, human and nonhuman. Dunn focuses on the latter. Having steered away from a "precise definition" of κτίσις in verses 19-21 (p. 469; see above), he makes a distinction similar to that of the KJV in verse 22, insisting that "here certainly it is nonhuman, and, as we would say, inanimate creation which is primarily in view" (p. 472).[38] Paul, in support of his metaphorical reflections on the κτίσις in verses 19-21, appeals here to something generally known and familiar to his readers in verse 22: "We know [οἴδαμεν][39] that the whole creation groans and travails together until now." He is still working with metaphor, but now with a metaphor widely used and accepted in both the Jewish and the Graeco-Roman world.[40] If, as "we know," the whole created order groans like a woman in labor to bring forth a new creation, then Paul can legitimately ascribe "eager expectation" and "hope" to the single created thing with which he is concerned in this passage: the much-despised body of sin and death. This he has done, with a brief explanation of its predicament (v. 20) and a glimpse of its hope of redemption and resurrection into sonship (v 21).

My proposal is that Paul is not introducing something new in Romans 8:19-22 (except very briefly, and almost as a truism, in v. 22), but making his third great affirmation (alongside 1 Cor 15 and 2 Cor 5) of the Christian hope of bodily resurrection. Such a proposal makes excellent sense of verse 23: "Not only so, but even those [καὶ αὐτοί] who have the firstfruits of the Spirit, even we ourselves [ἡμεῖς καὶ αὐτοί], groan within ourselves as we wait eagerly for adoption, the redemption of our body." The repeated καὶ αὐτοί corresponds to the καὶ αὐτὴ ἡ κτίσις of verse 21: *even* the κτίσις will be redeemed into sonship (*despite* being "subject to vanity"), and *even* we "groan within ourselves" (*despite* having "the firstfruits of the Spirit"). So far as the present is concerned, we are separated from our bodies, for we are God's "children" or "sons," and the body is merely God's "creature," formed from the dust of the ground. We look at the body now as something distinct from ourselves, as Paul did when he spoke of "the earthly tent we live in" (2 Cor 5:1). But in the future Paul sees us reconciled and reunited with our bodies, for we share with our bodies a common hope.

38. Zyro similarly advocates a widening ("Erweiterung") of the identification, not, however, to inanimate creation but to humankind, with particular emphasis on the Gentile world (*TSK* 18.1 [1845]: 413-15; 24.2 [1851]: 661-62).

39. For οἴδαμεν used rhetorically in Romans to introduce an unquestionable truth, cf. 2:2, 3:19, 7:14, and 8:28.

40. Fitzmyer comments that Paul borrows "a mode of expression from contemporary Greek philosophers who often compared the vernal rebirth of nature to a woman's labor" (p. 509), but most commentators accent rather the many Jewish parallels relating to the so-called "birth-pangs of the Messiah" (see Cranfield, 1.416; Dunn, pp. 472-73; Käsemann, p. 236; G. Bertram in *TDNT* [9]: 667-74).

The body's hope is to be "set free from slavery to corruption into the liberty of the glory of the children of God" (Rom 8:21), and "our" hope (that is, the hope of those already "in the Spirit" — cf. 8:9, 14-15) is for "adoption, the redemption of our body" (8:23).[41]

My purpose here is not to settle the interpretation of Romans 8:19-22. I am no more able to do so now than in 1955. It is rather to suggest that the identification of the κτίσις is very much an open question, not closed as most recent scholarship has assumed. I am also aware that the "body" interpretation does less than some might wish to further the cause of ecology, but other New Testament passages (Heb 1:10-12, for example; 2 Pet 3:7 and 10; Rev 20:11 and 21:1) also fall short in this respect.[42] But if the view proposed here is accepted, it can still be argued that Paul (perhaps more than some other biblical writers) does have a positive theology of creation. He hears creation's groans, but his resurrection hopes are not for the created order as a whole. Just as Paul believes in the redemption of humankind not in a universal sense but in a representative sense, with the church as humanity's representative, so he believes in the redemption of the created order in a representative sense, with a single created thing — the human body — representing the whole.[43] Creation is redeemed in that the crown of creation — what Irenaeus called "God's handiwork," or "the ancient formation of man" — is "set free from slavery to corruption into the liberty of the glory of the children of God."[44]

Irenaeus, perhaps, should be allowed to speak for himself. His comments on Romans 8:19-22 in Book V of his treatise *Against Heresies* display a certain ambiguity. First he says of the righteous (*Against Heresies* V, 32, 1):

> For it is just that in that very creation [*in qua enim conditione*] in which they toiled or were afflicted. . . . they should receive the reward of their suffering; and that in the creation [*qua conditione*] in which they were slain

41. Williams (p. 260) captures this mutuality of body and spirit: "Neither the spirit on the one hand, nor the body on the other, can realize the fullness of adoption without the other."

42. See Whitehouse, pp. 21-22; Williams, p. 255.

43. Young David Kern, in John Updike's early short story "Pigeon Feathers," agonizes at length over personal immortality and resurrection, but at the story's end, shooting pigeons in the barn, is "robed in this certainty: that the God who had lavished such craft upon these worthless birds would not destroy His whole Creation by refusing to let David live forever" (*Pigeon Feathers and Other Stories* [New York: Knopf, 1962], p. 150).

44. Paul's simultaneous awareness of the body and of creation as a whole is evident in Phil 3:20-21 (NRSV), where he speaks of "expecting" (ἀπεκδεχόμεθα) Jesus from heaven, who will "transform the body [τὸ σῶμα] of our humiliation that it may be conformed to the body of his glory, by the power that also enables him to make all things subject to himself" (καὶ ὑποτάξαι αὐτῷ τὰ πάντα).

> because of their love of God, in that they should be revived again; and that in the creation [*in qua conditione*] in which they endured servitude, in that they should reign. For God is rich in all things, and all things are His. It is fitting, therefore, that the creation itself [*ipsam conditionem*], being restored to its primeval condition, should without restraint be under the dominion of the righteous; and the apostle has made this plain in the Epistle to the Romans, when he thus speaks . . . [a quotation of Romans 8:19-21 follows].[45]

The Latin translation of Irenaeus uses a word, *conditio,* which refers unambiguously to the material creation as a whole, even though κτίσις in the Romans passage itself is consistently *creatura.* Later, however, at the very end of *Against Heresies* (V, 36, 3), Irenaeus seems to espouse a view closer to the one we have developed here:

> The apostle too has confessed that the creation [*creaturam*] shall be free from the bondage of corruption . . . into the liberty of the sons of God. And in all these things, and by them all, the same God the Father is manifested, who fashioned man [*plasmavit hominem*], and gave promise of the inheritance of the earth to the fathers, who brought it [*illam*] forth at the resurrection of the just, and fulfills the promises for the kingdom of His Son. . . . For there is the one Son, who accomplished His Father's will; and one human race, in which the mysteries of God are wrought . . . and they are not able to search out the wisdom of God, by means of which His handiwork [*plasma ejus*], confirmed and incorporated with His Son, is brought to perfection; that His offspring, the First-begotten Word, should descend to the creature, that is, to what had been molded [*in facturam, hoc est in plasma*], and that it should be contained by Him; and, on the other hand, the creature [*factura*] should contain the Word, and ascend to Him, passing beyond the angels, and be made after the image and likeness of God.[46]

Here the Latin version of Irenaeus avoids *conditio* in the sense of the whole natural creation, retaining instead *creatura* from the Romans passage as it would have appeared in Latin. *Creatura* is then defined by two other terms: *factura,* "that which was made," and *plasma,* "that which was formed," both referring, presumably, to the body made or formed from the earth. This is what God "brought forth at the resurrection of the just." While Irenaeus is quite capable of interpreting the κτίσις of Romans 8 as the whole creation (V, 32, 1), his last

45. The English is from *The Ante-Nicene Fathers* (Grand Rapids: Eerdmans, n.d.), I, p. 561, the Latin from W. W. Harvey, *Sancti Irenaei: Libros Quinque Adversus Haereses* (Cambridge: Typis Academicis, 1857), II, pp. 413-14.

46. *The Ante-Nicene Fathers,* I, p. 567; the Latin is from Harvey, II, p. 429.

word on the subject views it as the body — not the "body of sin and death" in the full Pauline sense perhaps, but the body as God created it (V, 36, 3).[47]

Even a number of modern scholars who identify the κτίσις unequivocally as the material creation are quick to recognize that what the passage is primarily about is the resurrection of the body. Douglas Moo, for example, admits that "While Paul obviously says some important things in this paragraph about the renewal of creation, his focus is consistently on anthropology."[48] C. K. Barrett comments that Paul's "main object in mentioning the creation is to emphasize the certainty of future salvation for Christians. He is not concerned with creation for its own sake, but evidently feels that the matter requires some further explanation."[49] Cranfield, while objecting to Barrett's comment that Paul is not concerned with creation for its own sake, nevertheless agrees that "Paul's main interest in these verses is in the certainty of the coming glory of believers" (1.415). Käsemann (p. 233) seems to be thinking out loud as he wavers back and forth among several options: "There can be no doubt that non-Christians are included. . . . Hence it is a mistake to speak of 'irrational creation' . . . and even the word 'nature' can hardly be used so self-evidently as modern man might think. Nature plays a very small role for the apostle. . . . All the same, the main emphasis today is rightly put on non-human creation . . . and the phrase πᾶσα ἡ κτίσις in v. 22 supports this." Finally, Merrill C. Tenney, without explicitly addressing the issue in his 1963 biblical-theological study of resurrection,[50] showed extraordinary sensitivity to Paul's priorities, citing Romans 8:19-22 seven times, but always in relation to the resurrection of believers, never to the "larger hope" of creation as a whole. From Irenaeus down to the present, I have sensed a certain ambivalence about this passage, and among some advocates of the "irrational creation" view a degree of unease about its implications. Perhaps it is time to reopen a very old interpretive question.

47. Whitehouse (pp. 50-53) makes a similar argument from Augustine, who is usually cited as favoring the identification of the κτίσις with humankind in general. This is the case, he notes, in Augustine's "Expositio Quarumdam Propositionum ex Epistola ad Romanos," 53 *(Omnem creaturam in ipso homine . . . cogitemus),* but Augustine goes on to explain *creatura* as "all which now in man travails and is liable to corruption" *(Quidquid nunc in homine laborat et corruptioni subjacet),* that is, Whitehouse suggests, the human body. Interestingly, Zyro too traces his interpretation back to Augustine (*TSK* 24.2 [1851]: 664.

48. *The Epistle to the Romans* (Grand Rapids: Eerdmans, 1996), p. 517, n. 50.

49. *A Commentary on the Epistle to the Romans* (New York: Harper & Brothers, 1957), p. 165.

50. *The Reality of the Resurrection* (New York: Harper & Row, 1963).

Paul and the Prophets: Prophetic Criticism in the Epistle to the Romans (with special reference to Romans 9–11)

Craig A. Evans

In his argument with the Corinthian Christians Paul states: "If anyone thinks he is a prophet or is spiritual, let him acknowledge that what I am writing to you is the Lord's command" (1 Cor 14:37). In light of what Paul had said earlier in 1 Corinthians 12:28 ("in the Church God has appointed first of all apostles, second prophets . . ."), Gordon Fee is led to suspect that Paul "seems to be arguing that he is first of all an apostle, that he is therefore also a prophet, and that thus he is 'writing to you the Lord's command.'"[1] Fee's interpretation of Paul's prophetic consciousness is probable and exposes an intriguing aspect of Paul's understanding of apostleship in general and of his call to mission in particular. This brief essay, written in honor of a master New Testament exegete and textual critic, will be principally concerned with an important feature of Paul's hermeneutic especially as it is displayed in Romans 9–11.

Twenty-five years ago Ferdinand Hahn made the intriguing suggestion that Christianity's concept of apostle is drawn from Isaiah 61:1.[2] Hahn's proposal has much to commend it. Jesus' apparently programmatic use of this text

1. G. D. Fee, *The First Epistle to the Corinthians* (NICNT; Grand Rapids: Eerdmans, 1987), p. 711.

2. F. Hahn, "Der Apostolat im Urchristentum: Seine Eigenart und seine Voraussetzungen," *KD* 20 (1974): 54-77, esp. 69-75.

(cf. Mt 11:5 = Lk 7:22; cf. Lk 4:16-30), as well as Paul's probable use of it, constitutes *prima facie* evidence for this hypothesis.

What is this evidence? In the context of Romans 10:15, where part of Isaiah 52:7 is quoted, we probably have allusions to Isaiah 61:1 as well. In v. 8 Paul refers to the word of faith "which we preach" (κηρύσσομεν). Again in v. 14 he asks, "How shall they hear without preaching?" (κηρύσσοντος). In v. 15 he asks, "How will they preach [κηρύξωσιν] unless they be sent [ἀποσταλῶσιν]?" This combination of κηρύσσειν and ἀποστέλλειν surely points to Isaiah 61:1: ". . . to proclaim good tidings to the poor he has sent [ἀπέσταλκε] me . . . to preach [κηρύξαι] release to captives. . . ."[3] The appearance of εὐαγγελίζεσθαι in the quotation of Isaiah 52:7 provides, of course, additional linkage with Isaiah 61, where the same verb occurs. In short, Paul's idea of apostleship does indeed appear to be based, at least in part, on Isaiah 61.

Peter Stuhlmacher has offered additional support to Hahn's proposal, by drawing our attention to tradition about the prophets of the latter days. This tradition, Stuhlmacher believes, clarifies the linkage between the "gospel" and the office of apostle. He appeals to targumic and rabbinic tradition.[4] Karl Sandnes agrees, adding that Paul's use of the plural form in his paraphrase of Isaiah 52:7 reflects tradition now preserved in the Isaiah Targum: "Get you up to a high mountain, prophets who proclaim good tidings to Zion . . ." (40:9); "The words of consolation which the prophets prophesied from the first to Zion, behold they come (to pass), and I will give to Jerusalem one who brings good tidings" (41:27).[5] Although neither the welcome herald in *Tg.* Isaiah 52:7 nor the "prophet" of *Tg.* Isaiah 61:1 is plural,[6] the appearance of "prophets" in the passages referred to above which speak of proclaiming the good tidings may very well reflect a tradition with which in an earlier form Paul was familiar.

The evidence suggests that for Paul the good tidings of Isaiah, especially Isaiah 52:7, formed the principal scriptural foundation of his understanding of

3. J. D. G. Dunn, *Romans,* 2 vols. (WBC 38a, 38b; Dallas: Word, 1988), vol. 2, p. 621.

4. P. Stuhlmacher, *Das Paulinische Evangelium I: Vorgeschichte* (Göttingen: Vandenhoeck & Ruprecht, 1968), esp. pp. 247-54; idem, "The Pauline Gospel," in P. Stuhlmacher (ed.), *The Gospel and the Gospels* (Grand Rapids: Eerdmans, 1991), pp. 149-72.

5. K. O. Sandnes, *Paul — One of the Prophets? A Contribution to the Apostle's Self-Understanding* (WUNT 2.43; Tübingen: Mohr [Siebeck], 1991), pp. 166-70.

6. *Tg.* Isa 61:1 reads: "The prophet said: 'A spirit of prophecy before the Lord God is upon me. . . .'" However, the idea of plural messengers or prophets is attested elsewhere. Commenting on Isa 52:7, one midrash states that "When the Holy One . . . will be king, they will all be messengers [מבשׂרים] proclaiming good tidings . . ." (*Midr. Ps.* 147.2 [on Ps 147:1]). The antiquity of this idea that the good tidings will be proclaimed by many is attested in the LXX (cf. Joel 2:32; Ps 67:11).

the εὐαγγέλιον that he so energetically proclaimed. Paul's experience of the risen Christ was essential, of course, and we must not discount the importance of the Jesus tradition itself. Indeed, as has already been suggested, it is probable that Jesus' proclamation of the good tidings of the kingdom of God and Paul's proclamation of the good tidings of Jesus are both informed by the same scriptural matrix.[7] Both phases of this proclamation are informed by the good tidings of Isaiah and certain aspects of the interpretive tradition that had grown up around the relevant passages.

If the New Testament idea of apostle is informed by Isaiah 61 and other Isaianic passages, passages which may also be understood in the more traditional prophetic sense, then we may be justified in looking for further linkage between the offices of apostle and prophet. It will be found that the association between apostle and prophet leads to important implications for understanding certain aspects of Paul's hermeneutics.

I. Relationship between Apostle and Prophet

Recent research has rightly recognized the close relationship between apostle and prophet.[8] Not only are prophets messengers and "seers," they are also those who have been "sent" (שלח/ἀποστέλλειν) by Yahweh. Isaiah, Jeremiah, and Ezekiel are "sent" by God to the people of Israel (Isa 6:8; Jer 1:7; Ezek 2:3). Throughout Israel's history God has sent his "servants the prophets to them" (Jer 7:25). Malachi prophesies that God will "send [his] messenger" (3:1) and "will send Elijah the prophet" (4:5). Similar language is employed in the New Testament, in reference both to Old Testament prophets and to Jesus' disciples/apostles (Mt 23:37; Mk 1:2; Lk 9:2; 10:3; 13:34; 22:35; Jn 1:6; 3:28; Rom 10:15). In the Old Testament the great lawgiver and prophet Moses is "sent" (Ex 3:10, 12-15; 4:28; 7:16; Deut 34:11). In later Jewish and Samaritan traditions Moses is also called a שליח (*Mek. R. Sim. Yoh.* on Ex 3:10-11; *'Abot R. Nat.* A 1; *Ex. Rab.* 3.4 [on 3:12]; 3.14 [on 4:10]; *Memar Marqa* 5:3; 6:3). In later traditions, the prophets are called "apostles" (cf. *Mek.* on Ex 12:1 [*Pisha* §1], where God says to Jonah: "I have other apostles [שלוחין] like you").

The linkage between apostle and prophet is in itself important. If a prophet is to proclaim the "good tidings" (as is explicitly expressed in *Tg.* Isa

7. See C. A. Evans, "From Gospel to Gospel: The Function of Isaiah in the New Testament," in C. C. Broyles and C. A. Evans (eds.), *Writing and Reading the Scroll of Isaiah: Studies of an Interpretive Tradition* (VTSup 70.2; FIOTL 1.2; Leiden: Brill, 1997), pp. 651-91.

8. F. H. Agnew, "The Origin of the NT Apostle-Concept: A Review of Research," *JBL* 105 (1986): 75-96, esp. 90-96; Sandnes, *Paul — One of the Prophets?*, pp. 17-20.

61:1-2), then the understanding of apostles as prophets provides the necessary warrant for apostolic proclamation of the good tidings. That Paul understood himself as a latter-day prophet seems probable, for, as we shall argue, his call, his visions, his manner of speaking about himself and his ministry, his sense of obligation, and his provocative comparison of himself to Elijah strongly suggest this.[9] It will be helpful to review briefly some of these elements. Paul's prophetic hermeneutic will be considered later in the study.

A. Prophetic Call

In Galatians Paul adopts prophetic language in describing his apostolic calling. His reference to God "who set me apart from my mother's womb and called me through his grace . . . that I might preach him among the Gentiles" (Gal 1:15-16) is clearly reminiscent of the call of Jeremiah (1:5: "Before I formed you in the womb I knew you. . . . I appointed you a prophet to the Gentiles") and of the language found in Second Isaiah (49:1, 5: "He called my name from my mother's womb . . . to gather Jacob and Israel to him").

B. Visions

The very nature of Paul's conversion invites comparison with the prophets. Just as the prophets received revelations and visions of God and/or heaven, particularly in connection with their call to prophetic office (Isa 1:1; 6:1-13; Ezek 1:1; 8:4; Obad 1; Nah 1:1; Hab 2:2), so Paul received revelations and visions (1 Cor 15:8; 2 Cor 12:1-4; Gal 1:12, 16; 2:2; cf. Acts 9:3-9; 22:6-11; 26:13-20). It is probable that the things Paul heard in Paradise "that no mortal is to repeat" and the "exceptional character of the revelations" (2 Cor 12:4-7) involved a vision of the divine throne room and the hearing of an angelic liturgy.[10]

9. See the especially helpful study by J. M. Myers and E. D. Freed, "Is Paul Also among the Prophets?" *Interp* 20 (1966): 40-53.

10. See J. M. Scott, "Throne-Chariot Mysticism in Qumran and in Paul," in C. A. Evans and P. W. Flint (eds.), *Eschatology, Messianism, and the Dead Sea Scrolls* (Studies in the Dead Sea Scrolls and Related Literature 1; Grand Rapids: Eerdmans, 1997), pp. 101-19, esp. pp. 107-8. For studies that take a similar tack, see C. Rowland, "The Parting of the Ways: The Evidence of Jewish and Christian Apocalyptic and Mystical Material," in J. D. G. Dunn (ed.), *Jews and Christians: The Parting of the Ways A.D. 70 to 135* (WUNT 66; Tübingen: Mohr [Siebeck], 1992), pp. 213-37; C. R. A. Morray-Jones, "Paradise Revisited (2 Cor 12:1-12): The Jewish Mystical Background of Paul's Apostolate, Part 1: The Jewish Sources," *HTR* 86 (1993): 177-217; idem, "Paradise Revisited (2 Cor 12:1-12): The Jewish Mystical Background

C. Manner of Speaking of Himself and His Ministry

Paul's criticism of his Galatian opponents (1:6-9: "there are some who trouble you and wish to distort the gospel of Christ. . . . But even if we, or an angel from heaven, should preach to you a gospel contrary to that which we preached to you, let him be accursed") echoes biblical language employed against false prophets and others who would encourage God's people to worship false gods (LXX Deut 13:12-18: "And if . . . evil men in one of your cities . . . say, 'Let us go and worship others gods . . . ,' you will curse it"; cf. 13:1-5, 6-11; 20:17-18). Prophetic language is also found in Paul's description before Herod Agrippa II of his Damascus road experience (compare Acts 26:16-17 with LXX Jer 1:7-8; Ezek 2:1-3).[11] Although the speech is a Lucan composition, the language probably accurately reflects Paul's sense of prophetic call and experience.

There is evidence, moreover, that prior to the Galatian crisis Paul understood himself as a prophet and that he did not adopt this vocabulary *ad hoc* to deal with the problem he faced in the churches of Galatia. His language in 1 Thessalonians, which is probably his earliest extant epistle, suggests that Paul's prophetic self-understanding originated with his apostolic calling. His expression of sincerity (1 Thess 2:4: "even as we have been tested by God," "God who tests our hearts") echoes the words of Jeremiah (LXX Jer 11:20: "Lord, who judges justly, testing the reins and the hearts . . ."). Both Paul and Jeremiah uttered these words in the face of opposition (compare 1 Thess 2:2 with Jer 11:19). Later Paul again takes up the theme of persecution (1 Thess 3:4: "For when we were with you, we told you beforehand that we were to suffer affliction, just as it has come to pass"; cf. 2 Cor 11:23-27), which recalls the tradition of the suffering and persecuted prophet (cf. Lk 13:33-34; *Pesiq. R.* 26.2: "Jeremiah said, 'Master of the universe, I cannot prophesy to them. What prophet ever came forth to them whom they did not wish to slay?"). Paul's eschatological warning (1 Thess 5:3: "When people say, 'There is peace and safety,' then sudden destruction will come upon them as travail comes upon a woman with child") echoes similar solemn warnings found in the Old Testament prophets (cf. Jer 6:14, 24; 8:11, 21; 14:13-14; Ezek 13:10, 16; Hos 14:1).

---

of Paul's Apostolate, Part 2: Paul's Heavenly Ascent and Its Significance," *HTR* 86 (1993): 265-92; M. Hengel, "'Sit at My Right Hand!' The Enthronement of Christ at the Right Hand of God and Psalm 110:1," in Hengel, *Studies in Early Christology* (Edinburgh: T. & T. Clark, 1995), pp. 119-225; A. F. Segal, "Paul and the Beginning of Jewish Mysticism," in J. J. Collins and M. Fishbane (eds.), *Death, Ecstasy, and Other Worldly Journeys* (Albany: SUNY Press, 1995), pp. 95-122.

11. See the parallels listed in Myers and Freed, "Is Paul Also among the Prophets?" pp. 45-46.

D. Apostolic Obligation

Paul's understanding of the apostolic obligation to proclaim the gospel is informed by the prophetic voice of Second Isaiah: "And how can men preach unless they are sent? As it is written, 'How beautiful are the feet of those who preach good news'" (Rom 10:14-17; cf. Isa 52:7; 53:1).[12] Moreover, when Paul says, "woe to me, if I should not preach the gospel" (1 Cor 9:16), he echoes the exclamations of the Old Testament prophets: "Woe is me!" (Isa 24:16; cf. Jer 13:27; Hos 9:12). Paul's anguish (Rom 9:2: "I have great sorrow and unceasing anguish in my heart"; 11:1: "Has God rejected his people?") also is reminiscent of prophetic anguish: "Hast thou utterly rejected Judah . . . ?" (Jer 14:19).

E. Comparison with Elijah

Despite the fact that relatively few Israelites had responded in faith to the Christian message, Paul was convinced that God had not rejected Israel (Rom 11:1-2). He grounds this conviction in the example of Elijah (Rom 11:3-4; cf. 1 Kgs 19:10, 18) and on Isaiah's remnant theology (Rom 9:27-29; 11:5; cf. Isa 1:9; 10:22). What is especially interesting here is Paul's comparison with Elijah. Evidently the apostle saw himself very much like Elijah of old, who felt alone and threatened. Just as God had preserved a remnant of the faithful in Elijah's time, so now in the eschatological period God once again has preserved a faithful remnant.

In the light of these observations on Paul's prophetic self-understanding, what are the implications for his interpretation of Scripture, especially those passages in which he engages in polemic against fellow Israelites who have rejected the gospel?[13] A number of important points need to be considered.

II. Hermeneutics of Prophetic Criticism

"True prophecy," as James A. Sanders has explained,[14] is theocentric, not ethnocentric. Unlike most of the "false prophets" who prophesied peace and

12. P. E. Dinter, "Paul and the Prophet Isaiah," *BTB* 13 (1983): 48-52, esp. 48.

13. Passages which some have taken as potentially anti-Jewish, even anti-Semitic, may on closer examination exemplify a type of hermeneutic adopted by Israel's classic prophets. On this matter, see D. A. Hagner, "Paul's Quarrel with Judaism," in C. A. Evans and D. A. Hagner (eds.), *Anti-Semitism and Early Christianity: Issues of Polemic and Faith* (Minneapolis: Fortress, 1993), pp. 128-50.

14. J. A. Sanders, "Canonical Hermeneutics: True and False Prophecy," in Sanders, *From Sacred Story to Sacred Text* (Philadelphia: Fortress, 1987), pp. 87-105.

safety, the true prophet understood sacred tradition and history from the divine point of view. What this often meant was that the great stories of the past, where God's power was displayed, did not offer assurance of Israel's victory (contrary to what the false prophets assumed and impressed upon wavering kings and princes). Rather, these stories tell more about God's sovereignty over his creatures than his obligations to them. In short, the same story could be interpreted in two radically different ways. As a result, the very story from which the false prophet gained his assurance could persuade the true prophet, through revelation, that Israel faced judgment. Nowhere can this be seen more clearly than in the prophets' respective interpretations and applications of Israel's sacred tradition. Several brief examples will illustrate this point.

One of the most startling examples comes from Isaiah, who alludes to two of David's great victories over the Philistines: "The Lord will rise up as on Mount Perazim [cf. 2 Sam 5:17-21], he will rage as in the valley of Gibeon [cf. 2 Sam 5:22-25]; to do his deed — strange is his deed! and to work his work — alien is his work!" (Isa 28:21).[15] But unlike the false prophets, Isaiah does not find in these victories assurance that Israel will once again be victorious against her enemies. On the contrary, Isaiah has "heard a decree of destruction from the Lord God of hosts" (Isa 28:22). God is angry and ready to defeat sinners on the field of battle; only this time the sinners are the Israelites, not their enemies!

Isaiah's allusion to the sacred stories of God's dealings with King David would have had a jarring effect upon his contemporaries. Surely these stories, which told of the defeat of the Philistines, should offer assurance of Israel's victory over the Assyrians (with Egypt's aid). But Isaiah saw in these stories, hermeneutically conditioned by his vision of God, the holiness and power of God. Because Israel has offended this holiness, God will turn his wrath against Israel.

Jeremiah tells his contemporaries not to listen to the false prophets who assure the inhabitants of Jerusalem that there is nothing to fear because of the presence of the Temple: "Do not trust in these deceptive words: 'This is the Temple of the Lord'" (Jer 7:4); and "No evil shall come upon you" (Jer 23:17). Through Jeremiah God tells his wayward people: "I will do to the house that is called by my name, in which you trust, and to the place that I gave to you and to your ancestors, just what I did to Shiloh. And I will cast you out of my sight, just as I cast out all your kinsfolk, all the offspring of Ephraim" (Jer 7:14-15). The presence of the Temple in Jerusalem will be destroyed and the people of Judah, like the northern tribes, will be carried off into captivity.

Ezekiel warns his contemporaries not to assume — contrary to what false

15. C. A. Evans, "On Isaiah's Use of Israel's Sacred Tradition," *BZ* 30 (1986): 92-99, esp. 96-97.

prophets would have them believe — that since "Abraham was only one man, yet he got possession of the land, [then] we [who] are many" will surely be able to possess the land (Ezek 33:24). Not so. Israel's arrogant self-assurance irritates God, who through his prophet asks rhetorically, "Shall you then possess the land?" (Ezek 33:25, 26). God answers his own question: "I will make the land a desolation and a waste" (Ezek 33:28, 29).

This hermeneutic, which Sanders has called the hermeneutic of prophetic criticism, is attested in the words of John the Baptist and Jesus of Nazareth. The Baptist angrily admonished those who approached him: "Do not presume to say to yourselves, 'We have Abraham as our ancestor'; for I tell you, God is able from these stones to raise up children to Abraham" (Mt 3:9 = Lk 3:8). John saw no guarantee of salvation in physical descent from the great patriarch. Indeed, his rhetoric about children being raised up from stones adumbrates Christianity's subsequent openness to the Gentiles (even if that was not John's point). Similarly, Jesus said to the congregation of Nazareth: "Doubtless you will quote to me the proverb, 'Doctor, cure yourself! Do here also in your hometown what you did in Capernaum'" (Lk 4:23). Jesus perceived that his kinsmen and neighbors assumed that messianic blessings (as described in Isa 61:1-2) were primarily for them. But Jesus warns them that they may not appreciate his understanding of Scripture, for "no (true) prophet is accepted in his hometown" (Lk 4:24). He implies, by examples from the ministries of Elijah and Elisha, that messianic blessings will be extended to Gentiles (such as the widow of Sidon) and even to Israel's enemies (such as Naaman the Syrian military leader). It should come as no surprise that the congregation reacted with anger. They believed that the messianic blessings were theirs, while judgment was reserved for their enemies.[16]

III. Prophetic Criticism in Romans 9–11

For reasons already stated, it is probable that Paul viewed himself as a prophet. What is of particular interest is the observation that in places Paul appears to be employing the hermeneutic of prophetic criticism, so common in the great

16. See J. A. Sanders, "From Isaiah 61 to Luke 4," in C. A. Evans and J. A. Sanders, *Luke and Scripture: The Function of Sacred Tradition in Luke-Acts* (Minneapolis: Fortress, 1993), pp. 46-69. For further discussion of prophetic criticism in John and Jesus, see B. D. Chilton and C. A. Evans, "Jesus and Israel's Scriptures," in Evans and Chilton (eds.), *Studying the Historical Jesus: Evaluations of the State of Current Research* (NTTS 19; Leiden: Brill, 1994), pp. 281-335, esp. pp. 309-33. Jesus' understanding of Isaiah 61 contrasts sharply with that presupposed by the author of 11QMelchizedek, which focuses on judgment upon Israel's enemies.

prophets of Israel's classical period, as detailed above. Like the "true" prophets of Israel's biblical past, Paul calls upon the sacred tradition to clarify the meaning of contemporary events and experience.[17] Like these prophets he finds in the sacred tradition evidence of God's freedom and sovereignty. This means that God may freely bestow his blessings on Israel's enemies and may pass judgment against Israel herself. As Paul Dinter has put it: "Paul's understanding of God's continuing activity was prophetic and dynamic. God could, as in the days of Isaiah, do a 'new thing.'"[18] The new thing that God was doing in Paul's time was to take a non-covenant people and make a people of God out of them (Rom 9:25-26; cf. Hos 1:10; 2:23). Imprecations originally uttered against Israel's enemies are applied against Israel herself: "Let their table become a snare and a trap, a pitfall and a retribution for them" (Rom 11:9-10; cf. Ps 69:22-23).[19] This remarkable application of the sacred tradition is not anti-Jewish — for Paul is a loyal Jew (cf. Rom 9:1-5; 11:1-2) — but rather prophetic in the same sense as we have seen in prophets like Isaiah, Jeremiah, and Ezekiel. Paul is no more anti-Jewish than were these great prophets of old. If Paul's interpretation and application of the Scripture of Israel are to be properly understood, it will be necessary to take into account the apostle's prophetic self-understanding.

The examples just cited are not unusual to Paul, but reflect a hermeneutic that underlies the whole of Romans 9–11, that strategic passage in which Paul deals with the vexatious question of how Gentiles have come to benefit from the promises and blessings originally extended to Israel and how Israelites find themselves for the most part estranged from these promises and blessings. The comments below are selective only, treating certain features of Paul's use of Scripture in Romans 9–11:

9:6b-8. Paul's hermeneutic of prophetic criticism manifests itself in his opening declaration: "For not all Israelites truly belong to Israel, and not all of Abraham's children are his true descendants; but 'It is through Isaac that descendants shall be named for you.' This means that it is not the children of the flesh who are the children of God, but the children of the promise are counted as descendants." The citation of Genesis 21:12 provides the necessary scriptural warrant. The point Paul makes is that not all those of physical descent from

17. See C. A. Evans, "Paul and the Hermeneutics of 'True Prophecy': A Study of Romans 9–11," *Bib* 65 (1984): 560-70. For a recent assessment of the major questions relating to Paul's use of the Old Testament in Romans, see R. N. Longenecker, "Prolegomena to Paul's Use of Scripture in Romans," *BBR* 7 (1997): 145-68.

18. Dinter, "Paul and the Prophet Isaiah," 52. J. D. G. Dunn (*Romans 9–16* [WBC 38b; Dallas: Word, 1988], p. 520) rightly comments that "scripture itself attests the two-sided character of God's dealings with his people, acting both as witness for Israel and accuser of Israel."

19. Evans, "Paul and the Hermeneutics of 'True Prophecy,'" pp. 567-68.

Abraham are genuine Israelites, that is, Israelites who have responded to the gospel of God in faith.[20] Their rejection of the gospel has cut them off from the great patriarch's wonderful legacy. The divine word that Abraham's descendants will be named through Isaac (and not Ishmael) proves the point that physical descent alone is not determinative. This note had already been sounded by John the Baptist and lies at the heart of Qumran's distinction between Israelites who are obedient and those who are not (cf. CD 5:15–6:11).

9:9-10. Paul's claim in v. 8 that only the "children of promise" are the true descendants of Abraham is justified by an appeal to Genesis 18:10, 14: "For this is what the promise said, 'About this time I will return and Sarah shall have a son'" (v. 9). That is, Sarah, not Hagar, will give birth to Abraham's heir. The same point may be claimed in the case of Rebecca's twins (v. 10), the younger of whom was chosen over the older (cf. Gen 25:21). By this argument Paul has established his theology of election as based on promise and not on mere physical descent or birth order.

9:11-18. In this passage God's sovereign choice is yet again witnessed in Scripture. Before Esau or Jacob had done anything, good or bad, God had made his choice: "the elder shall serve the younger" (v. 12; cf. Gen 25:23). Indeed, according to the prophet Malachi, whom Paul also quotes, God loved Jacob, but hated Esau (v. 13; cf. Mal 1:2-3). Although "hated" here is hyperbolic, meaning to "love less,"[21] the arbitrary nature of the choice is scarcely mitigated. On the contrary, God "will have mercy on whom" he wishes and "compassion on whom" he will have compassion (v. 15; cf. Ex 33:19). The point is driven home even more forcefully by the appeal to God's act of hardening the heart of Pharaoh (v. 17; cf. Ex 9:16). The implication of these comparisons is that unbelieving Israelites theologically play the role of Ishmael, Esau, and Pharaoh. The very persons on whom God's displeasure rests — as one would be tempted to read Scripture — are cited as exemplars of Israelites, on whom the blessings and promises of Scripture are supposed to be bestowed. This subversive application of the sacred tradition is a manifestation of the hermeneutic of prophetic criticism.

9:19-21. God's right to choose is grounded in his role as Creator. What is molded has no right to challenge him who does the molding. As had the prophets of old, Paul affirms God's sovereignty over his creation as surely as the potter has authority over the pots that he turns at his wheel (v. 21; cf. Isa 29:16; 45:9; 64:8; Jer 18:6). Some pots are for ordinary use, some are for special use. In either case it is the potter who decides, not the pot.

9:22-26. In pondering God's purpose for electing Gentiles, Paul speaks precisely to the point of the hermeneutic of prophetic criticism: "what if God,

20. So J. A. Fitzmyer, *Romans* (AB 33; New York: Doubleday, 1993), p. 560.

21. Fitzmyer, *Romans*, p. 563.

desiring to show his wrath and to make known his power . . . and what if he has done so in order to make known the riches of his glory . . . ?" (vv. 22-23). The protasis "what if . . . ?" has no corresponding apodosis, but it is not difficult to imagine what it must be: "It is God's right."[22] The ultimate purpose of God's election is not fairness (as humans usually expect — though only when the prospects appear favorable); rather, it is God's glory. Here the theocentric dimension of Paul's hermeneutic comes plainly into view. This theocentrism is what lies at the heart of prophetic criticism.

The rub for Paul comes at the end of v. 24, when the apostle says that God has called a people for himself, not only "from among the Jews but also from among the Gentiles." Paul builds his case for the inclusion of the Gentiles by appealing to two texts from Hosea: "Those who were not my people I will call 'my people' . . . they shall be called 'the children of the living God'" (v. 25-26; cf. Hos 2:23; 2:1 [LXX 1:10]). In the Hosean context the non-people are the northern tribes of Israel which had lost their covenant status because of idolatry. Because of God's redemptive mercy these lost Israelites, who had become in God's eyes pagans,[23] would be reclaimed and once again acquire the status of covenant people. Paul reasons that if God can reclaim a lost, non-covenant people once, he can do it again (cf. Isa 57:1-8, where the prophet envisions not only the regathering of Israel's exiles, but the gathering of eunuchs and foreigners to the Temple of Jerusalem). The citation of the passages from Hosea enables Paul to argue that "being the people of God is something brought about solely by God's invitation, that his call can completely transform what had appeared to be a clear-cut case of divine rejection."[24]

9:27-33. Unbelief will reduce Israel to a remnant (vv. 27-29; cf. Isa 10:22; 1:9). Paul's combination of Isaiah 8:14-15 ("a stone of stumbling") and 28:16 ("laying in Zion a stone . . . whoever believes in him [*or* it] will not be put to shame"), linked by the catchword "stone" (λίθος), clarifies both Israel's unbelief and stumbling, on the one hand, and the Gentiles' faith and righteousness, on the other. The stone that God has laid in Zion is the crucified and resurrected Christ,[25] which many ethnic Israelites have rejected and which many Gentiles have embraced in faith.

22. So E. Käsemann, *Commentary on Romans* (Grand Rapids: Eerdmans, 1980), p. 270.

23. The prophet depicts the northern kingdom as a harlot (1:2-3; 2:2-13; cf. 5:3-7), who is addressed: "You are not my people, and I am not your God" (1:9). Israel's sin is so severe that God promises to reverse the great act of salvation that was the exodus; Israel will be returned to slavery (11:1-7).

24. Dunn, *Romans*, p. 575.

25. I think Fitzmyer (*Romans*, p. 580) has misunderstood my point in referring to the Aramaic paraphrase of Isa 28:16, which speaks of a "strong king" — not a stone — appointed

10:1-17. Paul digresses from his principal line of argument to affirm his fidelity to ethnic Israel. His "heart's desire and prayer to God for them is that they may be saved" (v. 1). But Israel must respond to God's promise and its fulfillment in Christ in faith, as both Moses commands (vv. 5-9; cf. Lev 18:5; Deut 30:11-14)[26] and the prophets proclaim (vv. 10-17; cf. Isa 28:16; Joel 2:32; Isa 52:7; 53:1). The eschatological prophecy of the latter two passages from Isaiah, which, as we have seen, play an important role in defining early Christianity's concept of "apostle," underscores the need for faith and at the same time anticipates an unbelieving response on the part of many.

10:18-21. Paul returns to prophetic criticism in his citation of Moses (v. 19; cf. Deut 32:21) and Isaiah (vv. 20-21; cf. Isa 65:1-2). Moses had long ago prophesied that Israel would be provoked to jealousy by a non-covenant, foolish people. Indeed, according to Isaiah, God will be found by people who did not seek him. He will show himself to those who did not ask for him. Here again we have the theme of God's sovereign choice. The Gentiles will receive grace, but Israel will stubbornly refuse God's overtures (v. 21).

11:1-6. Israel's persistent unbelief notwithstanding, the nation is not rejected. God has preserved a remnant of the faithful, just as he did in the days of Elijah (1 Kgs 19:10, 18). The remnant itself reveals God's grace. However, the comparison between Israel of Paul's day with the Israel of Elijah's day would have been deeply resented by the Jewish religious leadership. The comparison of course implies that Israel is in a state of apostasy, with her priesthood leading the nation astray. Evidently, in Paul's eyes those who reject faith in Christ have in essence "bowed the knee to Baal" (v. 4). Clearly the Pharisees, of whom Paul once was a member, and all other Torah-observant Jews would identify with Elijah and the faithful seven thousand, not with the corrupt priesthood that along with Ahab and Jezebel worshiped Baal. Paul's comparison turns the ta-

in Zion (see Evans, "Paul and the Hermeneutics of 'True Prophecy,'" pp. 564-65 and n. 17). Although it is disputed, this may be in reference to a messianic figure. If so, the Aramaic tradition coheres with Paul's and early Christianity's messianic understanding of this Isaianic text. Paul certainly has not read the targum; the targum may preserve an exegetical tradition, with which in an earlier time Paul may have been familiar.

26. Again we have an interesting point of coherence between Paul and the Aramaic tradition. Whereas Lev 18:5 in the Hebrew only speaks of enjoying life in this world, if one is faithful to obey the Law, the Aramaic speaks of life in this world and in the world to come (cf. *Tgs. Onq.* and *Ps.-J.* Lev 18:5). See also Luke 10:25-28, where the lawyer's question and answer about what must be done to inherit "eternal life" are affirmed by Jesus with an allusion to Lev 18:5. Martin McNamara (*The New Testament and the Palestinian Targum to the Pentateuch* [AnBib 27a; Rome: Biblical Institute Press, 1978], pp. 70-78) has also shown how the Aramaic paraphrases of Deut 30:11-14 cohere with and probably clarify the nature of Paul's exegesis.

bles on his unbelieving kinsmen. According to his hermeneutic, it is they who worship Baal and persecute God's true prophets.

11:7-10. The elect of Israel obtained righteous standing before God, "but the rest were hardened" (v. 7). According to Paul, God rendered Israel obdurate, just as he did Pharaoh, Israel's great oppressor, and the feckless first generation of Israelites that escaped Egypt: "God gave them a sluggish spirit, eyes that would not see and ears that would not hear, down to this day" (v. 8). Paul has quoted a conflation of Deuteronomy 29:3 and Isaiah 29:10. By applying these texts to unbelieving Israel he has made comparison with notorious past generations of Israelites who lacked faith in God. So it is today, reasons the apostle. More shocking still, Paul quotes Psalm 69:22-23, originally uttered against Israel's enemies, and applies the text against Israel herself. Long ago David begged God: "Let their table become a snare and a trap . . . let their eyes be darkened so that they cannot see, and keep their backs forever bent." Paradoxically, the true enemies of Israel and of the Gentiles are the Israelites who reject the gospel.

11:11-16. Finally, Paul wrestles with the divine purpose of Israel's stumbling. Israel's "stumbling means riches for the world," the apostle believes, and "their defeat means riches for Gentiles." The benefit of the Gentiles' eventual "full inclusion" is unimaginable. Israel's rejection of the gospel has led to the reconciliation of the world; their acceptance will mean life from the dead (which is probably an allusion to the resurrection).

11:17-32. In this final section, Paul attempts to tie up some loose ends. In v. 25 Paul describes Israel's obduracy as a "mystery." He says "a hardening has come upon part of Israel, until the full number of the Gentiles has come in." Thus, the hardening of Israel not only has resulted in the salvation of many Gentiles, but it is only temporary. When the full number of Gentiles come in, then "all Israel will be saved" (v. 26). Paul justifies his hope by quoting a conflation of Isaiah 59:20-21 and 27:9, though with some interesting variations. We see here again Paul's prophetic perspective at work. Whereas the Hebrew reads "the deliverer will come to Zion" and the LXX reads "the deliverer will come for the sake of Zion," Paul says "the deliverer will come out of Zion." Paul's reading "out of" (ἐκ), in place of the LXX's "for the sake of" (ἕνεκεν), is not easily explained. In a recent study Christopher Stanley wonders if it is pre-Pauline and a reference to the place of Jesus' birth.[27] I wonder if it is not a change suggested by the messianically understood Numbers 24:17: "A star will arise from [ἐκ] Jacob, a man will arise from [ἐκ] Israel." Paul concludes his argument by reiterating his theme that Israel's folly has resulted in benefit for the Gentiles (vv. 28-32).

27. See C. D. Stanley, "'The Redeemer Will Come ἐκ Σιων': Romans 11.26-27 Revisited," in C. A. Evans and J. A. Sanders (eds.), *Paul and the Scriptures of Israel* (JSNTSupp. 83; SSEJC 1; Sheffield: JSOT Press, 1993), pp. 118-42, here p. 125, n. 26.

IV. Conclusion

Recently, Richard Longenecker has suggested that Paul's use of Scripture in Romans 9–11 may be a "polemical thrust against a Judaizing threat."[28] He may well be correct. This thrust appears to employ the hermeneutical strategy employed by most of Israel's classical prophets. For those steeped in Scripture, who would have led the opposition against the apostle, such a hermeneutical strategy would have been keenly felt. For those who had expressed faith in Jesus as God's Son and Israel's Messiah, the Pauline hermeneutic would have offered important assurance in light of their minority status and the growing criticism and occasional persecution they were experiencing.

But Paul's hermeneutical strategy may also have a significant bearing on the much larger and even more difficult twin problem of Israel's unbelief and Gentile entry into the church. Although Paul invokes the witness of Scripture, as seen especially in Romans 9–11, ultimately the apostle relies on the convicting power and witness of God's Spirit.[29] His reliance on the Spirit, of course, is consistent with the prophetic hope that God would someday pour out his Spirit on his people (Isa 32:15; 44:3; 59:21; Ezek 36:27; 37:14; Joel 2:28-29) and give them a new heart (Jer 31:33).

Paul's employment of the hermeneutic of prophetic criticism, seen so clearly in his use of Scripture in Romans 9–11, attests an important aspect of the apostle's understanding of his apostleship, as well as his assessment of the plight of Israel in his day. In short, Paul's calling placed him in the tradition of the prophets. But his continuity with this prophetic tradition was in one important sense different: whereas the prophets of old longed for the fulfillment of God's promises, Paul the "sent" prophet proclaimed Scripture's fulfillment in Christ. Thus, Paul joins the prophets who have been sent out into the world, bearing the good news foretold in Isaiah 52:7 and 61:1.

28. Longenecker, "Prolegomena to Paul's Use of Scripture in Romans," p. 167 (slightly adapted).

29. Here must be mentioned Gordon Fee's *God's Empowering Presence: The Holy Spirit in the Letters of Paul* (Peabody, Mass.: Hendrickson, 1994), esp. pp. 811-16.

Why Bring the Word Down? The Rhetoric of Demonstration and Disclosure in Romans 9:30–10:21

Edith M. Humphrey

Who will ascend into heaven, that is, to bring down an exegesis of Romans 10, *and who will descend into the abyss,* that is, to find its hidden treasure in a muddle of contradictory interpretations?

This is the very question that should not have been asked. But I have asked it, lured by an intimation of forbidden mysteries. Consequently, I have tripped over more than one stumbling stone: δικαιοσύνη θεοῦ, δικαιοσύνη ἐκ νόμου, τέλος νόμου, ῥῆμα Χριστοῦ, *pesher, midrash,* and other unutterable things. Nonetheless the search has gone on, motivated in my case by a fascination for New Testament texts that in various ways link vision with argument, evocative imagery with directive polemic.[1] Throughout the NT, vision-reports are embedded within their larger host genres. Thus, even where a vision-report

1. "To Rejoice or Not to Rejoice?: Rhetoric and the Fall of Satan in Luke 10:17-24 and Rev 12:1-17," Canadian Society of Biblical Studies Annual Meeting, 1993; "'I saw Satan Fall . . .' — The Rhetoric of Vision," *ARC: The Journal of the Faculty of Religious Studies, McGill University* 21 (1993): 75-78; "Collision of Modes? — Vision and Determining Argument in Acts 10:1–11:18," *Semeia* 71 (1995): 65-84; "In Search of a Voice: Rhetoric through Sight and Sound in Revelation 11:15–12:17," SBL Meeting, 1994 and forthcoming in L. Gregory Bloomquist and Greg Carey (eds.), *Vision and Persuasion: Rhetorical Dimensions in Apocalyptic Discourse* (Chalice Press, 1999); "Texts and Textures, Sights and Sound: Mary Visited and Revisited (Luke 1:5–2:40)," CSBS Meeting, 1995; "This Is the Word of the Lord — Or Is It a Vision? Rhetoric and Vision in Narratives of Paul's Conversion/Call," CSBS Meeting, 1996.

is located within a (literary) "speech," the exegete must go beyond a stylistic analysis which divorces the unit from its larger narrative or epistolary context: at every level a delicate balance of rhetorical and literary analysis is required. Preliminary results of these analyses have suggested that the vision-report is used in different ways in the NT, and to different effect. Several NT vision-reports, such as 2 Corinthians 12:1-8, emerge as carefully crafted pieces forming an integral part of the persuasive line. Other NT vision-reports, such as those found in the Lucan narratives, are rather more embryonic, and yet still make an interesting contribution to the rhetorical effect of each passage, at times even complicating the rhetorical direction of the discourse or narrative due to their centrifugal, evocative character.[2]

In the letter to the Romans, the techniques of persuasion and declaration apparently dominate over the symbolic and evocative; indeed, this epistle contains no "vision" as such. Yet, alongside multiple rhetorical questions, answers, and logical connectives (ὅτι, ἄρα, οὖν, ἀλλά, καθώς) Paul characteristically uses terms associated with vision and mystery (1:17, 18; 8:18, etc. — ἀποκαλύπτω; 2:5; [16:25] — ἀποκάλυψις; 3:21 *et passim* — πεφανέρωται; 11:25; [16:25] — μυστήριον). Moreover, by any definition,[3] it is clear that we also find in Romans "apocalyptic" motifs, such as seeing and hearing mysteries, glory, personal and cosmic transformation, judgment, ages, hidden wisdom, and knowledge. It is

2. See especially "Collision of Modes," pp. 80ff., where Peter's vision of the sheets in Acts 10:10-15 is seen to be "open" to an interpretation which deals with food regulations, while it is within *Luke*'s rhetoric carefully directed toward the more general question of the Gentiles and the gospel.

3. The careless use of "apocalyptic" (often as a synonym to "eschatological" and with an underlying assumption about "apocalyptic theology") with regard to Pauline thought has been well documented. See now the incisive remarks of R. Barry Matlock, especially on pp. 304-16 of his *Unveiling the Apocalyptic Paul: Paul's Interpreters and the Rhetoric of Criticism* (JSNTSupp 127; Sheffield: Sheffield Academic Press, 1996). I am myself more comfortable with avoidance of the term "apocalyptic" or at least with a definition of this as an adjective closely tied to actual examples of "apocalypses." The genre "apocalypse" has been fruitfully defined as "a genre of revelatory literature with a narrative framework, in which a revelation is mediated by an otherworldly being to a human recipient, disclosing a transcendent reality which is both temporal, insofar as it envisages eschatological salvation, and spatial, insofar as it involves another, supernatural world" (J. J. Collins, "Introduction: Towards the Morphology of a Genre," *Semeia* 14 [1979]: 1-20; p. 9). The adjective "apocalyptic" may therefore advisedly be used for passages which include a cluster of incipient motifs normally associated with the *content* of an apocalypse (i.e., those mysteries found on the "spatial" and "temporal" axes) or for passages which use a number of *formal elements* such as a mediating angel, visions, and the like. More frequently content motifs are found in the NT (especially those which might be placed in one of the four quadrants of the two axes, i.e., the eschatological); 2 Cor 12 provides an interesting example of a passage influenced by formal elements of the genre apocalypse, while refraining from providing content!

perhaps partly due to such a combination of styles that scholars such as Richard Hays and N. T. Wright[4] have successfully called attention to the underlying narrative of Paul's letters, and to their affinity with poetic rather than simply directive argument.

Romans 9:30–10:21 is a notoriously difficult passage. As such it provides an ideal test case for this characteristic of Paul's writing, that is, speech which brings together the poetic, the argumentative, and the visionary. How do these modes work together in Paul's rhetoric, or modify and even collide with each other? Key here to Paul's treatment of God, Israel, the Gentiles, Torah, Christ, righteousness, faithfulness, and the word seem to be three problematic verses, 10:6-8, in which the exploits of heaven and the abyss are contrasted with a word that is "near":

> And the Righteousness from faith speaks in this way: "Do not say in your heart, 'Who will ascend to heaven?'" (that is, to bring Christ down) "or, 'Who will descend into the abyss?'" (that is, to lead Christ up out of the dead). But what does she say? — "*Near* to you is the word, in your mouth and in your heart" (that is, the word of faith which we proclaim).[5]

I will seek to show that these troublesome three verses are best understood in the context not only of wisdom but also of the apocalypses and the Jewish mystical tradition; the significance of this insight will then be demonstrated within the rhetorical flow of 9:30–10:21; finally, I will consider the suitability of this esoteric motif for the purposes of Romans.

I. Romans 10:6-8; Ascent and Descent in Wisdom, Apocalypses, and Rabbinic Mysticism

Most commentators either ignore or lightly dismiss the imagery of Romans 10:6-7 on the assumption that its language about cosmic journeys is wholly metaphoric for the impossible. Such a demythologizing interpretation fits, to be sure, with the dominant intertextual link, Deuteronomy 30:11-14,[6] which

4. See the extensive treatment in Richard Hays, *Echoes of Scripture in the Letters of Paul* (New Haven: Yale, 1989) and the narratival approach of N. T. Wright, evident especially in "The Vindication of the Law: Narrative Analysis and Romans 8.1-11," *The Climax of the Covenant: Christ and the Law in Pauline Theology* (1991; Minneapolis: Fortress, 1992), pp. 193-216.

5. My own translation.

6. It is not entirely clear whether Paul is here informed by a Hebrew or old Greek text. The uncharacteristic use of *rhēma* (and not *logos*) may suggest indebtedness to a type of LXX

uses slightly different pictures to instruct the people that God's commandment is not infeasible nor distant from them ("not too hard, nor . . . too far away," 30:11). Indeed, use of the ascend/descend trope had become proverbial by later rabbinic times.[7] However, the composite nature of Paul's statement (more on this below!) and its adaptation to an underlying christological narrative indicate that Paul is neither using the image naïvely nor as an overused and dead metaphor. Paul stands neither with the Deuteronomist prior to the apocalypses which encoded tours of heaven and hell, nor in the time of the later rabbis, when such exploits were part of a currency that could enter into popular sayings. Rather, we find Paul thinking and writing in continuity with a growing tradition of discourse found in wisdom texts and in apocalypses: a discourse that debated, as it were, the reliability of esoteric journeys to search out God's purposes.

Hays is wry in his censure of those who, in their eagerness to acquit Paul of prooftexting, will not recognize the major allusion to Deuteronomy: "Sometimes the echo will be so loud that only the dullest or most ignorant reader could miss it (e.g., Rom 10:5-10)."[8] However, it is also clear that Paul is not relying *simply* upon Deuteronomy 30. After all, it is not specifically "Moses" who speaks here; rather, it is a new figure, the personified Righteousness. Her adapted words from Deuteronomy 30 are prefaced by a phrase found twice in that same book — "do not say in your heart" (Deut 8:17, 9:4). In Deuteronomy, this refrain is coupled with an insistence on God's initiating benediction of Israel and covenant with her, and the corollary, that the people are not to boast of their *own* power, possessions, accomplishments *or righteousness* (cf. Deut 9:4). Nor is Paul the only commentator to have associated Deuteronomy 30:12-13 with a feminine figure. We find in Baruch 3:29-30 a rhetorical rendering of the same two questions, in connection with hidden Wisdom (identified with Torah in Baruch 4:1): "Who has gone up into heaven and taken her and brought her down. . . . Who has gone over the sea, and found her . . . and will gain her?" Baruch's questions are not wholly rhetorical: the text hastens to add that "the one who knows all things knows her. . . . This is our God . . . who found the whole way to knowledge and gave her to his servant Israel" (3:32, 35-36). If

text, but Paul's lack of "in your hands" (cf. Masoretic Text) might counterbalance this. But the ambiguity of the LXX's phraseology "It is not up in heaven, *saying . . .*" (vs. MT: *"so that you must ask,"*) may well have given Paul an opportunity for his particular commentary, since in the LXX the Torah appears to be speaking, much as "Righteousness from faith" will speak in Romans.

7. See the reference to a rabbinic decision regarding a charming use of the trope in the relationship between a demanding suitor and his would-be bride in M.-J. Lagrange, *Épître aux Romains* (Paris: Études Bibliques, 1914), p. 255.

8. Hays, *Echoes*, p. 29.

both Deuteronomy and Baruch inform Paul's text, then we know the reason why *his* Righteousness from faith forbids such journeys: God is the initiator, alone giving Torah/Wisdom to his people.

So far we have traced the Pauline method dubbed by Hays "textual triple-exposure."[9] I am in agreement both with both Hays and Jack Suggs that "Paul's filtered citation of Deuteronomy echoes these Wisdom traditions, in which Wisdom is identified with Israel's Torah."[10] Both scholars point out that there are a number of Wisdom texts in addition to Baruch 3–4 which follow a similar theme of hidden or inaccessible wisdom, among them Job 28:12-14 and Sirach 24. Of these two texts, it seems to me that the latter is especially relevant:

> Alone I compassed the vault of heaven and traversed the depths of the abyss; over waves of the sea, over all the earth, and over every people I have held sway. Among all these I sought a resting place: in whose territory should I abide? The creator of all things gave me a command, and my creator chose the place for my tent. He said, "Make your dwelling in Jacob." (Sirach 24:5-8)

It is only here that personified Wisdom actually speaks, as is the case with Paul's "Righteousness." Here, too, is found a closer parallel to Paul's vertical dualism (the depths of the abyss).[11] Here we also see a more direct connection with Paul's own exegesis of the text: both Sirach, through the direct statement of Wisdom, and Paul, through his parenthetic exposition of Righteousness' words, warn that only one (besides God) has a direct right to secrets above and below. In Sirach, Wisdom alone has dwelt in highest heaven and was enthroned on the *shekina* of God (24:4); in Romans, the forbidden questions and their *pesher*-like explanations imply that Christ has dwelt in heaven and need not be brought down, and that he alone has come up from the abyss, from the realm of the dead. This intertextuality is confirmed by the emphasis in Sirach 24 on other themes consonant with Pauline discourse: Israel's privilege (24:11-12), obedience that does not lead to shame (24:22), and the identification of wisdom with

9. Hays, *Echoes,* p. 78.

10. Hays, *Echoes,* p. 80, so summarizes the discussion of M. Jack Suggs, "'The Word is Near You': Rom. 10:6-10 within the Purpose of the Letter," *Christian History and Interpretation: Studies Presented to John Knox,* ed. W. R. Farmer, C. F. D. Moule, R. R. Niebuhr (Cambridge: Cambridge University Press, 1967), pp. 289-312.

11. Note, however, that, some connection with Deuteronomy is retained and transformed in verse 6 ("over the sea") of Sirach's text. Paul's "descent to the abyss" departs in a marked way from any extant version of Deuteronomy, although Dunn remarks that "the possibility cannot be excluded that there was a text form" of this sort, now lost: James D. G. Dunn, *Romans 9–16,* WBC 38b (Dallas: Word, 1998), p. 606.

"the book of the covenant of the Most High" (24:23), not known fully by "the first man," i.e., Adam (24:28).

Paul, then, views the Deuteronomy texts not simply through the lens of Baruch and the general tradition of wisdom, but explicitly through Sirach. The canny reader, aware of these echoes, is supplied with various implied reasons for Paul's suppression of the quest (and questions) by Righteousness. Do not say in your heart, "Who will ascend and descend?" — because God's will is neither hard nor far away; because God's Wisdom/Torah is sought and found only by God, who has given her to his people; because Wisdom declares herself to be the esoteric visitor *par excellence,* who nonetheless prefers a humble tent among God's people to the vault of heavens or the mystique of the abyss. All these answers have been given in the context of wisdom passages which highlight God's initiating covenant, and so are apposite to Paul's concerns in Romans. As Jack Suggs argues, the (seeming) "tension between Gospel and Law [read *Torah*] is resolved by the identification of Christ with Wisdom-Torah."[12]

So far we have come only part of the way in tracing the impulse of apocalypses and the rabbinic mystics.[13] We go on to note that there are other significant ancient commentaries on Deuteronomy 30:11-14, notably several allusions to it in Philo[14] and a creative adaptation of the passage in the *Targum Neofiti.*[15] Philo, in *Post.* 84-85 parses Torah as "the good" and explains that it is near, not to be sought in heaven or on the other side of the sea; the targum speaks of the law as a nearby word that need not be sought by "another like Moses" who would ascend to heaven, nor by another "like Jonah" who would descend to the depths. With all this background we can conclude with Dunn that "Deut 30:11-14 was a subject of considerable reflection among Jews both in Palestine and the diaspora."[16]

However, is Dunn also correct to suggest that "a complete context" for our understanding has been provided, and to dismiss the suggestion by A. M. Goldberg[17] that Romans 10:6-7 is informed by a knowledge of apocalyptic mysticism? The following observations suggest not. In the first place, the characterization in the targum of "another like Moses" or "like Jonah" moves the identity of the "quester" away from an ineffable figure like Wisdom (cf. Sir 24) and implies that the rabbis were in fact responding to traditions about Moses

12. Suggs, "'The Word Is Near You,'" p. 311.

13. It is now generally accepted that wisdom was one of the tributaries that fed into these traditions, alongside prophecy.

14. See especially *Post.* 84-85, *Virt.* 183; *Mut.* 236-37; *Praem.* 80.

15. M. McNamara, *The New Testament and the Palestinian Targum to the Pentateuch* (AnBib 27A; Rome: Pontifical Biblical Institute, 1978), pp. 70-81.

16. Dunn, *Romans 9–16,* p. 604.

17. A. M. Goldberg, "Torah aus der Unterwelt? Eine Bemerkung zu Röm 10,6-7," *BZ* 14:1 (1970): 127-31.

and others following, or like him who would mediate transcendent realities. Attention has recently been called to the *Midr. Psalm* 68.19 by J. M. Scott in his discussion of another Pauline letter. That text preserves a tradition about Moses ascending and receiving the Torah as a "gift" for Israel, in a *Merkabah*-like encounter with God on Sinai.[18] If Moses, alongside other noteworthies such as Enoch, Ezra, and Ezekiel, was being viewed by some visionaries as a paradigmatic precursor of mystical "descent" to the chariot, then Goldberg's reading of the targumim is important.[19] The pertinent question is not what is "necessary" to provide "a complete context" for understanding Paul's strange departures from the Deuteronomy text. It is more a question of which traditions were actually current in Paul's day, and how the ascent and descent motifs might have been heard at that time.[20]

Perhaps Goldberg's arguments appeared too early to be taken seriously. Less than a decade later, however, scholars such as Ithamar Gruenwald[21] and Alan Segal[22] more extensively explored the close relationship between early rabbinic mysticism and the apocalypses, with Alan Segal presenting Paul as our sole concrete example[23] for the existence of a mystic tradition in the first century C.E.[24] These and other studies have continued to distinguish apocalypses

18. J. M. Scott, "The Triumph of God in 2 Cor 2:14," *NTS* 42 (1996): 270. See also later *hekhalot* texts, helpfully analyzed by Peter Schäfer in *The Hidden and Manifest God: Some Major Themes in Early Jewish Mysticism,* trans. Pomerance (Albany, N.Y.: SUNY, 1992). In some of these the adept calls upon the "Prince of the Face" in order to gain possession of the Torah.

19. Strangely, Dunn goes on in his commentary (p. 605) to link Romans 10:6b with "the desire of the ancients to explore the heavens and learn its secrets (by vision or heavenly journey)" and the polemic about this in John 3:13 and 6:62! He seems to be affirming instinctively what he has denied with regard to Goldberg's analysis.

20. Goldberg argues cogently that the *Neofiti Targum* (and also the *Fragment Targum*) on Deut 30 reflect underlying concepts of mystical ascent to the heavenlies and possibly even descent to the abyss — concepts which were important to mystical traditions, but dangerous in the eyes of some rabbis. Goldberg can adduce dubiously dated (3rd century C.E.?) references to heavenly ascent and theurgy (e.g., b. Hagiga 13a-15a), but must appeal to the frequent underworld journeys of the apocalypses (e.g., 1 Enoch 17:10-16) as background for the second half of the equation. On underworld journeys, see Martha Himmelfarb, *Tours of Hell: An Apocalyptic Form in Jewish and Christian Literature* (Philadelphia: University of Pennsylvania Press, 1984).

21. *Apocalyptic and Merkavah Mysticism* (Leiden: Brill, 1980).

22. *Two Powers in Heaven: Rabbinic Reports about Christianity and Gnosticism* (Leiden: Brill, 1977).

23. See especially *Paul the Convert: The Apostolate and Apostasy of Saul the Pharisee* (New Haven and London: Yale, 1990).

24. Recent scholarship has been rightly cautious in distinguishing between outright *Merkabah* texts and earlier expressions of mysticism. But see D. Dimant and J. Strugnell,

from early rabbinic mysticism as mentioned in the talmud and mishnah, because they are related to two different genres of literature, with disparate dating. Nevertheless, fewer and fewer scholars now characterize the visions represented in the apocalypses as wholly literary affairs; moreover, some Jewish mystical texts include apocalyptic elements or conform to the apocalypse genre (e.g., *Sefer Hekhaloth= 3 Enoch*). As Segal argues, both types of literature reflect "not unrelated experiences" although in the mystical tradition ecstatic "out of body" visions are more frequent, while in apocalypses bodily ascension followed by transformation is more common (e.g., 1 Enoch 14–15 and the probably later chapter 71, 3 Baruch 1, 2 Enoch 3, 7, 8, 11).[25] With the careful underpinning of such studies, and the proliferation of other analyses,[26] Goldberg's intuitions about the targumim's response to early mystical ascent (and possibly descent) traditions and their parallel reflection in Paul's thought find a stronger base. As he suggested, the targumim in question seem to be not merely employing a well-known *image* in their exposition of Deuteronomy, but displaying here a polemic tendency against apocalyptic or mystical practice.[27] Why might Paul not be doing the same in *his* exposition of this well-worn Deuteronomic text?

It is perhaps surprising that Segal's *Paul the Convert* does not treat Rom 10:6-7 in relation to esoteric experience alongside other Pauline texts such as 2 Corinthians 3–4 and 2 Corinthians 12. However, his omission is consonant with his particular aim: to establish Paul as a first-century mystic, an early instance of a developing tradition. Thus, he establishes Paul's ecstasy in *direct* relation to the paradigmatic biblical (e.g., Ezekiel and Daniel), apocalyptic *(1 Enoch, Apocalypse of Abraham, Ascension of Isaiah)*, and mystical material, al-

---

"The Merkavah Vision in Second Ezekiel (4Q385 3)," *RevQ* 14 (1990): 331-48 for a discussion of 4Q354 and *Merkabah*-like motifs in the late Hasmonean or even early Herodian ages.

25. That there was a complex relationship between mystical practice and the experiences implied by the apocalypses is demonstrated by the interesting ambivalence of a text not so far removed in time from Paul's day: 4 Ezra. In this late first-century-C.E. apocalypse, we note both a strong reserve toward esoteric journeys (4 Ezra 4:7-8) and an implied visit to the celestial Jerusalem (10:55). 4 Ezra also demonstrates that preparatory techniques for such experiences were not the preserve of the mystics alone, but find their way into the apocalypses (4 Ezra 3:1-2; 5:21; 6:35; 9:26-28). See also ch. 14, in which distinctions are made between the seer Ezra and his inspired scribes (who experience special illumination) and the people.

26. See, for example, David Halperin, *The Merkabah in Rabbinic Literature* (New Haven: American Oriental Society, 1980); Tryggve N. D. Mettinger, *The Dethronement of Sabaoth: Studies in the Shem and Kabod Theologies* (CBOT Series 18; Lund: Gleerup, 1982); Ira Chernus, *Mysticism in Rabbinic Judaism: Studies in the History of Midrash* (Berlin: de Gruyter, 1982); Peter Schäfer, "New Testament and Hekhalot Literature: The Journey into Heaven in Paul and Merkavah Mysticism," *JJS* 35 (1984): 19-35.

27. Goldberg, "Torah aus der Unterwelt?", p. 131.

though he does from time to time note "a special Christian cast."[28] Without detracting from the value of Segal's fine analysis, it seems important to highlight also the reserve with which Paul handles such experiences. This is most evident in 2 Corinthians 12, where Paul plays against, and not only with, the apocalyptic form,[29] refusing to give content to the vision, introducing a comic and diabolic *angelus interpres* ("a messenger from Satan, a thorn in the flesh"), spurning twice the fine distinctions of the mode of ascent ("whether in or out of the body, I don't know, God knows"), and using the entire episode, against its grain, as a stunning conclusion to his fool's speech. The final "unveiling" in all this is not an esoteric mystery, but rather the underlying message of Paul's gospel and a major theme of his correspondence to the Corinthians — that God's strength is made perfect in weakness.

In 2 Corinthians 3–4, Paul's point is more subtle, as is his imagery. I perceive here, in concert with Segal, Ezekiel-like language, imagery, and experience. Ezekiel, in his epiphany, beheld an exceptional vision of "the appearance *of* the likeness *of* the glory *of* God" (1:28): his language carefully distances the seer from the God whom no one can see and live. Paul, in speaking of the common sight of believers, also uses a string of linked terms: "For God, who said, 'Let light shine out of darkness,' made his light shine in our hearts, to give us the light *of* the knowledge *of* the glory *of* God in the face of Christ."[30] It seems, however, that Paul has reversed the direction or the impact of the mystical sequence. That is, the *light* of the *knowledge* of the *glory* of God are not distancing, but *approaching* terms; Paul clinches his anti-esoteric stance in insisting that the epiphany is commonly seen "in the face of Christ" and understood in "our hearts" (ἐν ταῖς καρδίαις ἡμῶν, 2 Cor 4:6).[31]

By oblique reference to Ezekiel (along with the direct reference to Moses) Paul evokes the same awesome presence of the LORD. Segal is probably also correct that Paul's choice of terminology reflects his own visionary experiences, to which he will later testify (reluctantly) in the letter; yet, the thrust of Paul's polemic is to emphasize neither the ineffability of revelation, nor his special apostolic privilege. Rather, he underscores the intimacy of the dwelling of the glory (now identified with Jesus and the Spirit) with all of God's people. Something has happened so that the light of the knowledge of the glory of God has been

28. Segal, *Paul the Convert*, p. 38.

29. See my analysis in "'I Saw Satan Fall . . .' — The Rhetoric of Vision," pp. 75-88.

30. Interestingly, Paul includes not only the typical *merkabah* themes of mysticism, but also the *bereshit* themes, implying a new creation.

31. That this is *not* a royal or apostolic "we" is clear from Paul's argument, which extends the transformation attendant upon this vision to "us all" (2 Cor 3:18) and which distinguishes between those whose eyes are veiled and those for whom the veil has been removed.

brought near in the face of Christ; that same glory, says Paul, is still vibrantly present to the whole community through the Holy Spirit (2 Cor 3:17). Segal recognizes this dynamic without emphasizing the reserve of Paul in using his own ecstatic visions as authoritative proof for this new state of affairs:

> [Paul's] point is that some Christian believers also make such an ascent and that its effects are more permanent than the vision that Moses received. The church has witnessed a theophany as important as the one vouchsafed to Moses, but the Christian theophany is greater still, as Paul himself has experienced.[32]

However, in the light of Paul's reticence, it seems more accurate to reverse Segal's statement: Paul's point is that the church has witnessed a theophany greater (and more intimate) than that of Moses, and that some, like Paul, have done so through ecstasy, but all are *together* promised the resultant transformation.[33]

With these wisdom, apocalyptic, and mystical traditions as background, and with Paul's own reserved testimony to visionary experience in place, we may now return to Romans 10 and tease out Paul's purpose in referring to ascent and descent. Given the witness to ascents in the apocalypses, some rabbinic literature, and Paul's own letter to the Corinthians, and the more muted witness to descents in the apocalypses and in the targumim, it is highly unlikely that Paul would allude to these matters solely as a matter of literary convention. It is far more likely that Romans 10:6-7 presents Paul's most extreme statement of reserve concerning the glorification of visionary privilege. Such a treatment differs from his ironic self-reference in 2 Corinthians, but is consonant with his characteristic ambivalence concerning such matters. It is not exactly, as Goldberg suggests, that Paul mirrors the absolute proscription of some rabbis against these endeavors; rather, the quests and their significance are strongly relativized by Paul's greatest mystery, a mystery which concerns God's people and whose content and mediator is Jesus the Christ.

32. Segal, *Paul the Convert,* 60.

33. Note also the emphasis upon *suspect* transformation in 2 Cor 11:13-15 as Paul moves into the polemic conclusion of his "boasting" section. The super-apostles claim to be μετασχηματιζόμενοι (2 Cor 11:13), just as Satan "transforms himself into an angel of light" (!) — and are thus "transformed" into seeming "ministers of righteousness." They will, ironically, be judged on the basis of their works (works that include apocalyptic exploits?; cf. 12:11-12) — presumably because this is the apt fulfillment *(telos)* of what they have emphasized in their pursuit of righteousness.

II. The Ascent/Descent Quest Denied within the Argument of Romans 9:30–10:21

The centrality of christology to Paul's argument becomes apparent when we place verses 6 and 7 within their immediate context. Not all have agreed with such an emphasis. Dunn insists that Paul's concern in Romans 10 is "not so much christological as soteriological, or salvation-historical";[34] Richard Hays has argued similarly that Paul's interpretations of the Old Testament here and elsewhere should be understood as "ecclesiocentric" rather than "christocentric,"[35] but has since qualified this remark.[36] The cautionary remarks of Dunn and Hays are helpful as a response to the charge that Paul is arbitrary in his exegesis of the Old Testament texts, prooftexting in order to make his christological claims.[37] Nonetheless, an analysis of the rhetoric of Romans 9:30–10:21 shows the centrality of Christ's role to Paul's thought, including his reading of the Old Testament.

By the time we come to this part of Paul's argument, he has already given ample indication of the centrality of Christ Jesus in his exposition of the gospel which reveals the "righteousness of God . . . from faith to faith" (1:16-17). His particular concern in chapters 9–11 is no excursus, but deals with an apparent and significant difficulty in understanding God's faithfulness, that is, the seeming failure of God's plan in relation to Israel. Chapter 9:1-29 has already laid out his thesis (9:6: "It is not as though God's word had failed"), and moved toward answering the problem by highlighting God's covenant with Israel (which culminates in the Christ, 9:5), by setting forth the theme of a remnant (9:6-18, 27-29) and by emphasizing God's surprising mercy toward the Gentiles (vv. 19-26). However, in order to demonstrate God's justice, Paul needs to establish clearly how his readers are to view the present circumstances of Israel's stumbling. In verses 30-31, Paul thus lays down two secondary propositions which have been intimated by these preliminary arguments of 9:1-29: "What are we to say? *Gentiles,* who did not strive for righteousness have attained it . . . but *Israel,* who did strive for righteousness . . . did not apprehend it." He then proceeds to explain why this is so.

34. Dunn, *Romans 9–16,* p. 605.

35. Hays, *Echoes,* pp. 84-87.

36. Hays, "On the Rebound: A Response to Critiques of *Echoes of Scripture in the Letters of Paul,*" in C. A. Evans and J. A. Sanders (eds.), *Paul and the Scriptures of Israel* (JSNTSupp 83; Sheffield: JSOT, 1992), pp. 77-78 and "Three Dramatic Roles: The Law in Romans 3–4," in James D. Dunn (ed.), *Paul and the Mosaic Law* (Tübingen: Mohr, 1996), pp. 151-64, esp. p. 160.

37. See, for example, the remarks of M. Black regarding Romans 10 in "The Christological Use of the Old Testament in the New Testament," *NTS* 18:1 (1971): "The Old Testament text serves as little more than a scriptural base for christological doctrine" (p. 9).

Although it will become apparent that Paul does not conform strictly here to the methods of Graeco-Roman classical rhetoric, comparison of 9:31–10:13 with the "complete argument" is helpful, for it demonstrates that Paul's thought is not simply circular, nor resting on the sheer force of assertion.[38] While the rhetoric is complicated by circular clarifications and enriched by subtle allusions, it is nevertheless carefully directed. We begin by noting that Paul's summary (9:30-31) of his introductory argument (9:1-29) functions as a *double* proposition: grace has been given to the Gentiles, while frustration has been the experience of Israel. This observation gives rise to the following flow of argument:

I. *Introduction:* rhetorical question, "What then shall we say?" (9:30a)
II. *Double Proposition:* (9:30b-31)
   A. The Gentiles who did not seek righteousness attained it. (30b)
   B. Israel who sought it did not. (31)
III. *Rationale:* (9:32-33) *"for"* Israel sought it the wrong way and predictably stumbled.

It is surprising, but in line with the general theme of the section, that Paul, at this point in the rationale, only pursues his second proposition, that is, Israel's frustration, without yet giving a reason for the "success" of the Gentiles. Moreover, he also interrupts the argument with an impassioned reflection on Israel's failure. This hiatus, along with the introductory remarks to the larger section (i.e., 9:1-3), might seem to be for the purposes of establishing *ethos:* Is Paul baring his heart in order to connect with the reader? Rather, Paul may well be intending to model what ought to be the faithful response to this stumbling of Israel: godly (i.e., Mosaic)[39] grief and prayer. This is a subtle foreshadowing of an important subtheme that will be sounded later in Paul's argument, as he chastises his (mostly Gentile?) readers for their arrogance and lack of concern for Israel (11:17-25). As such, the present reflection on Israel adds a deliberative flavor to what is more properly part of a judicial argument about God's righteousness. Yet even this parenthesis is not tangential to Paul's overall rhetoric: he is about to expound the antipathy of righteousness to arrogance of any sort, and so here embodies in his response to Israel's plight the very faithfulness and humility of which he will speak.

38. *Pace* Hays, *Echoes,* p. 82.

39. I am indebted to Terry Donaldson for pointing out in conversation that this Mosaic stance is consonant with the righteousness of faith. Paul thus stands in contrast to Mosaic pretenders in pursuit of ecstatically induced transformation and privileged inclusion ("righteousness").

Paul resumes his rationale in 10:3, answering more fully to proposition B, and distinguishing between God's righteousness and Israel's ignorance of this. He explains Israel's pursuit of righteousness by works as a search for her "own" righteousness and an ignorance of God's purposes. Torah itself was truly a Torah "of righteousness" which both marked out the covenant people and proceeded from the God of righteousness (9:31); but Israel's search, "as if it were works" (9:32) and in order to establish a righteousness peculiar to herself,[40] has caused her to stumble. Paul then provides the substantive reason (10:4) for Propositions A and B, a statement that is introduced as the rationale for this line of thought, but which finally makes explicit the major premise that has remained unstated.

> *Reason:*
> Answering to Proposition B,
>> "*for* **they** were ignorant of God's righteousness, seeking to establish their own"
>
> Answering to *both* propositions:
>> "*for* Christ is the fulfillment/end of the law, for righteousness to **all** who believe"

The underlying major premise, then, which explains Israel's ignorance of God's righteousness, is that *Christ* is the righteousness of God, both the goal toward which Torah was pointing and the unequivocal end of any misplaced search not proceeding from a confidence in God's own righteousness. It seems probable, then, that those like N. T. Wright who see Israel's "stumbling stone" as *both* the Torah and Christ[41] are correct. Those in Israel who have sought the Torah of righteousness "as if out of works" are unlikely to recognize that Christ is "the fulfillment of the Torah," for they have been seeking to establish a righteousness unique to themselves — that is, a national privilege — and have not recognized the righteousness of God. It is at this point that Paul brings together his two propositions, joining the unsought "success" of the Gentiles and the stumbling of Israel into one proposition, in 10:4. Linking together what Paul has said in 9:31-33 with his interjection of sorrow for Israel at 10:1-3, and with the explanation he now supplies (10:4), we see two complementary ideas. First, the Torah of righteousness was a suitable object of pursuit up until the coming of Christ, *but it had to be sought as if by faith,* and not by "works," because it was *God's* gift of righteousness, not a covenant membership to be established as Israel's own *by means of* observing its boundary markers. But, secondly, *it is futile*

40. Wright, *Climax,* pp. 242ff.
41. Wright, *Climax,* pp. 240-42.

now to search either for evidence of God's faithfulness or for the means to establish a covenant relationship with God. Why? *Because God's righteousness,* toward which the Torah was always pointing, has been openly demonstrated in Jesus Christ, *for righteousness to all who believe.* This yields the following double-headed argument, which focuses on God's righteousness but which entails the righteousness of his people:

> *Introduction:*
>
> *What then shall we say?* (That God is unjust? No, rather . . .)
>
> *Proposition:*
>
> *His righteousness* is not something to be sought out (as seen in the unexpected "success" of the Gentiles and in the stumbling of Israel)
>
> *Reason:*
>
> *Because* Christ is the fulfillment/end of the Torah *for righteousness* to all believing ones.

Paul then goes on to amplify his arguments, giving analogies, examples, citations, and the conclusion of his argument. Many[42] have been convinced that verses 5 and 6 are to be played off against each other, with a strong contrast intended between Moses' written words regarding "righteousness out of the law" and the spoken words of "Righteousness out of faith."[43] We might, in fact, expect such a contrast within the logical progression, given that the "opposite" or "contrary" is usually presented at this point in an elaborated thesis. However, Paul's thesis does not concern *legalistic* works, and so he is unlikely to cite Moses here as a negative example. In fact, he has just recently characterized the Torah in connection with righteousness (9:31) and does not introduce verse 5 as any sort of *contender* to the righteousness of God about which he has been speaking. Verse 5 does not present itself as a radical contrast to the following verses.

Rather, verses 5-7 are to be seen together as an explanation of his statement in verse 4, that Christ is the *telos* of the law. In this way, verse 5 becomes a clear illustration of Paul's initial statement that the righteousness of God is witnessed to in the law and the prophets (Rom 3:21), and verses 6-8 fill in the meaning of that righteousness, that is, *what it means to do these things and so live by them.* The amplification is given both positively and negatively: the ascent/descent motif rejects a futile and redundant activity that will not lead to

42. See especially Dunn, p. 602, and Stephen Westerholm, "Paul and the Law in Romans 9–11," in *Paul and the Mosaic Law,* pp. 215-38, esp. p. 231.

43. See especially Ernst Käsemann, "The Spirit and the Letter," in *Perspectives on Paul* (1969; Philadelphia: Fortress, 1971), p. 157.

life; the final words of Righteousness explain what is left to be "done," since all has already been spoken and done — what remains is the human confession of a near word from the lips and the holding of the near word in the heart (v. 8). Paul extends his argument into a concrete example, enjoining the readers to embrace his redefinition of "doing these things"[44] — confessing Jesus with the mouth and believing in the heart (vv. 9-10). Finally, he cites Scripture to indicate that anyone who does so shall not be ashamed, and concludes with his major and minor premises: Jesus is Lord and there is no distinction in his mode of faithfulness to either Jew or Gentile.

What emerges from this analysis is a rhetorical line with the following sequence:

Introduction, 9:30:
 What then shall we say? (That God is unjust? No, rather . . .)
Proposition, 9:30–10:3:
 His righteousness is not to be sought out, by Israelite or Gentile.
Reason, 10:4:
 Because Christ is the end of Torah, for righteousness to all believing ones.
Extended Analogy with Its Contrary:
 v. 5 Moses on righteousness: "you shall live by doing them"
 vv. 6-8 Righteousness says: doing them means not to quest *(contrary).*
 Righteousness says: doing them means to trust the word on lips and in heart.
Example, vv. 9-10:
 Therefore, you "do": confess and believe in Jesus/God.
Citation, v. 11:
 "No one who believes in him will be put to shame."
Conclusion, vv. 12-13:
 There is no difference between Jew and Greek.
 Jesus is Lord and "rich" (more than just) to all for salvation.

It is always in the area of explanation that Paul's christological emphasis is evident. The reason for his proposition is the relationship of Christ to Torah; the analogy intimates (perhaps humorously)[45] the past unique exploits of Christ; the example is centered around the confession of Christ; and the conclusion

44. It is not necessary to follow those who champion the omission of αὐτά and read αὐτῇ instead of αὐτοῖς; cf. Käsemann, Cranfield, and the RSV translation.

45. Hays, *Echoes,* p. 79.

transmutes the question of the justice of God into the generosity of the "Lord" who has been named. Paul's underlying question, in the light of God's covenant with Israel and with those who believe, is the problem of theodicy; the answers are given on the basis of a christological confession, that is, Paul's gospel. It is that word which is near to Paul's mouth and in his heart, and which is at hand to answer the explicit questions he has been asking.

Some have gone on to assume that chapter 10 largely emphasizes *human* confession and proclamation of the gospel, with verse 10 as the climax, and the ensuing verses, 14-18, as the result of this activity. But this is not likely, considering the manner in which Paul circles back to his major question about the justice and generosity of God in verses 19-21. The linked verses (14-17) dealing with the proclamation of the gospel are intimately connected with the issue of God's loving overtures to his people. Moreover, they focus upon the *rhēma* of Christ (17), the same *rhēma* which has been proclaimed to be "near" by the "Righteousness from faith," because Christ neither needs to be brought down nor up from the dead.

While it is not customary to speak of Jesus himself as *rhēma,* we need to give special attention to the implications of the story line of 10:6-7. What is *not* to be sought because it is near (the Torah, or wisdom) here gives way to Jesus, who is not to be sought. Christ, the unsought subject, merges with *rhēma,* the near gift, and so we are perhaps to think of the actual content of the word, Jesus himself, as taking precedence even over the human proclamation of the gospel. At the very least, *rhēma* is here ambiguous. After all, Wisdom proceeded from the mouth of God, and quested through heaven and the abyss to find her dwelling, just as (according to Paul's gospel) the "wisdom of God," Christ Jesus, has come to be near (Phil 2:5-11; 1 Cor 1:30; 2:1-13). Moreover, there is a strange kink in the link of Paul's chain at the end of verse 17: "faith comes from what is heard, and what is heard comes *through the word of Christ* [*alt:* God]." Why add this redundant agency, if "what is heard" *is* the *rhēma* about Christ — unless, of course, the alternate sources are instinctively right in their emendations ("word of God"), and the "word" is also to be identified with Christ himself?

Richard Hays, in contrasting Paul's hermeneutic with that of later rabbis, suggests, "for Paul the Word of God is Jesus Christ as experienced in the Spirit-filled Christian community. . . . Paul gains leverage on the [Deuteronomic] text by claiming immediate revelatory illumination."[46] This is very near the mark, except that Paul does not claim that this "immediate" illumination is peculiar to him; rather, it is shared by the whole community of God, because the "Word" has been brought down by God, and because he has come up triumphant from

46. Hays, *Echoes,* p. 4.

the abyss.[47] No ascent is necessary, for One has already been vindicated; nor do judgment and death present an insurmountable danger, since the abyss has already been plumbed. To claim, along with the Righteousness from faith, that there is no pursuit left to make is to severely radicalize any quest for a righteousness specific to Israel — and this would include the kind of separatist tendencies of "the wise" or visionaries who seem to have expected transformation as a result of what they had seen. Paul's "word," then, contrasts strongly with God's closing injunction to "Ezra" regarding the distinction between the Tanakh and the esoteric books:

> Make public the twenty-four books that you wrote first and let the worthy and unworthy read them. But keep the seventy that were written last, in order to give them to the wise among your people, for in them is the spring of understanding, the fountain of wisdom and the river of knowledge. (4 Ezra 14:45-47)

There is no special transformation for the wise, that they may seek it or have it mediated by a confidante especially privy to God's mysteries, for now the One who has been vindicated and has challenged death is more than near to the whole community.[48]

III. Complexity in Paul: Complementary Modes of Argument and Context

It will be apparent to the discerning reader that I have had to work reasonably hard to extract a direct line of argument from Paul's own richly connotative images and arguments. Paul's circling method and constant return to themes, his arguments within arguments for the purposes of explication, and his subtle reading of Old Testament texts through the lens of other traditions means that the reader may at times be tempted to leave the main line of his argument and go off on intriguing tangents — for example, the implied practices of mystics and apocalyptic visionaries. At other times, it is the implicit point, the one which is suggested and which must be inferred, which discloses what is essen-

47. *Pace* Dunn and others, the inference of the incarnation seems unavoidable in 10:6, and it seems likely that the irony of verse 7 is complete if we are meant to envisage Christ not as "led," but leading others from the realm of the dead (cf. Eph 4:8).

48. Against this tendency, see again the drive in other "questing" apocalypses (e.g., *1 Enoch, Ascension of Isaiah 6–11, Apocalypse of Paul*), which set apart the seers and which in the transformation of these noteworthies literalize Daniel's vision that "the wise shall shine like stars."

tial to Paul's meaning — in Romans 10:6-7, the unspoken story of the Christ's own questing.

We began by noting that scholars such as Hays and Wright have drawn attention to the allusive and poetic nature of Paul's work. This is indeed most apparent in his creative adaptation of the Deuteronomic text, which is prefaced by 10:4 and leads to 10:9, 12-13, declarative statements on the significance of Jesus the Christ, the fulfillment of the Torah, and the beneficent Lord of both Israel and Gentiles. Yet Paul's argument does not rest squarely on assertion: he has already by the end of chapter 8 established the centrality of Jesus as demonstrating God's righteousness. Chapters 9–11 deal with a crucial subset of this same theme, employing declarative argument and disclosing allusion to lead the reader to evaluate various "searches" for righteousness (including esoteric questing) in the light of God's definitive act. The very allusiveness of Paul's argumentation in 10:6-7, and its christocentric parsing, discourage (in concert with Righteousness) a serious deviation from the rhetorical path.

What is not immediately apparent in this analysis, however, is why the esoteric would be of interest to those whom Paul was addressing. The opaque nature of the letter to the Romans is well known; it is not like reading the correspondence to the Corinthians, which at least gives us some teasing intimations of actual interest in "mystery," "knowledge," and spiritual exploits. Romans is a far more difficult case. Let us see the letter, however, not simply as general circular (though it may have become circular) but as integrally connected to the particulars illuminated in chapter 15 — Paul's coming journey to Jerusalem, and his plans to use Rome as a base of operations for a westward mission. In this case, the attitude of the Roman church toward Israel is critical, as confirmed by his correction of anti-Israel sentiments in chapters 9–11. Suggs sketches a suggestive portrait of the situation in Rome which coheres nicely with our reading of Paul's purposes in chapter 10. In Suggs's view, "the time leading up to the visit has not been characterized by peace."[49] Chapter 15, coupled with the warnings against Gentile arrogance in chapters 10–11, confirms at least in part Suggs's highlighting of the "persistent problems associated with Jew-Gentile, Gospel-Law tensions."[50] It is not necessary to accentuate these tensions, as does Suggs, nor to extend them so as to include a sharp division between Jewish Christian and Gentile Christian, in order to perceive a driving force behind Paul's careful explanations and polemic. That there was a danger of the gospel being misunderstood as an attack on Torah, that there were some in Jerusalem who were suspicious of practical and doctrinal tendencies in the diaspora congregations, that there might be some in the diaspora who har-

49. Suggs, "'The Word Is Near You,'" p. 311.
50. Suggs, "'The Word Is Near You,'" p. 311.

bored (to speak anachronistically) proto-"Marcionite" tendencies — all this would present a threat to the apostle, whose gospel mystery declared the fulfillment of God's holy Torah in Jesus, and the unequivocal unity of Jew and Gentile through the Christ.

Paul, then, is driven to clarify his understanding of the Law and Israel in such a way that "the unity symbolized by the offering is protected from Jewish animosities and Jewish-Christian suspicions."[51] Some of Paul's congregations were indeed characterized by party spirit, aggrandizement of τῶν ὑπερλίαν ἀποστόλων based on their particular exploits, and an extreme interest in ecstasy and the visionary (as the Corinthian correspondence indicates). Among the points of contention, then, may well have been the suspicion among some Jews that Gentile churches were putting away God's decorous and Israel-shaped revelation of his will and his nature for exuberant and idiosyncratic experiences. Paul does not have to bear witness against his own visions to grant common ground here. For he is in agreement with the reserve of those rabbis who downplayed or even sanctioned the drive to probe mysteries:

> Whoever gives his mind to four things it were better for him if he had not come into the world — what is above? what is beneath? and what was beforetime? and what will be hereafter? And whosoever takes no thought for the honor of his Maker, it were better for him if he had not come into the world. (m. Hag 2.1)[52]

Typically, however, Paul gives his own christologically shaped reason alongside the more general argument that "the Torah had already been given in Zion."[53] What the rabbis say of the Torah, Paul can say of Christ. Yet Paul's understand-

51. Suggs, "'The Word Is Near You,'" p. 311.

52. *The Mishnah,* trans. H. Danby (London: Oxford University Press, 1938), p. 213. Admittedly this is a later text, but nevertheless one that represents a particular view of some rabbis with regard to the esoteric, and seems to have become the mainstream or majority position, with time. Moreover, (if we argue from silence) this discomfiture with mystery may well represent the view of those who were instrumental in shaping the "canon" of both Jewish and Christian communities, since each collection includes only one outright "apocalypse" and both of these are rather tame in comparison to other noncanonical examples of the literature. We might add that in the Eastern Orthodox community even the Johannine Apocalypse is not read liturgically, presumably for fear of misappropriation, but incorporated into the acts of liturgy. This renders it a public document, without suggesting that the seer's particular experience is to be sought by others — precisely the effect traced in Paul's subtle treatment of such matters in 2 Cor.

53. See Hays's discussion of Baba Mesia 59b (*Echoes,* pp. 2ff.), which exegetes Deut 30 in a different manner from that of Paul. While agreeing that there is a marked contrast, I clearly draw the contours somewhat differently.

ing of the Spirit leads him not to reject transcendent experience totally, only to qualify its importance with regard to covenant membership (δικαιοσύνη).

The persistent theme of transformation in apocalypses suggest that visionaries sometimes quested not simply out of sheer intrigue (a perilous enough pursuit, in the eyes of some coreligionists), but even in pursuit of angelic-like transfiguration. Such activities, understood by other rabbis as impious, would have been seen by Paul as just another mode of searching ἐξ ἔργων to establish a "peculiar righteousness." If his own congregants held such pursuits in high regard, then they too had missed the boat. To search mystically for further confirmation of their standing in Christ would mean not to acknowledge that the critical quest had already been undertaken by the Anointed. Paul, faced with a Judaism whose zeal for God (10:2) led its rabbis not only to zeal for Torah but to flights of mystical experience and apocalyptic speculation, offers instead Christ, the τέλος νόμου and τέλος ἀποκαλύψεως — the end and fulfillment of the law, and the fulfillment (but perhaps not the very end) of apocalyptic spirituality. In so doing, he adds his witness to the *rhēma* of the one who in his coming, death, and resurrection demonstrated and enacted God's righteousness in the sight of all people, thus providing a light for *apokalypsis* to the Gentiles, and the glory of God's people, Israel.

Romans 13:1-7 and Paul's Missiological Perspective: A Call to Political Quietism or Transformation?

Philip H. Towner

Romans 13:1-7 continues to play an important role in modern discussions of the relationship of the church to the state. Seeking to address the related questions, numerous studies have examined the passage from various perspectives. Most of these have wrestled with the details of the passage — the identity of the ruling powers, the meaning of the phrase "bearing the sword," the structure of the argument — or have attempted to reconstruct the historical background in hopes of shedding light on the original intention of the instruction and its enduring relevance.[1] Such efforts are of course essential to an understanding of the teaching. Whether it is urged that the teaching is historically conditioned and therefore applicable only to the first-century situation, or universally applicable throughout the ages, on the whole the teaching is considered to be conservative, and to enjoin believers to adopt a posture of political quietism and/or social conformity.[2] However, there is a radical, subversive edge

1. See the bibliography in J. A. Fitzmyer, *Romans: A New Translation with Introduction and Commentary,* AB 33 (New York: Doubleday, 1993), pp. 671-76.

2. See N. Elliott, *Liberating Paul: The Justice of God and the Politics of the Apostle* (Maryknoll, N.Y.: Orbis, 1994), pp. 214-26; E. Schüssler Fiorenza, *Bread Not Stone: The Challenge of Feminist Biblical Interpretation* (Boston: Beacon Press, 1984/95), p. 72; J. D. G. Dunn,

to the instruction that has not received sufficient attention. To bring this to light requires an approach to the passage that is somewhat different from previous studies. As B. W. Winter points out, in addition to analyzing the details mentioned above, it is equally important to locate the teaching within its cultural milieu.[3] Yet the didactic function and meaning of the passage depends equally on its theological antecedents and literary character. The hypothesis of this study is that the fundamental intention of this parenesis lies submerged in a conceptual pool in which theological, literary, and cultural currents intersect. I shall try to show that the influence of these currents on the passage corresponds to key Pauline emphases, and that the interplay of these currents creates the deeper sense of the passage.

The study will proceed in three main steps. First, I will consider the overall thrust of Romans and particularly the missiological dimension of its message. Second, I will explore some controlling themes of the ethical section of the letter in which 13:1-7 is situated. These two stages will prepare the way for an investigation of the parenesis from the literary, theological, and cultural perspectives.[4]

I. Romans and Paul's Missionary Intentions

As is true of all Paul's letters, Romans has more than one purpose.[5] The point of the present discussion is not to settle all debate about this, but rather to extract from the ongoing discussion some of the less controversial conclusions about the intentions of Paul in writing this letter. To begin, structural and thematic features unify the major part of the letter; the two passages, 1:8-16a and 15:14-33, which each describe Paul's intention to travel to Rome and beyond in pur-

"Romans 13:1-7 — A Charter for Political Quietism?" *Ex Auditu* 2 (1986): 55-68; J. Friedrich, W. Pöhlmann, and P. Stuhlmacher, "Zur historischen Situation und Intention von Röm 13,1-7," *ZTK* 73.2 (1976): 131-66.

3. B. W. Winter, *Seek the Welfare of the City: Christians as Benefactors and Citizens* (Grand Rapids: Eerdmans, 1994), pp. 4-5.

4. It is a privilege to contribute to this volume in honor of Gordon Fee. My piece is offered in gratitude for his friendship and partnership, as well as for the model of responsible Christian scholarship he has represented. Although I am certain that he will not agree with all of my conclusions, I feel confident that he will appreciate the desire to integrate the various aspects of Pauline teaching in a way that does justice to the apostle's eschatological awareness and his related zeal to reach the world for Christ and to transform outmoded and divisive structures.

5. See A. J. M. Wedderburn, *The Reasons for Romans* (Edinburgh: T. & T. Clark, 1988); K. P. Donfried (ed.), *The Romans Debate: Revised and Expanded Edition* (Peabody, Mass.: Hendrickson, 1991).

suit of his mission to the Gentiles, form brackets around the long section 1:8–15:33. Within this unity J. D. G. Dunn has identified three purposes — missionary, apologetic, and pastoral — that complement one another and form a whole.[6] We will see that their interrelation establishes the parameters of the Pauline mission within which 13:1-7 must be interpreted.

Romans undoubtedly represents Paul's mature thinking about his unique calling and message. The driving force of Paul's ministry is the impulse to reach the Gentile world with his gospel. He thus characterizes himself as the apostle to the Gentiles (cf. 15:16-22) and understands his ministry to be integral to the goal of bringing the "full number" of Gentiles to faith (11:25). This calling incorporates ministry to both Jews and Gentiles (1:16; chs. 9–11, etc.). As his ministry unfolded and his missionary praxis developed, Paul's unique vision of God's people as a single "body" of Messiah's followers in which ethnic barriers (Jew/Gentile) had been transcended became ever clearer.[7] His letters show that this vision was not easily realized in the churches he planted; yet his persistence in setting this goal before the churches confirms further that the missionary impulse determined the directions and motives of Paul's life.

Paul's desire to visit Rome must be linked to his mission plans. This link is clearly visible in 15:24: ". . . I hope to see you on my journey [to Spain] and to be sent on by you, once I have enjoyed your company for a little while" (NRSV; cf. 1:10-13). Although Paul believes that he and the Roman Christians have much to learn from one another, he seems rather to conceive of Rome as a staging area for his next thrust westward. If R. Riesner is correct,[8] Paul's geographical sketch of the mission in 15:16-28 forges a link to the prophetic pattern enunciated in Isaiah 66:18-21, a link which is further underscored with explicit OT quotations (e.g., 15:9 [Ps 17:50], 10 [Deut 32:43], 11 [Ps 117:1], 12 [Isa 11:10]). Such literary devices in Romans combine to disclose a view of present mission activity which is the specific outworking of God's universal scheme of grace. The missionary interest in Romans is clearly intrinsic to the writing of the letter and to Paul's purpose in visiting Rome. But what relation does this bear to other concerns in the letter?

The long exposition of the gospel that follows the programmatic announcement of 1:16-17 is generally explanatory ("apologetic," Dunn) in func-

6. J. D. G. Dunn, *Romans 1–8,* WBC 38a (Dallas: Word, 1988), pp. liv-lviii.

7. See P. H. Towner, "Mission Practice and Theology under Construction (Acts 18–20)," in *Witness to the Gospel: The Theology of Acts,* eds. I. H. Marshall and D. Peterson (Grand Rapids: Eerdmans, 1998), pp. 417-36.

8. R. Riesner, *Die Früzeit des Apostels Paulus,* WUNT 71 (Tübingen: J. C. B. Mohr [Siebeck], 1994), pp. 216-27.

tion. In view of his travel plans, this exposition would have served several purposes: (a) It would encourage the acceptance of his mission in Rome, thus ensuring the assistance and support of the church necessary to take his mission to Spain. (b) It would foster supportive feelings among Roman believers for his upcoming trip to Jerusalem (15:25-27, 30-32). (c) It would also allow Paul to clear up some misconceptions that had arisen regarding his gospel or its implications (3:8). But as the argument of the letter is viewed as a whole, the exposition of the universal gospel of salvation to Jews and Gentiles (1:16b–11:36) is designed primarily to lay the theological basis for the extended parenesis of 12:1–15:13.[9]

The third main purpose — the pastoral purpose — unfolds in this latter section (12:1–15:13). Here Paul takes up various matters related to church stability, but at the center of it all is the Jew-Gentile question and the challenge it poses to Christian unity in Rome. The body metaphor (12:4) which stems from this debate provides the general starting point for the entire parenesis section that will argue for a unity which also embraces diversity.[10] The specific concerns of 14:1–15:13 reflect tensions that run along ethnic lines. Paul's personal knowledge of people in the Roman house churches seems apparent from chapter 16, so that the argument sometimes proposed that 12:1–15:6 is general parenesis with no specific relevance to the Roman situation can be set aside.[11] Furthermore, the theme of Jew/Gentile unity is so clearly the pastoral corollary to the theological exposition which has preceded it that the link between the two sections must be a substantial one (see further below).

These three purposes — missionary, explanatory, pastoral — are interrelated. Dunn's proposal is useful, and I adapt it here: Paul's missionary vision is by no means simply a matter of geography, as if the simple proclamation of the message in Spain will mean the mission's fulfillment. Rather, for Paul the goal was the realization of God's eschatological promises concerning Gentiles and Jews in the formation of a new people of God without ethnic division. The pastoral section presses for this realization within the practical contours of the Roman situation. Until the "body" nature of the church was understood and implemented, Paul's mission could not be regarded as finished. Thus the missionary purpose relates directly to the explanatory, which articulates the

9. Cf. Dunn, *Romans 1–8,* p. lxii.

10. But see G. D. Fee, *God's Empowering Presence: The Holy Spirit in the Letters of Paul* (Peabody, Mass.: Hendrickson, 1994), p. 605, who argues that gifting for ministry is a more dominant concern than unity (in contrast to 1 Cor 12).

11. For the "general parenesis" argument in its various forms, see R. J. Karris, "Romans 14:1–15:13 and the Occasion of Romans," in K. P. Donfried (ed.), *The Romans Debate* (Peabody, Mass.: Hendrickson, 1991), pp. 65-84.

theological basis for the mutual acceptance of Jews and Gentiles, and it relates directly to the pastoral appeal, which applies the theology in the practical setting. In all of this, one expected outcome of these three purposes for Paul's projected ministry should not be overlooked, namely, that a unified and stable Christian community would make a much better base from which to reach Spain than a church plagued by internal disruption. Yet in the convergence of these purposes, Paul also envisaged the Roman congregations' own responsibility within God's missiological program. The parenesis of 13:1-7 addresses this responsibility.

II. The Purpose of 12:1–15:13 in Paul's Strategy: Unity in the Church, and Stability in Society

13:1-7 is a short didactic paragraph within a broader section of parenesis, 12:1–15:13. It will be useful to observe its place within the larger context and among the various currents of interest at play in the section. These interests move in two directions: behavior among believers in the church (private or communal ethics) and behavior among unbelievers in the world (public ethics). 13:1-7 belongs principally to the latter category, but since Paul's approach to both spheres of behavior is intrinsically (though differently) linked to God's universal plan of salvation, and since the themes employed overlap, I will begin by summarizing Paul's treatment of the first category.

The Jew/Gentile issue, and tensions arising from it, provides the background to much of the material in 12:1–15:13. The transition from theology to parenesis in 12:1 continues to develop Paul's thinking about the Jew-Gentile issue, only now in terms of its outworking in community life within the church and in society. For the moment, I will pass over the opening exhortation of 12:1-2. From 12:4 onward the "body of Christ" is depicted as a unity that incorporates diversity ("one body/many members") as the hoped-for resolution of the Jew-Gentile issue. It is precisely this issue that Paul addressed in the closing quotations of the OT in 15:9-12 (LXX Ps 15:50; 2 Sam 22:50; Deut 32:43; Ps 117:1; Isa 11:10) and in the elaboration of his ministry to the Gentiles in 15:15-21 (citing Isa 52:15). The model is set up in chapter 12, while the practical circumstances needing to be overcome are addressed in chapters 14–15.

The unity/disunity theme ties together the whole of 12:1–15:13;[12] prob-

12. This is evident first of all in those parts of the discourse addressed to the church as a whole, through the repeated use of the reciprocal pronoun ἀλλήλων (12:5, 10[2x], 16; 13:8; 14:13, 19; 15:5, 7; also ὁμοθυμαδόν in 15:6). The theme of mutuality and harmony brackets a large part of the section (12:16: τὸ αὐτὸ εἰς ἀλλήλους φρονοῦντες; 15:5: τὸ αὐτὸ φρονεῖν ἐν

lems of disunity are to be overcome through mutuality of service. The basis for mutuality is developed in several ways. First, following the initial injunction to mutuality in 12:3, 12:4-8 employs the "body" metaphor to establish that the church is a unity composed of diverse members (cf. 1 Cor 12:12-26). Second, unity in diversity is grounded in Christ's lordship over "weak" and "strong" believers alike (14:9; see also vv. 4, 6, 8, 10-12), and in the servanthood of Christ (15:8). Then, the qualities of forbearance and service toward others (first toward the weak, 15:1, then generally toward others, v. 2) are likewise grounded in the model of Christ's own servant-like behavior (15:3-4, 7; cf. 14:3). The attitude underlying the prescribed behavior in 12:3-21, illustrated in Christ's own service, is expounded in 13:8-10: the command to love others is established as the fulfillment of the law. In this way, the hermeneutical transition is made from the theory and general instructions of 12:1–13:7 to the praxis and specific instructions of 14:1–15:7.[13]

The church's public behavior is perhaps a less dominant theme in the entire section. However, this dimension does emerge in 12:14 and then in 12:17-21. And in these instructions a determined posture toward evil and misfortune worked on believers by unbelievers is already visible. The desired response is characterized by blessing the persecutor, resisting revenge, and seeking peace with all people. All of this is summed up with the evil/good contrast: "doing good" will overcome evil (12:21). Use of this contrast of inward and outward behavior indicates that in Paul's mind both dimensions of Christian ethics (those exercised among believers and those exercised in the world) form a whole, the integrity of which he maintains in Romans.

This leads us back to the opening charge of 12:1-2. We have already seen how it introduces one of the unifying themes, i.e., "the good," that the section seeks to develop. But at this point we must see how the exhortation calls the Roman believers to a transformed view of existence. Using the language of the sacrificial cult ("present your bodies as a living and holy sacrifice"), Paul in v. 1 redefines sacrifice and worship for the people of God. What was before a matter for priests in the isolation of cultic purity is now a matter for ordinary people.

ἀλλήλοις) and grows out of the theological mutuality made possible in Christ (12:5; οὕτως οἱ πολλοὶ ἓν σῶμά ἐσμεν ἐν Χριστῷ, τὸ δὲ καθ' εἷς ἀλλήλων μέλη). The ethical obligation culminates in the application of the law in 13:8, which is also anticipated in 12:9, 10.

13. The subsections are linked by repetition of words for "love," the "evil/good" contrast, and in the last two texts the word "neighbor":

12:9-10 — Ἡ ἀγάπη ἀνυπόκριτος. ἀποστυγοῦντες τὸ πονηρόν, κολλώμενοι τῷ ἀγαθῷ· 10 τῇ φιλαδελφίᾳ εἰς ἀλλήλους φιλόστοργοι, τῇ τιμῇ ἀλλήλους προηγούμενοι,

13:9-10 — Ἀγαπήσεις τὸν πλησίον σου ὡς σεαυτόν. ἡ ἀγάπη τῷ πλησίον κακὸν οὐκ ἐργάζεται·

15:2 — ἕκαστος ἡμῶν τῷ πλησίον ἀρεσκέτω εἰς τὸ ἀγαθὸν πρὸς οἰκοδομήν.

What is more, the command calls for the sacrifice of the *sōma*/body, that is, the dedication of the person "in his concrete relationships within this world."[14] This is no call to dedicate one's spirit, soul, or heart to God, but a call to participate in the world in a living (ongoing) act of worship and service to God. Logically, the charge is the culmination of all that has preceded it, but especially of the exposition of God's universal plan of redemption in which the tearing down of barriers has begun. As a call to action, it sets a broad agenda, spelled out in 12:3–15:7, a section which demonstrates how people can remove the barriers that jeopardize unity.

The related command of v. 2 to resist conformity with this age (τῷ αἰῶνι τούτῳ) and to be transformed by the renewal of the mind has often been misunderstood to signal the reinforcement of the division between the sacred and the secular, that is, to endorse a separatism. Rather, it actually charts the course for the life of service in a much-widened understanding of the church's domain. "This age," according to Jewish thinking, depicts the present evil age in contrast to the age to come. As such it is a negative characterization of life, one in which Christ is not recognized as Lord; instead, one that is organized around a prevailing "worldview" with values and ways that are antithetical to the will of God. The NT writers elsewhere categorize it as evil (Gal 1:4; Eph 5:16; 1 Jn 5:19). It is a way of life still in effect. But the way has been opened for its transformation to begin through the influence of those who themselves have been transformed. The experience Paul alludes to is that experience of renewal through the Holy Spirit (Rom 8:1-11). Though it is clearly a "work in progress," nevertheless, the presence of the Spirit enables the believing community to apprehend "the will of God." It is because of what God has done in the world that believers are to participate in the transforming of the world, bringing sacred and secular under one roof. Just as the "one body" is the goal of Paul's mission in relation to Jews and Gentiles, so the Christian participation in the structures of society becomes an obligation. Subsequent references to persecution are clear indications of the tension that the Christ-event will cause in present life. "This age" remains a potent force, and Christian witness in any form will run up against opposition (12:14, 17-18). Nevertheless, the dual commitment to a holistic mission of a renewed people of God and a transforming presence within "this age" is not lessened by the difficulties encountered in either sphere. Thus Paul's call to commitment at the outset of the section we have been considering prepares the way for his teaching about unity among believers and participation within society.

14. Dunn, *Romans 9–16*, WBC 38b (Dallas: Word, 1988), p. 709.

III. The Transformational Intention of 13:1-7

Although it could be argued that the parenesis is general at 12:14, 17-18, the instruction given in 13:1-7 is surely not a universal theology of the state,[15] but rather is parenesis addressed to specific circumstances. With regard to those circumstances, the following can be reasonably deduced: it is likely that Paul wanted to avoid another edict of expulsion to match Claudius's earlier one, which might have affected Jewish Christians and the church as a whole; furthermore, he was aware that the payment of taxes was potentially a sensitive issue.[16] However, it is not the specific situation or application of the teaching to it that will explain the fundamental nature of the passage. 13:1-7 is exhortation that belongs to a broader stratum of ethical teaching that is crafted to direct Christians to participate in the world. Therefore, we will need to locate the teaching within its literary tradition and cultural environment, and identify its theological bearings. These three perspectives will converge to show that fundamentally 13:1-7 is part of a tradition designed to guide the church in a process of world transformation which depends upon its circumspect, enthusiastic, missionary involvement in the structures of society. From Paul's perspective, this involvement is the ethical and missiological corollary of God's plan of universal salvation.

A. 13:1-7 as Part of a Broader Program of Engagement in the World

13:1-7 is related to a wider body of teaching in the NT which is similarly structured and similarly rooted in a very basic and dominant element of the ancient Mediterranean worldview, namely, the household. In ancient Mediterranean culture, the most fundamental relationships were those of kinship[17] and the institution of the household (οἶκος, οἰκία, οἰκονομία, and related vocabulary), within which most of these relationships functioned.[18] Moreover, the social ex-

15. Proper observation of the verbal and thematic context of this passage rules out the interpolation theory (contra, e.g., W. Schmithals, *Der Römerbrief als historisches Problem* [Gütersloh: Gütersloher, 1975], pp. 191-97); see discussion in Dunn, *Romans 9–16*, pp. 758-59; Douglas J. Moo, *The Epistle to the Romans* (NICNT; Grand Rapids: Eerdmans, 1996), pp. 790-94.

16. See references above, n. 2.

17. See B. J. Malina, *The New Testament World: Insights from Cultural Anthropology*, rev. ed. (Louisville, Ky.: Westminster/John Knox, 1993), pp. 117-48; K. C. Hanson, "Kinship," in R. Rohrbaugh (ed.), *The Social Sciences and New Testament Interpretation* (Peabody, Mass.: Hendrickson, 1996), pp. 62-79.

18. J. H. Elliott, "Temple versus Household in Luke-Acts: Models for Interpretation," in J. H. Neyrey (ed.), *The Social World of Luke-Acts* (Peabody, Mass.: Hendrickson, 1991), pp.

pectations of the household exceeded the private sphere. The ancient household was regarded as the basic building block of society; its stability guaranteed the stability of the city-state. From the time of Augustus, the emperor was regarded as *pater patriae:* he was a father, and the state his household.[19] The effect of this cultural milieu on Paul is evident in both his conception of the church (Eph 2:19; Gal 6:10; cf. 1 Tim 3:15; 2 Tim 2:20-21) and ministry (1 Cor 4:1; 9:17; Col 1:25). In several places in the Pauline corpus, the term οἰκονομία θεοῦ depicts the faith in terms of "household management" (Col 1:25; Eph 1:10; 3:2, 9; 1 Tim 1:4).[20] In making the connection between household management and God's order of reality in the world, we are pushed back to the cultural background in order to understand the dynamics involved. In the Graeco-Roman culture the household and society were separated only by a very permeable barrier. It was a natural step — at least it was a natural step for those who attributed the basic structure of nature to a creating God — to expand the thought of the human *oikos* to an *oikonomia theou,* which would then cover the arrangements of the universe.[21] This is very much the thought of 1 Peter 2:13, and Paul's thought runs along similar lines in Romans 13:1-7. The melding of concepts that occurs in the NT description of the people of God *(oikos, ekklesia, naos)* reflects the same remapping of domains that we have already seen to be part of Paul's thinking in Romans — the same permeability existed between the church as "household" and society.

The corollary of this dominant image of the *oikos* in the early church is the use of what has come to be called the "household code," especially in Pauline and Petrine writings (Col 3:18–4:1; Eph 5:22-33; 1 Tim 2:8-15; 5:1-2; 6:1-2; Titus 2:1–3:8; 1 Pet 2:13–3:7).[22] There is not space here for a complete rehearsal of the history of research into this form.[23] But some conclusions of the schol-

---

224-38; D. L. Balch, "Household Codes," *Anchor Bible Dictionary* 3:318-20; P. H. Towner, "Households and Household Codes," *Dictionary of Paul and His Letters* (1993): 417.

19. Many of the functions and positions in relation to the state were derived from the "household" root: *metoikoi/paroikoi* ("resident alien"), *oikeios* ("native"), *katoikoi* ("military colonists"), etc.; Towner, "Household Codes," p. 417.

20. Modern translations render the term variously in these passages, for although "household management" is its first meaning, related ideas of "ordering" or "dispensation" can be drawn from it, thus losing the basic reference to the *oikos.* In doing so, the modern translations are not capable of retaining the link with the household management theme.

21. See the discussion in L. T. Johnson, "*Oikonomia Theou:* The Theological Voice of 1 Timothy" (Unpublished paper given at SBL, 1996, New Orleans).

22. Cf. *1 Clement* 1:3–2:1; 21:6-8; Ignatius, *Letter to Polycarp* 4:1–5:2; Polycarp, *Letter to the Philippians* 4:2–6:1; cf. *Didache* 4:9-11; *Barnabas* 19:5b, 7.

23. See Balch, "Household Codes," pp. 318-20; P. H. Towner, "Household Codes," in R. Martin and P. H. Davids (eds.), *Dictionary of the Later New Testament and Its Development* (Downers Grove, Ill.: InterVarsity, 1997).

arly discussion should be mentioned as I seek to establish the relationship of Romans 13:1-7 to this tradition. The most informed conclusion suggests that the NT household codes show an affinity to and were influenced by the secular discussion of the theme "concerning the household" *(peri oikonomos),* of which the relation of the household to ruling authorities (in the NT see Rom 13:1-7; Titus 3:1-2; 1 Pet 2:13-17; cf. 1 Tim 2:1-2) was a part.[24]

The content of the NT household codes indicates their interest in Christian behavior in typical life situations. Once the household metaphor is taken over as an expression of congregational identity, the same pattern of teaching can be applied to address life both in the broader Christian community and in relation to the world. L. Goppelt observed correctly that life, which engaged the various social roles, would bring Christians into daily contact with unbelievers, providing every kind of opportunity to testify to the faith.[25] But the question of the tradition's intention is much debated.[26] It will need to be answered on the

24. D. Lührmann, "Neutestamentliche Haustafeln und antike Ökonomie," *NTS* 27:1 (1980): 83-97; K. Thraede, "Zum historischen Hintergrund der 'Haustafeln' des NT," in E. Dassmann et al. (eds.), *Pietas, Festschrift für Bernhard Kötting* (Munich: JAC Ergänzungsband 8, 1980), pp. 359-68; D. L. Balch, *Let Wives Be Submissive: The Domestic Code in 1 Peter* (SBLMS 26; Chico, Calif.: Scholars, 1981); K. Müller, "Die Haustafel des Kolosserbriefes und das antike Frauenthema," in *Die Frau in Urchristentum,* eds. G. Dautzenberg, H. Merklein, and K. Müller, QD 95 (Freiburg/Basel/Vienna: Herder, 1983), pp. 263-319; H. von Lips, "Die Haustafel als 'Topos' im Rahmen der urchristlichen Paränese," *NTS* 40:2 (1994): 261-80.

25. L. Goppelt, *Theology of the New Testament, Vol. 2: The Variety and Unity of the Apostolic Witness to Christ* (Grand Rapids: Eerdmans, 1982), p. 170.

26. Most have sought the tradition's intention according to different understandings of circumstances being addressed, and numerous suggestions have been made: purposeful accommodation to secular ethics (M. Dibelius, and H. Greeven, *An die Kolosser, Epheser, an Philemon* [3d ed.; HNT 12; Tübingen: J. C. B. Mohr, 1953], and more recently E. Schüssler Fiorenza, *In Memory of Her: A Feminist Reconstruction of Christian Origins* [New York: Crossroads, 1983]); quieting enthusiastic unrest (J. E. Crouch, *The Origin and Intention of the Colossian Haustafel,* FRLANT 109 [Göttingen: Vandenhoeck & Ruprecht, 1972]; R. P. Martin, "Haustafeln," *NIDNTT,* 3:928-32); preventing internal disintegration brought on by outside pressures (J. H. Elliott, *A Home for the Homeless: A Sociological Exegesis of 1 Peter, Its Situation and Strategy* [Philadelphia: Fortress, 1981]); defense-apologetic (Balch, *Wives;* "Household Codes," *ABD,* pp. 318-20); mission (D. Schroeder, *Die Haustafeln des neuen Testaments* [Dissertation, Hamburg: Mikrokopie, 1959]; Goppelt, *Theology, Vol. 2: A Commentary on 1 Peter* [Grand Rapids: Eerdmans, 1993]; cf. Schüssler Fiorenza, *Memory).* In each case, whether the ethic represents a retrograde step (in relation, e.g., to Gal 3:28) back toward patriarchy, or a proactive step preparing the way for engagement in the social structure for mission (Goppelt), the emphasis has been on conformity. However, the diversity in the form the tradition takes and in the circumstances it addresses in the NT suggests that none of these explanations is really sufficient in itself for all applications of the tradition; probably a deeper foundation or multilevel strategy was in mind.

basis of context and other clues. What can be said, at least of those codes and related pieces that have the church's public behavior in mind (Rom 13:1-7; 1 Pet 2:13-17; Titus 3:1-2), and are not simply "in-house" concerns, is that the NT writers reflect sensitivity to the expectations of society at large and seem to encourage Christians to live according to patterns that were widely accepted as respectable. This is the first level on which the codes operate: they allow a dialogue of life to go on; they facilitate communication between Christians and those on the outside. The "conventional" nature of the teaching would foster stability, and so it could have served in some applications as a response to enthusiasm or emancipation tendencies. Yet none of the NT household codes reflects uncritical secularization or wholesale adoption of conventional ethics. It is where new patterns penetrate the conventional shape of the household ethos — patterns such as the emphasis on justice and fairness along with theological grounding — that a second more fundamental level of intention comes to light.

This second level of intention is that of being a transforming influence within society. The theological grounding in the codes reveals the belief in a God who has opened up the whole world to his program. God's *oikonomia* envelops the whole of life, and, corresponding to this, Christian living will need to be done within culture. Though "household" language is somewhat less noticeable in Romans, it is nonetheless present (cf. 14:4; 16:5, 23). But God's presence in this world aims at reformation and transformation of its structures, never uncritical acceptance of them (Rom 12:2). In general the household codes sought a creative middle ground between conformity to secular life and disengagement from the world. In all cases the entrance of Christian goals and values into otherwise secular structures produces tension (thus, e.g., Rom 12:14, 17-18). Paradoxically, the household codes aim to mitigate the effects of this tension while also sustaining it.

Romans 13:1-7 must be seen within a similar social-ethical and missiological program. Its own literary context is one completely devoted to the message that God's people must live conscious of being God's people in the world. Paul's outlook is missiological from start to finish, both geographically and theologically. Romans 13:1-7 must be allowed to interact with this strong flow of themes. It also has all the marks of the household code tradition,[27] conceived broadly enough to include the teaching on the relation to the state. The specific circumstances in Rome which occasioned Paul's parenetic choice determined the shape of the specific application (vv. 1, 5, 6, 7), but the more funda-

27. In comparing Rom 13:1-7 with 1 Pet 2:13-17, Goppelt suggested, "I Peter 2 follows the form of the station codes while Romans 13 prepares the way for this form structurally" (*I Peter*, p. 180).

mental goal is to direct the congregations to participate proactively in public life. The link with the household code tradition suggests that more than safe conservatism or adherence to a theoretical doctrine is at stake, and themes developed in Romans elsewhere corroborate this suggestion.

B. Rom 13:1-7 and the Interplay of Cultural Convention and Theology

At the outset, I suggested that the question of the fundamental meaning of Romans 13:1-7 must be answered on the basis of theological, literary, and cultural factors. The link to the household theme and literary tradition associated with it just observed provides one line of evidence that the passage enjoins a life of public participation and interface. While this is a critical observation, the cultural and theological contexts of the parenesis establish its deeper level of intention.

For the limited purposes of this study, I will consolidate the main points arising out of analyses of the teaching's discourse or rhetorical structure.[28]

a. The argument itself begins with the thesis statement (13:1a), its theological grounding (13:1b-c), and a statement of the logical consequences that will follow should the thesis be rejected (13:2a-b):

   (1a) Let every person be subject to the governing authorities;
   (1b) for there is no authority except from God,
   (1c) and those authorities that exist have been instituted by God.
   (2a) Therefore whoever resists authority resists what God has appointed,
   (2b) and those who resist will incur judgment.

b. Parallel to the theological basis is a practical basis for the thesis that returns to the topic of "doing what is good" (v. 3a). Shifting to diatribe style, positive and negative illustrations develop further the thought of "doing good" (vv. 3b-4e):

   (3a) For rulers are not a terror to good conduct, but to bad.
      (3b) Do you wish to have no fear of the authority?

28. See the thorough evaluation of recent structural studies (R. H. Stein, "The Argument of Romans 13:1-7," *NovT* 31.4 [1989]: 325-43; S. E. Porter, "Romans 13:1-7 as Pauline Political Rhetoric," *Filologia Neotestamentaria* 3 [1990]: 115-39; H. Merklein, "Sinn und Zweck von Röm 13,1-7," in H. Merklein [ed.], *Neues Testament und Ethik* [Freiburg: Herder, 1989], pp. 238-70) and fresh reconstruction of the argument in K.-W. Peng, "Structure of Romans 12:1–15:13" (Unpublished Ph.D. Thesis, University of Sheffield; 1997), pp. 105-14.

(3c) Then do what is good,
(3d) and you will receive its approval;
(4a) for it is God's servant for your good.
(4b) But if you do what is wrong,
(4c) you should be afraid,
(4d) for the authority does not bear the sword in vain!
(4e) It is the servant of God to execute wrath on the wrongdoer.

c. In order to make a transition from the general argument to the particular issue, v. 5 repeats the thesis as rationale for the practice of paying taxes (v. 6):

(5a) Therefore one must be subject,
(5b) not only because of wrath
(5c) but also because of conscience.
(6a) For the same reason you also pay taxes,
(6b) for the authorities are God's servants, busy with this very thing.

d. V. 7 closes the argument with a generalizing command concerning behavior in relation to "all."[29]

(7a) Pay to all what is due them —
(7b) taxes to whom taxes are due,
(7c) revenue to whom revenue is due,
(7d) respect to whom respect is due,
(7e) honor to whom honor is due.

On one level, the teaching represents a collection of readily understandable "commonplaces" that give the particular ethic a popular appeal and would encourage behavior that is acceptable to all people because it promotes stability. This is seen, for instance, in the way Paul employs terminology for the political (vv. 1, 3), legal (v. 4), and taxation revenue systems (vv. 6-7) — terminology that was typical for the Roman setting.[30] Second, woven into the

29. Fitzmyer (*Romans*, p. 670) suggests that this is the underlying principle for vv. 1-7, and the likelihood that the teaching of Jesus is alluded to here as a foundation (Mk 12:17 pars.) perhaps strengthens this view (see discussion in M. Thompson, *Clothed with Christ: The Example and Teaching of Jesus in Romans*, JSNTSupp. 59 [Sheffield: Sheffield Academic Press, 1991], pp. 111-20; Dunn, *Romans 9–16*, p. 768).

30. For the "ruled" (ὑποτασσόμενοι or *subjecti*) and the "rulers in authority" (ὑπερέχοντες), cf. the material cited in Friedrich, Pöhlmann, and Stuhlmacher, "Röm 13, 1-7," pp. 131-66; A. Strobel, "Zum Verständnis von Rm 13," *ZNW* 47 (1956): 67-93.

fabric of the parenesis is a pattern of cultural features which acknowledge the social rules and obligations of citizens of various ranks and economic standing. For example, the term "honor" (τιμή) occurs in the general conclusion of v. 7 (1 Pet 2:17), reflecting the "honor and shame" system of public recognition. Duly acknowledging one's status (whether a matter of birth and family or acquired by virtuous behavior) was the role of the good citizen in public life.[31]

"Praise" (ἔπαινος; v. 3) was also part of the cultural pattern of Hellenistic civic responsibility. It constituted the acknowledgment given to the good citizen by those in power.[32] In the configuration in which it occurs in v. 3 (τὸ ἀγαθὸν ποίει, καὶ ἕξεις ἔπαινον ἐξ αὐτῆς), "praise" and "doing good" tap into the equally prevalent concept of benefaction. Benefaction (the term for it is εὐεργεσία; 1 Tim 6:2; cf. Lk 22:25-27) is related to the concept of honor in that the public performance of a benefit by a benefactor brings a return of public acknowledgment.[33] I will return to the system known as benefaction below.

These conventional features make the parenesis intelligible within the Roman social and political context. At this linguistic and semantic level, the parenesis affirms some of the conventional institutions and instructs the church to live within the given social structure. At the practical level, this might quiet unrest or encourage a life of respectability. If the understanding of the instruction remains at this level, it might even seem to endorse a status quo that is at odds with certain Christian ideals. But here is where the theological grounding of the ethic takes over.

The NT household code tradition, to which this instruction is related, typically supplies theological rationale.[34] In this case, theology is applied in two ways. First, the thesis statement in 13:1 ("Let every person be subject to the governing authorities") is given immediate theological support ("for there is no

31. Malina, *New Testament World,* pp. 28-62; H. Moxnes, "Honor and Shame," in R. Rohrbaugh (ed.), *The Social Sciences and New Testament Interpretation* (Peabody, Mass.: Hendrickson, 1996), pp. 19-40; B. J. Malina, and J. H. Neyrey, *Portraits of Paul: An Archaeology of Ancient Personality* (Louisville, Ky.: Westminster/John Knox, 1996), p. 176.

32. Strobel, "Rm 13," pp. 84-89; cf. Philo, *Legatio ad Gaium* 7; *Letter of Aristeas,* 291-94.

33. See Winter, *Welfare of the City,* pp. 25-40; cf. F. W. Danker, *Benefactor: Epigraphic Study of a Graeco-Roman and New Testament Semantic Field* (St. Louis: Clayton Publishing House, 1982); J. H. Elliott, "Patronage and Clientage," in R. Rohrbaugh (ed.), *The Social Sciences and New Testament Interpretation* (Peabody, Mass.: Hendrickson, 1996), pp. 144-56.

34. This is done in various ways. Christological grounding establishes a higher authority under which all must carry out their mutual obligations, relativizing the burden that goes with submission (Col 3:18, 20, 22, 23, 24; 4:1). Or Christ is set out as an example for appropriate behavior (Eph 5:25). A traditional piece of theology forms the basis in Titus 2:1–3:2 (2:11-14).

authority except from God, and those authorities that exist have been instituted by God"). As the combination ἐξουσίαις ὑπερεχούσαις indicates, Paul is referring to those who bear official authority.[35] These officials have been established in their positions by God. The logic of what Paul is commanding is implicit in the word play between the command — ὑποτασσέσθω — and the reason — ὑπὸ θεοῦ τεταγμέναι εἰσίν — (from τάσσω). But the actual theological background to this reasoning is the development of thought in OT prophetic writings and Jewish Wisdom literature[36] which originated in Israel's exile and Diaspora experience. The message of God's uninterrupted sovereignty in spite of pagan dominion over Israel brought hope but also included the obligation to exhibit loyalty to the pagan state: "But seek the welfare of the city where I have sent you into exile, and pray to the LORD on its behalf, for in its welfare you will find your welfare" (Jer 29:7; cf. Ezra 6:9-10; 1 Macc 7:33).[37]

It was in Israel's exile and Diaspora experiences that the remapping of its religious world had begun. This OT prophetic and Wisdom background of Paul's instruction emerges in various ways: v. 4 relates these rulers to God as his servants (διάκονος; see Babylon in Jer 25:9; Cyrus in Isa 45:1; cf. Wisd Sol 6:4),[38] and the secular powers, or, in the OT, "the nations," exercise his wrath (Isa 5:26-29; 7:18-20; 8:7-8; 13:4-5). The use of the term "ministers" (λειτουργοί) in v. 6 invites the readers/hearers, similarly, to consider how in God's *oikonomia*, service to God and the responsible[39] exercise of civic powers by those in authority are coalescing.[40] The entire pattern, as epitomized in Isa-

35. See Diogenes Laertius 6.78 (LCL II, 81); G. Delling, *TDNT* 8:29-30; BAGD s.v.; cf. 1 Tim 2:2; 1 Pet 2:13. The suggestions that the "powers" are angelic (cf. W. Wink, *Naming the Powers* [Philadelphia: Fortress, 1984], pp. 45-47), or rulers of the synagogues in Rome (M. D. Nanos, *The Mystery of Romans* [Minneapolis: Fortress, 1996], pp. 289-336), are not easily supported from the language or the context.

36. Isa 41:2-4; 45:1-7; Jer 21:7, 10; 27:5-6; Dan 2:21, 37-38; 4:17, 25, 32; 5:21; Prov 8:15-16; Sir 10:4; 17:17; Wisd Sol 6:3.

37. See E. Schürer, *The History of the Jewish People in the Age of Jesus Christ (175 B.C. - A.D. 135)*, rev. ed. by G. Vermes, F. Millar, and M. Goodman (Edinburgh: T. & T. Clark, 1973-79), vol. 2, pp. 311-13.

38. The Greek term is sometimes used of civil or court officials; see H. W. Beyer, *TDNT* 2:82; Esth 1:10; 2:2 (LXX).

39. The same tradition also enunciated clearly the principle that those who exceed their authority or violate their "calling" were subject to God's wrath (Dan 4:13-17, 23-25; 5:20-21; Wisd Sol 6:4-5).

40. The term λειτουργοί in Rom 15:16 carries cultic meaning, and in Phil 2:25 may also belong to the vocabulary of Christian ministry. In this case, the reference may be first to public officers serving the community of people (Strobel, "Rm 13," pp. 86-87), but the further qualifier "of God" makes the convergence of ideas almost certain (cf. Dunn, *Romans 9–16*, p. 767).

iah and rehearsed in Romans, provides the critical redemptive-historical precedents: God's plan is a universal one — salvation will reach to all, and all, even the nations, may be appointed as servants (for "you"; v. 4).

Echoes of the Jesus tradition in the general statement of v. 7 reflect a second application of theology to the instructions.[41] There is no question of a direct and explicit quote of Jesus' teaching,[42] but the thought in Mark 12:17 (pars.) is close enough to suggest that Paul has contextualized the dominical material here, as he did in 12:14.[43] If that is the case, then grounds for the specific action of paying taxes to the empire are drawn from the Jesus tradition, and made continuous with broader OT and Wisdom developments.

The preparation for movement to a deeper level of intention, namely, transformation, is already evident in what has been seen thus far. First, the parenesis continues the remapping of God's domain and the process of subverting old boundaries already apparent in Romans and the OT. Second, within our passage the crossing of lines is announced in a number of subtle ways. The word play between the command ὑποτασσέσθω and the reason ὑπὸ θεοῦ τεταγμέναι εἰσίν at once brings into correlation ruling authorities, Christian believers, and God, who stands behind the command and over the authorities. Then, these rulers are related to God (and to the church) with the terms διάκονος and λειτουργοί, which contain a creative ambiguity in the way each term can function in both cultic/church and civic contexts. Here, the OT pattern just observed and the genitive θεοῦ combine to reflect the elevating of secular administration to the level of service for God.[44] The pattern within Romans merges the secular and the sacred as God's eschatological rule reaches the whole of creation (8:18-23, 31-39; 11:33-36), a corollary of the mission to the Gentiles.

The intention of the transformation is fully reached at the point in the passage which commissions the church to action. Recent studies of the rhetorical structure of 13:1-7 suggest that v. 3 expresses the central action in the

41. See discussion in Thompson, *Clothed with Christ,* pp. 111-20; Dunn, *Romans 9–16,* p. 768.

42. Goppelt (*I Peter,* p. 181) argued that Jesus' teaching about paying taxes to Caesar (Mk 12:13-17) is at least part of the origin of the parenesis concerning authorities (Rom 13:1-7; 1 Pet 2:13-17; Titus 3:1-2). See also D. Wenham, *Paul: Follower of Jesus or Founder of Christianity?* (Grand Rapids: Eerdmans, 1995), pp. 253-54, 259-61.

43. The fact that in both Rom 13 and Mk 12 the teaching about taxes is followed by an exposition of the Great Commandment should also be noticed. See L. Goppelt, "Die Freiheit zur Kaisersteuer: Zu Mk. 12,17 und Röm 13,1-7," in *Christologie und Ethik: Aufsätze zum Neuen Testament* (Göttingen: Vandenhoeck & Ruprecht, 1968), pp. 208-19; Dunn, *Romans 9–16,* p. 768.

44. Dunn, *Romans 9–16,* p. 767.

parenesis in the phrase "to do good."[45] This is confirmed by the change to diatribe style at v. 3, directing attention to this central imperative,[46] and by the way in which "doing good" continues the theme that is central in 12:1–15:13 and prominent throughout Romans.[47] It is in this imperative "to do good" that Paul "co-opts" the cultural convention known as benefaction in order to empower the church for the transformation of society.

B. W. Winter has argued persuasively that Romans 13:3-4 commands the practice of "benefaction," the social convention designed to ensure the welfare of the city through the contributions of well-to-do citizens.[48] The term "the good work" (τὸ ἀγαθόν; vv. 3-4) and the command "to do the good work" (τὸ ἀγαθὸν ποιεῖν; v. 4) feature in descriptions of benefaction,[49] and the term "praise" (ἔπαινος), as a reward from rulers to good citizens and one who does a beneficent work, belongs within the semantic domain of this social convention.[50] Within such a discussion of public responsibility, the Roman congregations would not likely have missed the reference.[51]

The question is: How is the convention employed? Winter concluded from a study of various NT passages employing the convention or elements of it that early Christian writers sought to underline the continuing obligation of converted benefactors to the *politeia* and the city. When the evidence as a whole is assessed, Winter discovers that the convention has been expanded, since the injunctions to serve in this way were grounded in the will of God and since benefaction became the obligation of "[a]ll able-bodied members of the Christian community [seeking] the welfare of others in the city."[52] However, in the

45. The four imperatives in 13:1-7 reveal the "prominent" logic: "be subject" (v. 1a), "do what is good" (v. 3c), "be afraid" (v. 4b), "pay to all what is owed" (v. 7a). "Subjection" is viewed from the perspective of "doing what is good," which is supported by the general imperative of v. 7a. The negative command, "be afraid" (v. 4b), functions in relation to the negative condition (to be avoided) that immediately precedes it, to highlight the contrasting (approved) positive command, "do what is good" (v. 3c). See Peng, "Structure," pp. 140-42.

46. See Peng, "Structure," p. 137; cf. Dunn, *Romans 9–16*, p. 763.

47. See 2:7, 10; 3:8; 5:7; 7:12, 13, 18, 19; 8:28; 9:11; 10:15; 12:2, 9, 21; 13:3, 4; 14:16; 15:2; 16:19.

48. Winter, *Welfare of the City*, pp. 25-40, esp. pp. 26-30, 33-38.

49. See Winter's citations in *Welfare of the City*, pp. 26-30, 34-35, n. 34.

50. Winter, *Welfare of the City*, pp. 33, 35-36, n. 36.

51. In fact a contrast such as Rom 5:7 introduces — between "the righteous" (δίκαιος) and "the good" (ἀγαθός) — almost certainly draws upon the categories of this convention in setting on a pedestal the one who has made a benefaction and so binding some recipient of it to himself (see ibid., p. 35, and sources cited there). The occurrence of the term ὁ προϊστάμενος in 12:8 may also fall within the scope of benefaction (discussion in *Welfare of the City*, p. 35, n. 35).

52. Winter, *Welfare of the City*, p. 209.

case of Romans 13, Winter suggests that it is the rich Christians who were to continue to serve the city as benefactors in order to demonstrate the Christian community's commitment to society as it sought the welfare of the city. The reasons offered for his conventional or "material" interpretation in this text are: first, the language would normally be understood as addressing the wealthy; second, the singular "you" (σοί) of v. 4, which is a shift from third person inclusive address (already made in θέλεις of v. 3), addresses the teaching to the Roman believers in a way that distinguishes certain individuals, namely, the rich, from the whole.

It is at this point that I diverge somewhat from Winter. Although a departure from the general address to an injunction directed to just one part of the congregation is not impossible at this place in the instruction, it seems more likely that the change of person in vv. 3-4 is due rather to the switch to diatribe style (cf. 1 Cor 7:21, 27-28). In this case, even where the second person singular is used, all believers continue to be addressed. And if this is so, not only must Paul reshape the convention in order to apply it to the entire Christian community, but its application would also suggest a surprising reversal of values.

The revision of the benefaction concept that, according to Winter, emerges from the NT as a whole, I would argue, also applies to Romans 13. In fact, given the particulars of the discussion — people in relation to ruling authorities — Paul's co-opting of the convention in this parenesis may strike an even more radical note. While some of his readers may well have been rich Christians who could perform benefaction in the form of material contributions to the city, most believers almost certainly were not. Yet, if the reading above is correct, "doing good" according to the benefaction convention is the obligation of all. For this to be possible, the benefaction concept must be contextualized, and for this there is another NT passage which may shed some light on the way in which such benefaction was exercised. In 1 Timothy 6:2, Christian slaves are called on to serve their believing masters in a way that reverses the benefaction convention and redefines it. First, that slaves are to be benefactors, as the passage indicates, is to reverse the typical order of the convention in a fairly radical way.[53] Second, that benefaction is defined in terms of "service" indicates the expansion of the convention. Precedents for this "Pauline" development may be found in Seneca[54] and in the Jesus tradition preserved by Luke:

53. See P. H. Towner, "Can Slaves Be Their Masters' Benefactors? 1 Timothy 6:1-2a in Literary, Cultural and Theological Context," *UBS Bulletin* 182/183 (1997): 39-52, which builds on observations of Danker, *Benefactor*, pp. 323-26 and L. T. Johnson, *Letters to Paul's Delegates: 1 Timothy, 2 Timothy, Titus* (Valley Forge, Penn.: Trinity Press International, 1996), pp. 190-92.

54. Seneca, *On Benefits*, 3.18-20, on which see discussion in Towner, "Slaves," pp. 46-47.

> And he said to them, "The kings of the Gentiles exercise lordship over them; and those in authority (ἐξουσιάζοντες) over them are called benefactors (εὐεργέται). But not so with you; rather let the greatest among you become as the youngest, and the leader as one who serves (ὁ διακονῶν). For which is the greater, one who sits at table, or one who serves? Is it not the one who sits at table? But I am among you as one who serves (ὁ διακονῶν)." (Lk 22:25-27)

In 1 Timothy 6:1-2a, benefaction, redefined in resonance with the Jesus tradition, places a subversive question mark over the social reality of slavery. Benefaction becomes humble service, the exercise of which places the slave spiritually in the role of the master. In God's surprising *oikonomia* slaves serve humbly from the position of power; in fact, nobility and honor, the rewards of benefaction, are accorded here to the slaves. In all of this, the privileges of honor which that culture reserved for well-to-do patrons, benefactors, and slave owners are not denied; nor are the obligations of slaves to their masters trivialized. But the meaning and value of life lived at that level are relativized by the more fundamental reality of the universal lordship of Christ.

The social reality addressed in Romans 13 is larger than slavery, but a similar revision of benefaction is employed to transform a structure of society. Most are agreed that the Roman congregations were in a tenuous and vulnerable social-political situation. Their identity was an ambivalent thing both for those inside the church (the Jew/Gentile tension) and for those outside, who would still probably have viewed the Christian community within Judaism.[55] If the church's self-preservation was Paul's goal, teaching designed to encourage political quietism or behavior that ensured stability in contrast to the generally experienced social, political, and religious unrest would make perfect sense. But this kind of purpose alone does not realize the potential of Paul's co-opting of benefaction here. The church's (presumed) position of weakness and what we know of the benefaction convention suggest that Paul intends to deliver at least a mild shock in this call to action. A convention normally associated with the powerful "haves" is co-opted for the "have-nots." For this, the conventional meaning of "doing the good thing" requires redefinition, and the use of the concept throughout Romans provides the direction, with 12:2, 9 and 15:2 leading the way. The degree to which the Jesus tradition preserved in Luke 22 might have been involved in the redefinition of the idea is difficult to calculate. But the similar language and concepts suggest that it belongs to the broader trend identified by Winter,[56] and it may have contributed a point to Paul's herme-

55. Elliott, *Liberating Paul,* pp. 221-24; Dunn, *Romans 1–8,* pp. xliv-liv.

56. If we also notice the similarity of Lk 22:25-27 and Rom 13:1-7 in the terms ἐξουσιάζοντες and ὁ διακονῶν (perhaps also in the reference to rulers), we might be justified

neutical compass. In any case, "the good" is to be understood as service on behalf of others, which in this context of a discussion about public responsibility finds practical expression in the paying of taxes and respect for those in authority (and, no doubt, for those for whom it is possible, through material gifts of benefaction).

But as we allow theological, literary, and cultural backgrounds to converge, the implications of the teaching for the church and society become even more radical. The remapping of domains charted in Romans, with roots in the Jewish exile and Diaspora experience, determines that these mundane acts of responsibility are consecrated as service (so too political leadership). The church — powerless, poor, marginalized, and without any official political status in the empire — is directed to participate in the public life of society through humble service, taking the role, again spiritually and in defiance of appearances, of the honorable benefactor. The good it dispenses will be "for the welfare of the city," but on God's terms the good goes beyond maintaining the city to transforming it. In an ideal setting, this doing of good might legitimate humble service in the public opinion and earn for the church the rewards of the benefactor. Such service might enhance the church's witness; the attitude enjoined might quiet any unrest in the church. But Winter is right to underline the paradoxical situation of the church — more evident in 1 Peter's description, but anticipated here as well in 12:14, 17-18 — which exists as a body of alien residents and foreigners in a foreign land. Whatever the circumstances, the call of the parenesis is the church's charter of public ministry. Grounded as it is in the will and salvation plan of God for the whole world, the command is at the same time a source of empowerment for difficult, sacrificial ministry (8:31-39). The call of God directs the church to engage fully in the world in order to bring about transformation of its ways and values.

Within that grander missiological and eschatological reality (e.g., chs. 9–11; 15:7-13), benefaction expands to become a responsibility of the church as a whole — even in this passage. It expands in meaning as "doing good" becomes reinterpreted as service done in love. Thus Paul's co-opting of the cultural convention serves to orientate the church in its transforming engagement in the world. Ideally, it will strengthen the church's public image. Practically, it may ensure the church a stable existence in society. But at the deepest level, service to the world in this way is the corollary of God's universal mission, which seeks to remove old barriers as it proclaims the redemption of the whole world.

---

in allowing for a broader use of the Jesus tradition in this passage. Mk 12:17 (pars.) is, as we have seen, often cited as the background to 13:7, and it is very likely in view. But Lk 22 takes up related themes in a way which may prepare the way for the reversal of roles that Paul effects here.

IV. Concluding Observations

13:1-7 is not simply a theoretical, universally unchangeable theology of the state. This parenesis is more than anything a retooling of the cultural convention of benefaction in light of theological realities. The first of these realities is the fact of God's universal mission to the world which develops thematically throughout Romans. Second, as a corollary of the first, salvation has burst through old religious and ethnic barriers and merged the secular and the sacred. Third, the church is obligated to minister in the whole world. Its relation to the state is, then, not a separate category, but one that is integrated into the whole missiological outlook of Romans which is itself the sequel to Isaiah's story. In this aspect of Christian existence, the requirement of "doing the good" means serving the city and the state in a way that corresponds to but radically exceeds the conventional pattern of benefaction. Now all people, poor and rich alike, take on the role of benefactors. Now benefaction takes the form of humble, sacrificial service. Paul envisages a best-case scenario — authorities who will fulfill their roles responsibly, who will even acknowledge (with praise) the church's benefaction. But it is not hard to imagine the even more radical turn benefaction will take when the church confronts evil empires with Christlike service and sacrifice.

I conclude, therefore, that 13:1-7 is not simply designed to bring about stability in a church on the brink of revolting. Public image matters, yes. Stability matters, true. And adoption of this teaching would probably ensure Paul a stable base from which to launch his mission to Spain. But Paul goes beyond these things to command a critical engagement in the existing *politeia:* the church is to take the lead in doing good; it is to claim the role of "the powerful"; but it is to do this by means of service in humility.

Romans 16:25-27 — An Apt Conclusion

I. Howard Marshall

Doxologies, i.e., ascriptions of glory to God or Christ,[1] are a characteristic feature of the New Testament, there being no less than 17 examples.[2] They usually occur within the texts of letters and of Revelation, but Romans, 2 Peter, and Jude are distinguished from all other New Testament letters by having a conclusion in the form of a doxology.

Admittedly, the original position of the doxology in Romans 16:25-27 as the final part of the letter is a well-known crux, since it and the closing benediction both "float" in the manuscript tradition. At the same time its authenticity, both as an integral part of the letter to the Romans and as a Pauline composition, is a matter of critical debate. The arguments concerning its authenticity and location in the document are not simply textual but are also concerned with the style and content, which are often thought to be non-Pauline in character. A widely held hypothesis is that the doxology was not composed by Paul and was not an original part of the letter but was added to it at some later stage, possibly in the second century. Even if this was so, the doxology is clearly in-

1. Although some texts ascribe or promise glory to human beings (Rom 2:10; cf. Lk 14:10), we understand a doxology to be an ascription of honor to a divine or heavenly being.

2. Lk 2:14; 11:36; 19:38; Gal 1:5; Eph 3:21; Phil 4:20; 1 Tim 1:17; 6:16; 2 Tim 4:18; Heb 13:21; 1 Pet 4:11; 5:11; 2 Pet 3:18; Jude v. 25; Rev 1:6; 5:13; 7:12. See also Mt 6:13 TR. There are also numerous examples in the Apostolic Fathers: 1 Clement 20:12; 32:4; 38:4; 43:6; 45:7; 50:7; 58:2; 64; 65:2; 2 Clement 20:5; Martyrdom of Polycarp 14:3; 20:2; 21:1; 22:1, 4; Ep. 4; Didache 8:2; 9:2, 3, 4; 10:2, 4, 5; Diognetus 12:9. Romans 9:5b falls outside of the pattern of the doxologies which are discussed in this essay.

tended to function as a conclusion to the letter and can justifiably be investigated from this angle.[3]

I. Recent Discussion of the Textual Problem

The textual evidence has been dealt with succinctly by L. W. Hurtado, who gives some account of the recent history of the debate.[4] Following H. Gamble he lists three explanations of the origin of the doxology:[5]

1. It was produced in Marcionite circles. In Hurtado's opinion this theory has been effectively demolished by various scholars, including H. Gamble, who have shown that there is nothing Marcionite about it. The positive attitude to the Old Testament is a clear indication that this is not the work of a Marcionite.

2. It was produced by an "editor" or "compiler" to conclude an early collection of Pauline letters. However, in content it is closely related to the contents of Romans and therefore appears to be meant as a part of Romans.[6]

3. Gamble's own view is that it was composed to form a suitable conclusion to a 14-chapter version of Romans.[7]

Hurtado then lists and criticizes three arguments developed in favor of Gamble's hypothesis that the doxology is not by Paul:

The first is that to end a letter with a doxology would be highly unusual for Paul, who normally concludes with a grace benediction. Hurtado responds that Paul is capable of acting abnormally, and on any view of the matter Romans 16 ends abnormally. We may add that it is also significant that Jude ends with a developed doxology. Whatever the relative dating of the two letters, Jude provides further evidence that a closing doxology was not considered improper.

3. B. S. Childs, *The New Testament as Canon: An Introduction* (London: SCM Press, 1984), pp. 254f.

4. L. Hurtado, "The Doxology at the End of Romans," in E. J. Epp, and G. D. Fee, *New Testament Textual Criticism: Its Significance for Exegesis. Essays in Honor of Bruce M. Metzger* (Oxford: Clarendon, 1981), pp. 185-99. The brief treatment in B. M. Metzger, *A Textual Commentary on the Greek New Testament* (Stuttgart: Deutsche Bibelgesellschaft/United Bible Societies, 1994), pp. 470-73, 476f., leaves the issue of its origin and placement undecided: this uncertainty reflected in a "{C}" rating and in printing the doxology at the end of the letter but in square brackets.

5. H. Gamble Jr., *The Textual History of the Letter to the Romans* (Grand Rapids: Eerdmans, 1977).

6. It is also not clear what a doxology intended to conclude a collection of Pauline letters would be doing at the end of Romans.

7. So C. E. B. Cranfield (*The Epistle to the Romans,* II [Edinburgh: T & T Clark, 1979], 808f.), who also mentions the possibility of a Marcionite basis which has received orthodox supplements, but rightly rejects this as unproven. He believes that it has a post-Pauline ring.

The second argument is that the style is un-Pauline. Hurtado states that this argument depends on assumptions about the origin of Ephesians, 2 Timothy, and Titus, so-called deutero-Pauline letters. Further, we may underline Hurtado's comment on Paul's use of liturgical tradition by adding that people's language changes from their normal spoken or written style when they move into prayer and similar genres; there are sufficient examples of lofty language in Paul which may or may not be based on traditional formulations to show that he was capable of rhetorical flourishes.[8]

Subsequent to Hurtado's brief comment came the detailed examination of the language by J. K. Elliott.[9] Elliott claims that there is too high a proportion of unusual and unique expressions in the doxology and that it belongs with the deutero-Pauline letters, especially the Pastoral Epistles.[10] But liturgical language is often different from normal speech and can use phrases which are not found in normal usage; used outside the prayer context some might even appear grotesque. Who ever referred to "traveling mercies" outside the language of prayer? And who ever talks about "John Smith and his dear wife" (dear to whom?) outside pious circles? We should be wary about deciding *a priori* what a writer, whose style we think we know, may do in a prayer context, especially if traditional forms are being incorporated.

The third critique of Gamble's position has to do with the text-critical issue. Here Hurtado argues that the manuscript evidence is stronger for connecting the doxology with the end of Romans 16 rather than Romans 14. He then supplements this argument by briefly showing that there are links in the doxology to Romans 15 as well as to the earlier part of Romans. In effect, according to Hurtado, the argument that the doxology was originally composed to fit a 14-chapter letter does not stand up to scrutiny. His own assessment is a cautious one, namely that the doxology may very well be Paul's own assessment of the entire letter, or that it may be a later composition to give a better conclusion than 16:23. Given the ambivalent nature of the data, he is even prepared to allow the least likely possibility to remain as an option, namely that it started life as a secondary conclusion to Romans 1–14. There the matter is left open.[11]

8. It is appropriate to mention here Gordon Fee's strong support for the view that Phil 2:5-11 is a Pauline composition. See G. D. Fee, "Philippians 2:5-11: Hymn or Exalted Prose?" *BBR* 2 (1992): 29-46.

9. "The Language and Style of the Concluding Doxology to the Epistle to the Romans," *ZNW* 72 (1981): 124-30.

10. Elliott draws attention particularly to χρόνοις αἰωνίοις, γραφῶν προφητικῶν, and κατ' ἐπιταγὴν τοῦ αἰωνίου θεοῦ.

11. Most scholars assume that the doxology is non-Pauline. Those on the other side include J. A. D. Weima, *Neglected Endings: The Significance of the Pauline Letter Closings*

II. The Structure of the Doxology

The present essay does not propose to enter further into the textual questions. It is devoted rather to examining the structure, content, and function of the doxology in comparison with other examples of the genre.

It may be helpful at the outset to set out the doxology in sense units.

Τῷ δὲ δυναμένῳ
ὑμᾶς στηρίξαι
κατὰ τὸ εὐαγγελιόν μου καὶ τὸ κήρυγμα Ἰησοῦ Χριστοῦ,
κατὰ ἀποκάλυψιν μυστηρίου
χρόνοις αἰωνίοις *σεσιγημένου*,
φανερωθέντος δὲ νῦν
διά τε γραφῶν προφητικῶν
κατ' ἐπιταγὴν τοῦ αἰωνίου θεοῦ
εἰς ὑπακοὴν πίστεως εἰς πάντα τὰ ἔθνη *γνωρισθέντος*,

μόνῳ σοφῷ θεῷ,
διὰ Ἰησοῦ Χριστοῦ,
ᾧ ἡ δόξα εἰς τοὺς αἰῶνας, ἀμήν.

This analysis shows that we have a complicated structure with two main elements.

The first main structure is an ascription of glory following the typical pattern "To X [be] glory forever." The doxology is developed by describing what the person does, which in effect states the reason for the glorification. It is typical to do this by an expansion of the name of the person glorified. In the present case this is achieved by using a participle (δυναμένῳ) to describe what God has done (ὑμᾶς στηρίξαι), but as in Ephesians 3:20f. and Jude 24f., the participle is followed by so long a chain that the author has to make a fresh start and get back on course by naming (and describing) the object of the doxology (μόνῳ σοφῷ θεῷ). In this case, however, the identification is followed by adding a relative clause (ᾧ ἡ δόξα εἰς τοὺς αἰῶνας), thus leaving the preceding material hanging and so causing an anacoluthon.

This expansion in the doxology elaborates on the revelation of the "mystery." This thought is developed by the tagging on of the phrase "once hidden but now revealed," a structure which is known from elsewhere in the New Testament. Thus we have a second traditional structure inserted within the tradi-

(Sheffield: JSOT Press, 1994), pp. 135-44, 229f.; D. Moo, *The Epistle to the Romans* (Grand Rapids: Eerdmans, 1996), pp. 936-41.

tional doxology form. The inserted structure departs from the basic pattern in that the "now revealed" section is bifurcated into "now revealed and made known. . . ."

III. Doxologies in the New Testament

We shall now briefly set the doxology in the context of other examples of the genre.[12] A conspectus of the New Testament examples will facilitate comparisons:

TABLE 1

(1) Lk 2:14 δόξα ἐν ὑψίστοις θεῷ καὶ ἐπὶ γῆς εἰρήνη ἐν ἀνθρώποις εὐδοκίας.[13]

(2) Rom 11:36 ὅτι ἐξ αὐτοῦ καὶ δι᾽ αὐτοῦ καὶ εἰς αὐτὸν τὰ πάντα· αὐτῷ ἡ δόξα εἰς τοὺς αἰῶνας, ἀμήν.

(3) Rom 16:25-27 Τῷ δὲ δυναμένῳ ὑμᾶς στηρίξαι κατὰ τὸ εὐαγγέλιόν μου καὶ τὸ κήρυγμα Ἰησοῦ Χριστοῦ, κατὰ ἀποκάλυψιν μυστηρίου χρόνοις αἰωνίοις σεσιγημένου, φανερωθέντος δὲ νῦν διά τε γραφῶν προφητικῶν κατ᾽ ἐπιταγὴν τοῦ αἰωνίου θεοῦ εἰς ὑπακοὴν πίστεως εἰς πάντα τὰ ἔθνη γνωρισθέντος, μόνῳ σοφῷ θεῷ, διὰ Ἰησοῦ Χριστοῦ, ᾧ ἡ δόξα εἰς τοὺς αἰῶνας, ἀμήν.

(4) Gal 1:5 ᾧ ἡ δόξα εἰς τοὺς αἰῶνας τῶν αἰώνων, ἀμήν.

(5) Eph 3:20-21 Τῷ δὲ δυναμένῳ ὑπὲρ πάντα ποιῆσαι ὑπερεκπερισσοῦ ὧν αἰτούμεθα ἢ νοοῦμεν κατὰ τὴν δύναμιν τὴν ἐνεργουμένην ἐν ἡμῖν, αὐτῷ ἡ δόξα ἐν τῇ ἐκκλησίᾳ καὶ ἐν Χριστῷ Ἰησοῦ εἰς πάσας τὰς γενεὰς τοῦ αἰῶνος τῶν αἰώνων, ἀμήν.

(6) Phil 4:20 τῷ δὲ θεῷ καὶ πατρὶ ἡμῶν ἡ δόξα εἰς τοὺς αἰῶνας τῶν αἰώνων, ἀμήν.

(7) 1 Tim 1:17 τῷ δὲ βασιλεῖ τῶν αἰώνων, ἀφθάρτῳ, ἀοράτῳ, μόνῳ θεῷ, τιμὴ καὶ δόξα εἰς τοὺς αἰῶνας τῶν αἰώνων, ἀμήν.

(8) 1 Tim 6:16 ὁ μόνος ἔχων ἀθανασίαν, φῶς οἰκῶν ἀπρόσιτον, ὃν εἶδεν οὐδεὶς ἀνθρώπων οὐδὲ ἰδεῖν δύναται· ᾧ τιμὴ καὶ κράτος αἰώνιον, ἀμήν.

(9) 2 Tim 4:18 ᾧ ἡ δόξα εἰς τοὺς αἰῶνας τῶν αἰώνων, ἀμήν.

12. Cf. especially Weima, *Endings*, pp. 135-44.

13. Lk 19:38 (λέγοντες, εὐλογημένος ὁ ἐρχόμενος, ὁ βασιλεὺς ἐν ὀνόματι κυρίου· ἐν οὐρανῷ εἰρήνη καὶ δόξα ἐν ὑψίστοις) echoes Lk 2:14 and we should probably supply θεῷ after ὑψίστοις as the indirect object, thus forming a complete doxology. Analysis of the doxologies will be simpler, however, if we omit this one from the list.

(10) Heb 13:21 ᾧ ἡ δόξα εἰς τοὺς αἰῶνας [τῶν αἰώνων], ἀμήν.

(11) 1 Pet 4:11 ἵνα ἐν πᾶσιν δοξάζηται ὁ θεὸς διὰ Ἰησοῦ Χριστοῦ, ᾧ ἐστιν ἡ δόξα καὶ τὸ κράτος εἰς τοὺς αἰῶνας τῶν αἰώνων, ἀμήν.

(12) 1 Pet 5:11 αὐτῷ τὸ κράτος εἰς τοὺς αἰῶνας, ἀμήν.

(13) 2 Pet 3:18 αὐξάνετε δὲ ἐν χάριτι καὶ γνώσει τοῦ κυρίου ἡμῶν καὶ σωτῆρος Ἰησοῦ Χριστοῦ. αὐτῷ ἡ δόξα καὶ νῦν καὶ εἰς ἡμέραν αἰῶνος. [ἀμήν.]

(14) Jude 24-25 Τῷ δὲ δυναμένῳ φυλάξαι ὑμᾶς ἀπταίστους καὶ στῆσαι κατενώπιον τῆς δόξης αὐτοῦ ἀμώμους ἐν ἀγαλλιάσει, μόνῳ θεῷ σωτῆρι ἡμῶν διὰ Ἰησοῦ Χριστοῦ τοῦ κυρίου ἡμῶν δόξα μεγαλωσύνη κράτος καὶ ἐξουσία πρὸ παντὸς τοῦ αἰῶνος καὶ νῦν καὶ εἰς πάντας τοὺς αἰῶνας, ἀμήν.

(15) Rev 1:6 καὶ ἐποίησεν ἡμᾶς βασιλείαν, ἱερεῖς τῷ θεῷ καὶ πατρὶ αὐτοῦ, αὐτῷ ἡ δόξα καὶ κράτος εἰς τοὺς αἰῶνας [τῶν αἰώνων]· ἀμήν.

(16) Rev 5:13 καὶ πᾶν κτίσμα ὃ ἐν τῷ οὐρανῷ καὶ ἐπὶ τῆς γῆς καὶ ὑποκάτω τῆς γῆς καὶ ἐπὶ τῆς θαλάσσης, καὶ τὰ ἐν αὐτοῖς πάντα, ἤκουσα λέγοντας, τῷ καθημένῳ ἐπὶ τῷ θρόνῳ καὶ τῷ ἀρνίῳ ἡ εὐλογία καὶ ἡ τιμὴ καὶ ἡ δόξα καὶ τὸ κράτος εἰς τοὺς αἰῶνας τῶν αἰώνων.

(17) Rev 7:12 λέγοντες, ἀμήν, ἡ εὐλογία καὶ ἡ δόξα καὶ ἡ σοφία καὶ ἡ εὐχαριστία καὶ ἡ τιμὴ καὶ ἡ δύναμις καὶ ἡ ἰσχὺς τῷ θεῷ ἡμῶν εἰς τοὺς αἰῶνας τῶν αἰώνων· ἀμήν.

From this conspectus we can see that the doxology in Romans has its closest parallels in Jude, Ephesians, and 1 Timothy and also that the basic form of the doxology is "to X [is] glory for ever and ever, amen." However, this basic form is subject to variation at every point.

1. The normal object of the doxology is God himself, who is specifically named in Lk 2:14; Phil 4:20; 1 Tim 1:17; Jude 24f.; Rev 7:12. In other cases God is clearly identifiable as the object by the context: Rom 11:36; Gal 1:5; Eph 3:20; 1 Tim 6:15-16. There is less certainty in 2 Tim 4:18; Heb 13:21; 1 Pet 4:11; 5:11; Rev 1:6 (the consensus on these verses is: God: Heb 13:21; 1 Pet 5:11; Christ: 2 Tim 4:18; 1 Pet 4:11; Rev 1:6). Christ is certainly the object in 2 Pet 3:18; God and Christ are named together in Rev 5:13.

2. The object may be specifically identified by name. God is named as θεός in Lk 2:14; Phil 4:20; 1 Tim 1:17; Jude 24f.; Rev 7:12. Christ is not named in any of the doxologies. The doxology may also have a third person pronoun substituted for the name of God/Christ (Rom 11:36; 1 Pet 5:11; 2 Pet 3:18; Rev 1:6); in three other cases the third person pronoun is inserted to pull the doxology back on track after a lengthy description (Rom 16:25-27; Eph 3:20f.; Jude 24f.). In the remaining cases the doxology is tied to what precedes by a relative pronoun (Gal 1:5; 1 Tim 6:16; 2 Tim 4:18; Heb 13:21; 1 Pet 4:11). Romans

16:25-27 is anomalous in that after the recapitulation there is an inserted relative pronoun which causes anacoluthon. The anacoluthon is avoided in some MSS, which either omit the relative pronoun or replace it with a personal pronoun.[14]

3. The description of God, which indicates the reasons for ascribing glory to him, can be expressed in two ways. The first is a string of epithets or other titles (Rom 16:25-27; Phil.4:20; 1 Tim 1:17; Jude 24f.; Rev 7:12). These may also be present in the context. The second way is to use a participial phrase (Rom 16:25-27; Eph 3:20f.; Jude 24f.; cf. Rev 5:13).

4. The honor ascribed to God/Christ is generally said to be δόξα (Lk 2:14; Rom 11:36; 16:25-27; Gal 1:5; Eph 3:20f.; Phil 4:20; 2 Tim 4:18; Heb 13:21; 2 Pet 3:18). Various synonyms or similar terms may also be added to the mention of "glory": τιμή (1 Tim 1:17); κράτος (1 Pet 4:11; Rev 1:6); there are longer strings in Jude 24f.; Rev 5:13; 7:12, which in all cases include κράτος. Finally, in two cases δόξα is omitted and replaced by other words: κράτος (1 Pet 5:11; 1 Tim 6:16 [+ αἰώνιον]).

5. Usually there is no verb, but ἐστίν appears in 1 Pet 4:11 and is to be supplied elsewhere. (1 Clement 32:4 has the imperative form.)

6. The insertion of an intermediary "through Jesus Christ" is found in Rom 16:25-27 and Jude 24f., and there is something similar ("in the church and in Jesus Christ") in Eph 3:20f. See further 1 Pet 4:11, where God is glorified through Jesus Christ in the immediate context of a doxology. The same thought is expressed in relation to prayers (Rom 1:8; 5:11; 7:25); it is striking that the only other uses in Paul are in Romans.

7. The doxology is completed by a reference to the eternal character of the glory or praise which is ascribed (this is lacking in Lk 2:14; 1 Tim 6:16). The simplest form is εἰς τοὺς αἰῶνας followed by an ἀμήν (Rom 11:36; Rom 16:25-27; Heb 13:21 *v. l.;* 1 Pet 5:11; Rev 1:6 *v. l.*). The more elaborate form εἰς τοὺς

14. There is no simple answer as to why the author got himself into this anacoluthon. The best solution may be that originally there was no relative pronoun (as in B 630 f sy^{p}), but that it was inserted by a scribe who was familiar with the most common wording of doxologies and fell into a stereotyped form of words (cf. Gal 1:5). Alternatively, the author himself may have fallen into the pattern by some slip, but this is perhaps less likely; an author is likely to be more wide awake than a scribe at the end of a long document. Cranfield, *Romans*, II, pp. 813f., offers two other possibilities. One is that the relative refers to Jesus, and that the author has slipped from what was intended to be a doxology to God into one to Christ; this seems most unlikely. The other is that the relative functions as an emphatic or demonstrative pronoun, simply picking up the previous reference to God. (This view goes back at least to E. Kamlah, "Traditionsgeschichtliche Untersuchungen zur Schlüssdoxologie des Römerbriefes," [Diss. Tübingen, 1955] [as cited by E. Käsemann, *Commentary on Romans* (Grand Rapids: Eerdmans, 1980), 423].) Cranfield thinks that the usage in 1 Pet 4:11 and perhaps Heb 13:21 is similar. Neither parallel seems compelling.

αἰῶνας τῶν αἰώνων, ἀμήν occurs in Gal 1:5; Phil 4:20; 1 Tim 1:17; 2 Tim 4:18; Heb 13:21 *v. l.;* 1 Pet 4:11; Rev 1:6 *v. l.;* Rev 5:13 (omitting ἀμήν); and Rev 7:12.[15] There are even fuller forms in Eph 3:20f.; 2 Pet 3:18; and Jude 24f. The responsive ἀμήν is present in all of the examples except Rev 5:13 (where it is added by the TR).

So far as the present doxology is concerned we may now observe:

1. There is a great variety of wording between the doxologies. The two features that always occur are the person to whom glory is ascribed (dative) and the honor that is ascribed (usually, but not always "glory"). The wording that occurs most frequently is ᾧ ἡ δόξα εἰς τοὺς αἰῶνας τῶν αἰώνων, ἀμήν (Gal 1:5; 2 Tim 4:18; Heb 13:21). But it is evident that writers did not feel constrained by it. Any and every item in the basic structure is open to elaboration and change. Romans 16:25-27 falls into the category of the fuller doxologies represented by Eph 3:20f.; Jude 24f.; Rev 5:13; 7:12. It glorifies God and begins by describing the unnamed recipient of the honor (in this case without elaboration). In the second part God is named and said to receive δόξα, which is given to him through Christ and which is his simply "forever."

2. Doxologies are found in three places in Paul's acknowledged correspondence (Rom 11:36; Gal 1:5; Phil 4:20) and also in Eph; 1 Tim and 2 Tim. They also occur in Luke (but there as a reported spoken statement); Heb; 1 Pet; 2 Pet; Jude and Rev. Doxologies conclude 2 Pet and Jude. Doxologies are thus characteristic of the later books of the New Testament but are by no means confined to them. There is accordingly nothing strange about the occurrence of a doxology at the end of Romans.

3. Doxologies also feature in the Apostolic Fathers, where we have 24 examples (9 in 1 Clement; 1 in 2 Clement; 6 in M. Polycarp; 7 in Didache; and 1 in Diognetus). They are normally expressed to God, but sometimes there is ambiguity (1 Clement 20:12; 50:7). In some cases the ascription is through Jesus Christ (1 Clement 58:2; 64; 65:2). In 1 Clement they follow references to the greatness and power and creative acts of God (1 Clement 20:12; 32:4; 38:4; 43:6; 45:7). Usually they are simple in form. But interestingly, two of the examples of final doxologies, including one which is attached to the closing benediction in 1 Clement 65:2, are slightly more elaborate in form; evidently liturgical fullness was appropriate at this point. 2 Clement 20:5 closes the homily with an elaborate doxology. The third example of a final doxology in Diognetus 12:9 is a simple one. There is an elaborate doxology in M. Polycarp 20:2 which is reminiscent of Jude, and others in 22:1. M. Poly-

15. A decision on the original text of Heb 13:21 and Rev 1:6 is not easy. Since the longer form is the more common, the shorter form of the two disputed readings is perhaps more likely to be the original and to have been conformed to the "normal" pattern.

carp is further distinguished by trinitarian doxologies in 14:3 ("through whom to you [God] with him [Christ] and the Holy Spirit be glory . . .") and 22:3 ("Jesus, to whom with [the] Father and [the] Holy Spirit is glory for ever and ever, Amen." Cf. the Moscow MS: "to whom with the Father and the Son and the Holy Spirit is glory for ever and ever, Amen"). Finally, in the Didache the Lord's Prayer concludes with a doxology (8:2) and the prayers of thanksgiving contain what may be a repeated responsive set of doxologies (9:2, 3, 4 and 10:2, 4, 5. In both cases the third doxology uses the genitive σοῦ rather than the customary dative σοί).

Some of the Apostolic Fathers thus show a tendency to an increased use of doxologies. Some of the usage is stereotyped but other examples are more elaborate and creative. It is noteworthy that three of the documents close with doxologies. This evidence shows that the inclusion of doxologies in Christian writings continued into the second century. In itself, of course, this does not constitute a case for saying that the doxology in Romans must also belong to the second century, as the phenomenon is also attested in the New Testament.

4. The function of a doxology is primarily to ascribe praise and honor to God for who he is and for what he does; sometimes the reason for the ascription is contained in the immediate context, but at other times it is included within the doxology itself. It is an expression of thanksgiving and awed wonder at the graciousness and greatness of God. Thanksgiving and worship belong together.

5. At the same time the purpose of a doxology is partly parenetic, in that it reminds the readers of important facts. This is particularly obvious in the expanded doxologies in Eph 3:20f. and Jude 24f., which develop the thoughts of God's mighty power and his ability to preserve his people respectively. Together with Rom 16, these doxologies show a close parallelism in structure and content, in that all of them are concerned with what God is able to do in the lives of believers. They appear to represent variant forms, appropriate to each individual epistolary context, of a common structure praising God for his saving power.

In Romans 16:25-27 the paraenesis lies in the reminder that God is able[16] to strengthen the readers to stand fast. The verb "to strengthen" expresses a major purpose of Paul's pastoral dealings (Rom 1:11; 1 Thess 3:2; *et al.*), an activity which both in Romans and elsewhere is also ascribed to God (1 Thess 3:13; 2 Thess 2:17; 3:3; 1 Pet 5:10). It is entirely in keeping with Paul's habits elsewhere to refer at the same time to both the human and divine aspects of

16. The doxology begins with the set phrase "he who is able." This is also found in Eph 3:21 and Jude v. 24; M. Poly 20:2; cf. Acts 20:32. It is evidently a set form.

strengthening in this way (cf. 1 Thess 3:2, 13; note Rom 14:4 for a similar thought).

This, then, is a natural pastoral concern that does not need any particular motivation; it places this doxology alongside the ones in Heb 13:20f.; 1 Pet 5:10f.; 2 Pet 3:18; and especially Jude 24f., and it corresponds to a similar concern displayed without the use of the doxology form at the conclusion of other letters (1 Thess 5:23f.; cf. 1 Cor 15:58; 2 Cor 13:9; Eph 6:22; Phil 4:7; Col 4:8; Jas 5:8; 1 Pet 5:10; 1 Jn 5:18-20).

6. In addition to the parenetic element there is also an element of a more doctrinal nature in Romans 16:25-27. The readers are reminded that the strengthening takes place in accordance with the gospel preached by Paul and the proclamation of Jesus Christ. κατά is a notoriously difficult preposition to interpret. In other occurrences of the phrase κατὰ τὸ εὐαγγέλιόν μου, it appears to mean "in accordance with what my understanding of the gospel teaches" (Rom 2:16; 2 Tim 2:8; cf. 1 Tim 1:11, "according to the gospel of God"). It is thus a strengthening that has its basis in Christian salvation rather than any general sort of "You will be able to stand firm because God is on your side."[17] The implication is that the gospel teaches that God is able and willing to sustain his people, exactly as Jude 24 teaches.[18] One could also say that the thoughts expressed in Romans 8 regarding perseverance are summed up here.

The gospel is described as "my gospel" and further defined by a second phrase, "the preaching of Jesus Christ," which must mean the preaching whose content is Jesus Christ. This emphasis on the gospel preached by Paul is comprehensible at the end of a letter which has been devoted to setting out "my gospel" (Rom 2:16; cf. Gal 2:2; 2 Tim 2:8). "Preaching" (κήρυγμα) is a characteristically Pauline term (1 Cor 1:21; 2:4; 15:14; 2 Tim 4:17; Titus 1:3; cf. Mt 12:41 par. Lk 11:32), and the object is generally the gospel or Christ. The word itself is surprisingly rare in Pauline literature. In 1 Cor 1:21, 2:4, and 15:14, it is the content of what Paul preaches; in 1 Cor 1:21 its content is also said to be folly to unbelievers; in Titus 1:3 (cf. 2 Tim 4:17) it is the message entrusted to Paul. There is apparently a thin line between the message itself and the activity of preaching it. In Romans 16, a significant part of the message is the fact that God strengthens his people.

7. A further element in the doxology is the description of God as the only God who is wise. These are standing epithets of God; "only" recurs in 1 Tim 1:17; Jude 25. "Wise" is not used of God elsewhere in the New Testament (ex-

17. In Eph 3:20f. The "power that is at work in us" is of course the power of the Holy Spirit, the indwelling of Christ, and the fullness of God (vv. 16-19).

18. Cranfield's view that it means that God will confirm them in their belief in the gospel does not do adequate justice to the phrase (p. 809).

cept Jude 25 TR, evidently by contamination with Rom 16). The phrase fits into the context of Romans with its stress on the fact that there is [only] one God who will justify both Jews and Gentiles on the same basis (Rom 3:30; cf. 1 Cor 8:4, 6; Gal 3:20; Eph 4:6; 1 Tim 2:5). Similarly, the reference to wisdom picks up on 11:33, where God's saving wisdom is the object of adoration.[19]

IV. The Embedded Once/Now Structure

The next part of the doxology seems to go off at a tangent. We have a second κατά phrase, which may parallel the first one or may qualify it. The difference in meaning is not great, whichever view of the syntax we adopt. The gospel (or what it teaches) is "according to the revelation of the mystery." This indicates that the gospel is consonant with the mystery and implies that through the preaching of the gospel the "mystery" is made known.

Pauline usage establishes that the "mystery" is primarily the content of God's purpose to save humanity, and specifically to include both Jews and Gentiles in this salvation (Col 1:26f.; Eph 3:3-7; cf. Rom 11:25-32 for further discussion of the "mystery" of the place of the Jews alongside the Gentiles). The mystery is the saving plan of God now revealed to Paul and other stewards of the mysteries of God (1 Cor 4:1). It has been made known so as to lead to the obedience of faith (cf. 1:5) for all the nations.[20] Here is the universal note which is characteristic of Paul and which is particularly central in Romans.

But to speak of a "mystery" in this way is to imply that previously it was not revealed, and this leads the writer directly into the traditional structure of once/now or promised-hidden/fulfilled/revealed, which can be expressed in various ways (1 Cor 2:7-10; Col 1:26; Eph 3:4-7; 3:8-11; 2 Tim 1:9f.; Titus 1:2f.; 1 Pet 1:20). Basically, it contrasts the statements that the mystery was once hidden but is now revealed, or that salvation was once promised but has now been revealed. The present passage is particularly close to Titus 1:2f.

The hidden aspect is here expressed by the phrase "kept silent for eternal times,"[21] the only use of this verb in this context in the New Testament (other-

19. Cranfield, *Romans,* II, p. 814, suggests that the compound phrase has the force "who alone is wise," a thought that would fit in with Rom 11:33-36.

20. It is not clear whether "to all the nations" is governed by the participle ("made known to all the Gentiles . . . to bring about the obedience of faith," NRSV) or by the phrase "for obedience of faith" ("made known . . . so that all the nations might believe and obey him," NIV). γνωρίζω generally takes the dative of the indirect object; Phil 4:6 is in the special context of prayer. Therefore the NIV rendering is preferable.

21. "Eternal times" is a phrase found only in other expressions of the same structure (2 Tim 1:9; Titus 1:2).

wise it refers to human beings being silent). Elsewhere the word "hidden" is used (1 Cor 2:7; Col 1:26; Eph 3:9; "not made known," in Eph 3:5).[22]

The contrast is expressed by "revealed now," i.e., in the present age. We might have expected some account of how or where it has been made known in line with other examples of the same structure: "through the epiphany of our Savior Jesus Christ" (2 Tim 1:10); "he made known his word in the preaching" (Titus 1:3); "to us by the Spirit" (1 Cor 2:10); "now revealed to his holy ones" (Col 1:26); "now revealed to his holy apostles and prophets in the Spirit" (Eph 3:5); "made known now through the church" (Eph 3:10). Instead of this constant reference to what God is doing now through the Spirit in his (Christian) people, we appear to have the exegesis of "revealed" in the phrase that follows: "and made known through prophetic writings according to the command of the eternal God to [bring about] obedience of faith among all the nations." At first sight this is odd because it seems to place the making known in the time of the Old Testament rather than the New Testament. However, the comment fits in with the phrase "witnessed to by the law and the prophets" (3:21). To emphasize that it is the Scriptures through which the mystery is made known is highly appropriate in this context, given the concern in Romans to stress the Scriptural basis of the Pauline gospel. The Scriptures are seen as being/including prophetic writings in the sense that God announces in them what he is going to do, and Christian preachers like Paul believe that they can see the fulfillment of his promises taking place before their eyes. The nature of the gospel events is made clear by illumination, which indicates how those events are to be understood.[23] All this takes place in accordance with the express command of God. It is not that the evangelization of the Gentiles is an optional extra that the church, or some parts of the church, can carry out if it pleases: it is the express command of God that is to be carried out. The Gentile readers are assured that there is almost a divine "bias toward the Gentiles," despite the fact that the gospel comes "to the Jews first" and despite the intensity of Paul's concern for his own people. It is therefore significant that "eternal" brings out the fact that the same God who conceived his plan before time has now revealed it in accordance with his deliberate command, the same command that lies behind the commissioning of the apostle and his colleagues in the pastoral epistles ("by the command of the eternal God" is a phrase used elsewhere of God's commissioning of Paul as an apostle; 1 Tim 1:1; Titus 1:3). So the emphatic teaching is that the mission to

22. The significance of "silence" is discussed by L. M. Dewailly, "Mystère et Silence dans Rom. xvi.25," *NTS* 14 (1967): 111-18, who draws attention to the perfect participle as expressing an action by God himself creating a silence which is not abolished by the gospel revelation; God's secret remains God's secret even though it is revealed in Christ.

23. Cranfield, *Romans*, II, p. 812.

the Gentiles is not just a plan of God that he may suddenly have thought up; it is his settled purpose conceived in eternity and expressed prophetically in the Scriptures.

It may seem curious that nothing is apparently said about the present form of the revelation. The participle "revealed" is not qualified in any way. But in effect the qualification has already been expressed. God's purpose is being revealed in that gospel and in the preaching of it committed to Paul, in accordance with which he can be sure that God is able to strengthen his readers. Nothing more needed to be added to make the point clear. "According to the gospel" and "according to the revelation of the mystery" are complementary phrases. Thus the phrase "now revealed" recapitulates "according to my gospel and the preaching of Jesus Christ." There is thus a plasticity of expression which shows that the writer is not hidebound by the traditional structures he is using.

All this confirms what has been said by others, namely that the thought fits in aptly with the letter. Nevertheless, there may be evidence that suggests later compilation. Traces of the structure have been detected in Ignatius, *Mag.* 6:1 ("Jesus Christ, who was with the Father before the worlds and appeared at the end of time"), and Hermas, *Sim.* 9:12 ("The Son of God is older than all his creation. . . . He was made manifest in the last days of the consummation"). However, M. Wolter assigns this material together with 2 Timothy 1:9f. and 1 Peter 1:20 to a variant form of the scheme which lacks the "once hidden/now revealed" structure and stresses rather the eschatological time point of Christ's appearing.[24] The nearest we come to it is in Diognetus 8: "And having conceived a great and unutterable scheme he communicated it to his Son alone. For so long as he kept and guarded his wise design as a mystery, he seemed to neglect us and to be careless about us. But when he revealed it through his beloved Son, and manifested the purpose which he had prepared from the beginning, he gave us all these gifts at once, participation in his benefits, and sight and understanding of (mysteries) which none of us ever would have expected."[25] This is a very free use of the structure which is still fairly rigidly preserved in Romans 16. There is nothing here to suggest that the Romans structure belongs to the later period. Rather, the closest links of Romans 16 are with 2 Timothy and Titus. It is significant that the once/now structure is confined to the Pauline material and 1 Peter in the New Testament, including those books which may have been worked up by the followers of Paul rather than Paul himself. As Hurtado previously observed, the links between the doxology and the so-called

24. M. Wolter, "Verborgene Weisheit und Heil für die Heiden: Zur Traditionsgeschichte und Intention des 'Revelationsschemas'," *ZTK* 84 (1987): 297-319 (313).

25. Translation from J. B. Lightfoot and J. R. Harmer, *The Apostolic Fathers* (Grand Rapids: Baker, 1984 reprint), pp. 301-2.

"deutero-Paulines" "can be used against the authenticity of the doxology only if one can be certain that all these letters in no way come from Paul."[26] But that is something of which we cannot be certain. It is equally possible that the later letters preserve a genuine Pauline structure and were deeply influenced by it, whether or not they are directly from the pen of Paul.[27] In short, so far as the once/now structure is concerned, the later occurrences of the motif in no way affect the possibility that the motif is original to Romans.

V. Conclusion

I conclude that the doxology fits aptly at the end of Romans, a conclusion I recognize as in no way original but nonetheless worth restating. It does so, whether or not it was composed by the author of the letter. But the way in which it is composed, that is, in a highly allusive kind of way, rather suggests that it was not composed by a later hand but was the work of Paul himself, who was perfectly capable of adapting such so-called "liturgical" material, i.e., forms of words that were based on material spoken in the church meetings or that were intended to form a basis for such use.[28] In any case, the fact that the nearest parallels to both the doxological structure and to the "once hidden/now revealed" structure are found in Ephesians, the Pastoral Epistles, and Jude strongly suggests that the composition belongs to this period rather than to a later date in the second century.

The effect of the doxology is to gather together the main themes of the letter regarding God's plan of salvation for the Gentiles in accordance with the gospel revealed to Paul.[29] In accordance with his plan, expressed in the gospel, the readers can be sure of God's mighty action to strengthen them in their faith, as promised at the outset of the letter (1:11), and they are rightly called to ascribe praise and glory to this God, confirming the doxology with their responsive "Amen." Already at an earlier point in Romans, Paul had given vivid expression to his wonder at the ways of God (11:33-36). It is not surprising that at the

26. Hurtado, "The Doxology at the End of Romans," p. 191.

27. If the doxology should in fact go back to Paul himself, this would indicate that some of the material in the letters commonly termed "deutero-Pauline" stands closer to him than sometimes supposed.

28. Without committing himself on the matter, J. A. Ziesler (*Paul's Letter to the Romans* [London: SCM Press, 1989], pp. 356f.) observes that "there is nothing in the passage that is at odds with [Paul's] thought, or indeed that he might not have adapted from liturgical tradition."

29. For a similar conclusion see Weima, *Endings*, 229f.; cf. also J. R. W. Stott, *Romans: God's Good News for the World* (Downers Grove, Ill.: InterVarsity Press, 1994), pp. 405f.

end of the letter he is moved to praise God and to gather up some of the main themes of the letter in his own expression of praise, which the readers are invited to echo.[30]

May these few thoughts express my thanks to a scholar whose work of interpretation has always had as its goal that the readers of the New Testament may similarly be moved to praise and thanksgiving to God the Savior.

30. Cf. Childs, *The New Testament as Canon,* p. 254, for the insight that "the doxology is not a liturgical response of the letter's recipients to Paul's words, but a liturgical response of Paul to the subject of his book."

THEMATIC ESSAYS

Reasoned Eclecticism and the Text of Romans

Michael W. Holmes

The circumstance that the two most widely used editions of the Greek New Testament (the Nestle-Aland and United Bible Societies editions)[1] present an identical text makes it easy for some readers to conclude that the wording of the various documents comprising the New Testament has been definitively established. In the case of Romans, however, there is yet room for discussion at a number of places, and even where the printed text is not in question, an examination of variants in the apparatus is instructive with regard to the history of the transmission of the text, its interpretation, and text-critical methodology. Since all of these topics have been for many years of more than passing interest to our honoree, I am glad to offer some brief observations on various passages in Romans in recognition of his deep interest and high achievements in the field of New Testament textual criticism.

In what follows, the overarching concern may be indicated by a question: Within the framework of a reasoned eclecticism,[2] where, with respect to

1. Since the third UBS edition (1975) and 26th Nestle-Aland edition (1979), both have been edited by the same editorial committee (originally K. Aland, M. Black, C. M. Martini, B. M. Metzger, and A. Wikgren; for the fourth UBS and 27th Nestle-Aland editions [both 1993] B. Aland and J. Karavidopoulos replaced retired members Black and Wikgren).

2. By "reasoned eclecticism" I mean an approach to New Testament textual criticism that seeks to take into account all the evidence, both external and internal, on a passage-by-passage basis. It stands in contrast to, on the one hand, "rigorous" or "thoroughgoing" eclecticism (which relies almost exclusively on internal considerations, as in the work of G. D. Kilpatrick or J. K. Elliott), and, on the other hand, a "documentary" approach (which seeks to

Romans, does the ultimate weight lie, with external or internal considerations? In section I, an analysis of discussions of the text of Romans 5:1 (and others) suggests that the decisive criteria involve internal, rather than external, evidence or considerations. In section II it is argued that such an approach — one that gives careful consideration to external evidence but frequently bases a final decision on internal evidence — is required by the textual history of Romans. Section III then offers a reexamination of some variants in Romans in light of the considerations set out in sections I and II, and section IV suggests some wider implications of the discussion.

I

One of the better-known and widely debated textual problems in Romans involves the variation between indicative and imperative in 5:1 (ἔχομεν 01^1 B^2 F G P Ψ 0220^{vid} 1505.1506.1739^c.1881.2464 *pm* vg^{mss} sa; NA^{27}] ἔχωμεν 01* A B* C D K L 33.1739* *pm* f g vg bo $Mcion^T$; WH). The comments in the UBS *Textual Commentary* make the case for the indicative: "Although the subjunctive . . . has far better external support than the indicative . . . a majority of the Committee judged that internal evidence must here take precedence. Since in this passage it appears that Paul is not exhorting but stating facts ("peace" is the possession of those who have been justified), only the indicative is consonant with the apos-

eliminate any appeal to internal considerations and to base a decision solely on external evidence, as in the "majority text" theory). For a brief introduction to this approach focused on the Pauline letters, see M. W. Holmes, "Textual Criticism," in G. F. Hawthorne, R. P. Martin, and D. G. Reid (eds.), *Dictionary of Paul and His Letters* (Downers Grove, Ill.: InterVarsity Press, 1993), pp. 927-32; for fuller treatments see Gordon D. Fee, *New Testament Exegesis: A Handbook for Students and Pastors,* rev. ed. (Louisville, Ky.: Westminster/John Knox, 1993), pp. 81-91, and especially Bruce M. Metzger, *The Text of the New Testament,* 3d, enlarged ed. (New York and Oxford: Oxford University Press, 1992), pp. 207-46. For a critical analysis of this approach, consult Michael W. Holmes, "Reasoned Eclecticism in New Testament Textual Criticism," in Bart D. Ehrman and Michael W. Holmes, *The Text of the New Testament in Contemporary Research: Essays on the* Status Quaestionis (Studies and Documents, 46; Grand Rapids: Eerdmans, 1995), pp. 336-60.

See also Gordon D. Fee, "Rigorous or Reasoned Eclecticism — Which?" reprinted in Eldon Jay Epp and Gordon D. Fee, *Studies in the Theory and Method of New Testament Textual Criticism* (Studies and Documents, 45; Grand Rapids: Eerdmans, 1993), pp. 124-40 (a classic critique of "rigorous" eclecticism); J. Keith Elliott, "Thoroughgoing Eclecticism in New Testament Textual Criticism," in Ehrman and Holmes, *The Text of the New Testament in Contemporary Research,* pp. 321-35 (a sympathetic statement by its leading practitioner); and Daniel B. Wallace, "The Majority Text Theory: History, Methods, and Critique," in Ehrman and Holmes, *The Text of the New Testament in Contemporary Research,* pp. 297-320 (a withering critique).

tle's argument. Since the difference in pronunciation between ο and ω in the Hellenistic age was almost non-existent, when Paul dictated ἔχομεν, Tertius, his amanuensis (16.22), may have written down ἔχωμεν."[3]

On the other hand, Fee has argued (in classic Fee style and tone) on behalf of the subjunctive: "the original text in v. 1 is ἔχωμεν . . . and not the poorly attested ἔχομεν of the later Greek tradition. . . . The latter is usually preferred (1) on the (false) basis of the frequency of an omega/omicron interchange[4] in the textual history of the NT . . . and (2) on the (presumptuous) basis that the context demands the indicative, which seems to be a polite way of saying that scholars have difficulty believing that Paul would argue differently from themselves. . . . Better by far to go with Paul, whose use of the subjunctive here functions as an "imperative" only in a more distant sense. Indeed, most such subjunctives in Paul *assume* the prior indicative and thus embrace it as part of the exhortation. . . . Paul's point is application, pure and simple."[5]

These arguments parallel those of earlier generations. Like Fee, Sanday and Headlam preferred the subjunctive: "Clearly overwhelming authority for ἔχωμεν. It is argued however (i) that exhortation is here out of place . . . (ii) that ο and ω are frequently interchanged in the MSS. . . . (iii) it is possible that a mis-

3. Bruce M. Metzger (on behalf of and in cooperation with the Editorial Committee of the United Bible Societies' Greek New Testament), *A Textual Commentary on the Greek New Testament,* 2nd ed. (Stuttgart: Deutsche Bibelgesellschaft, 1994), p. 452.

4. Regarding the question of *omicron-omega* interchange, see the exploratory note by Ian A. Moir ("Orthography and Theology: The Omicron-Omega Interchange in Romans 5:1 and Elsewhere," in E. J. Epp and G. D. Fee [eds.], *New Testament Textual Criticism: Its Significance for Exegesis. Essays in Honour of Bruce M. Metzger* [Oxford: Clarendon Press, 1981], pp. 179-83) and the evidence collected by F. T. Gignac (*A Grammar of the Greek Papyri of the Roman and Byzantine Periods,* vol. 1: *Phonology* [Testi e documenti per lo studio dell'antichià, 55/1; Milan: Cisalpino-La Goliardica, 1976], pp. 275-77), which includes examples such as λέγο (for λέγω) and ἀπώ (for ἀπό). One apparent consequence is the relativization of the manuscript evidence: even if an autograph were available, writes J. H. Moulton, "it would be no evidence as to the author's grammar if he dictated the text" (*A Grammar of New Testament Greek,* vol. 1: *Prolegomena,* 3d ed. [Edinburgh: T. & T. Clark, 1908], p. 35; but cf. also vol. 2, p. 74). Therefore, the Alands conclude, "we can be certain only that the correctors of [01] and B intended ἔχομεν when they emended the ἔχωμεν of their exemplars. The external criteria yield no certainty here, so that internal criteria become determinative" (K. Aland and B. Aland, *The Text of the New Testament: An Introduction to the Critical Editions and to the Theory and Practice of Modern Textual Criticism,* 2nd rev. and enlarged ed. [Grand Rapids: Eerdmans; Leiden: Brill, 1989], p. 286). Other instances of this interchange in Romans include, in addition to 14:19 (discussed below), 3:28 (λογιζόμεθα] λογιζώμεθα K P 1175.2464 *al*); 3.29 (μόνον] μόνων B 945 1739^{c} *pc* Cl); 6:22 (ζήσομεν 01 A B D 1739.1881 Maj latt Cl] ζήσωμεν P^{46} C F G L Ψ 33.81.1241.2464 *al*).

5. Gordon D. Fee, *God's Empowering Presence: The Holy Spirit in the Pauline Letters* (Peabody, Mass.: Hendrickson, 1994), p. 495, n. 66.

take might have been made by Tertius. . . . But these reasons seem insufficient to overthrow the weight of direct testimony. (i) St. Paul is apt to pass from argument to exhortation . . . (ii) in ἔχωμεν inference and exhortation are really combined: it is a sort of light exhortation, 'we *should* have'. . . ."[6] Scrivener, however, argued for the indicative: while granting, with regard to external evidence, that "the case for ἔχομεν is much weaker," nevertheless it is to be preferred, "for the closer the context is examined the clearer it will appear that *inference* not *exhortation* is the Apostle's purpose. . . . Here, as in 2 Cor. iii.3, we find the chief uncials supporting a reading which is manifestly unsuitable to the context, although, since it does not absolutely destroy the sense, it does not (nor indeed does that other passage) lack strenuous defenders."[7]

It is remarkable how closely the two recent representative statements echo the earlier discussions (an indication, perhaps, of how little the discussion has advanced or the evidence changed over the last century or so). Of more interest are the kinds of arguments offered, an analysis of which indicates that internal criteria play the decisive role. To be sure, one side contends (and the other side concedes) that the weight of external evidence here favors the subjunctive. But elsewhere — e.g., Romans 14:19, διώκωμεν C D Ψ 33.1739.1881 Maj latt co; WH NA[27]] διώκομεν 01 A B F G L P 048.0209.6.326.629 *al* — virtually the same combination of external evidence is (rightly, in my judgment) set aside by those who insist that it be followed here (e.g., Westcott and Hort, Fee)[8]. This circumstance strongly indicates that external evidence plays a supporting, rather than a primary, role in the decision regarding the text. The really decisive criterion involves an internal consideration, in this instance how one reads the flow of Paul's argument (compare, e.g., the comments of Scrivener and Fee above).[9]

6. W. Sanday and A. C. Headlam, *A Critical and Exegetical Commentary on the Epistle to the Romans,* 5th ed., ICC (Edinburgh: T. & T. Clark, 1902 [1st ed. 1895]), p. 120.

7. F. H. A. Scrivener, *A Plain Introduction to the Criticism of the New Testament for the Use of Biblical Students,* 4th ed., 2 vols., ed. Edward Miller (London & New York: George Bell & Sons, 1894), vol. 2, pp. 379-80.

8. See *Presence,* pp. 621, 449, 596. Sanday and Headlam, who characterize the subjunctive in 14:19 as a "somewhat obvious correction" (p. 392), nonetheless in their (paraphrasing) translation of the text ("Let us . . .") appear to follow it (*Romans,* p. 383).

9. See also the discussions of 5:1 and 14:19 by Cranfield, who offers excellent examples of internal considerations trumping external evidence (C. E. B. Cranfield, *A Critical and Exegetical Commentary on the Epistle to the Romans,* ICC, 2 vols. [Edinburgh: T. & T. Clark, 1975, 1979], vol. 1, p. 257, n. 1; vol. 2, pp. 720-21).

With regard to the question of the indicative vs. the imperative and the flow of Paul's argument, it may be observed that apart from 5:1, the instance in contention (and setting aside for obvious contextual reasons 3:8), there are no hortatory subjunctives in Romans 1–9. It may be further observed that apart from 3:4 (which has no bearing on the issue in question), there are no imperatives in chs. 1–10 outside of a cluster of five in ch. 6

Similarly, the priority of internal considerations over external attestation is clearly evident in the UBS Editorial Committee's treatment of 3:7 (δέ 01 A 81.365.1506 *pc* bo Aug; NA[27]] γάρ B D G K L P Ψ 6.33.1241.1739.1881.2464 Maj lat sy sa Origen[lat]): "A majority of the Committee, feeling that Paul's argument requires a parallel between verses 5 and 7, preferred the reading εἰ δέ and regarded εἰ γάρ as a rather inept scribal substitution, perhaps of Western origin."[10] Here a reading with very strong external support from all three extant textual traditions (Alexandrian [B.33.1739 sa], Western [DG lat], and Byzantine [K L P Maj]) is (rightly, in my opinion) set aside entirely on the basis of internal considerations.

II

An approach such as this, which gives careful and deliberate consideration to external evidence (i.e., the evidence provided by the manuscripts and other witnesses) but not infrequently bases a final decision on internal evidence (i.e., transcriptional considerations, dealing with habits and practices of copyists, and intrinsic considerations, involving authorial style, vocabulary, argument, etc.), is required in large part by the very nature of the textual history of the Pauline corpus and of Romans in particular. Consider the following examples of variation in Romans (in each instance the genuine reading is given first, followed by secondary variants; the lemmas are from NA[27]). In particular, observe the shifting patterns of alignment among the manuscript witnesses, and how the same groups of witnesses variously support both genuine and secondary readings.

3:28 [. . . λογιζόμεθα γὰρ δικαιοῦσθαι πίστει ἄνθρωπον . . .]
γάρ 01 A D* F G Ψ 81.630.1506.1739.1881 *al*] οὖν B C D² K L P 6.33.1175.1241.2464 Maj.[11]

(6:11, 12, 13, 13, 19). Hesitant though I am to disagree with Fee, I am nonetheless inclined to view these observations as evidence favoring the indicative in 5:1.

10. Metzger, *Textual Commentary*, p. 448; so also Lagrange (M.-J. Lagrange, *Saint Paul: Épître aux Romains*, 6th ed. [Paris: Gabalda, 1950], p. 66). In favor of the alternative reading (adopted in the UBS first edition) see Cranfield, *Romans*, vol. 1, p. 185, n. 3.

11. The UBS *Textual Commentary* (p. 450) follows closely Lagrange: "lire γάρ *(Ti., WH.)* et non pas οὖν *(Soden)*. οὖν indiquerait que Paul cite cette conséquence pour la première fois; ce qui est contre tout le contexte. Il entend plutôt donner la raison de son affirmation, d'après ce qu'il a déjà ét abli. Dès lors λογιζόμεθα ne signifie pas 'nous inférons', mais 'nous tenons, nous pensons'" (*Romains*, p. 79); cf. Cranfield: "The reading οὖν is perhaps to be explained (as Bengel suggested . . .) as an accidental repetition of the οὖν of the previous verse" (*Romans*, vol. 1, p. 220, n. 4).

4:19 [καὶ μὴ ἀσθενήσας τῇ πίστει κατενόησεν τὸ ἑαυτοῦ σῶμα [ἤδη] νενεκρωμένον . . .]

(a) τῇ πίστει *rell*] ἐν τῇ πίστει D* F G.

(b) κατενόησεν 01 A B C 6.81.1506.1739 *pc* m sy^{p} co] οὐ κατενόησεν D F G K L P Ψ 33.1175.1241.1881.2464 Maj it syh.

(c) *omit* ἤδη B F G 630.1739.1881 *pc* lat sy^{p} sa] *include* ἤδη 01 A C D K L P Ψ 6.33.81.1175.1241.1506.2464 Maj m sy^{h**} bo.

[Only the rejected reading in (a) is properly labeled "Western," and, like so many Western readings, involves an adaptation of the text (in this case, the addition of a clarifying preposition). Neither of the other two variants are "Western" in any meaningful sense of the term; both may be traced back to a second-century "reservoir" (Zuntz's term) of readings out of which the various textual traditions later emerged.[12] What is interesting is the alignment of the various textual traditions. The Western readings (here preserved by F G) align with the earliest strand of the Alexandrian tradition (B 1739) in (c) but not (b), while the bulk of the Alexandrian witnesses (01 A etc.) oppose F G in both instances. The Byzantine tradition, reversing the pattern of B 1739, joins F G in (b) but not (c). In short, in both (b) and (c) the Byzantine tradition preserves readings that are sensible and superficially attractive, but secondary; the original readings are likely preserved by B 1739.[13]]

5:6 [ἔτι γὰρ Χριστὸς ὄντων ἡμῶν ἀσθενῶν ἔτι κατὰ καιρὸν . . . ἀπέθανεν.]

(a) ἔτι γὰρ . . . ἔτι] 01 A C^{vid} D* 81.1241.1506 *pc* Epiph

(b) ἔτι γὰρ . . . *omit*] D^{2} K P Ψ 6.33.1175.1739.1881.2464 Maj

(c) εἴ γε . . . ἔτι] B 945 vg^{mss} sa (bo) Aug

(d) εἴ γάρ γε . . . ἔτι] 1852 vg^{mss}

12. G. Zuntz, *The Text of the Epistles. A Disquisition upon the* Corpus Paulinum (London: British Academy, 1953), pp. 265-66.

13. Regarding (b) see Metzger, *Textual Commentary*, p. 451. With respect to ἤδη, only a majority of the Editorial Committee thought that "[t]he predominant weight of manuscript evidence . . . favors the retention" of the word, which "gives the impression of a certain heightening of the account. Moreover, who would have omitted the word had it stood in the text originally?" The brackets around the word reflect "the conflict between external evidence and internal considerations" (*Textual Commentary*, pp. 451-52). In the other occurrences of ἤδη in the Pauline corpus (Rom 13:11; 1 Cor 4:8; 5:3; 6:7; Phil 3:12; 2 Thess 2:7; 1 Tim 5:15; 2 Tim 2:18; 4:6), the term typically emphasizes something that is happening unexpectedly early or before its expected time — which hardly seems to be the case in 4:19, especially in light of the following explanatory clause ("since he was about a hundred years old"). Moreover, the combination of Alexandrian (B 1739 sa) and Western (F G lat) witnesses supporting the omission of the word is not inconsequential. Thus I am inclined to omit the word.

(e) εἰς τί γὰρ . . . ἔτι] D^1 F G lat Ir^{lat} Ambst Pel
[Here the tradition simply fragments; in the opinion of the UBS Editorial Committee, it is possible that none of the extant readings is original.[14]]

6:8 [εἰ δὲ ἀπεθάνομεν σὺν Χριστῷ, . . .]
δέ *rell*] γάρ p^{46} FG 945 *pc* vg^{mss}

6:11 [. . . λογίζεσθε ἑαυτοὺς [εἶναι] νεκροὺς μὲν . . . ζῶντας δὲ . . . ἐν Χριστῷ Ἰησοῦ.]
(a) εἶναι P^{94vid} 01* B C 81.1506.1739.1881 *pc*] *place after* μέν 01^2 D^1 Ψ Maj lat; *omit* P^{46vid} A D* F G 33^{vid} *pc* Tert.
(b) ἐν Χριστῷ Ἰησοῦ P^{46} A B D F G Ψ 630.1739* *pc* it sy^h sa Tert] + τῷ κυρίῳ ἡμῶν P^{94vid} 01 C K L P 6.33.81.1241.1506.1739^c.1881.2464 Maj bo Ambst; *omit* Ir^{lat} $Origen^{lat9/11}$ Amb Jer Aug.
[Notice the split between P^{46}/DFG and B 1739 in the first variant, and their agreement in the second (with 33 doing the opposite); also, P^{94} 01 C 81.1506.1881 are against the papyrus in both places (splitting with B 1739 in the second variant).]

6:12 [μὴ οὖν βασιλευέτω ἡ ἁμαρτία ἐν τῷ θνητῷ ὑμῶν σώματι εἰς τὸ ὑπακούειν ταῖς ἐπιθυμίαις αὐτοῦ, . . .]
(a) ταῖς ἐπιθυμίαις αὐτοῦ] P^{94} 01 A B C* 6.81.1506.1739.1881 *al* lat sy^p co (Or) Did
(b) αὐτῇ P^{46} D F G b Ir^{lat} Tert Ambst
(c) αὐτῃ ἐν ταῖς ἐπιθυμίαις αὐτοῦ] C^3 K L P Ψ 1175.1241.2464 Maj sy^h
(d) αὐτοῦ ἐν ταῖς ἐπιθυμίαις αὐτοῦ] 33.1912 *pc*
[Here the differing forms of the text reflect different interpretations of its meaning: in (a) the antecedent of αὐτοῦ is σώματι ("body"), while in (b) the antecedent of αὐτῇ is ἁμαρτία ("sin").]

6:21 [. . . τὸ γὰρ τέλος ἐκείνων θάνατος. [22]νυνὶ δὲ . . .]
τὸ γὰρ 01* A C D^2 Ψ 33.1739.1881 Maj Cl] τὸ μὲν γὰρ P^{94vid} 01^2 B D*F G 1505 *pc* sy^h.
[As Cranfield observes, the μέν "is not likely to be original: it is inappropriate here, and was probably introduced by mistake as correlative to the first δέ of v. 22."[15]]

14. "[T]he reading adopted as text seems to be the earliest attainable reading preserved in the manuscripts; whether it originated as a primitive error in the exemplar of the first collection of the Pauline Letters, or whether it arose when, as one may assume, Paul repeated ἔτι, perhaps for the sake of emphasis, while dictating to Tertius . . . it is impossible to say" (Metzger, *Textual Commentary*, p. 453).

15. Cranfield, *Romans*, vol. 1, p. 327, n. 5.

7:6 [. . . ὥστε δουλεύειν ἡμᾶς ἐν καινότητι πνεύματος . . .]
ἡμᾶς 01 A C D Ψ 33.1739.1881 Maj] ὑμᾶς 1505 *pc; omit* B F G 629
[Notice both here and in 6:21 the B + Western (FG) agreement, neither of which was preserved by the ancient ancestor of 1739.]

8:23 [. . . ἡμεῖς καὶ αὐτοὶ ἐν ἑαυτοῖς στενάζομεν υἱοθεσίαν ἀπεκδεχόμενοι . . .]
(a) ἡμεῖς καὶ αὐτοί P^{46} 01 A C 81.1506. 1739.1881 *pc*] καὶ ἡμεῖς αὐτοί 33 (630) Maj (sy^{h}); καὶ αὐτοί B 104 *pc* lat; ἡμεῖς αὐτοί Ψ d* g Ambst; αὐτοί D F G *pc* vg^{ms}.
(b) υἱοθεσίαν *rell*] *omit* P^{46vid} D F G 614 t Ambst

8:24 [ὃ γὰρ βλέπει τίς ἐλπίζει;]
(a) τίς P^{27vid} P^{46} B* 1739^{marg} m* bo] τις τί B^{2} D F G *pc* lat Or Cyp; τις καί 01* 1739^{txt} *pc;* τις, τί καί 01^{2} A C K L P Ψ 6.33.81.1241.1506.1881. 2464 Maj b sy^{h} sa Cl Did.
[With respect to the reading of P^{46} B, Zuntz notes that "[t]he striking conciseness . . . is characteristically Pauline; its various expansions are due to the lack of punctuation (after βλέπει) and accentuation (τίς)."[16]]
(b) ἐλπίζει *rell*] ὑπομένει 01* A 1739^{mg} sy^{p} co.[17]

8:28 [. . . πάντα συνεργεῖ εἰς ἀγαθόν . . .]
συνεργεῖ 01 C D F G Ψ 33.1739.1881 Maj latt sy bo Cl] + ὁ θεός P^{46} A B 81 sa

11:1 [. . . μὴ ἀπώσατο ὁ θεὸς τὸν λαὸν αὐτοῦ . . .]

(a)	τὸν λαὸν	αὐτοῦ	01* B C 33.1739 *rell* vg $sy^{p,h}$ sa bo
(b)	τὸν λαὸν	αὐτοῦ ὃν προέγνω	01^{2} A D [*cf. 11:2*]
(c)	τὴν κληρονομίαν	αὐτοῦ ἣν προέγνω	P^{46}
(d)	τὴν κληρονομίαν	αὐτοῦ	F G b Ambst Pel

11:6 [. . . ἐπεὶ ἡ χάρις οὐκέτι γίνεται χάρις.]
γίνεται χάρις P^{46} 01* A C D F G P (81) 629.630.1739.1881 *pc* lat co Or]
+ εἰ δὲ ἐξ ἔργων οὐκέτι ἐστὶ χάρις, ἐπεὶ τὸ ἔργον οὐκέτι ἐστὶν ἔργον 01^{2} Ψ 6.33^{vid} (365) Maj vg^{ms} (sy);
+ εἰ δὲ ἐξ ἔργων οὐκέτι χάρις, ἐπεὶ τὸ ἔργον οὐκέτι ἐστὶν χάρις B
[Here B preserves a singular subvariation of the Byzantine textform.]

16. Zuntz, *Text,* p. 80, n. 2.

17. Zuntz considers ὑπομένει to be a "serious competitor" for ἐλπίζει: "If this less obvious but suitable verb was not original, whence could it come? . . . Paul could here use it for the sake of stylistic variation" (*Text,* p. 80, n. 2).

11:17 [. . . καὶ συγκοινωνὸς τῆς ῥίζης τῆς πιότητος τῆς ἐλαίας ἐγένου . . .]
τῆς ῥίζης 01* B C Ψ 1175.1506.2464 *pc* b] + καί 01^2 A D^2 33.81.1739.1881 Maj vg sy; *omit* P^{46} D* F G bo^{ms} Ir^{lat}

11:31 [. . . ἵνα καὶ αὐτοὶ [νῦν] ἐλεηθῶσιν . . .]
νῦν 01 B $D^{*.c}$ 1506 *pc* bo] ὕστερον 33.88.365 *pc* sa; *omit* P^{46} A D^2 F G Ψ 6.630.1739.1881 Maj latt

[In both 11:17 and 11:31, the variant readings are, in the words of the Editorial Committee, "suspicious as ameliorating emendations."[18] Notice how A 1739 Maj oppose P^{46} FG in 11:31 but join them in 11:17.]

12:14 [εὐλογεῖτε τοὺς διώκοντας [ὑμᾶς] . . .]
omit ὑμᾶς P^{46} B 6.1739 vg^{ww} Clem Or] include ὑμᾶς 01 A D Ψ 33^{vid} 88.1881 Maj t vg^{cl} sy.[19]

14:10 (. . . βήματι τοῦ θεοῦ . . .)
θεοῦ 01* A B C* D F G 630.1506.1739 *pc* lat co] Χριστοῦ 01^c C^2 Ψ 048.0209.6.33.1881 Maj r vg^{cl} sy Polyc $Mcion^T$ Ambst

[While Χριστοῦ is almost certainly secondary (a harmonization to 2 Cor 5:10), its presence already in Polycarp and Marcion indicates that it is nonetheless a very ancient variant.[20]]

14:12 [ἄρα [οὖν] ἕκαστος ἡμῶν περὶ ἑαυτοῦ λόγον δώσει [τῷ θεῷ].]
(a) *omit* οὖν B D* F G P* 6.630.1739.1881 *pc* lat] include οὖν 01 A C D^2 Ψ 0209.33 Maj sy^h
(b) δώσει 01 A C D^2 Ψ 33.1739.1881 Maj] ἀποδώσει B D* F G 326 *pc*
(c) *omit* τῷ θεῷ B F G 6.630.1739.1881 *pc* r Polyc Cyp] *include* τῷ θεῷ 01 A C D L P Ψ 0209.33 Maj lat sy co

[With respect to (a), in Romans (other than in this passage), the combination ἄρα οὖν occurs seven times (5:18; 7:3, 25; 8:12; 9:16, 18; 14:19), whereas ἄρα alone occurs only twice, in 7:21 and 10:17 (where FG *pc* add οὖν).[21] This circumstance alone makes it much more likely that οὖν would have been added to ἄρα by a copyist than vice versa. Moreover, when ἄρα (which when alone functions as an inferential particle) is used in combination with οὖν, ἄρα "expresses

18. Metzger, *Textual Commentary*, p. 464 (discussing 11:17).

19. In a long list of general terms, the specificity given to this one phrase by ὑμᾶς is clearly out of place; the addition of the pronoun is almost certainly due to the influence of Mt 5:44 // Lk 6:28 (cf. Zuntz, *Text*, p. 80; Lagrange, *Romains*, p. 305).

20. See further Zuntz, *Text*, pp. 224, 231, n. 1.

21. The remaining occurrence of ἄρα in Romans is in 8:1, where it occurs in conjunction with νῦν.

the inference and οὖν the transition" (BAGD, p. 104, s.v. ἄρα) — a pattern which fits the other occurrences of ἄρα and ἄρα οὖν in Romans. Here in 14:12 Paul is simply drawing a conclusion (as in 7:21 and 10:17); the οὖν, therefore, is out of place. Its secondary character here in 14:12 is confirmed by the presence of the transitional οὖν at the beginning of 14:13. In (b), the reading of B D* F G (which in this case are not supported by 1739) is suspect as a harmonization of δίδωμι + λόγον, which apparently is a New Testament *hapax legomenon,* to the more customary New Testament formulation of ἀποδίδωμι + λόγον. As for (c), there is no obvious reason why τῷ θεῷ, if it were original, should have been omitted (either intentionally or accidentally);[22] on other hand, its addition — repeating exactly the last two words of verse 11 — makes explicit what is clearly implicit in the context (vv. 10-11). As in (a), it appears that B 1739 F G have here preserved the correct reading.]

In these few but representative examples one may observe a wide range of combinations of witnesses arranging themselves in support of both genuine and secondary readings. P^{46} B, for example, preserve, against virtually all of the other witnesses, genuine readings (8:24, 12:14) and also secondary corruptions (8:28), and occasionally even a tertiary reading is found in one or the other (B, 11:6). The same goes for P^{46} DFG (original: 13:12 [discussed below]; secondary: 6:8, 6:11a, 8:23, etc.), or B DFG (original: 4:19c, 14:12a, c; secondary: 6:21, 7:6, 14:12b), or a small segment of the Alexandrian tradition in opposition to P^{46} and/or B + D(F)G + Maj (original: 3:7, 8:11 [discussed below]; secondary: 14:21 [discussed below]). For other combinations, one need only read through the apparatus of NA^{27}. In short, it appears that virtually every combination of witnesses that at one or more points preserves the original text also preserves at other points readings that are indisputably secondary.

In view of this phenomenon it is clear why Zuntz stated so forcefully his judgment that while documentary or external considerations can "throw a very considerable weight into the scales of probability," they cannot, by themselves, "suffice to determine [a] choice between competing readings."[23] This is because, as Hort pointed out, the most that can be obtained on the basis of external evidence alone

22. A point the UBS Editorial Committee recognizes; but "the combination of such witnesses as [01] A C D 33 81 614 and most versional testimony makes it difficult to reject" the two words in question (Metzger, *Textual Commentary,* p. 469).

23. Zuntz, *Text,* p. 282.

> is the discovery of what is relatively original: whether the readings thus relatively original were also the readings of the autograph is another question, which can never be answered in the affirmative with absolute decision except where the autograph itself is extant. . . . Even in a case in which it were possible to shew that the extant documents can be traced back to two originals which diverged from the autograph itself without any intermediate common ancestor, we could never be quite sure that where they differed one or other must have the true reading, since they might independently introduce different changes in the same place, say owing to some obscurity in the writing of a particular word.[24]

This means, as Zuntz points out, that "*Recensio* alone can no longer settle any really problematical point. There is no *règle de fer,* no divining-rod to save the critic from the strain of labor and thought."[25] In short, it is the character of the textual history of Romans that requires the textual critic to utilize a reasoned eclecticism in which external evidence plays a very important but nonetheless secondary role to internal evidence and considerations.[26]

III

With these considerations in mind, it may be worthwhile to reconsider at some points, primarily by way of illustration, the text of Romans as printed in the UBS^4 and NA^{27} editions.[27] There are a number of places in Romans where the Committee has placed brackets around words, indicating substantial uncertainty on their part as to whether the words so enclosed belong in the text. Some of these have been discussed above (4:19c; 12:14; 14:12a, c), where it was suggested that in these specific instances the bracketed words are not part of the text.

In other instances, it may be suggested that readings now in the apparatus are more likely to be original than the readings printed as the text. A variation in 8:11 (ὁ ἐγείρας Χριστὸν ἐκ νεκρῶν ζῳοποιήσει . . .) offers a case in point. The following readings are found in the manuscripts:

24. B. F. Westcott and F. J. A. Hort, *The New Testament in the Original Greek,* [2] *Introduction* [and] *Appendix* (Cambridge: Macmillan, 1881), p. 66.

25. Zuntz, *Text,* p. 283.

26. See further on this point Holmes, "Reasoned Eclecticism," pp. 346-49.

27. In keeping with the intention of the Editorial Committee, which views the results of its labors as "a working text . . . it is not to be considered as definitive, but as a stimulus to further efforts toward defining and verifying the text of the New Testament" ($Nestle\text{-}Aland^{27}$, p. 45*).

(a) ἐκ νεκρῶν Χριστὸν Ἰησοῦν] 01* A (C 81) 630.1506.1739.1881 *pc*
(b) Χριστὸν ἐκ νεκρῶν] B D^{2} F G *pc* m sa $Mcion^{T}$ Ir^{lat} Spec; NA^{27}/UBS^{4}
(c)τὸν Χριστὸν ἐκ νεκρῶν] 01^{2} Ψ 33 Maj
(d) Χριστὸν Ἰησοῦν ἐκ νεκρῶν] D* (104 lat sy^{p}) bo

As noted, the Editorial Committee adopts (but does not discuss in the *Textual Commentary*) reading (b), with the support of B F G *pc* etc. But Fee argues persuasively for (a),

> the text of Egypt . . . which has both the "addition" of Ἰησοῦν and the unique word order ἐκ νεκρῶν Χριστὸν Ἰησοῦν (found nowhere else in the corpus). This seems to represent the original text on all counts: external evidence (B has clearly abandoned its tradition here) and transcriptional probability — it is the one reading that explains how the others emerged. The editors of NA^{26}/UBS^{4} opt for Χριστὸν ἐκ νεκρῶν (with B F G and the MajT [which adds τόν before Χριστόν]) as "the least unsatisfactory reading," considering the "addition" of "Jesus" as possibly due to assimilation to the immediately preceding clause. . . . But that scarcely explains the unique word order, or why, if assimilation were at work, there was not a simple substitution of "Jesus" for "Christ."[28]

Moreover, Cranfield points out that the position of ἐκ νεκρῶν after the name could well be the result of assimilation to the word order of the preceding clause.[29]

In 13:12 (ἀποθώμεθα οὖν τὰ ἔργα τοῦ σκότους), what the *Textual Commentary* characterizes as "several Western witnesses" — P^{46} $D^{*,3}$ F G Old Latin vg — read ἀποβαλώμεθα instead of ἀποθώμεθα (01 A B C D^{1} Ψ 048.0285^{vid} 33.1739 (1881) Maj Cl). "Since the use of ἀποθέσθαι is normal in formulas of renunciation . . . and since the verb ἀποβάλλειν recurs nowhere else in the Pauline Epistles and its middle voice is entirely absent from the New Testament, a majority of the Committee preferred the reading ἀποθώμεθα."[30] Zuntz, however, analyzing exactly the same data, comes to a different conclusion:

> As long as the variant ἀποβαλώμεθα was known from D FG only, it was quite naturally dismissed as a specifically Western error, due perhaps to the faulty retranslation of the Latin *abiciamus*. In fact, however, the Greek original of the Old Latin must have had the same reading as D FG, for the three other Pauline instances of ἀποτίθεμαι (Eph iv.22 and 25, Col iii.8) are ren-

28. Fee, *Presence*, p. 543, n. 204.
29. Cranfield, *Romans*, vol. 1, pp. 390-91.
30. Metzger, *Textual Commentary*, p. 467.

> dered by *depono*. Now P^{46} shows that ἀποβαλώμεθα is not a specifically Western reading. It was known about A.D. 200 in Egypt. Could it even be original? The verb recurs nowhere else in the Pauline Epistles and its middle voice is entirely absent from the New Testament. Even so, it suits the context quite excellently. It seems possible, then, that a Pauline *hapax legomenon* has here been ousted by a verb which was familiar from many similar passages.[31]

Indeed, if we ask which reading best explains the rise of the other, it is difficult to avoid Zuntz's conclusion that here P^{46} $D^{*.2}$ F G latt, over against the bulk of the surviving witnesses, preserve the original text. If the more familiar ἀποθώμεθα were original, how would it ever get displaced by the unusual ἀποβαλώμεθα? On the other hand, it is easy to understand how the latter (which occurs in the middle voice in Prov 28:24 LXX) could be dislodged by the former to the extent that ἀποθώμεθα now dominates the textual tradition.[32]

At 14:21 (. . . μηδὲ πιεῖν οἶνον μηδὲ ἐν ᾧ ὁ ἀδελφός σου προσκόπτει), the manuscripts preserve at the end of the verse a multitude of readings:

(a) προσκόπτει	ἢ σκανδαλίζεται	ἢ ἀσθενεῖ	P^{46vid} 01^2 B D F G Ψ 0209.33.1881 Maj lat sy^h sa Ambst
(b) προσκόπτει			01^2 A C 048.6.81.945.1506.1739 *pc* r sy^p bo Mcion
(c) λυπεῖται			01*
(d) λυπεῖται	ἢ σκανδαλίζεται	ἢ ἀσθενεῖ	P
(e) προσκόπτει		ἢ ἀσθενεῖ	sy^{pal}
(f) σκανδαλίζεται ἢ προσκόπτει		ἢ ἀσθενεῖ	1984 1985 m Chrys

The six forms of this passage essentially resolve into a choice between (a) and (b).[33] On behalf of the shorter reading the *Textual Commentary* suggests that the longer text is "a Western expansion . . . which gained wide circulation ($[01]^C$ B D G Y 0209^{vid} 33 . . .). Other variations in various witnesses suggest that the original text was modified or expanded by copyists who recollected 1 Cor 8.11-13."[34] But this is unconvincing, in two respects. First, it will not do

31. Zuntz, *Text*, p. 94.

32. One may compare 4:1, where προπάτορα (01* A B C* 6.81.365.1506 *pc* sa Or^{lem}), a NT *hapax legomenon*, has been displaced by πατέρα, the customary NT designation for Abraham, in 01^1 C^3 D F G Ψ 33.629.1739.1881 Maj latt.

33. Reading (c) is likely a variant form of (b) due to the influence of 14:15; (e) and (f) appear to be variant forms of (a); and (d) apparently conflates elements of both (c) and (a).

34. Metzger, *Textual Commentary*, p. 469; cf. Cranfield, *Romans*, vol. 2, p. 725, n. 1.

to label the longer text a "Western expansion"; it is a very early reading that has both strong early Alexandrian (P^{46vid} B) and Western (D F G) support, and therefore, as Zuntz has shown, must date from a time before the two traditions separated.[35]

Second, it is highly unlikely that ἢ σκανδαλίζεται ἢ ἀσθενεῖ is due to the activity of "copyists who recollected 1 Cor 8.11-13." For the relevant verbal forms we find there are ἀπόλλυται (v. 11) and σκανδαλίζει/σκανδαλίσω (v. 13); ἀσθενέω is used only adjectivally (v. 11, ὁ ἀσθενῶν; v. 12, συνείδησιν ἀσθενοῦσαν; cf. the adjective in vv. 7, 9, 10), as in Romans 14:2, ὁ ἀσθενῶν (cf. 14:1). Moreover, in 1 Corinthians 8 Paul uses terms singly (either πρόσκομμα, v. 9, or ἀπόλλυται, v. 11, or τύπτοντες, v. 12, or σκανδαλίζει/σκανδαλίσω, v. 13; cf. μολύνεται, v. 7); only here in Romans 14 does he combine terms (14:13, πρόσκομμα . . . ἢ σκάνδαλον; 14:21, μὴ φαγεῖν κρέα μηδὲ πιεῖν οἶνον μηδὲ ἐν ᾧ . . . ; cf. 14:17). So, it is quite unlikely that the longer reading is an expansion based on 1 Corinthians 8.

On the other hand, if the longer text (a) — whose external support is nothing to sneeze at — is original, the rise of the shorter reading is very easily accounted for as the result of one of the most common and basic scribal slips, homoioteleuton. The ideas and terms in the longer phrase are characteristically Pauline, yet they are distinctively used in a manner that cannot be derived from other Pauline texts, thus ruling out the idea that the longer text is a scribal insertion.[36] The original text in this instance is preserved by p^{46} B D F G Maj.

IV

In addition to whatever contribution this survey of some textual variants in Romans, brief and highly selective though it obviously is, makes to the discussion of the overarching question posed at the beginning of the essay, it also reminds us of how much there is still to learn about the transmission of the Pauline corpus in the second century. How is it that a very few witnesses (e.g., P^{46} + B, or either one + DFG) can at times, against the rest of the tradition, preserve original readings, and also preserve obviously secondary corruptions that the rest of the witnesses have managed to avoid? Who (or what) was responsible for the early creation of so many sensible but secondary readings in Romans? How are we to understand, and what ought we to infer from, the constantly shifting alignments between witnesses within the Alexandrian tradition? As a disci-

35. See Zuntz, *Text,* pp. 265-66.

36. Scribal insertions from other passages tend to be imitative rather than creative.

pline, we are still attempting to improve upon Zuntz's answers to these questions, and in many respects have not yet done so.[37]

Even as the survey reminds us of how much is yet to be learned, it also highlights the significant extent to which the analysis of individual variants is shaped and influenced by one's understanding of the history of the text's transmission.[38] Whether one views, for example, an agreement between P^{46} and DFG as due to the infiltration of a "Western" reading into the early Alexandrian tradition (as some of the comments in the UBS *Textual Commentary* would appear to imply), or (following Zuntz) as the survival in two separate traditions of a very old reading, has a critical influence on how one evaluates a variant such as 14:21. One cannot study individual stones in isolation from the mosaic of which they are a part.

Finally, we are reminded of the close and synergistic relationship between textual criticism and exegesis. On the one hand it is clear (quoting once more our honoree) "how integral to exegesis the questions of textual criticism are."[39] Obviously one cannot exegete a document until its text has been determined, and in some cases the choice one makes regarding the text will significantly determine or shape how one interprets the text. In Romans 5:1, e.g., the choice between indicative and subjunctive will determine to a large extent how one reads the whole of 5:1-11 and their place in the flow of the letter. More than that, however, the attempt to establish the text often forces one to investigate matters (such as style, word usage, syntax, flow of thought, etc.) that are central to exegesis. In other words, textual criticism and exegesis deal with questions that are not so much discrete and isolated as they are overlapping and complementary. In a day when the closest some commentaries come to textual criticism is an occasional quotation from the UBS *Textual Commentary*, this is a point worth reaffirming.

37. See Zuntz, *Text*, pp. 263-83. See now, however, on some of these questions G. Quispel ("Marcion and the Text of the New Testament," *Vigiliae Christianae* 52 [1998]: 349-60), who highlights the significance of the studies of John J. Clabeaux (*A Lost Edition of the Letters of Paul: A Reassessment of the Text of the Pauline Corpus Attested by Marcion* [Washington, D.C.: Catholic Biblical Association of America, 1989]) and especially Ulrich Schmid (*Marcion und sein Apostolos. Rekonstruktion und historische Einordnung der marcionitischen Paulusbriefausgabe* [Berlin and New York: de Gruyter, 1995]) for our understanding of the early history of the Pauline text and its transmission.

38. Zuntz has described the relationship between the evaluation of individual variants and one's understanding of their place in the larger picture as a fruitful circle (rather than a vicious one) (*Text*, p. 13). See further on this point Holmes, "Reasoned Eclecticism," pp. 349-53.

39. Fee, *New Testament Exegesis*, p. 91. For an extended discussion of the relationship between exegesis and textual criticism, see Gordon D. Fee, "On Text and Commentary on 1 and 2 Thessalonians," in Eugene H. Lovering, Jr. (ed.), *Society of Biblical Literature 1992 Seminar Papers* (Atlanta: Scholars Press, 1992), pp. 165-83.

On the other hand (and of more significance for the present discussion), it is also clear, particularly in the case of the Pauline letters, that exegetical considerations are not infrequently determinative for textual questions (see, in addition to 5:1, the discussions of 14:12, 14:19, and 4:19 above). External evidence can take us a long way toward the recovery of the original text, but in many cases it is only internal evidence and considerations that enable us to make a choice between competing readings. Of the two kinds of internal evidence, transcriptional and intrinsic, it is specifically the latter (which involves matters of authorial style, vocabulary, argument, etc.) that brings us deep into the area of exegesis. In short, the determination of the text of the NT will never be a mechanical procedure separable from the determination of its meaning; to pursue either one is necessarily to pursue the other, as our honoree has so often and so fruitfully demonstrated.

"Mercy upon All": God as Father in the Epistle to the Romans

Marianne Meye Thompson

In theological discussions in recent years, the significance of calling God "Father" has been much in debate, with far-reaching theological claims being made for the designation. T. F. Torrance writes,

> When we turn to the Scriptures of the New Testament, we find a radical deepening of the Old Testament doctrine of God, for "Father" is now revealed to be more than an epithet — it is the personal name of God in which the form and content of his self-revelation as Father through Jesus Christ his Son are inseparable.[1]

Or, in the words of Claude Geffre,

> The name "Father" is the one best calculated to manifest the novelty of the God of Jesus, as compared not only with the God of the Greeks but with the God of the Jews. . . . Compared with the God of Israel the God of Jesus represents a revolution in so far as God is the God of grace before being the God of the law.[2]

1. "The Christian Apprehension of God the Father," *Speaking the Christian God: The Holy Trinity and the Challenge of Feminism,* ed. Alvin F. Kimel, Jr. (Grand Rapids: Eerdmans; Leominster, U.K.: Gracewing, 1992), p. 131.

2. "Father as the Proper Name of God," in *God as Father?,* ed. Johannes-Baptist Metz and Edward Schillebeeckx; *Concilium* 143: *Dogma* (Edinburgh: T. & T. Clark; New York: Seabury, 1981), pp. 44-45.

Not only theologians but also biblical scholars have advanced similar arguments for the meaning and significance of the designation of God as Father in the NT. For example, Rudolf Bultmann once wrote,

> [In Judaism] God had retreated far off into the distance as the transcendent heavenly King, and His sway over the present could barely still be made out. For Jesus, God again became *a God at hand*. . . . This contrast finds expression in the respective forms of address used in prayer. Compare the ornate, emotional, often liturgically beautiful, but often over-loaded forms of address in Jewish prayer with the stark simplicity of "Father"![3]

Similarly, in his article on *abba* for the *Theological Dictionary of the New Testament,* Gerhard Kittel wrote,

> Jesus' term for God . . . shows how this Father-child relationship to God far surpasses any possibilities of intimacy assumed in Judaism, introducing indeed something which is wholly new.[4]

The contemporary assertion that "Father" implies a new understanding of the nearness of God which enables a sense of intimacy with God is particularly indebted to the arguments of Joachim Jeremias regarding the novelty of Jesus' address to God as *abba.* While an enormous structure has been built on the foundation of Jesus' use of *abba,* that term actually occurs only three times in the New Testament and, of those three uses, only one is found on the lips of Jesus (Mk 14:36). The other two instances are attributed to Christian believers in Paul's letters to the Galatians (4:6) and to the Romans (8:15). Interpretation of these passages has, however, been unduly shaped by a misinterpretation and misapplication of Jeremias's arguments regarding Jesus' use of *abba.* In order, then, to sharpen our interpretation of God as "Father" in Romans 8, we shall first briefly suggest how scholars have drawn unfounded conclusions from Jeremias's hypothesis and applied them to Paul's assertions regarding the confession of God as Father.

Jeremias contended that Jesus' use of the reverent and familial term *abba* revealed his own consciousness of a special relationship to God. Jeremias did *not* argue that Jesus' address to God as *abba* embodied a radically new conception of God.[5] Quite the contrary: according to Jeremias, Jesus' conception of

3. *Theology of the New Testament,* 2 vols. (ET New York: Scribner's, 1951, 1955), vol. 1, p. 23; emphasis his.

4. "αββα," *TDNT* 1.6.

5. Thus Willem A. Van Gemeren wrongly criticizes Jeremias for asserting "that Jesus' teaching on the Fatherhood of God is a completely new revelation" ("'*Abba*' in the Old Testament?" *JETS* 31 [1988]: 385-98, esp. 388).

God as Father had much in common with the portrayal of God as Father in the OT and Judaism, where the two aspects of God's fatherhood that were particularly stressed were God's tenderness and "absolute authority." Jesus' use of *abba* not only revealed his distinctive filial consciousness, but also showed his "complete surrender" in obedience to the Father, as the prayer in Gethsemane most vividly demonstrates.[6] His personal and direct address to God as *abba* further reveals his conviction that "the expressions of God's fatherly goodness are *eschatological events*," and that Jesus granted to his disciples "the community of the *time of salvation*," a share in his own relationship with God.[7] For Jeremias, Jesus' eschatological convictions and filial consciousness were linked together. In other words, Jeremias was simply inquiring whether Jesus' own consciousness and convictions with respect to his mission might be inferred from the use of *abba*. Indeed, Jeremias claimed to have found in the use of *abba* the *ipsissima verba* of Jesus, and so also a secure starting point for understanding the mission of Jesus.[8]

In light of Jeremias's stress on Jesus' *filial* consciousness as the basis of his mission, it is surprising that Jeremias left undeveloped the notion of the father as the founder of a clan or head of a family who bestows an inheritance on his son and so also on subsequent generations. Although the depiction of God as Father is somewhat infrequent in the OT, when it is used it typically entails the portrayal of God as the ancestor of the "clan" who bequeaths an inheritance to Israel (Deut 32:4-6; cf. Deut 32:18; Jer 3:19; 31:9; Isa 61:7-10; 63:16; 64:8; Zech 9:12). Accordingly, in those sources of second-temple Judaism which both characterize and invoke God as Father, such imagery tends to be grounded in the special election by God of Israel, or even of a faithful remnant within Israel.[9] In the Gospels, Jesus

6. Jeremias, *Prayers of Jesus* (ET Philadelphia: Fortress, 1967), pp. 11-12, 62. J. M. Oesterreicher appropriately translates Jesus' petition in Mk 14:36 as "Abba, You all-powerful One!" in "Abba, Father! On the Humanity of Jesus," in *The Lord's Prayer and the Jewish Liturgy*, ed. J. J. Petuchowski and M. Brocke (London: Barnes & Oates, 1978), p. 132. On the father as a figure of authority to whom Israel owes obedience and faithfulness, see Hos 11:1, 3, 4; Jer 31:9, 18, 20; and Rex Mason, *Old Testament Pictures of God* (Regent's Study Guides; Oxford: Regent's Park College; and Macon: Smith & Helwys, 1993), esp. p. 68.

7. *Prayers of Jesus*, pp. 43, 63; emphasis added.

8. Jeremias, *New Testament Theology: The Proclamation of Jesus* (ET New York: Scribner's, 1971), pp. 36-37; 42-68.

9. For texts which speak of God as Father, see Wis 2:16, 14:3; Sir 23:1,4, 51:10; 3 Macc 6:3, 8; *Jub.* 19:29; *460*, f. 5, I:5; *382*, f. 55, II:1-9; *379*, f. 6, I:1-7; *Jos. As.* 12:8-15. Texts which speak of God as the Father of the nation include 1 Chr 29:10 (LXX); Tob 13:4; Wis 11:10; 1QH 9:35; *Ant.* 2,6,8; 3 Macc 2:21, 5:7, 7:6; *Jub.* 1:25, 28; *Apocryphon of Ezekiel*, fragment 2. For further discussion, see Dieter Zeller, "God as Father in the Proclamation and in the Prayer of Jesus," in *Standing before God: Studies in Prayer and in Tradition with Essays in Honor of John M. Oesterreicher*, ed. A. Finkel and L. Frizzell (New York: KTAV, 1981), pp. 117-30, esp. p. 9.

speaks of God as his Father, and of those who gather around him and do the Father's will as his family (Mk 3:35; Lk 8:21; Mt 12:50). Not only does Jesus speak of the gracious provision of the Father for his own (Mt 6:25-32), but he also promises that his Father will grant this family an inheritance: "Fear not, little flock; it is the *Father*'s good pleasure to give you the *kingdom*" (Lk 12:32).[10]

It is this very notion of God as a father who gives his children an inheritance which is crucial to Paul's declaration in Romans 8 that God the Father has, through the Spirit, made Jews and Gentiles together "heirs of God and fellow heirs with Christ" (Rom 8:16-17). These assertions, however, have too often been taken as the perfect corollaries of Jeremias's stress on Jesus' sense of his relationship with God, with the result that Romans 8 is read primarily in terms of the believer's experience and sense of intimacy in relationship to God. In this manner, Jeremias's argument regarding Jesus' sense of sonship has been transferred wholesale to believers — thereby eviscerating his hypothesis regarding Jesus' *distinctive* filial consciousness and, often, ignoring its concomitant *eschatological* context as the basis of Jesus' mission. But although the eschatological framework of the confession of God as Father has disappeared in some modern interpretations, it remains crucial for Paul, for whom confession of God as Father rests on the fundamentally eschatological conviction that, in Christ, God's purposes for the salvation of all the world are being brought to their completion.[11] The invocation of God as "Father" acknowledges both the divine initiative in salvation, construed as God's gracious bestowal of his inheritance on and through Jesus Christ, God's Son, as well as the status of those who are heirs with Christ. These twin affirmations, and not the filial sensibilities of believers or some newly benign view of God, comprise the substance of the invocation of God as "*Abba!* Father" in the Epistle to the Romans, to which we now turn.

I. The Epistle to the Romans

God is explicitly called "Father" only a handful of times in Romans (1:7; 6:4; 8:15; 15:6), but the relatively infrequent use of the term belies its centrality for understanding Paul's view of God's saving activity. Briefly, one may character-

10. Antoinette Clark Wire's translation of *basileia* as "inheritance," while playing down too much the sense of "dominion" inherent in the term, captures the emphasis on God's bestowing a kingdom or inheritance, and provides a connection between the image of God as king and God as Father. See "The God of Jesus in the Gospel Sayings Source," in *Reading from this Place,* vol. 1: *Social Location and Biblical Interpretation in the United States,* ed. Fernando F. Segovia and Mary Ann Tolbert (Minneapolis: Fortress, 1995), p. 281.

11. Edgar Krentz, "God in the New Testament," in *Our Naming of God,* ed. Carl E. Braaten (Minneapolis: Fortress, 1989), pp. 75-90, esp. pp. 89-90.

ize Paul as contending that those who invoke God as Father thereby manifest their part in God's eschatological purpose of adopting Jew and Gentile into one family, and thus also their participation in God's purposes for the salvation of all in Jesus Christ. Paul links together the fatherhood of God, the inheritance to be received by Jesus and those who are "joint heirs" with and through him, and the work and role of Spirit, who brings the dead to life, sets slaves free, and adopts them as God's own children. Paul's understanding of God as Father has less to do with certain attributes or characteristics that might be assigned to God, and much more to do with the way in which God's mercy and faithfulness persistently seek out a people as heirs of the divine promises.

A. Romans 1:7

The first reference to God as Father appears in Paul's greeting to the Christians at Rome: "To all God's beloved in Rome, who are called to be saints: Grace to you and peace from God our Father and the Lord Jesus Christ" (1:7).[12] With three simple strokes, this pithy opening adumbrates the key elements of Paul's understanding of God as Father in Romans.

(1) Crucial to understanding God as Father in Romans is the affirmation that God is the Father of Jew and Gentile alike (3:29-30; cf. 1:16). Already at the outset, the epistle's inclusive emphasis is distilled in its address to *all* those who are in Rome (πᾶσιν τοῖς οὖσιν ἐν ῥώμῃ), and its affirmation of God as "*our* Father" (πατρὸς ἡμῶν).

(2) Those who know God as Father are "God's beloved" (ἀγαπητοῖς θεοῦ). For Paul, it is through the Spirit that "God's love (ἀγάπη τοῦ θεοῦ) is poured into our hearts" (5:5), and that the adoption of the children of God is effected. This adoption is permanent, so that nothing is "able to separate us from the love of God (τῆς ἀγάπης τοῦ θεοῦ) in Christ Jesus our Lord" (8:39). Paul does not claim that God's love has been transferred from Jews to Gentiles, or from Jews to Christians, for Israel remains "beloved for the sake of their forefathers" (11:28).[13] Rather, the very love and mercy of God that elected Israel

12. In all 13 canonical Pauline epistles, God is identified as Father in the prescript of the letter: 12 times Paul sends his greeting from "God the Father . . ."; in 1 Thessalonians, Paul identifies the addressees as "the church of the Thessalonians in God the Father and the Lord Jesus Christ" (cf. 2 Thess, which names God as Father both in the identification of the church and in the greeting itself). In Galatians Paul opens with an assertion of his calling through "Jesus Christ and God the Father who raised him from the dead" (1:1), and also sends greetings "from God the Father and our Lord Jesus Christ" (1:3).

13. See N. T. Wright, "Romans and the Theology of Paul," in *Pauline Theology*, vol. 3: *Romans*, ed. David M. Hay and E. Elizabeth Johnson (Minneapolis: Fortress, 1995), p. 54:

now elects all those in Christ, so that those who were "not my people" have been called "my people," and those who were "not beloved" have been called "my beloved" by God (9:14-18; 9:25-26; 11:1-2; 11:29-32). The terms previously applied to Israel — "my people," "my beloved," "children of the living God" — now include the Gentiles as well. Paul's emphasis on those in Christ as God's beloved foreshadows a dominant theme of Romans, reinforced strongly in 9–11, that the righteousness of God has been revealed through the manifestation of his mercy in the calling of a people, Jew and Gentile together.

(3) Those who are God's beloved are "*called* to be saints" (κλητοῖς ἁγίοις), a phrase that not only echoes the description of Paul as one "*called* to be an apostle" (1:1), and of believers as those "*called* to belong to Christ Jesus" (1:6), but does so by accentuating God's initiative: God has called them to be saints, to belong to Christ.[14] "Called" does not simply mean "renamed." That those who were "not my people" and "not beloved" have been *called* "my people," "children of the living God," and "my beloved," does not imply that God has given the Gentiles a new *name,* but that in adopting them as heirs God has granted them a new *status* as part of a new family (9:7, 11, 26).

These three elements — the corporate identification of God as "our Father," and of believers both as "beloved" and as "called" — lead us to the heart of Paul's understanding of the "fatherhood of God," which will be more fully explicated in Romans 8. While God is referred to as "Father" only once (Rom 6:4) between the epistle's prescript and Romans 8, the intervening chapters nevertheless chart a trajectory along which Paul's understanding of God as Father must be plotted. This will become clearer as we explore Paul's argument in chapters 4 and 6.

B. Romans 4; 6:4

Paul advances his argument that Jew and Gentile are called together to belong to the family of God, and are destined as God's beloved to receive the divine inheritance, by showing how Jew and Gentile alike are descended from Abraham, the forefather of the people of Israel. As we shall see, Romans 4 and Romans 8 together comprise a diptych: Romans 4 names *Abraham* as the father of Jew and Gentile, while Romans 8 names *God* as the Father of Jew and Gentile. Thus

---

"Paul is careful not to say, or imply, that the privileges of Israel are simply 'transferred to the church,' even though, for him, the church means Jews-and-Gentiles-together-in-Christ. . . . All that the new family inherit, they inherit in him."

14. C. E. B. Cranfield, *A Critical and Exegetical Commentary on the Epistle to the Romans,* 2 vols., ICC (Edinburgh: T. & T. Clark, 1975), vol. 1, p. 69.

to establish that God is the Father of both Jew and Gentile, Paul first argues that Abraham is the forefather of both Jew and Gentile.

In Romans 4, Abraham serves as the prime example of one who is justified by God's grace, through faith (4:3), and not by works (4:2). To score the point, Paul quotes Genesis 15:6, "Abraham believed (ἐπίστευσεν) God, and it was reckoned to him as righteousness." But while Abraham serves as an instance of exemplary trust in the promises of God, his designation as "our forefather" points to his role as the progenitor of many people who, as his offspring, are also his heirs.[15] If, for Paul, Abraham were only an example of faith, then Paul would not need to argue that Abraham was the father of all who believe (4:11-12, 16-18), and that Abraham's descendants (4:13, 16, 18) would inherit the promises made to him (4:13, 14). Paul's persistent use of metaphors of family and inheritance, together with his argument that Gentile believers are true heirs and descendants of Abraham, indicates that not only do the Gentiles share Abraham's faith, but that "their destiny is prefigured in him."[16] Gentiles who receive and trust the promise of God belong to Abraham's family. The Gentiles have in Abraham a forefather, not by virtue of physical descent from him — which they cannot claim — but because they are heirs of the promise made to him who trusted in the promises of God.

But this is exactly the way in which Paul envisions Abraham to be the forefather of the Jews as well: he is their forefather as the recipient of a promise given to him by the God in whom he trusted (cf. 9:6-8).[17] Paul wants his Jewish readers to "reconsider any view of Abraham as simply 'our forefather according to the flesh.'"[18] Abraham is "the father of us all" (4:16), because Jew and Gentile alike are heirs through the promise made to Abraham and his seed (4:13), *not* because Jews are descended from Abraham "according to the flesh" (κατὰ σάρκα). Accordingly, there are not two ways of becoming part of Abraham's family: there is only one, and it is according to grace (κατὰ χάριν; 4:16), not according

15. On Abraham as example of faith and forefather of the Jewish people, see James D. G. Dunn, *Romans 1–8* and *Romans 9–16* (WBC 38A and 38B; Dallas: Word, 1988), vol. 1, p. 200, for discussion and references to primary literature; J. C. Beker, *Paul the Apostle: The Triumph of God in Life and Thought* (Philadelphia: Fortress, 1980), p. 99; and Leander Keck, "What Makes Romans Tick?" in *Pauline Theology*, p. 25.

16. Richard B. Hays, *Echoes of Scripture in the Letters of Paul* (New Haven: Yale, 1989), p. 56; idem, "'Have We Found Abraham to Be Our Forefather according to the Flesh?' A Reconsideration of Romans 4:1," *NovT* 27 (1985): 76-98; and Wright, "Romans and the Theology of Paul," p. 40. But for salient objections against Hays' way of punctuating Romans 4:1, see Dunn, *Romans 1–8*, 199.

17. See Wright, "Romans and the Theology of Paul," pp. 39-42.

18. Andrew T. Lincoln, "From Wrath to Justification: Tradition, Gospel, and Audience in the Theology of Romans 1:18–4:25," in *Pauline Theology*, p. 152.

to fleshly descent (κατὰ σάρκα; 4:1), for Abraham is "the father of us all" (4:16).[19]

While Jews might appear to have a "natural" (κατὰ σάρκα) claim on Abraham's inheritance, they inherit in precisely the same way as do the Gentiles: by means of the promise made to Abraham. Thus, although the Israelites are Paul's "kinsmen by race" (κατὰ σάρκα; 9:3) and are those from whose lineage the Messiah comes (ὁ Χριστὸς τὸ κατὰ σάρκα; 9:5) and are even the offspring of Abraham (σπέρμα Ἀβραάμ), they are not Abraham's children (τέκνα; 9:7) so long as they are "children of the flesh" and not "children of the promise." As Paul writes, the promise that Abraham and his descendants would "inherit the world" did not come through the law, but through the righteousness of faith (4:13), for faith or trust corresponds to promise. Therefore, God justifies the circumcised ἐκ πίστεως (by faith) and the uncircumcised διὰ τῆς πίστεως (through faith; Rom 3:30).[20] Paul establishes the equal status of Jew and Gentile before God by contending that all who trust in God's promises are true heirs of Abraham.[21] That this promise has been carried out through Christ testifies to the faithfulness of God, the one who gives life to the dead.

Indeed, underlying the whole argument about Abraham is the view of the father as the one who gives life. The contrast between death and life figures in important ways here in chapter 4, as well as in the reference to God as Father in 6:4, and again in Romans 8. In 4:17 God is described as the one who "gives life to the dead" (τοῦ ζῳοποιοῦντος τοὺς νεκρούς) and "calls into existence the things that do not exist" (καλοῦντος τὰ μὴ ὄντα ὡς ὄντα). God's life-giving power is operative both in causing Abraham, whose body "was as good as dead" (τὸ ἑαυτοῦ σῶμα [ἤδη] νενεκρωμένον), to become a father first of Isaac, and subsequently "of many nations," and in the raising of Jesus from the dead (τὸν ἐγείραντα Ἰησοῦν τὸν κύριον ἡμῶν ἐκ νεκρῶν). Similarly, Abraham "is the father of us all" (4:16), the "father of many nations" (4:17), because he gave life to a son and, through him, to

19. Wright, "Romans and the Theology of Paul," p. 40.

20. Stanley K. Stowers contends that Paul deliberately uses the two different prepositions to show that the Gentiles are taken up into the heritage of the Jews (*A Rereading of Romans: Justice, Jews, and Gentiles* [New Haven: Yale, 1994], pp. 238-39). The preposition ἐκ, used in philosophical discussions of descent and paternity, implies that faith is the generative cause of God's justifying act, whereas διά connotes the instrumentality of faith. But C. K. Barrett (*The Epistle to the Romans,* rev. ed. [Peabody, Mass.: Hendrickson, 1991], p. 80), Cranfield (*Romans,* 1.22), and Joseph A. Fitzmyer, *Romans: A New Translation with Introduction and Commentary* (AB [New York: Doubleday, 1993], pp. 365-66), label the variation as purely rhetorical; see also Dunn, *Romans,* 1.189-90.

21. See here N. T. Wright, *The Climax of the Covenant: Christ and the Law in Pauline Theology* (Minneapolis: Fortress, 1992), p. 167.

many offspring. God is the Father of Jesus Christ, whom he raised from the dead, and through whom believers "walk in newness of life" (6:4; cf. 10:9).[22] With the designation of God as Father, Paul underscores with one stroke both the life-giving power of God and the ways in which believers find their destiny prefigured in the death and resurrection of Jesus, the ultimate heir of the promise made to Abraham. In Romans 8 this trajectory is traced out even more fully.

C. Romans 8

The promise made to Abraham was fulfilled, first, through the birth of a son and heir, "our forefather Isaac" (9:10), who in turn becomes the forefather of those who are children of the promise (9:6-9), but ultimately through the birth, death, and resurrection of God's own Son (8:3), through whom one receives adoption and so enters into the promised inheritance (Rom 8:17: heirs of God, and fellow heirs with Christ; cf. Gal 4:15-18). This narrative explains the varying designations of God as simply "the Father" (Rom 6:4; 1 Cor 8:6; Gal 1:1), "the God and Father of our Lord Jesus Christ" (Rom 15:6; 2 Cor 1:3; 11:31), and "God our Father and the Lord Jesus Christ" (Rom 1:7; 1 Cor 1:3; 2 Cor 1:2; Gal 1:3, passim). God is "our Father" because God is "the Father of our Lord Jesus Christ," the Son and heir, through whom his true offspring also become heirs of God's inheritance.

Paul explicitly locates the believer's address to God as "*Abba!* Father!" in the work of the Holy Spirit (8:15). This passage, together with Galatians 4:6, is the *locus classicus* for understanding the fatherhood of God in Paul. Unfortunately, discussion of this invocation has been too quickly severed from its context in the argument of Romans regarding the revelation of God's righteousness to Jew and Gentile alike and moved into the realm of the believer's subjective experience of God. In support of this interpretation, Paul's use of the unusual verb κράζειν has been taken to point to the emotional, enthusiastic, or spontaneous prayers of believers, while the address to God as *abba* has been read, in light of Jeremias's arguments about Jesus' use of the term, to refer to the believer's sense of intimacy in relationship with God. Thus it is the reality of this intimate relationship to which the Spirit "bears witness" within the realm

22. Dunn, *Romans,* 1.315, comments that usually in resurrection formulas, agency is not specified, whereas here it is. It is not surprising that the agent of raising Jesus to life is the *Father,* for in Romans "fatherhood" is particularly associated with the creation and procreation of life. See also the comments of Andrew T. Lincoln, "Abraham Goes to Rome: Paul's Treatment of Abraham in Romans 4," in *Worship, Theology and Ministry in the Early Church: Essays in Honour of Ralph P. Martin* (JSNTSupp. 87), ed. Michael J. Wilkins and Terence Paige (Sheffield: Sheffield Academic Press, 1992), pp. 163-79, esp. pp. 176-78.

of the individual's experience or faith.[23] Such interpretations find a natural home in those outlines of Romans that posit a sharp break between the argument for "justification by faith" in Romans 1–4 and the description of the life of faith in Romans 5–8.[24]

Such factors have contributed to reading Romans 8 primarily in *individualistic, subjective,* and *experiential* terms, when it should be read first in *cosmic, corporate, eschatological,* and *theocentric* terms. Furthermore, this division effectively severs Romans 8 both from Paul's argument in Romans 4 that God's righteousness has been revealed in adopting Jew and Gentile together into one family, as well as from Romans 9–11, which takes up the issue of God's faithfulness to Israel in part because of the fact that the "adoption" rightly belongs to it. But confession of God as Father highlights God's mercy to Israel as well as to the Gentiles in adopting them into one family who, as descendants of Abraham, inherit together in Jesus Christ (15:8-9). God's creation of that one family finds its proper place within the larger narrative of God's redemption of the whole world.

Romans 8:15 places particular emphasis on the agency of the Spirit in the creation of that people. The emphasis on the work of the Spirit is borne out by the use of the term κράζειν, whose sense is disputed. While some take it as introducing a "brief, ejaculatory utterance" which in turn reflects the "deeply emotional or enthusiastic character of earliest Christian experience and worship,"[25] others construe it as a technical term for acclamation, whose proper setting is a liturgical event within the life of the congregation.[26] Paul's use of κράζειν, rather than a word for confess, speak, or pray, is indeed striking.[27] κράζειν is also found in Galatians 4:6, where, however, the subject of the verb is not the believer, but the Spirit ("God has sent the Spirit of his Son into our hearts, crying, '*Abba!* Father!'"; κρᾶζον, Αββα ὁ πατήρ). Romans 9:27 contains the only other use of κράζειν in the Pauline correspondence. There it refers to Isaiah's prophetic speech and is used interchangeably with προείρηκεν (predict, foretell; in 9:29), indicating the Spirit-inspired nature of Isaiah's speech. On the basis of Galatians 4:6 and

23. It is telling, for example, that in Dunn's massive tome on the theology of Paul, discussion of God as "Father" finds it place under the heading of "God in experience." See Dunn, *The Theology of Paul the Apostle* (Grand Rapids: Eerdmans, 1998), p. 49.

24. See, e.g., the magisterial commentary by Cranfield, which follows just this division, with appropriate labels: "The revelation of the righteousness which is from God by faith alone — 'He who is righteous by faith' expounded (1:18–4:25)"; "The life promised for those who are righteous by faith — 'shall live' expounded (5:1–8:39)."

25. Dunn, *Romans,* 1.453.

26. Ernst Käsemann, *Commentary on Romans* (ET Grand Rapids: Eerdmans, 1980), p. 228.

27. But see Mk 14:36: καὶ ἔλεγεν· αββα ὁ πατήρ.

Romans 9:27, it seems likely, therefore, that the verb κράζειν is used because the Spirit is the ultimate source of these words, rather than because they signify the interior or emotional state of those who are speaking, or a particular setting of prayer or worship.[28] When Dunn writes that "In Rom. 8.16 Paul speaks *explicitly* of a *sense of sonship* to God as Father," one hears the echoes of Jeremias's contention that Jesus' distinctive filial consciousness found expression in his prayer to God as *Abba*.[29] But Romans 8:16 speaks *explicitly* of the work of the Spirit, not of the "sense of sonship" which believers have.

While Paul's discussions elsewhere of the Spirit in corporate worship (e.g., 1 Cor 12–14) may well suggest that the setting for such Spirit-inspired prophecy lies within the context of corporate worship, it is the *corporate* dimension of acknowledging God as "Father" which sheds further light on Paul's use of the term and his argument in Romans 8. Paul's concern is not so much with the individual's experience of God, nor with the Spirit's activity within the individual — often referred to as "the inner testimony of the Holy Spirit" — but with the unity of Jew and Gentile, who, in Christ, call out to the one God with one acclamation: "*Abba!* Father!"[30] Three factors testify decisively to the corporate, rather than individualistic, dimension implicit in Paul's assumptions about the significance of this address to God. First, the pronouns and verbs from Romans 8:1 through the end of the chapter are almost all plural, including those assertions which refer explicitly to the Spirit's indwelling (8:9, 11), bearing witness (8:16), intercession (8:26-27), and to reception of the Spirit (8:15, 23). Second, the family imagery points not to an agglomeration of individuals, but to a greater, corporate reality. Third, the link between becoming part of Abraham's family (ch. 4) and God's family (ch. 8) underscores the point that just as the Gentiles are Abraham's heirs, so too they are "heirs of God and joint heirs with Christ" (8:17). In short, Paul's declaration that through the Spirit those in Christ know and acknowledge God as Father does not speak only of one of the benefits of being in Christ, but further advances the whole thrust of the argument in Romans that in Christ God has abolished the divisions between Jew and Gentile and adopted them together into one family.

In this light, it can scarcely be forgotten that the whole of Romans 8 is framed, on the one side, by chapter 7, with its exposition of the power of sin and the consequent limitations of law, and, on the other side, by chapters 9–11,

28. See also Gordon D. Fee, *God's Empowering Presence: The Holy Spirit in the Letters of Paul* (Peabody, Mass.: Hendrickson, 1994), p. 567. Moreover, it is not at all clear that even if Jeremias's arguments regarding Jesus' use of *abba* were true, one can legitimately transfer Jesus' sense of consciousness to believers.

29. *Theology of Paul*, p. 49; my emphasis.

30. See Fee, *Empowering Presence*, p. 569.

with its impassioned demonstration of God's ongoing faithfulness to Israel. It is in fact the whole discussion of Romans 1–8, with its argument that God has brought the Gentiles into the elect family of God, along with Israel, to whom "the adoption properly belongs," which then requires that Paul establish that God has actually confirmed "the promises given to the patriarchs . . . in order that the Gentiles might glorify God for his mercy" (15:8-9). The evidence that God has now also adopted the Gentiles into the family to share the inheritance of Israel lies in the empowering presence of the Spirit by which believers, Jew and Gentile alike, cry out and acknowledge God as Father. The ultimate question of how God brings people into right relationship is answered in two ways: positively, in terms of adoption as children; and negatively, in terms of the law. To paraphrase Paul, God has done what the law could not do: by sending his own Son he created a family of Jew and Gentile together, adopting them as his own, not through the law, which could not effect unity, but through the Spirit. Calling God "Father" cannot therefore be reduced to the external characterization of an internal experience; rather, the accent falls, as it does throughout Romans, "not on the subjective experience of believers but on God's saving power through Christ's act *pro nobis*."[31]

Paul sets this whole argument within a larger cosmic framework. The human dilemma, described in Romans 8 in terms of slavery and bondage, cannot be isolated and analyzed apart from the cosmic sweep of the power and effects of sin, death, and decay. "We know that the whole creation has been groaning in travail together until now; and not only the creation, but we ourselves" (8:22-23). Human beings will and do participate in God's liberation of *all* creation, of which the adoption of the children of God is but one facet. "The glorious liberty of the children of God" belongs in the cosmic frame of God's intent and promise that "the creation itself will be set free from its bondage to decay" (8:21).[32] Moving out from this sweeping cosmic framework, Paul contends that in the human realm God has dealt with slavery to sin through the emancipation of the slaves — not only obtaining their freedom, but further adopting them into one family as his own children.[33] As J. Louis Martyn sharply phrases it, "The gospel is about the divine invasion of the cosmos (theology), not about human movement into blessedness (religion)."[34]

31. Richard B. Hays, "Adam, Israel, Christ: The Question of Covenant in the Theology of Romans: A Response to Leander E. Keck and N. T. Wright," in *Pauline Theology*, p. 75.

32. The universal scope of God's redemption is emphasized by Ernst Käsemann in his commentary on Romans; cf. the comments of Hays, "Adam, Israel, Christ," p. 74.

33. Dunn, *Romans*, 1.452.

34. Martyn, "The Abrahamic Covenant, Christ, and the Church," in *Theological Issues in the Letters of Paul* (Nashville: Abingdon, 1997), p. 170.

Paul also speaks of the freedom for all creation in the context of eschatological hope, even as he does of the "glorious liberty of the children of God." While he writes "you *have received* (ἐλάβετε) the spirit of adoption" (Rom 8:15) and "we *are* children of God (ἐσμὲν τέκνα θεοῦ)" (8:16), and while he testifies to the freedom of the children of God who are heirs and not slaves (Rom 8:2, 15), he also speaks of groaning "as we *wait for* adoption" (υἱοθεσίαν ἀπεκδεχόμενοι; 8:23), implying that present adoption anticipates full adoption in the future. Similarly, while in Romans 9:6 Paul speaks of "adoption" as properly belonging to the Israelites, he has already stated that this privilege now belongs to those who receive their inheritance through the one true heir, Jesus, rather than by virtue of genealogy. And yet, contending that the gifts and the call of God are irrevocable (Rom 11:29), Paul holds on to the hope of the future "adoption" of Israel as children of God. He envisions the gathering of Jew and Gentile together who "may with one voice glorify the God and Father of our Lord Jesus Christ" (15:6; cf. 15:7-13). Ultimately the harmonious glorification of "the God and Father of *our* Lord Jesus Christ" summarizes not only the purpose of Romans, but indeed the purpose of the gospel, the revelation of the righteousness of God for all who believe, both Jew and Gentile (1:16-17; 15:8-9).

II. Summary: Mercy upon All

The adoption of Jew and Gentile as heirs of the promise made to Christ should not be construed simply as a result or "benefit" of the cosmic, theocentric, Pauline gospel — although adoption is surely not less than that. Rather, the adoption of the children of God is the gospel, now expressed in the language of family and inheritance, and testifies to God's faithfulness to the Jews, the children of Abraham, and God's mercy to the Gentiles, also the children of Abraham. To speak of God as Father is to underscore God's faithfulness to Israel, "to whom belongs the adoption," and God's mercy toward the Gentiles, who, as the heirs of God through Christ, have received adoption as children and the promised inheritance — an inheritance sealed to believers by the Spirit of God. What lies at the core of Paul's convictions that God is the Father of all who are children of Abraham and heirs with Christ is the belief that, in Christ, God has had "mercy upon all" (Rom 11:32).

Confession of God as Father finds its proper place in the narrative of God's faithfulness and mercy to Israel, which comes to its climax when God did not spare his own Son (8:3) but gave him up in love "for us all," thus including Gentiles in the mercy of God. Any abstraction of the confession of God as Father from this narrative, presupposed in and made explicit by Romans, runs the risk of losing sight of the promise of the inheritance that is granted by God to

Christ and those who are joint heirs with him. If this movement from promise to fulfillment is lost, then God's initiative, faithfulness, and mercy in adopting the heirs of Abraham in Christ, all become mere ciphers, without the evidence in human life of which Paul speaks: the confession of the community that the Father, through the Spirit, has adopted heirs of the Son. Even as the "mercies of God" are manifested through the adoption of the Gentiles to be God's children, so Paul implores them "by the mercies of God" (12:1) to live together in the unity appropriate to a family created by God's gracious act.

And the underlying narrative does not cease with the movement from promise to fulfillment. For Paul, the fulfillment of the promise opens up, rather than forecloses, the orientation toward the future; God's fulfillment of the promise to Abraham becomes the ground for hope that God will complete this act of adoption. That future orientation precludes any triumphalist claim of an assured status which is vested in the individual believer, rather than in the God who brings the dead to life and calls believers together into one family. The very narrative which moves from promise to fulfillment unfolds toward the future with hope as its leitmotif — hope that by the mercy shown to the Gentiles, the Jews also may receive mercy (11:30-31).

The narrative context of the confession of God as Father decisively shapes our understanding of both this confession and its content. A backward glance catches sight of God's faithfulness and mercy, and therefore a look toward the future confidently expects the same. To acknowledge God as Father is therefore to acknowledge oneself beholden to the mercy and grace of God, and as trusting in the faithfulness of God. Those who approach God as Father do so as those who "have hope for the future, and . . . who can confidently look forward to life and glory."[35] That confidence is constantly directed toward the God who is the life-giving, faithful, and merciful Father. The invocation of God as Father belongs in the narrative of God's saving mercy to "the Jew first and also the Greek," a narrative which moves into the future with constant hope of that same mercy. Because of that mercy, and in the hope of that mercy, those who are heirs with Christ call on God as "*Abba!* Father."

35. C. K. Barrett, *Romans*, p. 153.

Jesus' Divine Sonship in Paul's Epistle to the Romans

L. W. Hurtado

The language expressive of Jesus' divine "sonship" has received a good deal of attention in scholarly analyses of Paul's christology.[1] At least three

1. I have offered a general analysis of Jesus' divine sonship in Paul elsewhere: "Son of God," *Dictionary of Paul and His Letters*, ed. G. F. Hawthorne, R. P. Martin, and D. G. Reid (Downers Grove, Ill./Leicester, U.K.: InterVarsity Press, 1993), pp. 900-906. In addition to the other scholarly literature cited there, note also W. Grundmann, "Sohn Gottes," *ZNW* 47 (1956): 113-33; C. Dietzfelbinger, "Sohn und Gesetz: Überlegungen zur paulinischen Christologie," *Anfänge der Christologie*, ed. C. Breytenbach and H. Paulsen (Göttingen: Vandenhoeck & Ruprecht, 1991), pp. 111-29.

It is a great pleasure to offer this essay in tribute to my longtime friend, Professor Gordon Fee. We first made acquaintance in 1968, when I wrote him to ask advice on doctoral studies. His advice to a then unknown inquirer was (as is characteristic of his judgments) forthright and accurate, and I am grateful for the encouragement he gave. My Ph.D. thesis adapted an approach to establishing textual relationships first fully employed by him, and over the years I have learned much from his text-critical studies and his exegetical contributions to the understanding of Paul. I am also grateful for his friendly encouragement over the years since that letter asking advice about my own academic plans. The following essay arises from the research program with which I have been occupied for a number of years now on "Christ-Devotion in the First Two Centuries." I have described this program in another essay: "Christ-Devotion in the First Two Centuries: Reflections and a Proposal," *Toronto Journal of Theology* 12 (1996): 17-33. I plan to produce a book-length study on this subject.

widely varying views have been taken, however, as to the importance and meaning of the references to Jesus' divine sonship in Paul's religious thought. In this essay, I wish to focus on the role and meaning of references to Jesus as God's Son in Paul's epistle to the Romans.[2] But before we turn to an analysis of Jesus' divine sonship in the epistle to the Romans, it will be helpful to review briefly the scholarly discussion about the christological category of divine sonship in Paul.[3]

I. Three Alternative Views

The great exponent of the old history-of-religions school, Wilhelm Bousset, asserted that Jesus' divine sonship was central to Paul's religious message and represented the key means by which Paul communicated Jesus' divine status to his Gentile converts and justified to them the worship of Jesus.[4] Bousset claimed that in Paul's writings the meaning of the references to Jesus' divine sonship was taken directly from the pagan religious environment where sons of gods were themselves divine beings. Paul thus appropriated a religious category from the pagan religious setting of his converts to promote reverence for Jesus in terms that they could readily appreciate. Bousset's view was also repeated in the writings of other very influential scholars such as Bultmann[5] and Schoeps.[6]

2. The New Testament treats women as well as men as recipients of God's love and as heirs of salvation, but in its language the New Testament reflects the linguistic conventions and cultural patterns of its time, including what we have come to see as "androcentric" terminology. Thus, mixed groups of Christian women and men are referred to and addressed as "brothers" *(adelphoi),* and in their redeemed relationship to God as "sons [*huioi*] of God." Because this essay involves as close an analysis of the Greek of Romans as possible, the translations of phrases will reflect the androcentric nature of the Greek original. It is right that in our modern speech we should consider ways of avoiding gender-exclusionary expressions. I intend no opposition to this in the rendering of New Testament passages in this essay.

3. In addition to scholars reviewed in this essay, J. D. G. Dunn (*Christology in the Making* [London/Philadelphia: SCM/Westminster, 1980; 2nd ed., 1989], pp. 12-64) could also be mentioned as offering a noteworthy discussion, but it is focused heavily on the question of whether Paul and other New Testament writers believed in Jesus' "preexistence."

4. Wilhelm Bousset, *Kyrios Christos,* trans. J. E. Steely (Nashville: Abingdon Press, 1970 [German 1913]), esp. pp. 91-98, 206-10.

5. Rudolf Bultmann, *Theology of the New Testament* (2 vols.; New York: Charles Scribner's Sons, 1951, 1955), vol. 1, pp. 128-29.

6. H. J. Schoeps, *Paul: The Theology of the Apostle in the Light of Jewish Religious History* (Philadelphia: Westminster, 1959), pp. 149-59.

In Bousset and others as well, two questions seem to be conflated and confused: (1) Was there an influential precedent or pattern of usage for "Son of God" becoming a christological title and category, and if so, was it Jewish messianism or pagan traditions? (2) When earliest Christians used the rhetoric of divine sonship for Jesus, what did they mean to say? Rightly for his time, Bousset noticed that there was little to connect the "Son of God" title with Jewish messianism (although recent discoveries and analysis suggest that divine-sonship language may have been somewhat more associated with messianism than previously thought);[7] however, he did find examples of the rhetoric of divine sonship applied in pagan circles to figures treated as objects of cultic devotion. Consequently, he quite understandably (but wrongly, as we shall argue) concluded that this pagan usage must have been both the impetus and the meaning for early Christians in referring to Jesus as God's "Son."

But we must de-couple the two questions and make initial the semantic one, that is, the question as to how the New Testament authors used the language of Jesus' divine sonship. Subsequently, we can explore possible influences from Jewish and pagan traditions. When we proceed in this way, making the semantic question initial and deciding it on the basis of analysis of the sentences in which divine-sonship language is used, we find that Paul's usage shows clear derivation from the Old Testament and Jewish traditions where the language is applied to the devout, righteous individual as well as to Israel collectively, particularly in the second-temple period.[8] Paul's reference to Jesus in divine-sonship language involves primarily connotations of God's direct involvement in Jesus, Jesus' special status with God, and consequent honor and authority (as we shall see below in our analysis of references in Romans).[9] Along with other factors, this in turn suggests that the impetus for employing the language of divine sonship did not come primarily from pagan traditions of divinized heroes. But although Paul's meaning seems heavily dependent on Jewish usage of divine-sonship language, the impetus for attributing divine sonship to Jesus seems to have been heavily indebted to internal considerations, arising from the desire and need to assert both God's direct involvement in Jesus and his own fa-

7. See now John J. Collins, *The Scepter and the Star: The Messiahs of the Dead Sea Scrolls and Other Ancient Literature* (New York: Doubleday, 1995), pp. 154-72.

8. See, e.g., Gerhard Delling, "Die Bezeichnung 'Söhne Gottes' in der jüdischen Literatur der hellenistisch-römischen Zeit," *God's Christ and His People: Studies in Honour of Nils Alstrup Dahl*, ed. J. Jervell and W. A. Meeks (Oslo: Universitetsforlaget, 1977), pp. 18-28. Also still worth consulting is the concise discussion of NT christological titles and their background by E. D. Burton, *A Critical and Exegetical Commentary on the Epistle to the Galatians* (ICC; Edinburgh: T. & T. Clark, 1921), pp. 392-417, "son(s) of God" on pp. 404-17.

9. Hurtado, "Son of God"; Michael Theobald, "'Sohn Gottes' als christologische Grundmetapher bei Paulus," *Theologische Quartalschrift* 174 (1994): 185-207.

vor with God, the latter perhaps in part because of the negative connotations of a crucified messiah and leader.

In short, Bousset seems to have been right to attribute importance to divine-sonship language in Paul's references to Jesus, but Bousset was wrong in thinking that Paul's intention was primarily to attribute divinity to Jesus after the pattern of divinized demigods of the pagan traditions.

On the other hand, in his study of the major christological titles used by Paul, Werner Kramer presented the view that Jesus' divine sonship was not in fact very important in Paul's thought. Kramer rested his argument on two main bases. First, he noted the relative infrequency of Pauline references to Jesus' divine sonship in comparison with the many Pauline uses of the titles *Kyrios* and *Christos.* Secondly, Kramer argued that the few references to Jesus' divine sonship that are found in Paul's letters were all remnants of "pre-Pauline" tradition and echoed by Paul simply as familiar religious rhetoric but not very significant as disclosing Paul's own christological emphases.[10]

The logic Kramer employed in this latter argument, surprisingly common in traditio-historical studies, is that, if one can find in a writer such as Paul what appear to be remnants of an earlier tradition, these remnants should be subtracted from the data to be used for portraying the religious emphases of the writer whose text(s) one is studying. That is, whatever is judged to be "tradition" cannot be used to characterize the author's own thought. But surely to identify this procedure is immediately to communicate its absurdity.[11] If a writer incorporates into his/her text without refutation or criticism elements of a tradition, this is surely because the author accepts these elements and indeed regards them as expressive of his/her own thoughts. Consequently, in drawing up the data to be used for characterizing Paul's christological thought, it is irrelevant whether a given phrase is Paul's own coinage or is appropriated from the wider Christian tradition. All that Paul says about Jesus without criticism is directly indicative of Paul's christological beliefs, whether particular statements are original with him or echo the statements and formulas of others also. If the question were to determine Paul's *originality,* then demonstrably "pre-Pauline" material might well be set aside; but if the question is what was of christological significance for Paul, then all the data he employs to express his views are relevant to the discussion.

10. Werner Kramer, *Christ, Lord, Son of God* (London: SCM, 1966), pp. 183-94, esp. p. 189. But Kramer did note that the one factor that may have influenced Paul occasionally to employ references to Jesus as God's "Son" was that "the title suggests the Son's solidarity with God" (p. 185).

11. Theobald (191, n. 33) refers to Kramer's approach as "methodische verfehlt."

12. Martin Hengel, *The Son of God: The Origin of Christology and the History of Jewish-Hellenistic Religion* (ET; Philadelphia/London: Fortress Press/SCM, 1976; rev. ed., 1977; German, 1975).

The third major approach to the significance and meaning of divine-sonship language in Paul's christology is represented best by Martin Hengel.[12] Hengel shows persuasively that the divine-sonship category and rhetoric are in fact significant in Paul's view of Jesus, and that pagan traditions fail to account for Paul's usage.[13] Moreover, Hengel notes that Paul's references to Jesus as God's Son appear "most frequently in the letters where the controversy with the Jewish tradition is at its height" (Romans and Galatians), which both militates against Bousset's claim that Paul used divine sonship as a kind of "marketing device" for promoting worship of Jesus among Gentile converts in terms they could appreciate, and suggests that Paul uses the category quite deliberately and with connections to particular themes and emphases[14] (I judge Hengel's basic conclusions to be sound and therefore adopt his broad view of matters as the basis for proceeding in an inquiry about Jesus' divine sonship in Paul).

II. Jesus' Divine Sonship in Paul — General Observations

In an earlier study, I analyzed Paul's references to Jesus as God's Son with a view toward establishing the patterns of usage and connotations involved.[15] As a basis for our analysis of references in Romans, I briefly repeat from this article some of my observations about Paul's christological use of divine-sonship language.

In the traditional 13-epistle Pauline corpus, there are 17 references to Jesus' divine sonship (15 references if we omit the disputed epistles to the Ephesians and the Colossians). The actual title "Son of God" appears only four times among these references and with variations in the Greek word order (*tou . . . huiou theou,* Rom 1:4; *ho tou theou . . . huios,* 2 Cor 1:19; *tou huiou tou theou,* Gal 2:20; *tou huiou tou theou,* Eph 4:13).[16] In the remaining 13 references, Jesus is referred to as "his [God's] Son" (Rom 1:3, 9; 5:10; 8:29, 32; 1 Cor 1:9; Gal

13. Hengel, *The Son of God,* esp. pp. 7-15 on Paul, and pp. 21-56 on the religious backgrounds.

14. Hengel, *The Son of God,* p. 7. The major christological title Paul used in cultic formulas and contexts was not "Son of God" but *Kyrios.* See, e.g., my article on this title: "Lord," *Dictionary of Paul and His Letters,* ed. G. F. Hawthorne, R. P. Martin, and D. G. Reid (Downers Grove, Ill.: InterVarsity Press, 1993), pp. 560-69.

15. Hurtado, "Son of God," esp. pp. 903-6.

16. In Gal 2:20, the reading *theou kai christou,* supported by P46, B, D*, F, G, and other witnesses, is likely to be explained as resulting from faulty copying of the reading given above (see B. M. Metzger, *A Textual Commentary on the Greek New Testament* [London/New York: United Bible Societies, 1971], p. 593). In Eph 4:13, the variant reading of F, G, b and others, which involves the omission of *"tou huiou,"* likewise probably resulted from a copying error.

1:16; 4:4, 6; 1 Thess 1:10), and also as "his own Son" (Rom 8:3), "the Son" (1 Cor 15:28), and "the Son of his love" (Col 1:13). As I noted in my previous study, "The conviction that Jesus is God's Son was apparently what mattered to Paul, not so much the christological title or the fixed verbal formulas to express that conviction."[17]

The one consistent syntactical feature in all these references to Jesus' divine sonship is the use of the definite article. This suggests that Paul was concerned to attribute to Jesus a unique kind of sonship, and not merely to include him in a class of those (such as the righteous, great men, wonder workers, etc.) who can be referred to as "sons/children" of God, as in Jewish sources (e.g., Wis 2:12-20; 5:1-8). In fact, whether one presumes a Jewish or pagan background for the language of divine sonship, Paul's consistent use of the definite article seems intended to make a strong distinction between the use of divine-sonship rhetoric for others and what he intends to assert as true of Jesus.

Furthermore, as Hengel noted, these references to Jesus' divine sonship are not distributed randomly but cluster in two epistles, Romans (seven references) and Galatians (four references), which between them account for 11 of the 15 references in the undisputed epistles (or the 17 in the entire Pauline corpus). This clustering of references in these two epistles suggests that Paul used divine-sonship rhetoric deliberately and likely in connection with particular themes and emphases, not casually or merely as stock christological rhetoric.[18] The concentration of divine-sonship references in these two epistles makes it reasonable to inquire what specific thematic connections there are that drew Paul to use this christological rhetoric with such frequency in these writings. In the epistle to the Romans alone, there are seven references to Jesus' divine sonship, by far the largest number of occurrences among Paul's epistles. It is appropriate, therefore, to focus on the use of divine-sonship rhetoric in this epistle. In what follows, we shall examine relevant references in Romans with a view to establishing what divine-sonship rhetoric meant for Paul and specifically how it functions in the emphases and dynamics of this epistle.[19]

17. Hurtado, "Son of God," 903.

18. I have characterized the main themes as follows: "The Gospel and the Son" (Rom 1:9; Gal 1:15-16); "The Royal Son" (Rom 1:3-4; 1 Thess 1:9-10; 1 Cor 15:24-28; Col 1:13), "The Sacrificed Son" (Rom 8:32; 5:10; Gal 2:20), "The Son and the Torah" (Gal 4:4; Rom 8:3), and "The Son and God's Sons" (Gal 4:5; Rom 8:1-29; 1 Cor 1:9; 2 Cor 1:19-20; Eph 4:13). See Hurtado, "Son of God," 903-6.

19. Cf. J. A. Fitzmyer's survey of christological titles and roles attributed to Jesus in Romans: "The Christology of the Epistle to the Romans," *The Future of Christology: Essays in Honor of Leander E. Keck*, ed. A. J. Malherbe and W. A. Meeks (Minneapolis: Fortress Press, 1993), pp. 81-90.

III. Jesus' Divine Sonship in Romans

The first thing to note is that references to Jesus' divine sonship in Romans are not randomly distributed but appear at particular points. There is a cluster of references in Romans 1 (vv. 3-4, 9), a single reference in 5:10, and another cluster in Romans 8 (vv. 3, 29, 32). Both the comparatively greater number of references in Romans and the distribution of them prompt the hypothesis that divine-sonship rhetoric may play a significant role and may be connected with particular themes. To anticipate the following analysis of these references, I propose three major points about Paul's use of divine-sonship language: (1) Divine-sonship rhetoric is clearly intended, at least in part, as honorific of Jesus; (2) the rhetoric carries a strongly *theocentric* force that emphasizes God's involvement in Jesus; (3) divine-sonship rhetoric is also used to link the salvation of the elect with the status of Jesus. Given that I wish to demonstrate how divine-sonship rhetoric is employed in Romans in connection with the larger dynamics and themes of the epistle, it will be simplest to examine the references to Jesus' divine sonship in the order in which they occur.

A. Romans 1:1-17

Perhaps the most well-known and most investigated references are in Romans 1:1-7.[20] It is widely thought that this paragraph contains a "pre-Pauline" creedal fragment in vv. 3-4, where we have the two balanced lines referring to Jesus as "of the seed of David according to the flesh, and designated the Son of God in power according to the Spirit of holiness by resurrection from the dead."[21] Hengel and Scott, however, have both noted that attempts at reconstructing a pre-Pauline creedal statement from these verses have produced unverifiable and divergent hypotheses, which does not promote much confidence in the enterprise.[22] In any case, as my concern here is with the way Paul employs references to Jesus' divine sonship in the context of this epistle, it is not necessary to pursue attempts to excavate the passage for pre-Pauline "artifacts." In this paragraph, where Paul refers to Jesus as "Christ Jesus" (v. 1), "Jesus Christ" (v. 6), "Jesus Christ our Lord" (v. 4), and "(the) Lord Jesus Christ" (v. 7), why does he also use the language of divine

20. "In recent years, more has been written about this than about any other New Testament text": Hengel, *Son of God,* p. 59.

21. See, e.g., the discussion of the passage (and bibliography) in J. D. G. Dunn, *Romans 1–8,* Word Biblical Commentary 38A (Dallas: Word, 1988), pp. 3-26. Theobald (193, n. 42) attempts a reconstruction of the putative creedal statement.

22. Hengel, *Son of God,* 59; James M. Scott, *Adoption as Sons of God* (WUNT 2/48; Tübingen: Mohr [Siebeck], 1992), p. 236.

sonship in vv. 3-4? As is sometimes suggested, is Paul merely showing an acquaintance with "non/pre-Pauline" (i.e., "Jewish-Christian") tradition to impress his Roman readers? Or does Paul employ the rhetoric here with more theological intentionality? I suggest that, in fact, there is more here in terms of meaningful use of divine-sonship rhetoric than is sometimes recognized.

It is important to note that, from the paragraph's opening words onward, there is a "binitarian" perspective, with Jesus and God both referred to and linked. Paul is both a slave of Jesus and called and set apart by God (v. 1). In the sonorous "grace and peace" salutation that rounds off this paragraph (v. 7), common in Paul's letter openings and generally accepted as derived from early Christian liturgical usage, both God and Jesus are invoked as sources of these blessings. The liturgical derivation of the expression reflects how Jesus was linked with God in the devotional life of early Christians.[23] Moreover, between the opening words and the invocation of this blessing in v. 7, the binitarian note is sounded. The "gospel of God" (v. 1) foretold through God's prophets (v. 2) concerns God's Son, "Jesus Christ our Lord" (vv. 3-4), through whom Paul is commissioned to bring about obedience of the Gentiles "for his name's sake" (v. 5). In this way, Jesus is certainly highlighted and by being associated so directly with God is given the highest status imaginable for a monotheist. At the same time, this honoring of Jesus is done precisely by placing him in the center of God's redeeming purposes, which means that there is a *theocentric* "context," so to speak, within which Jesus' significance is expressed.

Indeed, this theocentric tone characterizes the epistle as a whole. In the context of 1:1-17, for example, Paul's thanks are directed to God through Jesus (v. 8), and God is witness of Paul's service to God (v. 9). Paul prays that God's will may lead him to Rome (v. 10). Concluding this passage are the familiar Pauline statements about the gospel as the "power of God unto salvation," and about the "righteousness of God" being revealed in it (vv. 16-17). Along with the central role of Jesus in the salvific drama, therefore, we must not overlook the primacy of God. In 2:16, for example, God will judge human secrets according to Paul's gospel through Christ Jesus. In the well-known 3:21-26, where Jesus' death is so central, note that it is God's righteousness that is revealed (vv. 21-22, 25-26), that sinners fall short of God's glory (v. 23) and are justified by God's gift (v. 24), and that it is God who put forth Jesus as atonement (v. 25). The two lyrical passages that are commonly recognized as the major points where Paul's discussion reaches important climactic moments and gathers up all that has preceded — 8:31-39

23. I have emphasized the historical significance of the "binitarian" pattern of early Christian devotional practice in the context of ancient Jewish concern about the uniqueness of God in *One God, One Lord: Early Christian Devotion and Ancient Jewish Monotheism* (Philadelphia/London: Fortress Press/SCM, 1988) esp. pp. 93-124.

and 11:33-36 — are both clearly theocentric. In 8:31-39, to which we shall return later, there is certainly a binitarian tone, with Jesus' importance clear, but the primacy of God undeniable. In 11:33-36, God alone is praised as the origin and source of all things (esp. v. 36). In light of this theocentric emphasis in Romans, the reference to Jesus as God's "Son" in the opening paragraph (vv. 3-4) seems intended to make a christological statement that "situates" Jesus honorifically within the frame of God's primacy and purposes.

The same is true of the other reference to Jesus' divine sonship in this chapter (1:9). Here Paul's service is directed to God, while the message with which this service is concerned is "the gospel of his Son" *(to euangelion tou huiou autou)*. This corresponds interestingly to the phrasing in 1:1, "the gospel of God." Together, these two characterizations of the message make God the author and the one whose purpose is served in proclaiming it, with Jesus being its material content and focus. In using divine-sonship language to characterize the message here, Paul emphasizes both that the message involves proclaiming Jesus' significance in the divine plan ("the Son") and that Jesus' significance has to do with his relationship to God.

As *the* Son of God (N.B., as already mentioned, the definite article in vv. 3-4 as well as in v. 9), Jesus is certainly singled out for special honor and status. Divine-sonship language is used honorifically of various figures in ancient Jewish as well as pagan traditions, but Paul's syntax in all these references communicates a *sui generis* status for Jesus, distinguishing him from any others to whom divine-sonship language might be applied (e.g., the pious or Israelites generally, angels, holy men). In the biblical and Jewish traditions of the time (the revered traditions Paul drew upon and refashioned in his ministry), sonship to God means God's favor and approval (upon the pious/Israel), and/or God's authority (e.g., upon the Davidic king as in Ps 2). Thus the force of Paul's phrasing seems to claim for Jesus a unique favor, approval, and authority. Indeed, Paul's consistent use of the definite article may presuppose prior usage of divine-sonship language and signal Paul's desire to make a special claim for Jesus. Divine-sonship language, thus, is used to signify Jesus' high status. But the effect of divine-sonship language is to emphasize that this uniqueness has to do with Jesus' standing with God. The "Son" here is God's unique agent, whose significance is set within the context of God's purposes.

It is often thought that the two balanced lines in vv. 3-4 are to be taken as directly contrasting each other: "seed of David" contrasted with "Son of God," and "according to the flesh" in contrast with "according to the Spirit of holiness." Dunn, for example, refers to the two lines as "in antithetic parallelism."[24]

24. Dunn, *Romans 1–8*, pp. 5, 12; but Dunn does express caution about "interpreting the formula itself in a rigidly antithetical way . . ." (p. 23).

There is, to be sure, a measure of contrast, but "antithetic" may exaggerate and even distort it.[25] Jesus' Davidic descent is of course not the final thing to be said about him, but neither is it to be taken here as in any way negative, as if "seed of David" were something untrue, misleading, or to be transcended. In Romans 15:7-9, Paul positively refers to Jesus' Jewish descent and ministry-orbit, making it all part of the divine plan both for fulfillment of "promises of the fathers" and the enfranchisement of Gentiles. It therefore seems reasonable to consider whether the "seed of David" motif in 1:3 likewise plays a more positive role than some have granted.

The *kata sarka* ("according to the flesh") in 1:3 should not necessarily signal something negative. In 9:3, Paul refers to fellow Jews as *"syngenōn mou kata sarka,"* which should probably be taken as "my physical/natural kin," distinguished from his spiritual "brothers/sisters" but with no negative connotation necessary (contra Dunn).[26] The whole of Romans 9:1-5 refers to the Jewish people in quite positive terms, one of the things attributed to them being that "from them is the Christ/Messiah as to physical descent [*ho Christos to kata sarka*]" (v. 5).[27] Here again, it seems to me unnecessary to read into *kata sarka* anything particularly negative or critical (again, contra Dunn).[28] To be sure, *kata sarka* is a delimited sphere and not the fullest measure of things. When it comes to ethical effort, living *kata sarka* (e.g., Rom 8:4-5, 12-13) is hopelessly inadequate, and in Paul "flesh" can certainly bear negative overtones in statements dealing with moral/ethical questions (e.g., Gal 5:13-24). But, as with all words, it is the particular statement in which a word is used that gives the particular connotation of the word, the primary semantic unit being the statement, not individual words — as if the words were bearers of unvarying semantic values.[29] Thus, in Romans 1:3, where the questions of sin and God's righteous demands and such things are not under discussion, *kata sarka* need

25. I am pleased to point to Professor Fee for support of my view (*God's Empowering Presence* [Peabody, Mass.: Hendrickson, 1994], pp. 478-84, and esp. pp. 479, n. 18 and 480, n. 20).

26. Dunn (*Romans 9–16,* Word Biblical Commentary 38B [Dallas: Word, 1988], p. 525) sees in all occurrences of the phrase "negative overtones," here "a too restricted understanding of the family who are God's people."

27. On the syntactical significance of the neuter article in the phrase *to kata sarka,* see BDF para. 266.2 (p. 139).

28. Ibid., 528. Dunn sees *kata sarka* in 9:5 as "denoting a seriously inadequate understanding of the term or relation so qualified" (in this case, *ho Christos*).

29. On the linguistics theory behind my statement here, see, e.g., Moisés Silva, *Biblical Words and Their Meaning: An Introduction to Lexical Semantics* (Grand Rapids: Zondervan, 1983), esp. pp. 138-43; Peter Cotterell and Max Turner, *Linguistics and Biblical Interpretation* (Downers Grove, Ill.: InterVarsity Press, 1989); Arthur Gibson, *Biblical Semantic Logic* (Oxford: Blackwell, 1981).

express nothing more than Jesus' physical lineage, and the relationship between the two balanced lines in vv. 3-4 may better be taken as climactic or progressive parallelism rather than antithetic.[30] In further support of this, I note that, had Paul intended the two lines to be antithetical, we should have expected the particle *de,* which usually implies contrast. This particle does appear where Paul clearly makes an antithetical contrast, e.g., 8:5-6, 9, 13, making its absence in Romans 1:3-4 the more relevant for understanding these verses.

In short, Davidic descent characterizes Jesus positively as far as ordinary human reckoning and identification are concerned, and it expresses his historical appearance in honorific terms within the history of his Jewish people. "The Son of God in/with power [*en dynamei*]" is clearly a sequentially subsequent characterization arising from Jesus' resurrection (v. 4, *ex anastaseōs nekrōn*), and, of course, is a still more honorific status indicating much more fully Jesus' significance in the divine plan. But Jesus' physical birth of Davidic stock, though less striking in its honor, is still meaningful in the overall context of the epistle. His Davidic descent and messianic role (9:5) are both his *kata sarka,* through his physical/historical connection with Israel, and in this epistle where there is such emphasis upon the salvation-historical purposes and plans of God, Jesus' historical/physical derivation is relevant. The divine plan involves the broadening of the elect beyond historical Israel to take in Gentiles as well (esp. 11:11-32; 15:7-33), and so in the opening paragraph of Romans Paul refers to Jesus' physical descent from the royal-messianic line of Israel and to his divinely signified role as "the Son of God." In the sequence of the manifestation of his own significance, Jesus prefigures and embodies the divine purpose that involves fulfillment of promises to Israel and the widening of the children of God to include all who trust in the gospel of God's Son, including Gentiles, who are specifically mentioned in 1:5.[31]

To recognize this is to see the christological rhetoric of divine sonship here as related to the soteriological theme of the epistle, this relation providing another reason for Paul invoking divine-sonship rhetoric at the letter opening. In Romans, Paul not only refers to Jesus in divine-sonship rhetoric, he also employs this language to describe the salvific destiny of the elect. I shall delay further discussion of this, however, until we turn to the references to divine sonship in Romans 8.

30. Cf. Josef Blank, who likewise denies that Davidic descent and divine sonship are antitheses, and notes that both are messianic. As Davidic seed, Jesus is "Messias designatus," and as Son of God *in power* he is "Messias Rex" (*Paulus und Jesus* [SANT 16; Munich: Kösel, 1968], p. 254). Note also C. E. B. Cranfield, *The Epistle to the Romans, Vol. 1: Romans 1–8* (ICC; Edinburgh: T. & T. Clark, 1975), pp. 59-60.

31. See also Fee, p. 484.

Before proceeding with other references to divine sonship in Romans, however, one last observation from Romans 1:3-4 is in order. The controversy over whether to understand *horisthentos* in 1:4 as "appointed/installed" or "declared" cannot be addressed adequately here. On the one hand, for Paul Jesus is to be thought of as God's Son from the outset, as the references to God sending his Son indicate (Rom 8:3-4; Gal 4:4-6). On the other hand, in 1:4 the resurrection clearly seems to be seen as a salvation-historical event that places Jesus in a new position as the Son *in power*, appointed to rule on God's behalf, as is reflected also elsewhere in Paul (e.g., 1 Cor 15:20-28).[32] But I want to point out something else. It may be significant to observe that Paul uses cognate words to refer to his own appointment to apostleship (1:1, *aphorizein*), Jesus' appointment as Son-in-power *(horizein)*, and the foreordination of the elect for divine sonship (8:29, *proorizein*). Though each of the words has its own particular connotation, the aural similarity would not be so easily missed in Greek (particularly when Romans was read aloud) and the wordplay/association may be intentional. If so, this could be a device Paul uses to signal that the divine sonship of Jesus is vitally related to Paul's authority as apostle, and also to the divine sonship of believers that he discusses later in Romans 8.

B. Romans 5:1-11

In Romans 5:1-11, we have a very interesting example of Paul's use of christological rhetoric, and another case where a reference to Jesus as God's Son seems deliberate and meaningful. The passage is concerned with the relationship with God given to the elect through Jesus, who is referred to in the liturgical-sounding phrasing "our Lord Jesus Christ" in 5:1 and 5:11 in statements which frame the passage. In v. 6 and v. 8, it is simply "Christ" who died for the "impious/ungodly" and "sinners," the term "Christ" frequently used by Paul in creedal-like statements referring to Jesus' death and resurrection.[33] Is there a reason for the reference to Jesus as "his Son" in 5:10?

An affirmative answer is justified by the immediate context. In 5:1-7, Jesus is the subject of the main verbs, the principal actor in view. But in v. 8, it is God who "commends his own love to us" through Christ's death for sinners,

32. Dunn claims that taking *en dynamei* ("in power") as qualifying "the Son of God" in Rom 1:4 is "generally accepted to be the most obvious reading of the phrase," and describes Paul's meaning as follows: "Jesus did not first become God's Son at the resurrection; but he entered upon a still higher rank of sonship" (*Romans 1–8*, 14). Similarly Cranfield, *The Epistle to the Romans*, pp. 61-62.

33. Kramer, *Christ, Lord, Son of God*, pp. 19-64.

and in v. 10 the focus is on *reconciliation with God.* The reference to Jesus' death as "the death of his Son" fits with the theocentric focus of vv. 8-10. This phrasing both communicates the significance of Jesus under God and reveals the divine "investment," so to speak, in this death: We are reconciled to God through the death of *God's Son.* The emotive connotation of this phrasing was no doubt fully intended.[34]

So, in Romans 5:1-11, the variation in christological rhetoric is not at all random but subtly and yet eloquently meaningful. Again, divine-sonship rhetoric is invoked here most obviously to connote the connection between Jesus' death and the divine purpose which is so much the emphasis in this epistle.

C. Romans 8

Through Romans 8 the language of divine sonship runs like a silver thread.[35] The newly explicit feature of this chapter, however, is that in addition to its christological use divine-sonship language is also used to portray the salvation of the elect. I have suggested earlier in the discussion of Romans 1:1-7 that divine-sonship rhetoric there anticipates the soteriological themes developed later in the epistle. In Romans 8 we have the clearest justification for this suggestion.

There are three christological statements employing divine-sonship language in this chapter. In the first (8:3-4), God sends "his own Son" with a view to making it possible for those who "walk according to the Spirit" to fulfill the "righteous demand of the Law." Here the sending of God's Son is contrasted with the "inability of the Law on account of the weakness of the flesh" (v. 3a). Again, as in the earlier references in Romans, here God is the actor and God's Son the unique agent of the divine purpose. But, furthermore, the mention of the Son having been sent "in likeness to sinful flesh and concerning sin" (v. 3b) associates this Son with those for whom he is sent and with their earthly condition. In this first use of divine-sonship language in the chapter, theological, christological, and soteriological concerns are all reflected.

Everyone acquainted with Paul's letters will immediately see the similarity of this passage to Galatians 4:1-7. There also, Paul says that God sent his Son in full human condition ("born of a woman, born under the Law," Gal 4:4), as in Romans 8:3. It is frequently asserted that these two passages are evidence of a

34. Dunn refers to the phrase as giving "clear indication that this was not simply God's initiative, but God's own action through his Son (cf. 2 Cor 5:19)" (*Romans 1–8,* p. 260).

35. On Romans 8, see Fee's discussion (pp. 515-91), which, though focusing more on Paul's references to the Spirit, gives much useful comment about christological and soteriological matters as well.

christological "sending formula" that was perhaps "pre-Pauline." But the claim far exceeds the warrants for it.[36] For our purposes, the more relevant matter is that Galatians 4:1-7 shows that for Paul the link between Jesus' divine sonship and the divine sonship of believers was not an *ad hoc* motif in Romans but likely was a significant theme in his religious thought.[37] Thus, in Galatians 4:5, the object of God sending his Son is that believers might receive "sonship/ adoption" *(huiothesia)*, and in 4:6, as God's sons, believers are given the Spirit of his Son, thereby being prompted to address God from the heart as "*Abba*, Father" (the Aramaic term here likely alluding to an early Christian tradition of Jesus' prayer habits).

The next reference to Jesus as God's Son is Romans 8:29, where the soteriological application of Jesus' divine sonship is explicit, even primary. The elect are destined by God to be "conformed to the image [*eikonos*] of his Son so that he might be the firstborn among many brothers." Between the references to God's sending of his own Son in 8:3 and 8:29, Paul develops the theme of the divine sonship of believers, and it is likely significant that here as well as in Galatians 4:1-7 the divine sonship of believers is addressed only after referring to Jesus as the divine Son.[38]

The divine sonship of believers in both the Romans and the Galatians passages is clearly derivative of Jesus' sonship. In Galatians 4:6 God sends "the Spirit of his Son,"[39] and in Romans 8:16-17 believers are "heirs of God, co-heirs with Christ" as divine sons/children.[40] The primacy of Jesus' divine sonship is

36. E.g., Kramer, *Christ, Lord, Son of God*, pp. 111-15. Kramer quite properly makes "fixed key words" a requirement for claiming to have found a "formula" (p. 112), but fails to show any verbal links between Gal 4:4 and Rom 8:3 other than God and the Son! The verbs differ (Rom 8:3, *pempein;* Gal 4:4, *apostellein*), as do all the other qualifying phrases (e.g., Rom 8:3, "in the likeness of sinful flesh and for sin"; Gal 4:4, "born of [a] woman, born under [the] Law").

37. On the divine sonship/adoption of believers in Paul's thought, see now esp. Scott, *Adoption as Sons of God;* and Brendan Byrne, *Sons of God — "Seed of Abraham"* (AnBib 83; Rome: Biblical Institute Press, 1979).

38. Thus, I must dissent from Fee's comment (p. 565) that, unlike Gal 4:4-6, in Rom 8:14-16 there is "no close tie between 'sonship' and Christ as God's 'Son.'" The immediately relevant context for Paul's reference to believers as "sons" in Rom 8:14-16 does not begin in v. 14 but at v. 1, and so the designation of believers as "sons" follows closely after the reference to Jesus as the "Son" sent from God to establish them in relationship with God (vv. 3-4). Moreover, it does seem to me a bit artificial to take 8:14-16 as downplaying the relevance of vv. 16-17, where the association of the sonship of believers and that of Jesus is explicit.

39. The omission of "his Son" *(tou huiou)* in P46 notwithstanding, the phrase probably belongs to the original text.

40. Paul uses *huioi theou* in 8:14, 19, and *tekna theou* in 8:16-17, 21, apparently with no sharp distinction intended here.

undeniably explicit in 8:29. He is the image to which believers are to be conformed, and he is to be the "firstborn," holding the special rank connoted by that title among all the other sons of God.[41] For those readers/listeners acquainted with ancient Jewish tradition, "firstborn" may well have echoed with its use for Israel (e.g., Ex 4:22; Jer 31:9; Sir 36:17; *Pss Sol* 18:4) and perhaps for the Davidic king (Ps 89:27), with whom Jesus has been associated in Romans 1:3. In this light, "firstborn" would imply that Jesus is the criterion and pattern for all the elect ("many brothers"), designated in a traditional honorific term for Israel as God's chosen one. By applying the term to Jesus, Paul makes him the chosen one around whom and after whom the entire company of the redeemed are formed.

I have suggested earlier in this essay that this association of Jesus as divine Son and the elect as sons of God by derivation from him is anticipated and alluded to right from the opening reference to Jesus' divine sonship in Romans 1:3-4. In Romans 8, as well as in Galatians 4:4-6, we have clear proof that this theme was part of Paul's repertoire of teachings. Given the accumulated scholarly demonstrations of Paul's fondness for anticipating in letter openings the themes he later addresses in the letter bodies, it seems entirely reasonable to grant that the explicit discussion in Romans 8 is evidence that the references to Jesus' divine sonship in the opening chapter of this epistle were intended in part to prepare readers for the more developed discussion later in the letter-body here. Just as Jesus was appointed/declared "Son" in divine power (*en dynamei,* 1:4) by the divine Spirit[42] and through his resurrection, so believers are to be resurrected by God's Spirit (8:11) and revealed in glory (8:18) as sons of God (8:19, 21, 23). In other words, there is a symmetry between Jesus' glorification as divine Son and the glorification of believers in divine sonship, a symmetry that is, however, explicitly disclosed only in Romans 8, but likely anticipated from the opening of the epistle.

The final reference to Jesus' divine sonship comes just a few verses later, in Romans 8:32, where we read that God "did not spare his own Son but gave him over/up for us all." As already indicated, 8:31-39 is a clearly theocentric passage, as the opening words signal: "If God is for us, who [is there] against us?" (v. 31b).[43] In terms that are often recognized as echoing the story of the offering

41. See, e.g., K. H. Bartels, "First, Firstborn," *NIDNTT* 1:664-70. Cf. the christological use of the term in Col 1:18.

42. See the detailed discussion of "Spirit of holiness" in 1:4 by Fee (pp. 482-83).

43. To be sure, there is a "binitarian" theme as well, as reflected in the alternation between God and Christ in the rhetorical questions in vv. 33-34, and in the concluding words of v. 39, "the love of God in Christ Jesus our Lord." In v. 35, in spite of the support of Sinaiticus for *agapēs tou theou* ("love of God"), it is probable that "love of Christ" is to be preferred as original. But, as v. 39 makes plain, the love of Christ is God's love manifested through him.

of Isaac (Gen 22:12, 16), Romans 8:32 emphasizes God's hand in Jesus' redemptive death.[44] Both the reference to Jesus as God's "own Son" and the allusion to the Abraham/Isaac story are probably intended to bring a powerful emotive force to the statement, emphasizing God's great generosity and the lengths he went to in order to secure redemption for the elect. On the basis of this astonishing act of God, Paul completes the sentence in a rhetorical question giving assurance that God will bestow on the elect "all things with him [Christ]."

In this verse, therefore, we have the theocentric tone characteristic of Paul's references to Jesus' divine sonship, and in the rhetorical question in v. 32b an allusion to the idea that Jesus' divine sonship, though unique in some ways, is also generative of, and the pattern for, the divine blessings to be given to the elect, blessings which include divine sonship. Surely, in the context of Romans 8, the "all things with him" to be given by God have been specified as including the glorious revelation and full possession of divine sonship (vv. 18-23) that is patterned after Jesus' sonship (v. 29).

IV. Conclusion

It is commonly recognized that in Romans 1–8 Paul develops and defends for his readers the theological rationale for his ministry to the Gentiles. After having done so, he then turns in chapters 9–11 to the logical questions that have to do with Israel in the light of the large-scale rejection of the gospel among the Jews. Romans 9–11 is not, as it has often been treated in Christian tradition, a parenthesis, but integral to the understanding of God's great salvific program as presented in Romans, and as it must have been operative in all Paul's activities and thought.[45] But Romans 1–8 unfolds Paul's arguments for the enfranchisement of Gentiles into the community of the redeemed on the basis of Jesus Christ. It is, therefore, understandable that references to Jesus' divine sonship are found in these chapters in Romans. Paul wishes to justify his mission, which

44. The *ouk epheisato* of Rom 8:32 echoes the *ouk epheisō* of LXX Gen 22:12, 16. The *tou idiou huiou* may echo *tou huiou sou tou agapētou*. It also bears noting that the *paredōken* of Rom 8:32 echoes the ominous use of the same word in the same epistle for God's judgment upon the disobedient in 1:24, 26, 28, as well as the other use in making reference to Jesus' redemptive death in 4:25. Cf. Gal 2:20, "the Son of God who loved me and gave himself [*paradontos heauton*] for me."

45. For a vigorously argued attempt at a coherent analysis of Romans, see S. K. Stowers, *A Rereading of Romans: Justice, Jews and Gentiles* (New Haven: Yale, 1994), and cf. the criticism by R. B. Hays, "'The Gospel Is the Power of God for Salvation to Gentiles Only'? A Critique of Stanley Stowers' *Rereading of Romans*," *CR* (1996): 27-44.

is directed toward winning the faithful obedience of Gentiles (1:5), and wishes to show that God's aim involves the adoption into divine sonship of all those who put their trust in the gospel message that concerns Jesus Christ, God's paradigmatic and unique Son. Consequently, in the letter opening Paul asserts Jesus' divine sonship, along with the mention of Jesus' historical connection with Israel through the line of David. As both seed of David and Son of God, Jesus thus unites in himself the two major dynamics that run through the epistle to the Romans: (1) God's faithfulness to historic Israel, in spite of the unbelief and disobedience of many in Israel, and (2) God's great generosity in annexing Gentiles into the company of the redeemed, making them sons of God, even though the privileges of Israel (9:1-5) are not theirs by natural rights.

Though Paul was surely echoing the christological rhetoric of wider Christian circles and "pre-Pauline" tradition in referring to Jesus as God's Son, Paul's use of divine-sonship language is not to be accounted for simply as a somewhat passive use of traditional categories with little significance for his own view of Jesus' meaning. Paul used divine-sonship language for Jesus especially when he wished to portray Jesus' significance *with reference to God.* Jesus is "Lord" of believers. He is "Christ" as the eschatological redeemer. He is "the Son" in relation to God, as uniquely honored by God and unique agent of God. Also, when Paul wanted to emphasize God's direct involvement in Jesus' redemptive work, divine-sonship language was effective, perhaps particularly on the emotive level, portraying God as sending Jesus, even giving him up (with a judicial connotation) for the sake of the elect. Furthermore, as clearly shown in Romans and Galatians, when Paul wished to assert the fullness of the divine enfranchisement given to all who put faith in the gospel, including particularly Gentiles in spite of their godless past, he spoke of Jesus' as God's Son. Though unique, this Son is also the pattern and basis for the filial intimacy with God that is to be given to all who trust in him.

I hope also to have shown that in the epistle to the Romans Paul's references to Jesus' divine sonship are meaningfully placed, both reflecting and contributing to the dynamics of the epistle, particularly in the presentation of God's salvific purposes in chapters 1–8.

From Romans to the Real World: Biblical Principles and Cultural Change in Relation to Homosexuality and the Ministry of Women

R. T. France

I. Introduction

My cumbersome title attempts to set out clearly the aim of this paper. It is about hermeneutics, how we get from an authoritative ancient text (specifically Romans) to practical decisions relating to the real world in which we live today. The paper considers the tension which often arises between the desire to maintain biblical principles and the need to relate biblical values appropriately to a changing culture, and recognizes the sharply contrasting conclusions which equally convinced Christians therefore often draw from the same biblical texts. I propose to examine the subject with reference to two of the most controversial areas in the Christian church in the Western world today, the issues respectively of homosexuality and of the ministry of women in the church.

The two issues are of course quite separate. Why then am I attempting to deal with them in a single article? In Britain (and I have no reason to think we are unique in this respect) those Christians who, like myself, have argued from Scripture for the appropriateness of ordaining women to positions of leadership in the church have often been confronted by other Christians with the assertion that if our hermeneutical principles can lead us so clearly to discard the plain injunctions of Scripture on this one issue, we are bound also to approve homosexual practice, since the same principles apply.[1] This assertion is usually offered as a self-evident conclusion, if we are to be hermeneutically consistent. How can one with integrity adopt a "liberal" position on the ministry of women and remain "conservative" in relation to homosexual practice?

In fact, however, while I do believe that it is right in the light of Scripture to ordain women to positions of leadership in the church, I cannot find similar scriptural warrant for approving homosexual practice. How can I be so "inconsistent"? This has led me to examine again the hermeneutical basis for my conclusions on these two issues.

I know that these issues are of great interest to Gordon Fee (though as a matter of fact our personal discussions have focused more on the ministry of women than on homosexuality).[2] I hope therefore that it may not be too impertinent for me to conduct my hermeneutical self-examination in his Festschrift. The editors have decided that the focus of the volume is to be on Romans, and it so happens that within this one letter there are substantial passages which contribute significantly to the debate on these two issues. The total scriptural evidence is of course much wider in each case, but I hope that by discussing homosexual practice in the light of Romans 1:18-32 and the ministry of women in the light of Romans 16:1-16 we may uncover some useful hermeneutical pointers.

The two passages are of course very different in character, but that is precisely the point: not all of Scripture, even in Paul's letters, consists of specific injunctions or dogmatic propositions, but for a fully Christian view of the authority of Scripture all of it is at least potentially relevant for our guidance

1. Thus M. Tinker, replying to an article by me on the ordination of women in *Churchman* 108 (1994): 234-41, writes "Formally the arguments and methodology used by Dr. France in his paper are exactly the same as those used for legitimizing homosexual practice. Is it not time to question seriously an hermeneutic which leads to such results?" (*Churchman* 108, p. 246). See, by contrast, the following statement from the report of the 1997 consultation (at Kingston, Jamaica) of the Evangelical Fellowship in the Anglican Communion: "Attempts have been made to link the blessing of homosexual unions and ordination of practicing homosexuals with the ordination of women in one agenda of 'liberation'. However, proposals for the ordination of practicing homosexuals and for the blessing of homosexual unions attract two questions. Firstly, are homosexual acts sinful, forbidden by God? Secondly, if they are sinful, may the church formally bless and ordain people to live in unrepented and continuing sin? These questions have no parallel in the debate which surrounded the ordination of women. The state of being female is nowhere regarded in Scripture as sinful. The attempted linkage is disingenuous" (*Anvil* 14/3 [1997]: 217).

2. Gordon would not wish to conduct the discussion in terms of "ordination" as such; the issue for him, as for me, is that of leadership in the church. I use the terminology of "ordination" simply because that is the form in which the issue has arisen in the particular branch of the church to which I belong.

today. It should therefore be illuminating to explore how these two very different passages fit into the wider debate. If in the process we discover that within the compass of this one letter Paul appears to be, like me, "conservative" in relation to homosexual practice and "liberal" in relation to the ministry of women, I shall not wish to resist that conclusion!

II. Setting the Scene

I approach these issues in the context of the Church of England, which in 1994 for the first time ordained women to its priesthood, and in which there is at the time of writing (late 1997) a vigorous debate on the issue of homosexuality, with special reference to whether it is right for known practicing homosexuals to be ordained.

Opposition to the ordination of women to the priesthood has come from two different quarters: from the catholic wing of the church mainly on the grounds that it is a departure from the tradition of the church (both Orthodox and Catholic), and from the evangelical wing on the quite different grounds that Scripture explicitly forbids women to have authority over or to teach men. The alliance of these two contrasting strands of opposition succeeded in preventing earlier attempts to have the measure approved by the church's General Synod, but in 1992 the necessary two-thirds majority was achieved with a number of evangelicals, who would previously have been expected to oppose the measure, now voting in favor. While it has been easy to caricature their change of mind as a capitulation to pressure from the church's leadership and/or an unprincipled bowing to secular culture, what has in fact happened is that a significant hermeneutical reappraisal has been taking place. What had appeared to be the "plain teaching of Scripture" has been seen to be less one-sided than was previously thought. The division among evangelicals has been not on the basis of greater and less fidelity to Scripture, but rather on that of a genuine disagreement over how the varying strands of Scripture evidence relating to this issue should be applied to the current scene.

The resultant polarization of evangelical views has been an uncomfortable experience (though not a new one — evangelicals have seldom been a totally united body!). It has resulted in the setting up of a pressure group (called "Reform") dedicated to preventing any further erosion (as they see it) of traditionally held evangelical positions. And many believe that the next step on the downward slope is likely to be the open recognition of homosexual practice as compatible with Christian discipleship, and therefore as acceptable in an ordained minister.

This article is not written only for Anglicans, and these issues will arise, if they arise at all, in different forms in different church contexts. But I suspect that there is enough common ground in principle for most readers to recognize the relevance of our Church of England debates to their different contexts. It may help if, before we turn to the examination of the issues, I try to clarify some terms.

The specific area of dispute with regard to women in the Church of England has been their ordination to the priesthood. For a good number of years women have been licensed as lay workers and as Readers (lay people authorized to conduct services and to preach), and since 1987 have been ordained as deacons (with the title "Reverend" and the use of the clerical collar). Ordination to the priesthood authorizes certain additional functions (presiding at the Eucharist, and the pronouncing of absolution and blessing), but more significantly from the evangelical point of view it opens the way to appointment as incumbent or priest-in-charge, that is, as the leading member of the local ministry team (or "senior pastor"), and thus raises the question of a woman holding authority over men. It is here that some evangelicals feel obliged to draw the line, on the grounds that "Scripture forbids it."

With regard to homosexuality it is important to stress that what is under discussion is not homosexual orientation but homosexual practice. No doubt the distinction is oversimplified, but it marks a real difference in focus. The debate as to whether a homosexual orientation is innate or acquired will continue, and evangelicals will no doubt continue to be divided over these matters. But the issue from the point of view of scriptural authority is whether sexual activity between people of the same sex can be approved, and whether when such activity is acknowledged this should be regarded as a bar to ordained ministry.

With these broad definitions of the issues involved, we proceed to look from a hermeneutical point of view at each of the two questions in turn, before briefly comparing the two debates and drawing out the implications for evangelical hermeneutics. In the space available all that can be offered is a broad-brush treatment, but I hope that its very lack of sophistication may make it easier to focus on the basic issues raised.

III. The Ministry of Women

I have recently discussed the hermeneutical issues relating to the question of women's ministry in the church in a series of lectures published under the title *Women in the Church's Ministry: A Test-case for Biblical Hermeneutics.*[3] Those

3. The Didsbury Lectures 1995, published by Paternoster Press, Carlisle, 1995, and by Eerdmans, Grand Rapids, 1997.

lectures were specifically devoted to teasing out the basis of disagreement among evangelicals in this debate, and to highlighting the hermeneutical issues raised. That book therefore covers the subject of this first main section of the present paper more fully than is here possible, and I shall content myself with summarizing its argument, with the hope that any reader who wishes to explore the basis for the following remarks will be prepared to look up that fuller treatment.

A. *The Shape of the Debate*

Those who argue from Scripture that women should not be ordained usually rely on two separate but related lines of argument. The first is that there are two passages in Pauline letters which explicitly command women to be silent (1 Cor 14:34-35) and to refrain from teaching or having authority over men (1 Tim 2:11-12). The second is that in several places women are instructed to "be in submission" (ὑποτάσσομαι) to men. This injunction is explicit in Ephesians 5:22; Colossians 3:18; Titus 2:5; 1 Peter 3:1, 5, and is also incorporated into the two texts just mentioned (1 Cor 14:34; 1 Tim 2:11). In one of these passages Paul uses the metaphor "head" to describe the relation of man to woman, and the same metaphor is used also in 1 Corinthians 11:3, though there without explicit use of language of "submission."

To take the second line of argument first, there is no doubt that in the New Testament, and especially in Paul, there is a strong sense of a God-given "order" in society and in the church, which includes the relationship of the sexes. What is not so clear is the sphere(s) of life to which this principle applies. Almost all the passages listed above use ὑποτάσσομαι with specific reference to the marriage relationship, and it is at least arguable whether the principle may rightly be extended more generally to the relations of men and women in society or in the church. The ambiguity of the Greek terms ἀνήρ (man *or* husband) and γυνή (woman *or* wife) compounds the uncertainty. Where, as in most of the above passages, the context is specifically of marriage, the domestic focus seems clear, but in 1 Corinthians 11:2-16 and 1 Timothy 2:9-15, passages which speak of church life, it remains to be decided whether Paul is speaking of a woman's silence and submission in relation to other men in general or only in relation to her husband.

As for the metaphor "head," I am constantly amazed at the confident way in which people speak of a "principle of headship" in the New Testament, apparently unaware that there is no such abstract noun in the Greek New Testament, and that the noun "head," which is twice used metaphorically of man in relation to woman, is also used metaphorically of a variety of other relationships in ways that do not suggest a single unambiguous concept of "headship." Moreover, one of the two metaphorical uses of "head" for a man (Eph 5:23) is explicitly concerned with the marriage relationship rather than with society in general. Clearly the metaphor must be understood in relation to its context; it does not in itself import a specific ideology.

Thus there is no doubt that the New Testament includes a principle of the "submission" of woman to man (though also of mutual submission, Eph 5:21), but there is room for considerable uncertainty about just what this "submission" involves, and about how far it can legitimately be invoked outside the marriage relationship.

Returning now to the other line of argument, the two Pauline "prohibition texts," we find that most of the emphasis falls on 1 Timothy 2:11-12. This is because everyone seems to find 1 Corinthians 14:34-35 hard to interpret in its context, and some (among whom Gordon Fee is prominent) doubt whether these verses, which seem awkwardly to interrupt the flow of Paul's thought, were originally a part of the letter.[4] Those who believe that Paul really did instruct the Corinthian women to be silent in church must also face the embarrassment that in 1 Corinthians 11:5 he accepts without comment that women were praying and prophesying in that same church. The fact that in 14:35 he goes on to mention specifically their desire to ask questions, and instructs them to do so with their husbands at home, suggests to others that verse 34 was not in fact meant to be a blanket ban on all vocal activity in church, but rather a call for silence in certain particular circumstances. He has already issued such an injunction to tongue-speakers and prophets in vv. 28 and 30 without suggesting that they be permanently silent.

1 Timothy 2:11-12 thus remains as the one apparently clear case of Paul's imposing a ban on women's ministry. There has been much debate on what sort of "teaching" and "authority" is involved, especially in view of the use of the rare verb αὐθεντέω rather than the normal language of authority (ἐξουσία), and over whether here too γυνή and ἀνήρ refer specifically (and only?) to "wife" and "husband," as may be suggested by the illustration drawn from the story of Adam and Eve (and finding the solution in childbirth) which follows in vv. 13-15.

But most interpreters have agreed that Paul (if we may assume, with Gordon Fee,[5] that it *was* Paul!) does here prohibit teaching and authority for the women of the church in Ephesus. Much energy has then been devoted to discerning whether this was the result of problems specific to that particular

4. G. D. Fee, *The First Epistle to the Corinthians* (Grand Rapids: Eerdmans, 1987), pp. 699-705.

5. G. D. Fee, *1 and 2 Timothy, Titus* (NIBC; Peabody Mass.: Hendrickson, 1984), pp. 23-26.

church at that time, or whether Paul would have said the same to women in other churches at other times as well. In particular much has been made of Paul's concern over apparently Gnostic teaching in the church in Ephesus, the instruction to Timothy to oppose those who devalue marriage, and the presence in that church of certain women who were going about "saying what they should not say" (5:13). On such grounds Gordon Fee has argued persuasively that the instructions in 2:11-12 relate to the specific local situation rather than laying down a universal rule, and that their status is comparable with that of the remarkably parallel rules for the treatment of widows in 5:11-15, which are not generally treated as normative for modern church life.[6]

Those who are unpersuaded that the matter is settled by these two traditional lines of argument (a general New Testament principle of female submission, and the presence of two passages prohibiting women's speaking/teaching/authority) typically respond by appealing to a wider pattern in life and thought of the New Testament church. They point out Jesus' positive attitude toward women, particularly when seen against the background of contemporary Jewish and pagan attitudes. They note the prominent role which several women played in the life and ministry of the New Testament church, including in some cases apparently the holding of recognized offices in local congregations. Paul himself not infrequently refers appreciatively to the role of women whom he regards as in some sense colleagues in his gospel work, and in Galatians 3:28 famously declares that in Christ there is "no longer male and female." On such grounds they may speak of a development or "trajectory" toward the elimination of discrimination between men and women in relation to Christian ministry which, even if not fully effective within the New Testament period, was inevitably destined to lead to women taking a full and leading role in the life of the churches. Some draw attention to the elimination of slavery as a parallel example of a trajectory which was set up in the New Testament but did not find its full working out until many centuries later and in a different social and cultural context.

It is within this wider perspective that a remarkable passage in Romans comes into play, and it is to this that we now turn as the first of our two soundings in Romans.

B. Romans 16:1-16

Nowhere else does Paul include such a long list of greetings in his letters. Perhaps it is because he is writing to a church which he has not yet visited that he

6. G. D. Fee, *Gospel and Spirit* (Peabody Mass.: Hendrickson, 1991), pp. 52-65.

feels it necessary to establish how many of its members he has already met and worked with on their travels in other parts of the empire. For whatever reason, he mentions no fewer than 27 individuals in these verses, together with general greetings to the households of Aristobulus and Narcissus. These 27 are friends and in many cases explicitly designated as his coworkers. This passage therefore serves as a sort of roll call of Paul's colleagues in ministry.

Its relevance to our present subject lies in the fact that ten of the 27 people named are women. That in itself is remarkable in the context of what has often been assumed to be a predominantly male-led movement. It becomes the more remarkable when we note the expressions that Paul uses to describe a number of these women.

Four of them (Mary, v. 6; Tryphaena, Tryphosa, and Persis, v. 12) are described as having "worked hard"; the verb κοπιάω is used elsewhere of Paul's own apostolic ministry in evangelism and church building (1 Cor 15:10; Gal 4:11; Phil 2:16, etc.), and of the parallel labors of his associates (1 Cor 6:16; 1 Thess 5:12). While the verb is not in itself very specific, the addition of ἐν κυρίῳ with reference to the labors of Tryphaena, Tryphosa, and Persis, and of εἰς ὑμᾶς with regard to Mary's work, suggests that he refers to specifically Christian ministry. For some of the others the nature of that ministry is more explicit.

Prisca (v. 3) and her husband Aquila are described as Paul's συνεργοί, the term he uses elsewhere for others who were his chief associates in his apostolic mission (Timothy, Titus, Mark, Luke, Philemon, etc.). From other references to Prisc(ill)a, who is normally mentioned before her husband, we gain the impression of a woman with a significant and authoritative ministry, including the principal role in instructing the formidable Apollos in the faith (Acts 18:26)! Phoebe (vv. 1-2) is a διάκονος of the local church, which suggests a recognized ministry comparable to that of the διάκονοι of Philippians 1:1 and 1 Timothy 3:8-13. She is also described by Paul as προστάτις of himself and others, a term which is probably best translated as "benefactor," or perhaps "patron," and thus presumably a leading member of the congregation. But the most remarkable is Junia (v. 7), who is described as Paul's "fellow-prisoner" but also as "prominent among the apostles."[7] So do we have here a female "apostle"?

The term ἀπόστολος is of course used of other Christian leaders of the first century besides the twelve and Paul (Acts 14:4, 14; 2 Cor 8:23, etc.), but it is certainly a title of leadership. So Western Christians have tried to evade the

7. The rendering "highly regarded *by* the apostles" has been suggested, but it may fairly be concluded that this unnatural reading derives not from linguistic probability but from apologetic embarrassment. It has not been adopted in any English version that I have seen.

force of Paul's language by turning Junia into a man, Junias. We cannot pursue the linguistic argument here;[8] suffice it to say that I have seldom known Gordon Fee (who is not noted for muting his views) more irate than on this chauvinist subterfuge! His robust and irresistible campaign to restore the female name Junia in the "inclusive language edition" of the NIV was matched only by his incredulous disappointment when the majority voted to leave the indefensible masculine alternative in a footnote. His anger was particularly directed against the entry 'Ιουνιᾶς in the Bauer Lexicon, which prefers this supposed masculine form, admittedly "not found elsewhere," to the female name (which it grudgingly admits "from a purely lexical point of view deserves consideration") without pointing out that the latter is not only commonly found in Greek writings of the period, but is the unanimous interpretation of all ancient translators and commentators. The first evidence for the name being taken as (masculine) Junias comes from the late thirteenth century, and in the East it was not until the nineteenth century that this idea emerged.[9] This, for Gordon, is not lexicography!

The cumulative impression from Romans 16:1-16 is that Paul numbered women among his closest fellow workers in his apostolic mission, that they held positions of recognized authority in his churches, and that they were engaged in teaching and indeed "apostleship." And Romans 16:1-16 does not stand alone: other references in Acts and in other epistles reinforce this impression. All this seems to be a different world from 1 Timothy 2:11-12, and hard to square with the belief that Paul's principle of female "submission" extends outside the marriage relationship to include the prohibition of authoritative ministry in the church. Could these verses have come from the same Paul who forbade Ephesian women to teach or have authority?

C. Weighing the Evidence

The problem cannot be solved by arguing that either Romans 16:1-16 or 1 Timothy 2:11-12 was not written by Paul (there is scholarly support for either proposal),[10] since neither passage stands alone. They are merely prominent outcrops of two underlying strata of the New Testament, one restricting the role of

8. C. E. B. Cranfield, *The Epistle to the Romans,* vol. 2 (ICC; T. & T. Clark, 1979), pp. 788-89 is probably the best easily accessible discussion.

9. So K. E. Bailey, *Anvil* 11 (1994): 11-13.

10. Arguments for the non-Pauline authorship of the Pastoral Epistles are too well-known to need documentation here. For the authenticity of Romans 16:1-16, see again Cranfield's commentary (*Romans,* vol. 1 [1975], pp. 5-11).

women in at least certain spheres of church life, the other celebrating their role in ministry and leadership.

The interpreter is therefore left with a choice as to which of these two contrasting strands in the New Testament should take priority in drawing out guidance for modern church life. Hence the fundamental disagreement between equally sincere interpreters of Scripture over the ministry of women. It derives from opposite choices on this basic dilemma.

Some base their hermeneutic on their apparently clear "prohibition" texts, understood in the light of a wide-ranging principle of male "headship," and so regard the prohibition as still valid for the church today. They must then deny that Paul's declaration "no longer male and female" is relevant to ministry, and must find ways of reading texts like Romans 16:1-16 which maintain a distinction in principle between what men and women were allowed to do in the church.

For others the principle of "no longer male and female" is fundamental, extending beyond simply the sphere of salvation to that of ministry in the church, and support for this is found in the New Testament evidence as to what women did in fact do (apparently with Paul's approval) in the first century. They must then question how widely Paul's principle of female submission can legitimately be extended, and must conclude that the prohibitions issued on women's activities in Corinth and Ephesus related to specific problems which had arisen in those particular situations. They will argue that the "trajectory" of New Testament thought is clearly in the direction of greater equality between the sexes rather than toward a permanent male supremacy.

There seems no incontrovertible way of deciding which choice is right. Responsible hermeneutics is not an exact science, and equally convinced champions of the authority of Scripture for Christian life and thought today will no doubt continue to come to opposite conclusions in this area where each viewpoint can fairly claim to have Scripture on its side. While it may be obvious to some which is the "basic principle,"[11] the opposite may be equally obvious to others.

The choice is often made not so much on the basis of an "objective" hermeneutic as in the light of the tradition within which the interpreter has grown up and now operates. Change is also possible, however, as various outside influences are brought to bear and cause the interpreter to reexamine his or her hermeneutical assumptions. I have myself changed my mind on the issue, as have those evangelicals who voted in 1992 for the ordination of women. But in matters of religion change usually comes slowly, if at all! Meanwhile, we must agree to differ.

11. E.g., F. F. Bruce, *Commentary on Galatians* (Exeter, U.K.: Paternoster, 1982), p. 190.

IV. Homosexual Practice

The preceding section was a very bald summary (oversimplified to the point of distortion) of an argument I have conducted in more detail elsewhere. Here I venture into new ground, at least in terms of any argument formulated for publication, but still with the same constraint on space. I can only apologize in advance for what will no doubt come across as a quite simplistic statement of my basic approach.

A. What Does Scripture Offer?

In the previous section I argued that the disagreement over the ministry of women arises from the fact that material can be found from Scripture in support of either viewpoint, leaving the interpreter the ultimate decision on which takes priority. Is this the case with regard to homosexual behavior?

Biblical passages which refer directly to homosexual behavior are not many, and all can be briefly mentioned here.

In the Old Testament there are two stories of attempted homosexual rape (Gen 19:1-11; Judg 19:22-30), each of which serves as the trigger for severe punishment, whether by God (Sodom) or by his people (Gibeah). In each case there was also a flagrant breach of the laws of hospitality, but from the way the story is told it is clear that the attempted sexual assault is the focus of the judgment. It would, however, be as illegitimate to argue from these passages for a prohibition of any homosexual activity as to conclude from the condemnation of heterosexual rape that intercourse between men and women is forbidden. They certainly give no encouragement to loving homosexual behavior, but neither do they directly condemn it.[12]

More relevant are two passages in the law which prohibit male homosexual practice ("lie with a male as with a woman") and declare it to be an "abomination" (Lev 18:22; 20:13). These passages, brief and undeveloped as they are, are quite unequivocal. They occur in the setting of other laws against sexual misconduct such as adultery, incest, and bestiality, listed as the sort of behavior for which the pagan nations have been driven out of the land. The

12. The reference in Jude 7 to the sin of Sodom and Gomorrah as "indulging in immorality and [literally] going after another flesh" reflects the story of attempted homosexual rape in Gen 19, and is widely assumed to locate the sin of the men of Sodom particularly in their homosexual inclination. Some commentators argue, however, that it refers rather to their desire for sexual relations with *angels;* so, e.g., R. J. Bauckham, *Jude, 2 Peter* (Word Biblical Commentary; Waco: Word, 1983), p. 54. "Other flesh" would be a strange term for fellow men. The passage is too obscure to be used confidently on either side of the debate.

penalty in Leviticus 18 is to be "cut off from their people" and in Leviticus 20 is death.[13]

Deuteronomy 23:17-18 prohibits Israelites from being male prostitutes, and declares their earnings "abhorrent to the Lord your God." The Book of Kings condemns the presence of male prostitutes in Judah as an aspect of pagan worship, and an offense in the sight of God (1 Kings 14:24; 15:12; 22:46; 2 Kings 23:7). Again, as with the stories of attempted homosexual rape, we must be aware of equating prostitution with homosexual activity in general, but it seems clear that the homosexual activity involved in male prostitution was not acceptable and was particularly associated with pagan worship.

In the New Testament we find similar brief and undeveloped condemnations of homosexual behavior in 1 Corinthians 6:9-10 and 1 Timothy 1:9-10. In the former passage μαλακοί and ἀρσενοκοῖται are among the immoral people who will not inherit the kingdom of God, while in the latter ἀρσενοκοῖται are among a similar list of those who engage in unrighteous practices (including also parricide, murder, and slave trading) which are "contrary to sound teaching." While there is room for debate over the meaning of μαλακός ("soft," "effeminate," but sometime used more specifically of the younger partner in a pederast relationship, or a male prostitute),[14] there seems little doubt that ἀρσενοκοῖται ("those who go to bed with males," echoing terms of LXX Lev 18:22) in both passages is intended to cover male homosexual activity in general rather than only pederasty or male prostitution (for each of which more specific Greek words were available).[15]

And that, apart from Romans 1:18-32, to which we shall turn shortly, is all that can be reasonably claimed as direct reference to homosexual activity in the Bible. It is, it will be noticed, uniformly hostile. These few references must, moreover, be set alongside the underlying biblical assumption from Genesis 2:24 onward that God's purpose for human sexuality is to be found in the heterosexual union of man and woman. The fact that so few references to homosexuality occur suggests perhaps not that the matter was of little consequence, but that homosexual behavior, so common in the pagan world both of Old and New Testaments, was simply alien to the Jewish and Christian ethos.

Where then can those who wish to argue on biblical grounds for the legitimacy of homosexual activity turn for support? They can of course attempt to

13. A further law in Deut 22:5 condemns transvestism as "abhorrent to the Lord," but without exploring the motive behind it; this law may relate to homosexual activity, but the background is obscure.

14. G. D. Fee, *The First Epistle to the Corinthians*, pp. 243-44.

15. See the full study of the word by D. F. Wright, *Vigiliae Christianae* 38 (1984): 125-53.

deflect the negative verdict drawn from the above passages by arguing that they refer not to loving homosexual relations but to perversions such as pederasty, prostitution, and rape. In the absence of more detailed description in the relevant passages this is a hazardous enterprise, even though the very brevity of the references perhaps leaves scope for constructing such an argument (essentially an argument from silence) for each passage taken alone. But in view of the overall negativity of these passages taken together, such an attempt is not likely to convince in the absence of any overt encouragement to homosexual love to counterbalance these references. Can any such encouragement be found in the Bible?

Appeal is made in this connection particularly to the love of David and Jonathan: Jonathan "loved David as his own soul" (1 Sam 18:1-4), "as he loved his own life" (1 Sam 20:17); they wept and kissed each other at their parting (1 Sam 20:41), and David declared Jonathan's love for him "wonderful, passing the love of women" (2 Sam 1:26). There is, however, no indication of sexual activity between them (kissing between men was common, as it is in many cultures today, and had no necessary sexual connotations); their "love" was a firm, loyal, and unselfish friendship, expressed in a "covenant" (1 Sam 18:3; 20:8, 16-17, 42) which led Jonathan to prefer David's interests to his own. It is perhaps not surprising that the strong emotional language (and especially the phrase "passing the love of women") has been taken in our culture to suggest something more sexually expressed, but this remains speculation, and speculation which finds no support in the general pattern of sexual relations in Israel as far as we can discern it from the Old Testament. The stories of David provide ample evidence of his heterosexual orientation!

The fact that Jesus was, as far as we know, unmarried (and that celibacy was unusual in Jewish culture) has led some to speculate that he was homosexual in orientation. His selection of an all-male group of disciples can be no cause for surprise in the culture of his day, but one of them was singled out in the Fourth Gospel as the disciple "whom Jesus loved," and this close relationship (including his reclining at the last supper "on Jesus' chest," Jn 13:23, 25) has led some to suggest that he was not only a specially close friend but a sexual partner. We are again confronted by the difficulty of deciding what would be the force of such expressions in a cultural context different from our own, but here too it must be insisted that no hint of sexual interest, let alone sexual activity, is found in the gospel text.[16] Only a culture that has difficulty in appreciat-

16. The expression "reclining on the chest of" is rightly translated by modern versions by some such phrase as "reclining next to," indicating the position to Jesus' right at a formal meal (using something like the Roman triclinium arrangement, where guests reclined at table supported by their left elbow).

ing close friendship between men on any other basis would think of importing a sexual element into this language.

But if there is no evidence of approved homosexual activity in the Bible, might it be possible to argue for it on more general grounds of a Christian ideal of love and acceptance and of tolerance of differing views within the church (as in Rom 14), together with the fact that cultural attitudes have changed, and that these ideals must now be expressed in a way appropriate to our culture, even if it would have been unacceptable in that of the Bible? Does cultural relativity allow us to condone or even promote what the biblical writers condemned? It seems that this must ultimately be the basis of an attempt to provide scriptural support for homosexual behavior.

B. Romans 1:18-32

Other biblical references to homosexuality are, as we have seen, very meager. But here is a passage which not only offers a more explicit description of homosexual behavior, but also sets it deliberately in a theological context. This, therefore, has rightly become the central passage in any discussion of biblical teaching on homosexuality.

The passage as a whole is a denunciation of human "ungodliness and unrighteousness." It forms the first element in Paul's cumulative argument that "the whole world is held accountable to God" (3:19), since "both Jews and Greeks are under the power of sin" (3:9). In 1:18-32 the focus is on Gentile sinfulness, before turning to the Jews especially in chapters 2 and 3.

The essence of Gentile sin is their refusal of the evidence of creation and their consequent idolatry, worshiping the creature rather than the Creator (vv. 18-23). Homosexuality is brought into the argument to show the result of the essentially perverted orientation expressed in idolatry. It is one of the vices to which in consequence "God gave them up." Many other aspects of sinful behavior are listed in vv. 29-31, but it is their sexual activity which is picked out for special condemnation.

In verse 24 there is a broad statement about their "uncleanness and dishonoring their bodies among themselves," which is not expressed in specifically homosexual terms. But in verses 26-27 Paul is quite explicit. The terms he uses are heavily loaded ("natural"/"unnatural"; "burning with desire for each other"; "committing shameless acts"; "due penalty for their error"), but his target cannot be mistaken. He is describing same-sex sexual activity, and uniquely in the Bible he specifies female as well as male homoerotic behavior. There is no qualification in terms of whether the relationship is one of love and consent or of exploitation and violence. It is the "unnatural" sexual activity which is itself the evidence of the "God-forsaken" state of such people, and of their liability to God's wrath. They know that such behavior deserves death, yet they not only practice it but even applaud it (v. 32).

The total condemnation of homosexual behavior seems inescapable. And Paul has stated his argument with clarity and force. How then can those who wish to claim that homosexual activity is compatible with biblical values evade the force of this passage? One strategy is to regard the passage as no longer ethically relevant: it is simply an expression of the limited outlook of Jews and Christians in biblical times which must now be set aside in favor of a proper expression of Christian love and tolerance in a culturally altered world. We shall return to this argument shortly. But is there anything in the passage itself which may give us pause? Two aspects of the passage have been appealed to.

One is the observation that this is a Jew writing about Graeco-Roman culture. The language of these verses reflects a conventional Jewish critique of pagan idolatry and ethics.[17] But what was abhorrent to Jewish thought (as the few Old Testament references noted above indicate) was widely accepted and prized in the Graeco-Roman world. Homosexual partnerships, whether pederastic or between adults, are accepted without comment, and described with appreciation, across a wide range of Greek literature. What to the Jew was "unnatural" and repulsive was to the Greek noble and praiseworthy. Paul, as a Jew, simply did not understand, and what we find in Romans 1:26-27 is merely Jewish cultural prejudice.

Such argument raises in acute form the issue of biblical authority. The Bible message is encapsulated in a specific culture, and the attempt to extricate it is hazardous, especially when, as is this case, a substantive Bible passage is not merely sidelined but declared to be quite wrong. If we were dealing with a passing illustration, this might seem less drastic (though it would still raise important questions about where the authority is located); but this is an essential plank in Paul's central theological argument, presented in detail and with passion. Jew or not, he writes as God's apostle and with deliberate emphasis. If *this* passage can be set aside on the grounds that its author was Jewish, what other part of the Bible is safe?

The second argument against accepting this passage as a total ban on homosexual activity for Christians focuses on Paul's terms "natural" and "unnatural." On this view "unnatural" sexual acts are indeed to be condemned, but for the true homosexual, homoerotic behavior is entirely natural. Indeed, for someone of such orientation, attempting heterosexual intercourse would be

17. Cf. Wisdom 14:12-31, which includes in v. 26, among many other evil results of idolatry, γενέσεως ἐναλλαγή, usually translated "sexual perversion" (cf. Paul's use of μεταλλάσσω in Rom 1:26).

"unnatural," and it would be this rather than their homosexual behavior which would properly incur the condemnation of this passage.

Paul is not speaking, however, about the "nature" of an individual, which may differ from that of another.[18] Rather φύσις refers to "nature" in general, the established order of God's creation. Paul uses the same term of the laws of horticulture in Romans 11:24 and of the difference between the sexes in 1 Corinthians 11:14. φύσις in these passages seems to mean something like "the pattern of God's created world," "the way things ought to be." Homosexuality, on this understanding, runs counter to the way God has designed human sexuality. It is thus in essence a misuse of God's creation, whatever the personal inclinations of an individual.[19]

C. Toward a Biblical Understanding of Homosexuality

On the issue of the ministry of women we came to the conclusion that each side of the current debate could find relevant scriptural support, and that in the end it comes to a decision as to which strand of biblical evidence should take priority. In such a situation those who claim to be subject to the authority of Scripture may justly conclude that the "innovation" of ordaining women is a proper outworking of biblical principles, even though they would be unwise to claim that their position is the only one open to an honest evangelical. The question which now confronts us is whether there is a comparable choice to be made with regard to the acceptance of homosexual practice. Does the Bible here also leave us with a dilemma?

Wolfhart Pannenberg answers that question decisively: "The Bible's assessments of homosexual practice are unambiguous in their pointed rejection, and all its statements on this subject agree without exception."[20] Our survey of the biblical material above supports his conclusion, which has also been the overwhelming consensus of Christian tradition through the ages. The situation is thus decisively different from that with regard to the ministry of women. On homosexual practice the Bible speaks with a consistent voice.

18. Cf. M. Vasey, *Strangers and Friends* (London: Hodder & Stoughton, 1955), p. 131.

19. The overall tenor of the passage in relation to homosexual practice is well summarized by J. D. G. Dunn, *Romans 1–8* (Word Biblical Commentary; Dallas: Word, 1988), pp. 73-74.

20. Taken from a brief summary article published in the *Church Times* of June 21, 1996, under the title "*Amor vincit omnia* — or does it?" Pannenberg concludes that a church which "ceased to treat homosexual activity as a departure from the biblical norm . . . would stand no longer on biblical ground but against the unequivocal witness of scripture" and "would thereby have ceased to be one, holy, catholic and apostolic"!

Christian arguments in favor of homosexual practice have therefore (not surprisingly) tended not to focus much on Scripture. There have been attempts, as we have noted above, to suggest that one or another biblical passage does not mean what it has generally been understood to mean. But more often the argument has been that the biblical condemnation of homosexual practice, clear as it is for its own day, does not apply to ours. For some this view may take the form of a simple rejection of any authority for the Bible in deciding on contemporary issues: to appeal to the Bible at all is an anachronism.

But evangelical Christians do not have the luxury of such a simple cutting of the hermeneutical knot. For them there are two main lines of defense against this apparently total biblical condemnation, which reinforce one another. One is to argue that the cultural change has been so great that the sort of homosexual practice promoted today is quite different from that which the Bible writers attacked. The other is to apply to this issue more general biblical principles of love and tolerance which, while admittedly not applied to this issue within the Bible, may nonetheless be felt to be relevant to it.

The former view, that loving homosexual relationships as we know them today are in principle quite different from what the Bible writers condemned, suggests that modern studies of homosexuality have invalidated the ancient understanding of it. They have certainly introduced new terminology, and have put the whole issue on a more sophisticated basis of experimental evidence and of psychological explanation (though their conclusions in these areas are far from unanimous). But it is not true that the ancient world knew nothing of loving homosexual relationships, even if it may have lacked the scientific expertise to interpret them as we would. The approval of homosexual feelings and behavior in the Graeco-Roman world was based on the view that, where not abused, they are good and loving. They were not regarded as in themselves "perverted." And Paul, as a well-educated Hellenistic Jew from Asia Minor, could not have been unaware of this evaluation among his Greek fellow citizens, which is well known to any classical scholar. If Paul then chose to bracket all homosexual acts together as "against nature," it was not because he was unaware of a less negative view, but because he deliberately chose to oppose it. He is not an innocent abroad, but a clear-sighted and radical critic of an aspect of local culture that he knew well, but believed to be incompatible with the purpose of God for his creation.

The appeal to the primacy of love in this connection may seem to take us straight back to the ethical debates of the sixties, and in particular to the contention of "Situation Ethics" that the principle of love overrides moral rules, that whatever in a given situation is perceived to be the most loving course is right, even if it may run counter to sexual or other rules (such as prohibition of adultery) which have traditionally been derived from the Bible. We need not return to that debate; suffice it to say that the main stream of Christian ethical thinking has not been convinced that moral rules are so easily discarded.

This is not to devalue the primacy of love, but to argue that its primacy does not leave it as the *only* relevant ethical principle. The real world is not so simple, and moral choices are regularly made in situations where biblical principles are found to be in tension with one another and to point to differing directions. In such cases "love" may often be the arbiter, though to determine what is the most loving course can be an extremely subjective decision. But the biblical material relating to homosexuality does not seem to admit such arbitration. When all the specific material relevant to the issue in Scripture seems to point in the same direction, have we the right to define "love" in such a way as to overturn that consistent witness?

It is important to recognize that the biblical witness to which I refer is not only the handful of "negative" texts we have looked at above, but also (a) the absence of any "positive" texts on the subject, and, more importantly, (b) the general tenor of biblical teaching and example which indicates that God has designed human nature for heterosexual love and intercourse. It is against this consistent background that the negative references to homosexual behavior find their proper place.

Ultimately, then, we must decide what are the acceptable limits of the argument from cultural change. Social conventions are different in our day from biblical times, and homosexual behavior has achieved greater social acceptance in modern Western society than it has ever known before within the Judaeo-Christian tradition. In such a situation is it appropriate to apply the greater biblical principles of love and tolerance to this particular aspect of human choice even though it would have been unthinkable so to apply it within the cultural context of first-century Christianity? If in this case the principle of love appears to be in tension with the Bible's heterosexual understanding of God's purpose, may the latter be legitimately subordinated to the former?

Or is it after all possible to uphold the biblical sexual ethic without thereby forfeiting the claims of love toward the homosexual? Can love coexist with ethical disapproval? I hope it will be clear from the above that I believe that it can and should, and that a responsible understanding of the authority of the Bible for ethics cannot afford to discard the Bible's consistent witness on this controversial issue.

V. Conclusion

I must conclude, painfully aware how many important issues I have either omitted or oversimplified. My own conclusion is that in attempting to be guided by the Bible we find a significantly different situation with regard to homosexuality from that with regard to the ordination of women. In the former case we find a consistent, if limited, pattern of biblical teaching and example which indicates that homosexual activity, however loving and well motivated, is not in accordance with God's design for human creation. In the latter we are confronted with a tension between two strands of biblical material which appear to lead us in different directions. In such a situation we cannot escape the need to make a decision as to which of these strands should be regarded as expressing the more fundamental principle, and should therefore take priority in formulating a biblical attitude for today. But in the case of homosexual behavior there seems to be no such divergence in the biblical witness, and so no comparable hermeneutical decision to be made.

Why then is it suggested, as we noted at the beginning, that the same hermeneutical principle governs the two issues, and that those who conclude that women should be ordained to positions of leadership in the church are bound also to conclude in favor of homosexual activity? I would judge that the suspicion underlying this assertion is that on both issues a vote for change from what has been the traditional Christian position is simply a capitulation to the "spirit of the age," a weak acquiescence with the strident propaganda of the feminist and homosexual lobbies, and an unwillingness to risk being seen as "negative" and "old-fashioned" by upholding biblical standards.

No hermeneutical activity takes place in a cultural or historical vacuum. The history of biblical interpretation is the story of new insights discovered often under the pressure of changing circumstances and of cultural shift; the eventual abolition of slavery is a celebrated example. The increased recognition of the "positive" strand of biblical thinking about the ministry of women has undoubtedly been triggered by wider debate about the place of women in society, and the recognition that a church which refuses to ordain women was finding itself increasingly out on a limb and subject to misunderstanding and abuse from a more "liberal" culture. But it has been the result not of apologetically discarding the biblical witness, but of reexamining it in light of the changing agenda and of discovering there things we had not previously sufficiently noticed.

But to reexamine our position in the light of the secular agenda is not necessarily to change it. In the case of the role of women it has led many of us to change, because, we believe, a balanced understanding of the Bible itself demands it. But in the case of homosexuality the reexamination of the Bible has not had the same result. Rather, it has led us to reaffirm the traditional Christian view, because we find that this is what the Bible supports, and further study has served only to reinforce that conviction.

* * *

Our study has attempted, as the editors requested, to focus primarily on Romans. On each of the two issues studied, Romans offers a passage which contributes significantly to the debate. But the two passages are very different.

With regard to homosexuality, Romans 1:18-32 includes the most prominent biblical treatment on the subject, not at a narrative level but as a matter of theological reflection. Paul states his position forcefully and unambiguously, and his statement is agreed on all sides to provide a fundamental plank in constructing a biblical approach to the issue, whether the interpreter is sympathetic to Paul's expressive viewpoint or not.

With regard to the ministry of women, however, Paul makes no pronouncement on the subject in this epistle. What we find instead is an intriguing insight, apparently almost accidental, into Pauline church practice in the listing of some of Paul's fellow workers in Romans 16:1-16. It might then be objected that this passage is not suitable for use in trying to resolve a controversial issue in the way that Romans 1:18-32 is. Surely we should base our biblical principles on the overt theological pronouncements of the biblical writers, not on such *obiter dicta.*

But it is the contention of this paper that an evangelical hermeneutic must not confine itself to the overt pronouncements of the apostolic writers, but must be open to biblical evidence as a whole, including its narrative and incidental parts. When this broader approach is undertaken, it may lead us to reexamine the way we have understood some of the more "obvious" texts. If it is the case that Paul approved and valued the ministry of women alongside men in the way that Romans 16:1-16 reveals (and there is plenty of evidence elsewhere in the New Testament to support this conclusion), this poses important questions about our interpretation of the texts which have traditionally been supposed to prohibit any such activity on the part of women. If the Paul who wrote 1 Corinthians 14:34-35 and 1 Timothy 2:11-12 also wrote Romans 16:1-16 (and indeed 1 Cor 11:2-16), it is prima facie unlikely that he really meant that no woman must ever speak or exercise authoritative ministry in the church. Thus alongside the deliberate pronouncements of Romans 1:18-32, the "incidental" evidence of Romans 16:1-16 also has a vital, though different, role in a truly biblical hermeneutic. If this recognition makes the task of deriving guidance for the real world from the biblical text more complex than it might at first have seemed, so be it. Let us hope that by embracing the wider range of biblical evidence we are enabled to be more responsible in offering biblical guidance for the issues of our generation.

A Breaking of Expectations: The Rhetoric of Surprise in Paul's Letter to the Romans

Robert H. Gundry

> Change (τὸ μεταβάλλειν) also is pleasant, since change is in the order of nature; for perpetual sameness creates an excess of the normal condition; whence it was said: "change (μεταβολή) in all things is sweet" [Euripides *Orestes* 234]. . . . The same may be said of sudden changes (αἱ περιπέτειαι) and narrow escapes from danger; for all these things excite wonder.

Though Aristotle wrote the foregoing passage in his *Art of Rhetoric* 1.11.20, 24, he was not describing change and sudden changes as a rhetorical art. I wish to give them just that description, however, and call attention to instances of metabolic and peripetic turns of phrase in Paul's letter to the Romans, i.e., expressions in this letter that evoke surprise because they break the expectations of readers and listeners.[1] This breaking of expectations lends considerable force to the points that Paul makes in the texts concerned — indeed, those points often consist in such a breaking — and it provides both subject matter and an exemplary style for the enlivening of sermons in our own day.

1. Cf. Quintilian 9.2.22-23. It will be obvious that, as used in the present essay, rhetorical art includes matters of substance, not just of ornamentation.

Others will doubtless discover instances of the rhetoric of surprise that I have omitted or missed. Since the instances that I do discuss fail to fall into any discernible pattern, the discussion will proceed somewhat unpredictably from passage to passage. But this is just as well for an essay honoring a scholar who is markedly "born of the Spirit" and therefore comparable to the "wind/Spirit that blows where it wants to, and you hear its sound but do not know where it comes from or where it is going"![2]

Rom 3:27: "Where then is boasting? Through what kind of law has it been excluded? Of works? No; rather, through the law of faith." Paul has just written disparagingly about the person "who boasts in the law" (2:23; cf. 2:17) and contrasted "faith" with "works of the law" (3:20-22). Therefore it is surprising that Paul now hitches "faith" to "the law." Commentators have noted this peripety, but usually they get bogged down in debating the question whether "the law of faith" means the principle of faith or, as in v. 31c, the OT law as established through faith — not to mention other possibilities — or commentators try to blunt the expression by calling it "a play on words,"[3] or "an oxymoron" so that faith "is in reality no law at all,"[4] or by describing it as only a formal match for "the law of works" so that, in connection with faith, "the law" turns into a meaningless frill.[5] These efforts to tame the expression bear witness to the ferocity of its power. Left untamed, it presages Paul's vehement denial of antinomianism in v. 31a-b, "Do we then nullify the law through faith? Perish the thought!" and further such denials as, for example, in 6:1-3, "Should we remain in sin that grace might increase? Perish the thought! . . . Or are you ignorant . . . ?" and 8:4, where "the righteous demand of the law" is fulfilled "in us who walk not according to the flesh but according to the Spirit."

Rom 4:9: "For we say, 'To Abraham faith was reckoned as righteousness.'" Here Paul is quoting Genesis 15:6, as he has just quoted the same text in v. 3. But there he introduced the quotation with the question, "For what does the scripture say?" (cf. the introduction to a quotation of Ps 32:1-2 in v. 6a, "just as also David says . . ."). So we expect the requotation of Genesis 15:6 in v. 9 to be introduced with the clause, "For the scripture says" or, to give variety, "For Moses says" (as in 10:19, except for "First" instead of "For") or "For Moses writes" (as in 10:5) or "For it is written" (as in 12:19; 14:11; 1 Cor 1:19; 3:19; Gal 3:10; 4:22, 27, plus many passages where only "For" is lacking) — but not "For *we*

2. Jn 3:8. N.B.: the text says that this characteristic of the wind/Spirit applies also to the person born of the Spirit (cf. Rom 12:11: "fervent in spirit").

3. D. J. Moo, *The Epistle to the Romans* (Grand Rapids: Eerdmans, 1996), p. 250.

4. J. A. Fitzmyer, *Romans* (AB; New York: Doubleday, 1993), p. 363.

5. H. Lietzmann and M. Dibelius as cited by C. E. B. Cranfield, *A Critical and Exegetical Commentary on the Epistle to the Romans* (ICC; Edinburgh: T. & T. Clark) 1.219.

say," which Paul never uses elsewhere to introduce OT phraseology. So strongly has faith established the law that the words of the law have become the gospel-words of Paul and the Christian community.[6] No "that" (ὅτι) follows "For we say" to make the quotation indirect (as in 10:5; Gal 3:10; 4:22). The resultant directness of the quotation (as in vv. 3, 6-8 and elsewhere) adds to the startling effect of Paul's quoting Moses as a quotation of himself and his fellow Christians, so startling that A C D[c] F G Ψ 33 and the Majority Text insert ὅτι against א B D* 630 1739 1881 *pc.*

Rom 4:12 (in reference to Abraham): "and the father of circumcision to the ones [who are] not only of circumcision but who are also tracing the steps of the faith of our father Abraham, [which he had] in uncircumcision." What surprises in this convoluted set of phrases is Paul's putting "of the faith" after "the footsteps" — we expect "the footsteps of our father Abraham" — and Paul's making "in uncircumcision" modify "the faith" rather than "our father Abraham." It is as though Abraham's faith has transmuted him into faith itself, so that it, not he, makes the footsteps that others trace. And this transmutation goes so far as to attribute a state of uncircumcision to faith rather than to Abraham (N.B. the attributive position of ἐν ἀκροβυστίᾳ). So highly does Paul value faith!

Rom 4:13: "For the promise to Abraham, or to his seed, that he was to be heir of the world was not through the law, but through the righteousness of faith." At the end of this statement we expect Paul to say "through faith" (instead of "through the righteousness of faith") as an exact contrast to the phrase "through the law" (at the beginning in the Greek text). Our expectation gains strength from the earlier, multiple use of the phrase "through faith" in 1:12; 3:22, 25, 30, 31; and indeed the expectation will quickly find fulfillment in v. 14, and again in v. 16 where the promise is associated with faith as opposed to the law (cf. v. 20; Gal 3:14, 22). Instead, however, Paul carries "the righteousness of faith" over from v. 11 (cf. Phil 3:9) for a contrast with "the law." One could think the carryover to be unreflective on his part. But the association of the promise not just with faith but with the righteousness of faith probably signals that "through" (διά) has to do with attendant circumstance rather than with instrumentality. For Paul can hardly mean that righteousness constitutes the instrument through which the promise is received. Faith is the instrument

6. Of course, "we say" harks back to the question in v. 1, "What then shall we say . . . ?" But for two reasons this question does not evacuate the surprise in v. 9: (1) the conjunction "For" (γάρ) that goes with "we say" makes a reason for the immediately surrounding questions ("Therefore is this blessing on the circumcision or also on the uncircumcision?" [v. 9a] and "Therefore how was it [faith] reckoned [to Abraham], when he was in circumcision or in uncircumcision?" [v. 10a]), not an answer to the question in v. 1; (2) the wording that follows "For we say" does not echo the question in v. 1, which would have produced something like the answer, "We say that Abraham found . . ."; rather, as noted above, it echoes Gen 15:6.

through which righteousness is received, and that righteousness is the circumstance in which the promise is received.

Rom 5:3: "And not only [so], but also we boast in (ἐν) tribulations." Commentators regularly note that "in tribulations" very likely denotes the object of boasting, not the condition in which boasting is done,[7] and just as regularly note the surprise of tribulations as an object of boasting. Not so often mentioned is the heightening of this surprise by the immediately preceding v. 2b, "and we boast on the basis of (ἐπ') the hope of God's glory." Because of ἐπ', the hope of God's glory probably provides the basis for boasting. We therefore expect the object of boasting to be eternal life or the like (cf. 2:7; 5:17, 18; 6:22, 23). All the greater our surprise to read about quite the opposite, viz., present tribulations. On second thought, however, it is precisely the hope of enjoying God's glory in the future that makes possible not only the endurance of those tribulations but also a boasting in them; for, as Paul says (vv. 3b-4), they produce patience, which in turn produces character, which again in turn produces hope. To boast on the basis of hope, then, is to boast in the tribulations out of which that hope ultimately grows.

Rom 5:6: "For when we were still weak, still Christ died for the ungodly." Moo describes "weak" as "somewhat unexpected" and as "roughly synonymous" with "ungodly" and "sinful," and he defines weakness here as a "total incapacity for good."[8] Dunn gives a less vigorous definition: weakness has to do with creaturehood over against the Creator's omnipotence (cf. 1:20; 4:21) and begins a crescendo that builds up from weakness through ungodliness and sinfulness to enmity.[9] In any case, the association of weakness with wickedness, and the putting of weakness ahead of ungodliness and sinfulness, do cause some surprise. Moral weakness here prepares for the larger statement in 8:3: "For as to the incapability of the law, in that it was weak through the flesh, God by sending his own Son in the likeness of sinful flesh and as a sin-offering [or 'for sin'] condemned sin in the flesh." Our weakness, then, pairs up with the weakness of the law in that both weaknesses have to do with "flesh" (in the specially Pauline sense; cf. 6:19: "I speak in human terms because of the weakness of your flesh"). The unexpected use of "weak" in 5:6 telegraphs the later treatment.

Rom 5:15: "But not as the transgression, thus is also the gracious gift (χάρισμα)." "Righteousness" would make a much better antonym for "transgression" than "gracious gift" does. Indeed, Cranfield says that the gracious gift probably refers to righteousness before God.[10] Probably so, but we are still

7. Cf. 2:17, 23; 5:11; 1 Cor 1:31; 3:21; 2 Cor 5:12; 10:15, 16, 17; 11:12; Gal 6:13; Phil 3:3.

8. Moo, *The Epistle to the Romans,* p. 306.

9. J. D. G. Dunn, *Romans 1–8* (WBC 38A; Dallas: Word, 1988), p. 254.

10. Cranfield, *A Commentary,* 1.284.

faced with the question, Why does Paul not say "righteousness," as he will in succeeding verses? His choice of "the gracious gift" highlights and summarizes the theme of "this grace in which we stand" (5:2), the nature of which grace Paul has detailed in vv. 1-11. In view of his discussion of sin and transgression in vv. 12-21, moreover, "the gracious gift" emphasizes that "the gift of righteousness" (v. 17) is not only undeserved. It is ill-deserved. And so the theme of grace flowers throughout this passage (see vv. 15, 16, 17, 20, 21). Though Paul has mentioned grace before (1:5, 7, 11; 3:24; 4:4, 16; 5:2) and will later mention it a number of times (see the concordance s.v. χαρίζομαι, χάρις, and χάρισμα), it is the unexpected putting of "the gracious gift" over against "the transgression" that kicks off this flurry of references to amazing grace.

Romans 5:16 contains another unexpected turn of phrase that ratchets up the gracious gift to its highest possible level: "And the gift [is] not as through one who sinned. For the sentence of judgment had its origin in one [transgression], with the result of a sentence of condemnation; by contrast, the gracious gift had its origin in many transgressions, with the result of a sentence of righteousness."[11] Here "the gracious gift" stands in a more natural contrast with "the sentence of judgment." The surprise lies elsewhere, then. If only one transgression led to a sentence of condemnation, we expect many transgressions to multiply into many sentences of condemnation. But the glorious irony of divine grace shatters this expectation: further transgressions — beyond Adam's original sin and after the law came through Moses — triggered God's grace rather than hardening his condemnation and multiplying his judgments. Cranfield puts it well: "That one single misdeed should be answered by judgment, this is perfectly understandable: that the accumulated sins and guilt of all the ages should be answered by God's free gift, this is the miracle of miracles, utterly beyond human comprehension."[12]

Yet even Cranfield's fine statement may be too weak, for "answered by" seems not quite to satisfy Paul's ἐκ, "from, out of." That preposition indicates origin and shares the meaning of διά plus the genitive, as in 3:30: "if indeed there is one God who will justify the circumcision by (ἐκ) faith and the uncircumcision through (διά) faith." Justification has its instrumental origin in faith. οἱ ἐκ πίστεως (Gal 3:7) are not those who respond to faith; they are those who exercise it.[13] It would go too far to say that the many transgressions exercised grace (or that the one transgression exercised judgment), yet it may not

11. A more literal translation than "had its origin in" would read "is from" (ἐκ with an implied verb of being).

12. Cranfield, *A Commentary*, 1.286.

13. For other such uses of ἐκ in Romans alone, see 1:17; 3:26; 4:14, 16; 5:1; 9:30, 32; 10:6, 17; 14:23.

go too far to say that the gracious gift of God's righteousness came not just in answer to our many transgressions, but — strikingly and mysteriously — through them, by way of them, out of them. It is no mystery that the judgment should originate in a transgression. But that the gracious gift should originate in many transgressions — ah, there is mystery indeed (cf. 11:29-36)!

Rom 5:17: "For if because of the transgression of the one [Adam], death reigned through the one [Adam again], much more will they who receive the abundance of grace and of the gift of righteousness reign in life through the one, Jesus Christ." For perfect parallelism we expect that "life" will reign in contrast with the reign of "death." Why then does Paul speak about the reigning of people *in* life rather than about the reigning *of* life over people? He wants to stress again the grace of God, for these people who will reign are "the ones who receive the abundance of grace and of the gift of righteousness." Once subject to the reign of death, they will no longer be subjects at all; rather, rulers whose very domain will consist of life. Adam was the agent of death's reign ("through the one"), but the recipients of abundant grace and free righteousness will be more than agents of life's rule. They will themselves be rulers, and life the territory of their rule.[14]

Rom 5:18: Reigning in life leads now to another surprising turn of phrase: εἰς δικαίωσιν ζωῆς, "with the result of a justifying of life." The switch from δικαίωμα, "sentence of righteousness" (vv. 16, 18), and especially from δικαιοσύνη, "righteousness" (v. 17), to δικαίωσις, "justifying," does not surprise, for Paul has used δικαίωσις just recently (4:25). And he has also been talking about life. For two reasons, however, the addition of ζωῆς, "of life," does surprise: (1) the preceding εἰς κατάκριμα, "with the result of condemnation,"

14. Cf. Cranfield, *A Commentary,* 1.288. So unexpected is Paul's phraseology that Fitzmyer paraphrases him in terms of the expected rather than according to his actual words: "Whereas in v 14 Paul spoke of the reign of death, now he replaces that with the reign of life [*sic*], . . . (cf. 1 Cor 4:18 [*sic,* 4:8])" (Fitzmyer, *Romans,* p. 420). Moo sees the broken parallelism, but as an avoidance of universal salvation inasmuch as the abundance of grace and of free righteousness has to be received "through choice and personal decision," in contrast with death, which is "not a consciously chosen destiny" (*The Epistle to the Romans,* pp. 339-40). But Paul's other uses of λαμβάνω do not encourage an emphasis on choice and personal decision. In v. 11, for example, it seems unlikely that "we have now received the reconciliation" means we have chosen to be reconciled (see further the concordance, but esp. Rom 13:2 [where the "judgment" to be received is hardly chosen by its recipients]; 2 Cor 11:24 [where Paul hardly chose five times to receive thirty-nine stripes]). Even where λαμβάνω means "take," choice and personal decision seem not to be in view; rather, opportunity, privilege, possibility, qualification, or the like. The use of ἔλαβον in Jn 1:12 for choice and personal decision is Johannine, not Pauline; furthermore, the perfective force of παρ- in the παρέλαβον of v. 11 rubs off on ἔλαβον. To question Moo's use of Rom 5:17 against a Pauline doctrine of universal salvation is not to affirm that Paul taught such a doctrine, however.

parallels εἰς δικαίωσιν but lacks a following genitive; and (2) the recent and only other Pauline (or NT) use of δικαίωσις governs an objective genitive (διὰ τὴν δικαίωσιν ἡμῶν, "on account of [probably in the sense of having an end in view] the justifying of us" — 4:25 again), yet here in 5:18 an objective genitive would make no sense. Life is not justified. The action of justification produces life, as Paul goes on to say in v. 21: "through righteousness with the result of life eternal." So commentators correctly speak about a genitive of result in v. 18, but by treating Paul's turn of phrase as something of a puzzle they miss the rhetorical power of its unexpectedness.

Rom 5:19: "For just as through the disobedience of the one man [Adam] the many were constituted sinners, so also through the obedience of the one [man, Jesus Christ — see vv. 15, 17] the many will be constituted righteous." From v. 12 onward Paul has been using the vocabulary of sin and transgression over against righteousness, but now he introduces the vocabulary of disobedience and obedience. Cranfield comments truly, "The use of παρακοή and ὑπακοή . . . makes explicit the fact that Adam's παράπτωμα and Christ's δικαίωμα are both to be understood in relation to the revealed will of God."[15] But there is more to be said: this new vocabulary prepares for Paul's extensive discussion of obedience in chapter 6 and implicitly presents Christ as the great exemplar of obedience for "as many as have been baptized into him" (6:3).

Rom 5:21: Paul returns to the language of reigning. But whereas he earlier talked about death as reigning (vv. 14, 17), here he talks about the reign of sin: "just as sin reigned in death." Sin, the cause of death (v. 12), replaces death; and just as the recipients of abundant grace and free righteousness will reign "in life," so now sin is said to have reigned "in death" — death as the territory, the domain, of sin's reign of terror. This switch from the reign of death to the reign of sin prepares for a discussion of the reign of sin in one's mortal body (6:12: θνητῷ . . . σώματι, "a body subject to death") and the breaking of that reign "through baptism into [Christ's] death" (6:4 and the whole of ch. 6; N.B. esp. 6:23: "for the wages of sin is death").

Further in 5:21, we expect the mentioned righteousness to reign in opposition to the reign of sin (cf. 6:12-14). Instead, it is "grace" that "reigns through righteousness with the result of life eternal through Jesus Christ our Lord." And whereas in v. 17 it was "the ones who receive the abundance of grace and of the gift of righteousness who will reign in life through the one, Jesus Christ," here in v. 21 it is grace itself that reigns, righteousness becoming the instrument or, more probably, the surrounding condition of its reign, life eternal the result, and Jesus Christ remaining the personal agent. Thus Paul exalts grace to prepare for the question whether we should sin that grace may abound (6:1).

15. Cranfield, *A Commentary,* 1.291.

"Through righteousness" gives the answer in advance of Paul's "Perish the thought!" (6:2).

Rom 6:4: "Therefore we were buried with him [Christ] through baptism into death that just as Christ was raised from the dead through the glory of the Father, so also we might walk in newness of life." We usually associate the resurrection with God's power. Indeed, Paul wrote in 1 Corinthians 6:14 that "God has both raised the Lord and will raise us through his power (διὰ τῆς δυνάμεως αὐτοῦ)," and in 2 Corinthians 13:4 that Christ "was crucified out of weakness, yet he lives out of God's power (ἐκ δυνάμεως θεοῦ)" (cf. Rom 1:4: "marked out [as] God's Son with power . . . by resurrection from the dead"). But here the resurrection is said to have taken place through the Father's glory (cf. Jn 11:40). To be sure, numerous passages associate God's glory and power with each other (see, e.g., 2 Thess 1:9; Col 1:11),[16] and this association may well have led from "power" to "glory." But why the choice of "glory" *over* "power" here? I suggest that the reason lies, first, in Paul's having contrasted God's glory with the sinfulness of human beings — most forcefully and explicitly in 3:23: "for all have sinned and lack God's glory" (cf. also 1:23; 3:7) — and, second, in Paul's aiming to use Christ's resurrection as the entree of believers into a life free from sin and therefore full of its opposite, the glory of God.

Rom 6:6: "Knowing this, that our old person (ἄνθρωπος) was crucified with [Christ] in order that the body of sin might be nullified, so that we might no longer be slaves to sin." Why does Paul not say "sin" instead of "the body of sin"? Probably not only to highlight the body as the physical instrument through which sin acts, but also to stress that because of the believer's crucifixion with Christ, the body as dominated by sin is now dead so far as God is concerned (and the believer should adopt the same standpoint); for originally — in Homer, particularly — the word for body, σῶμα, stood for a dead body, a corpse.[17] Though σῶμα early came to be used also for a living body, the connotation of a corpse often lingered, as for example in Romans 7:4, ". . . you also have been put to death through the body [= corpse] of the Christ," and 8:10, "the body is dead because of sin."[18] Crucifixion with Christ has made a corpse,

16. See further J. A. Fitzmyer, *To Advance the Gospel* (New York: Crossroad, 1981), pp. 209-13. Paul also cites the Holy Spirit as the agent of resurrection in Rom 1:4; 8:11. In view of these passages, it is mystifying why Dunn (*Romans 1–8,* 315) thinks Paul avoids mentioning the Spirit in Rom 6:4 "probably deliberately, to avoid attributing Christ's resurrection to the Spirit . . . , thus indicating already an awareness that the relation of exalted Christ to Spirit of God was an issue of some theological sensitivity."

17. See LSJ s.v. σῶμα 1 with references; E. Schweizer, σῶμα κτλ., *TDNT* 8.1025-28.

18. Cf. R. H. Gundry, *Soma in Biblical Theology with Emphasis on Pauline Anthropology* (SNTSMS 29; Cambridge: Cambridge University Press, 1976; repr. Grand Rapids: Zondervan, 1987), pp. 9-15, 38-39, 56-58, 240.

inactive as all corpses are, out of the body of sin, "for the one who has died is released (δεδικαίωται) from sin" (Rom 6:7).

Rom 6:12-23: This paragraph abounds with unexpected twists and turns. As a contrast to presenting "your members as weapons of unrighteousness to sin" in v. 13, we expect a presentation to righteousness. Instead, we read of a presentation "to God" *(bis)*. Apparently Paul wants to emphasize that the one true God is our only legitimate slavemaster. Because "death" is the subject of "lording" (κυριεύει) in v. 9, we expect v. 14a to say that "death will not lord it over you." Instead it says, "For sin shall not lord it over you." This shift is due to the intervening exhortations not to let sin reign over your mortal body and not to present your members as weapons of unrighteousness to sin (vv. 12-13). As Paul himself immediately recognizes in v. 15 ("What then? Should we sin because we are not under law but under grace?"), his statement in v. 14b, "For you are not under law, but under grace," seems to violate the surrounding exhortations to sinless, righteous living. That is to say, being under the law would seem to equate with sinless, righteous living; for the law prohibits sin and commands righteousness. And being under grace would seem to equate with sinful, unrighteous living; for grace passes over sin. But Paul's emphasis on grace is so powerful that he reverses the expected associations almost brazenly, and waits till chapter 8 to introduce the Holy Spirit as the element that makes possible this reversal.

In view of presenting yourselves to God in v. 13, Paul might have repeated that phraseology in v. 16. Instead he speaks of presenting yourselves as "slaves . . . of obedience with the result of righteousness."[19] Commentators regularly note their surprise at "obedience," but just as regularly fail to note that "obedience" is doubly surprising in that not only does the preceding context lead us to expect "God," but also earlier in v. 16 obedience has both nominally and verbally appeared as equally associated with sin: "You know, do you not, that the one to whom you present yourselves as slaves with the result of obedience — you are slaves to the one whom you obey, whether [slaves] of sin with the result of death . . . ?" But now in the final phrases obedience stands unqualified as the alternative to sin: "or [slaves] of obedience with the result of righteousness." Subconsciously in Paul's mind, I suspect, obedience to sin is quickly overpowered by sin as disobedience to God and God's law, so that obedience no longer wears two hats, but only a white one.

Still in v. 16, Paul's concern with sanctification leads him to write "with the result of righteousness," whereas we expect "with the result of life" over against the earlier phrase, "with the result of death." Cranfield takes the antony-

19. A genitive of description, yielding the sense "obedient slaves," would leave unmentioned the slavemaster to be contrasted with "sin."

mous relationship with "death" as an indication "that δικαιοσύνη has here its forensic, rather than its moral, sense."[20] But then forensic righteousness would derive from the believer's "obedience" to God and God's law — hardly Paul's doctrine of justification! So Moo is correct to settle on the sense of moral righteousness, i.e., "conduct pleasing to God" (cf. Rom 8:4).[21] He goes on to write, "The objection that this does not make a natural contrast with 'death' is not a telling one, since the contrast 'sin' and 'obedience' has already disrupted a precise antithesis."[22] But the compound phrases follow one right after the other and in exact parallelism ("whether of sin with the result of death, or of obedience with the result of righteousness"); so I do not understand this defense. In any case it is unnecessary or, rather, both the objection and the defense miss the point that just as Paul's concern with sanctification leads him to use the formerly ambivalent "obedience" for a contrast with "sin," so that same concern leads him to use "righteousness," which in its moral sense he might have used for a contrast with "sin" (and will use thus in v. 18), for a somewhat ill-fitting contrast with "death." But though the somewhat ill fit highlights Paul's concern with sanctification, it also rests on a certain rationale. For if righteousness is the result of obedience, then unlike the obedience with which v. 16 begins, the obedience with which v. 16 ends cannot be ambivalent.

Commentators have done a good enough job of underlining the way in which Paul's stress on obedience leads him to speak in v. 17 of believers' being given over to the pattern of Christian teaching, as a slave is transferred from one master to another, rather than of that pattern's being given over to them, as a tradition is handed on.[23] We skip therefore to v. 18, where Paul speaks of "having been liberated (ἐλευθερωθέντες) from sin." This phraseology makes a good contrast with the following statement, "you have been enslaved to righteousness," but it marks a shift from his earlier phraseology, "released (δεδικαίωται) from sin" (v. 7). In particular, the shift in verbs represents a theological shift from status to behavior; and it may be that we are to detect some word play in the cognateness of the "righteousness" (δικαιοσύνῃ) to which believers have been enslaved and their having been "released" (δεδικαίωται) from sin. Likewise, enslavement "to righteousness" makes a good complement to liberation "from sin," but it marks a shift from presenting your members and yourselves "to God" (v. 13) and to presenting yourselves "as slaves to [and 'of'] obedience" (v. 16). As here in v. 18, the earlier contrasts were with "sin." So for a

20. Cranfield, *A Commentary,* 1.322n.4.

21. Moo, *The Epistle to the Romans,* pp. 399-400.

22. Moo, *The Epistle to the Romans,* p. 400.

23. See also F. W. Beare, "On the Interpretation of Romans vi. 17," *NTS* 5 (1958-59): 206-10.

contrast with enslavement to sin Paul has progressed from enslavement to God, through enslavement to obedience, and now to enslavement to righteousness. This progression is both materially and rhetorically understandable: materially in that enslavement to God requires obedience to the righteous demand of God's law (cf. 8:4 again), rhetorically in that being a slave of obedience has been said to result in righteousness (v. 16), so that righteousness itself becomes a slavemaster alongside, or synonymously with, God and obedience.

In v. 19 we see a progression on the opposite side, from enslavement to sin in earlier verses to enslavement "to uncleanness and lawlessness with the result of lawlessness." "Uncleanness" is used "particularly of sexual immorality."[24] But why bring in that particularity here? Well, Paul used the term "your members" twice in v. 13, and uses it again twice in v. 19. By referring to physical parts of the body, this term naturally calls to mind sexual behavior, as for example in 1 Corinthians 6:15, "Taking therefore the members of Christ, should I make [them] members of a prostitute?" and Colossians 3:5, "Therefore put to death the members on the earth, [viz.,] fornication, uncleanness, passion, evil lust. . . ." So apparently "your members" leads Paul to the particularity of sexual sin, indicated by uncleanness, already detailed in terms of sexual misbehavior (1:24 *et seqq.*), and about to be described as conduct of which believers "are now ashamed" (6:21; cf. also 7:5 and the possibility that Paul's exemplary problem in 7:7-25 had to do with sexual lust[25]).

Since it is precisely the law through which the passions of sin come about, it is striking that Paul pairs "lawlessness" with "uncleanness" (still in 6:19). But he is leading up to the argument of chapter 7 that apart from the Spirit the law as used by sin incites people to sin rather than deterring them from sinning. More striking is the addition of the phrase "with the result of lawlessness" (εἰς τὴν ἀνομίαν) right after "to lawlessness" (τῇ ἀνομίᾳ). Here, of course, Paul is leading up to the contrastive phrases, "to righteousness with the result of sanctification"; but there and in v. 16 the result is expressed with a noun different from the preceding one. Why the repetition here? Why did Paul not reserve "lawlessness" for the ecbatic phrase alone so as to avoid a compound object for εἰς and make a structurally closer parallelism with the following ("as slaves to uncleanness with the result of lawlessness . . . as slaves to righteousness with the

24. Cranfield, *A Commentary,* 1.122, citing 2 Cor 12:21; Gal 5:19; Eph 5:3; Col 3:5.

25. R. H. Gundry, "The Moral Frustration of Paul before His Conversion: Sexual Lust in Romans 7:7-25," *Pauline Studies: Essays Presented to Professor F. F. Bruce on His 70th Birthday,* ed. D. A. Hagner and M. J. Harris (Exeter, U.K.: Paternoster/Grand Rapids: Eerdmans, 1980), pp. 228-45. It is not to be denied that sin, using the commandment not to lust, aroused "every [kind of] lust" (πᾶσαν ἐπιθυμίαν). But that phrase may refer to every kind of sexual lust. Even if it has a broader reference yet, sexual lust might have been the first in Paul's experience of sin's coming to life.

result of sanctification")? Perhaps an answer lies in the counterintuitive indication that lawlessness, too, is a slavemaster. It is easy to understand uncleanness, especially in its sense of sexual lust, as enslaving. But lawlessness? It is more natural to think of that in terms of liberty and license. Not so, says Paul. Lawlessness, too, is enslaving, and as such is cause as well as effect. On the other side, it is easy to understand sanctification, i.e., holiness, as enslaving, so that Paul does not need to pair it with righteousness as a slavemaster and then repeat it in the ecbatic phrase ("as slaves to righteousness and sanctification with the result of sanctification"). Righteousness stands alone as the slavemaster, and in this respect echoes v. 18, where after appearing as the result of enslavement to obedience in v. 16 righteousness first took over the role of slavemaster. As compared with v. 16, sanctification in v. 19 replaces righteousness as an effect contrary to the uncleanness associated with lawlessness (cf. 1 Cor 6:9-11 for an association of sanctification with the washing away of sins, prominent among which are sexual ones such as uncleanness alludes to).

In v. 22, "having been liberated from sin" echoes v. 18 exactly, but "having been enslaved to God" differs from v. 18: "you have been enslaved to righteousness." This difference is not entirely surprising, because Paul has earlier told his audience to present themselves and their members "to God" (v. 13 *bis*) and because such a presentation has been equated with enslavement (vv. 16, 19). On the other hand, righteousness would have made a more exact contrast with sin, as in vv. 16, 18, 20. But self-presentation to God has connected with "coming to life from the dead" (v. 13), and Paul is about to describe "eternal life" as "the end" of having been enslaved to God (v. 22), and as the "free gift (χάρισμα) of God" (v. 23). So Paul turns God into a slavemaster to highlight God's grace as seen in the gift of eternal life, over against the miserliness of that other slavemaster, sin, who gives no gifts, only wages — and wages worse than nothing, viz., death (cf. 7:25 for another contrast between sin and God).

In 7:1-4 Paul speaks of dying (ἀποθάνῃ *bis*) as breaking the legal bond of marriage, but then switches to being put to death (ἐθανατώθητε) as the means by which believers are released from the law. Commentators often note this switch and usually explain it in terms of a Pauline stress on divine initiative. Well and good so far as that explanation goes. But it should be added that the echo of θάνατος in 6:1-5 *(tris)*, which deals with having been put to death with Christ, provides a further explanation for the switch in 7:1-4: Paul wishes to recall the believer's death not as a natural death but as a being put to death — i.e., executed, crucified — with Christ or, as he immediately goes on to say, "through the corpse (σώματος) of the Christ."

It is also surprising that in 7:4 believers correspond to both the husband who dies and the wife who lives to marry another man in vv. 1-3. Nowadays commentators try to skirt this oddity by denying allegory and affirming that

Paul makes only one point, i.e., that obligation to the law "ceases when death occurs."[26] In support of this denial-cum-affirmation, Cranfield notes that v. 4 starts with ὥστε, which introduces a conclusion ("So then"), not with οὕτως ("Thus"), which would have introduced a comparison.[27] But allegory will not go away so easily. ὥστε may introduce a conclusion, but the "also" (καί) before "you" (ὑμεῖς) draws a comparison; and the two-prongedness of this comparison — "you have been put to death [as the first husband died] . . . in order that you might become another's [as the widowed wife remarried]" — makes it allegorical and, contrary to expectations, makes believers like the widowed wife, who did *not* die though in fact believers *were* put to death. That Paul's allegory tolerates such astonishingly flagrant inconcinnities testifies to the overpowering strength of his teaching that believers were united with Christ in both his death and his resurrection.

To be mentioned only in passing are (1) "the law of the Spirit of life in Christ Jesus" (8:2), which Fitzmyer calls an "oxymoron" because "the Spirit . . . in his [Paul's] understanding is anything but 'law'" (though we should add that "the law is Spiritual" according to 7:14);[28] (2) "liberated you from the law of sin and of death" (8:2), which elaborates liberation simply from sin (6:18, 22) so as to incorporate the intervening discussion of the death-dealing effect of the law as used by sin; (3) the addition "and peace" where we expect only "life" as a contrast with "death" (8:6), the purpose of the addition being to set up a contrast with "hatred toward God" (8:7); (4) the switch to believers' being "in the Spirit" (8:9) from their being "in Christ Jesus" (8:1) for a contrast with being "in the flesh" (8:9); (5) the switch from your being "in the Spirit" to the dwelling of God's Spirit "in you" (8:9, 11 *bis*) to set up for Christ's dwelling "in you" (8:10); (6) the switch from "the Spirit of God" to "the Spirit of Christ" (8:9) to set up for the dwelling of "Christ" in you (8:10); (7) the switch to Christ's dwelling in believers (8:10) from their being "in Christ" (8:1) to match the indwelling of God's Spirit, who equates with Christ's Spirit; (8) the use of "life," a noun, in the statement, "the Spirit is life because of righteousness," instead of "alive," an adjective (in Greek a participle, i.e., a verbal adjective, of ζάω) that would match more closely the adjective "dead" in the contrastive statement, "the body is dead because of sin" (8:10), for Paul's point is not that the Spirit (alternatively, the human spirit) is alive, but that the Spirit has life to give believers because of the righteousness that is both a gift (justification) and an

26. Fitzmyer, *Romans*, p. 455; see also Dunn, *Romans 1–8*, pp. 368-70; Cranfield, *A Commentary*, 1.334-35 *et al.*

27. Cranfield, *A Commentary*, 1.334-35.

28. Fitzmyer, *Romans*, p. 482.

effect (sanctification); and (9) the switch from "the Spirit of God" and "the Spirit of Christ" (8:9) to "the Spirit of the one who raised Jesus from the dead . . . , the one who raised Christ from the dead" (8:11) to reflect the statement that "the Spirit is life because of righteousness" (8:10).

Rom 8:19: "For the eager expectation of the creation is awaiting the revelation of the sons of God." Since we are glorified only "with Christ" (8:17) and since the glory is going to be revealed "to us" (εἰς ἡμᾶς — 8:18), we might have expected to read in v. 19 about the revelation "of Jesus Christ" rather than "of the sons of God" (cf. 1 Cor 1:7; Gal 1:12; 2 Thess 1:7). But because God's sons belong to the created order, their revelation provides hope for the rest of creation, too.[29]

Paul has described human beings as "slaves of sin" (6:16, 17, 20); so now that he is describing the fallen state of creation he transmutes "slaves" into "slavery," and "of sin," which cannot apply to the world outside human beings, into "of decay" (8:21). And just as believers have been liberated from sin (6:18, 22) and from the law of sin and of death (8:2), so the creation will be liberated from the slavery of decay. The addition "of death" earlier in the chapter provides a middle term that oils the transition from "sin" to "decay" (cf. 1 Cor 15:42, 50). The liberty of God's children "into" (εἰς) which the creation will be liberated is no longer a merely negative liberty from sin and from the law of sin and death. It is a positive liberty, one "of glory" (cf. vv. 17-18, 30), the opposite of sin (see 3:23 again, and cf. Paul's associating glory with *in*corruption in Rom 1:23; 2:7; 1 Cor 15:42-43). All this talk of slavery and liberation then leads Paul to speak about "the redemption of our body" (8:23) rather than, as expected, about its "resurrection," for redemption means the manumission of a slave.

Finally in this connection, we may consider 8:24: "for we have been saved τῇ . . . ἐλπίδι." Favored nowadays is the modal dative, "in hope" (by way of manner), or the sociative dative, "with hope" (by way of accompaniment). Against the old instrumental interpretation, "by hope" (as a matter of means), it is argued that "Paul nowhere suggests that hope is a means of salvation."[30] But surely this is not a knockdown argument, for Paul talks about the ways and means of salvation with remarkable variety: We are saved by believing (Rom 1:16; 13:11; 1 Cor 1:21; 2 Thess 2:13; 1 Tim 4:10), by (ἐν) Christ's life (Rom 5:10), by confession with the mouth (Rom 10:10), and, in the case of Gentiles, by Israel's transgression (Rom 11:11). The Christian wife may save her husband, and the Christian husband his wife (1 Cor 7:16). Paul himself saves some

29. See Moo, *The Epistle to the Romans*, p. 513, for a good comment on Paul's writing that "the eager expectation of the creation," rather than the creation itself, is awaiting.

30. Moo, *The Epistle to the Romans*, pp. 521-22n.72.

(1 Cor 9:22). People are saved through (διά) the gospel (1 Cor 15:1-2), by apostolic endurance of afflictions (2 Cor 1:6; 2 Tim 2:10), by repentance (2 Cor 7:10), and by grace (simple dative) through (διά) faith, not of (ἐκ) works (Eph 2:5, 8); yet people work out their own salvation with fear and trembling by virtue of God's working in them (Phil 2:12-13). Salvation comes through the Lord Jesus Christ (1 Thess 5:9) and by the Spirit's sanctification (2 Thess 2:13). Christian women are saved through childbearing (1 Tim 2:15). You save yourself (1 Tim 4:16), and you are saved through scriptural instruction (2 Tim 3:15) and according to (κατά) God's mercy (Titus 3:5). Nearly all these ways and means of salvation have no support in Pauline literature outside the particular passages in which they occur. So why cannot salvation by hope be a variation among many others? Favoring this possibility are the close associations, almost equations, that Paul makes between hope and faith: "May the God of hope fill you with all joy and peace in believing, so that you may abound in hope by the power of the Holy Spirit" (Rom 15:13); "For by the Spirit we eagerly await through faith the hope of righteousness" (Gal 5:5; cf. 1 Cor 13:13; 1 Thess 1:3; also being justified πίστει [simple dative, "by faith"] in Rom 3:8 and being saved τῇ . . . πίστει [simple dative] in Rom 8:24). Salvation by hope replaces justification by faith, then, because the problem under discussion has shifted from guilt to the suffering of decay and death. The eschatological term "hope" has become appropriate.

Commentators often note that the Gentiles' not pursuing "righteousness" in Romans 9:30 leads us to expect a contrast in Romans 9:31 with Israel's pursuing "righteousness," but that Paul surprises with Israel's pursuing "a *law* of righteousness." But there is a further, double surprise: (1) the demotion of "righteousness" in v. 31 to become a genitive modifier of the direct object "law," whereas Paul might simply have omitted "righteousness" and left "law" to stand alone in contrast to "righteousness" in v. 30; and (2) the switch from κατέλαβεν, "laid hold of" (v. 30), to ἔφθασεν, "did [not] arrive at" (v. 31). But "righteousness" does not stand alone in v. 30. Paul repeats the word and adds the qualifier, "that [comes] from faith" (τὴν ἐκ πίστεως). The δέ which introduces the appositive phrase carries something of an adversative sense; i.e., it distinguishes this kind of righteousness from every other kind. All the more, then, why does Paul not speak of a contrastive righteousness deriving from the law? Why does he reverse righteousness and law in v. 31? Precisely because it is not Israel's pursuing righteousness in the law that he faults, for in the law they would have found testimony to the righteousness of God that comes from faith (1:17; 3:21; 4:3, 6-8). Rather, Paul faults Israel's pursuit of the law as such, for pursuing the law as such meant dependence on works for righteousness (v. 32) — hence, "a law of righteousness." And he says that Israel "did not *arrive* at" the law rather than that they "did not *lay hold* of" it, because ἔφθασεν connotes arrival before others.[31] Israel had an early start (3:1-2; cf. 1:16; 9:4-5; Acts 13:46), but sadly have not arrived at all, much less early. The late-starting Gentiles have preceded them (see esp. 11:25-27).[32]

After writing, "Thus we the many are one body in Christ" (Rom 12:5a), Paul writes, "but [we are] members one by one of each other" (Rom 12:5b). An adversative δέ, "but," draws contrasts between "many . . . one body" and "members one by one," and between "in Christ" and "of each other." What we expect after "one body in Christ," however, is "members of the body," or perhaps "members of Christ" as in 1 Corinthians 6:15. The phraseology that Paul does use stresses that the body is not a separate entity that we belong to. Rather, we *are* the body to the extent that, or in that, we belong to each other in Christ (cf. 1 Cor 12:27).

Rom 13:12c-d: "Therefore let us lay aside the works of darkness, but let us put on the weapons of light." The change from "works" to "weapons" is often noted, and explained as an echo of Paul's military imagery in 6:13 (cf. Eph 6:10-17). But there the weapons consisted of our body parts (μέλη); here — if we can judge from the antithetic parallel with "the works of darkness" (cf. v. 14b) — they consist of moral virtues (cf. Eph 4:24; 6:14; Col 3:5-14). And 6:13 talked about "weapons of unrighteousness" as well as "weapons of righteousness." For a better contrast with "the weapons of light," then, we might have expected Paul to speak here about "the weapons of darkness," not about "the works of darkness." But though "the night is far gone and the day has come near" (13:12a-b), it is still nighttime; and you wear armor in daytime, whereas nighttime is more suitable for practicing evil (1 Thess 5:7-8; cf. Jn 3:20 and, for another Pauline shift from evil "works" to a different figure of speech for virtues, viz., "fruit," Gal 5:19-23). The shift from weapons as body parts to weapons as virtues is then determined by the imagery of dressing and undressing. You do not put on a body part.

Neither do you put on another person. Yet surprisingly, Paul goes on to write, "But put on the Lord Jesus Christ, and do not make provision for the flesh to gratify its lusts" (13:14). The parallel with putting on the weapons of light as opposed to the works of darkness and the contrast with the flesh and its lusts strikingly gather up virtues into the very person of Christ. Just as justification is portrayed as a putting on of his person in baptism (Gal 3:27), so also is sanctification. In himself he outfits the whole of Christian experience.

Finally, in Romans 15:30 Paul beseeches his audience, as he says, "through

31. In 2 Cor 10:14 φθάνω connotes arrival before false apostles; in Phil 3:16 arrival at a point preliminary to the final goal; in 1 Thess 2:16 arrival of God's wrath prior to the last day; in 1 Thess 4:15 arrival of some prior to that of others (though such arrival is denied).

32. See R. H. Gundry, "Grace, Works, and Staying Saved in Paul," *Bib* 66 (1985): 16-18.

our Lord Jesus Christ and through the love of the Spirit to strive together with me in prayers to God for me." The phrase "the love of" damages the parallelism and makes commentators address the question, Is the Spirit the subject, the object, or the source of the mentioned love? Almost certainly the source, for 5:5 said, "God's love has been poured out in our hearts through the Holy Spirit that has been given us." To have mentioned "the love of Christ" in 15:30 as an echo of 8:35 would have connoted Christ's love for us, a thought unsuited to Paul's point here. What is that point, then, and why the mention of love at all? The point is that earnest prayer for another's Christian ministry must grow out of a Spirit-inspired love for that person. So as the Spirit has inspired Gordon Fee to minister to us, may that same Spirit inspire us to strive lovingly in prayer together with him.

Trustworthy Preaching: Reflections on John Chrysostom's Interpretation of Romans 8

Barbara Aland

It is not without reason that John Chrysostom is the most widely known preacher of the Church's early history. At the same time, the literature on Chrysostom frequently observes that his sermons contain very little systematic theological reflection. It seems impossible that preaching can have that sort of credibility unless it is rooted in solid theological thought. By examining a single section of one of his homilies, this study will focus on an important aspect of Chrysostom's work in order to illustrate how he managed to create credible, faith-provoking preaching.[1]

1. My discussion draws on the following works: R. Brändle, *Matth. 25,31-46 im Werk des Johannes Chrysostomos. Ein Beitrag zur Auslegungsgeschichte und zur Erforschung der Ethik der griechischen Kirche um die Wende vom 4. und 5. Jahrhundert* (Tübingen, 1979). R. Brändle: *Synergismus als Phänomen der Frömmigkeitsgeschichte, dargestellt an den Predigten des Johannes Chrysostomos,* in "Gnadenwahl und Entscheidungsfreiheit in der Theologie der Alten Kirche," Oikonomia v. 9, hrsg. von F. von Lilienfeld und E. Mühlenberg (Erlangen, 1980), pp. 69-89. R. Brändle, *Johannes Chrysostomos I,* RAC, Lfrg. 139/140 (1997), Sp. 426-503. I gladly admit that this study is inspired by Brändle's work, and I only hope to deepen our understanding of

Various people have helped me to translate the German text of my paper, especially Stefan Lukits and Scot Becker, as well as Hella Strothotte. Mary-Lyon Dolezal contributed many helpful suggestions to the final version. I am grateful to all of them for their friendly cooperation.

I. Preliminary Observations

1. Chrysostom uses the contemporary Byzantine form of the Pauline text with a consistency which is hardly seen among writers of his day.[2] When he quotes verses or phrases in the course of his exposition, he cites them accurately — so accurately, in fact, that by and large even these short quotations recall the Lemmata texts at the heading of his expositions. As a consequence, the texts of Lemma and exposition seem intimately related, which is helpful when using the Lemmata in text-critical studies.[3] This is not to deny that Chrysostom sometimes varies the text for the sake of style. In Romans 8:35, for example, he reads at the end of a longer passage οὐδὲν ἔστιν ὃ διαστῆσαι δυνήσεται instead of τίς ἡμᾶς χωρίζει.[4] The change is clearly stylistic and does not constitute a textual variant.[5] More-

Chrysostom on the basis of Brändle's writings. E. Jüngel, *Die Autorität des bittenden Christus. Eine These zur materialen Begründung der Eigenart des Wortes Gottes. Erwägungen zum Problem der Infallibilität in der Theologie,* in "Unterwegs zur Sache. Theologische Bemerkungen" (München, 1972), pp. 179-88. R. Kaczynski, *Das Wort Gottes in Liturgie und Alltag der Gemeinden des Johannes Chrysostomos,* Freiburger Theologische Studien 94 (1974). A. M. Ritter, *Charisma im Verständnis des Johannes Chrysostomos und seiner Zeit. Ein Beitrag zur Erforschung der griechisch-orientalischen Ekklesiologie in der Frühzeit der Reichskirche* (Göttingen, 1972). In recent years, important progress has been made in the study of the sociological situation in Antioch at Chrysostom's time, the pastoral role of preachers and their preaching, the use of rhetoric in homiletics, and the principles of Chrysostom's exegetical work. Whereas all these factors contribute to the trustworthiness of his preaching, our topic lies elsewhere. Therefore, I will mention here only a few works that have especially helped to understand the issue at hand: R. Hill, *Akribeia. A Principle of Chrysostom's Exegesis,* Colloquium 14 (1981) 32-36. P. Allen, *The Homilist and the Congregation: A Case Study of Chrysostom's Homilies on Hebrews,* Augustianum 36 (1996) 397-421.

2. In his discussion of Mt 25:31-46, Brändle (1979) arrives at different conclusions. The difference is mainly due to the fact that Chrysostom cites and alludes to this particular text frequently in the course of his exposition. Variation of expression is therefore a matter of course.

3. This is true even for those texts that have been edited only by the *Patrologia Graeca.* Our studies at the Institute for New Testament Textual Research in Münster have shown that for textual matters it is of no consequence if one looks at Migne's text or at one of the critical editions. In all of these editions, the scriptural quotations follow the Byzantine text of Chrysostom's time to the same degree. This text comes from an old tradition which mostly agrees with the best manuscripts. Only a number of characteristic variants depart from the "original" text.

4. The printed text of Chrysostom's homily says "χωρίζει." This is presumably a printing error for χωρίσει.

5. Rom. h. 16 (15),3 (PG 60,544). It is worth noting that the *Patrologia Graeca* does not count Chrysostom's praefatio as Homily 1. Consequently, the numbering of *Patrologia Graeca* [as well as the English *Library of the Fathers* edition — Tr.] is off by one compared to the numbering used in this article.

over, Chrysostom is acquainted with other variants and makes note of them. Commenting on Romans 8:35, he says: "'Who shall separate us from the love of Christ?' And [Paul] does not say 'of God' [so ℵ (B) 365 1506], so indifferent is it to him whether he mentions the name of Christ or of God."[6] This remark should not be overinterpreted in christological terms. Apparently, Chrysostom is aware of the variant θεοῦ and wants to show that it poses no substantial difference to the variant τοῦ Χριστοῦ.[7] His exegetical judgment is sound, in view of the humanity and divinity in the person of Christ.[8]

2. My second observation is that Chrysostom intends his preaching to be moral instruction and education. Such instruction was necessary because of the situation in the large city of Antioch.[9] Christians there were still exposed to attacks from the more numerous pagans and Jews. In addition, Paul himself commissions church leaders to give moral instruction. Chrysostom wants to teach his audience and to follow the example of Paul, who "worked harder" than anyone,[10] who loved his congregations as if he were their father, and even more than this,[11] who taught "all of humankind, whole cities and nations." Chrysostom likewise charges his listeners to lead their households, friends, and neighbors "on the right path." In this study, I am dealing with those aspects of his moral instruction only indirectly. Yet, it is necessary to examine his exhortation in order to understand how he made them believable in his preaching.

In the following discussion I will consider the synergistic problem only peripherally. It is widely agreed that Chrysostom expressed himself in terms which the Reformation theologians would have called synergistic. However, accusations of synergism cannot properly be brought against Chrysostom, because for him, obedience was the appropriate response to God's prevenient grace. Christian faith and credible preaching were unthinkable without such a response. As Brändle has shown, Chrysostom's preaching cannot be described in terms of the synergistic debate. Obviously, these categories are more our problem than

6. Rom. h. 16 (15),3 (PG 60,544).

7. Chrysostom knows the variant τοῦ θεοῦ. He quotes the verse eight times and in seven out of eight instances uses τοῦ Χριστοῦ, yet once he uses τοῦ θεοῦ (De laud. sancti Pauli apostoli h. 6,1). See also Rom 8:39.

8. I will look at this issue again at the end of this article.

9. Cf. among others J. H. W. G. Liebeschuetz, *Barbarians and Bishops: Army, Church and State in the Age of Arcadius and Chrysostom* (Oxford, 1990), pp. 166-88.

10. Rom. h. 1,1 (praef.) (PG 60,392).

11. Rom. h. 1,2 (praef.) (PG 60,394).

his. He held both sides together, classical synergism and the unequivocal primacy of grace.[12] Chrysostom deals with the question on his own terms. The degree to which his perspective moves toward a solution of the synergistic problem will be dealt with in the following discussion.

After some formal observations which show how important it was to Chrysostom to present the scriptural text credibly, I will divide our topic in three headings:

1. The Pleading Christ and His Authority
2. The Christological Basis
3. Preaching That Allows Free Acceptance

At several points in his *Homilies,* Chrysostom points out to his audience that, on their own, they would not be able to understand a certain verse. He then proceeds to explain a passage, paraphrasing freely for the sake of clarification.[13] For example, in Romans 8:36f., Paul seeks to assure his readers that despite their present suffering (8:36) they have received the victory of him who loves them (8:37). Chrysostom reminds them in his exposition that this promise is by no means unbelievable (μὴ τοίνυν ἀπιστήσῃς).[14] God is on our side (συναγωνιζόμενος),[15] so it is neither incredible nor paradoxical (θαυμαστὰ . . . καὶ παράδοξα) that he gives us the victory over our persecutors. Even as exiles, we are more powerful than they.[16] Chrysostom refers here to the "power and love of God" in order to reconcile his congregation to the otherwise shocking paradoxes of the Pauline text. More examples could be mentioned[17] that show how significant it was for Chrysostom that his readers understand the text. He also succeeded in explaining the credibility of the text itself: it demonstrates an authority which both asserts its claims on them and gives them full freedom to accept it.

II. The Pleading Christ and His Authority

Rudolf Brändle points to the end of the sixteenth homily on Romans as an example of an especially forceful formulation of Chrysostom's soteriological con-

12. See Brändle (1980), pp. 70-89.

13. For Rom 8:38-39 cf. h. 16 (15),4 (PG 60,546).

14. Rom. h. 16 (15),4 (PG 60,545).

15. Rom. h. 16 (15),4 (PG 60,545).

16. μὴ τοίνυν ἀπιστήσῃς . . . εἶ ἐλαυνόμενοι τῶν διωκόντων κρατοῦμεν. Rom. h. 16 (15),4 (PG 60,545). . . .

17. E.g., in his exposition of Rom 8:15. If it serves him well, John Chrysostom also uses sophisticated rhetorical devices to make his point.

cern. Chrysostom calls his concluding remarks περὶ τῶν ἐθικωτέρων[18] when he no longer treats the text phrase by phrase. They contain, however, more than ethical instruction. The passage follows Chrysostom's exposition of the powerful conclusion of Romans 8. It deals with the daily dying of Christians according to the example of the Crucified One. Without suffering, one cannot have the love and victory of Christ. Later, Paul concludes in two hymnic verses (Rom 8:38-39) that everything depends on where one's allegiance lies. If the Lord is Christ, then one is assured of conquering both death and life, present and future. By paraphrasing again Romans 8:39, Chrysostom makes it clear that even the throngs of apocalyptic powers are not able to separate one from the love of Christ.[19] Chrysostom adds a concluding section which continues the theme of the love of Christ. However, after Chrysostom's climactic exposition of the Pauline discourse, this postscript seems unimpressive.

Thus, the powerful Lord now appears weak. Paul has just depicted the Master of all powers; now Chrysostom presents an image of Christ as a poor and weak man, a homeless foreigner and prisoner. In each of these forms of poverty and helplessness, Christ is portrayed as pleading — pleading for mercy with his destitution, pleading for kindness with his homelessness and nakedness, and appealing for compassion by pointing to his own imprisonment. "If you will not thank me for having suffered for you, show mercy on me for my poverty. If you can have no mercy on my poverty, let my disease move you. . . . Have you no regard for these? Then let [the thought] of [human] nature itself stir you: if you see me naked, remember that nakedness in which I hung on the cross for you; or if not this, remember the nakedness which I now suffer through the poor."[20] This would appear to his audience as a poor, even pitiable speech. Does the Lord of all powers and authorities now come to them in humiliation, asking — even begging — for their kindness? Chrysostom concludes: "I then (τότε) suffered for you and still suffer for you (ἀλλὰ καὶ νῦν διὰ σὲ), so that whether you are moved by the former sufferings or the latter, you might show some pity. I fasted for you, now I hunger for you again. I was thirsty for you when hanging on the cross. I thirst now through the poor, so that by the former or by the latter, I may draw you to myself and make you charitable (φιλανθρώπως) — for your own salvation (ἐπὶ σωτηρίᾳ τῇ σῇ)."[21]

18. Rom. h. 17 (16),10 (PG 60,564).

19. Chrysostom understood well that it was God's love which does not allow any powers to separate the people from him. He emphasizes this after his citation of Rom 8:39. Directly following this, however, he describes how Paul responds to God's love with his passionate love for Christ (PG 60,546,36f.). Paul was willing to submit everything to his longing for Christ, even his hopes for heaven (PG 60,546,40-44).

20. Rom. h. 16 (15),6 (PG 60,547).

21. Rom. h. 16 (15),6 (PG 60,547-48).

This passage suggests why Chrysostom puts such a pitiable speech into Christ's mouth. He further develops this theme as he continues: In humble weakness, Christ asks not for grandiose gifts of obedience, but for small, freely given favors. He desires these gifts so that he might be a debtor and repay the faithful with a heavenly crown, which they then wear "by a certain free consent" (τὶς παρρησία). What Christ wants, as Brändle has rightly pointed out, is "not slaves at all, but friends whose mercy proceeds from love." He also states: "For John Chrysostom, human participation in salvation is a gift from God, not something that must be snatched from his hands at the cost of his honor."[22]

The cogency of Brändle's argument is apparent. In Chrysostom's view, the αὐτεξούσιον is a great gift from God which cannot be nullified in those who have received salvation from Christ. Therefore they should be allowed to participate in their salvation. This human cooperation does not compromise the prevenience of grace. The response to the generous offer of grace should come willingly and by one's own free will. Christ gives human beings the dignity to be able to freely accept his offer. It is only the invitation which permits the freedom to respond. With this request, Christ gives the faithful dignity to know that they are esteemed by God.

It is worth taking a closer look at the theological reflection which stands behind this particular image of Christ.[23] In the exposition of Romans 8:38-39, Chrysostom has discussed Christ as the Son of God who stands against all powers, so that nothing may separate those who believe from his love. The same Christ now presents himself in poverty, requesting charity. In misery and need, he subordinates himself to the people.

Despite the paradox inherent in this manner of speaking, the truth of the matter is not changed; rather, this form of speech enhances the way the truth is communicated. It comes as a request, the only kind of address which gives the listener enough room to encounter the truth freely. It gives him space to perceive the request's obviousness and to willingly assent to it. Truth, then, is rightly expressed as request; not demand, not expectation, not obligation — so that the audience is enabled to come and see the truth for itself. When it comes in this way, the listeners are brought inside the process of understanding Scripture, an understanding worked by the Spirit and apprehended by faith. It is here that preaching becomes credible.

Do such reflections underlie the final section of Chrysostom's homily,

22. Brändle (1980), p. 89: "Die Mitwirkung des Menschen am Heil ist für Johannes Chrysostomos nicht etwas, was der Mensch Gott auf Kosten seiner Ehre abtrotzt, sondern eine Gabe Gottes."

23. Cf. Jüngel (1972), pp. 181-84, 186-88.

or has it here been overinterpreted? To begin with, Chrysostom's frequent use of the pleading Christ motif supports this interpretation. His explication of the Last Judgment in Matthew 25:31-46 is a particularly good example. Rudolf Brändle, in his impressive monograph, is certainly correct that in Chrysostom's sermon on this particular passage in Matthew, his most profound meditations surround the image of the pleading Christ.[24] In addition, the pleading Christ motif is closely related to the principle of συγκατάβασις, God's condescension to humanity in Christ. Christ bows down and assumes human weakness so that the people might grasp the truth of his request and follow him. The principle of συγκατάβασις is comprehensive. In its primary sense, it describes how God extends himself for fellowship with the people and the world. It also speaks of the way in which, by analogy with the incarnation, Christ's followers conform themselves to those around them so that they may "by all means win some."[25] Therefore, συγκατάβασις is characteristic of every preacher who wants to open Scripture to the understanding of others. If this principle was important to Chrysostom, that is, if he developed and used it as a homiletical and hermeneutical principle,[26] then it is easy to accept that the preceding analysis does in fact describe Chrysostom's reflections behind his sixteenth homily. The pleading Christ is not accidental hyperbole — which would be hard to imagine anyway in view of the utter destitution of the request — rather, it is a deliberate homiletical construct. Chrysostom has carefully chosen the pleading Christ image to bring Paul's climactic speech *sub contrario* to his own congregation.

If Chrysostom used the image of the pleading Christ as intentionally as I have suggested, then it is useful to inquire whether he was influenced by some outside tradition. Of even more interest, however, is the christological basis for the motif of the pleading Christ. I will treat these two questions in turn.

The first question will be treated only briefly. It seems possible that Chrysostom's picture of the pleading Christ, as well as his comprehensive principle of συγκατάβασις, was influenced by Irenaeus. Like Chrysostom, Irenaeus writes, ". . . The Logos of God, Jesus Christ, our Lord, because of his overflowing love became what we are in order to make us completely into

24. Brändle (1979), p. 231, cites many parallels of the same theme. Cf. the concluding remarks to the 15th homily on Romans. Closely related to this is the often occurring theme that Christ is in each suffering fellow man.

25. Paul's accommodation to other people's weaknesses is a good example of συγκατάβασις. Cf. ep. ad Cor. I h. 21.1 and 23,1 (1 Cor 9:22-24) (PG 61,187). Cf. also Hebr. h. 13,3 (PG 63,106).

26. Regarding the principle of God's condescension cf. Kaczynski (1974), pp. 25-27; Brändle (1997), cols. 467-68 and cols. 485-86 with numerous references. Cf. also Hill (1982), pp. 32-36.

what he is."[27] Both authors develop the theme of God's total condescension by which he enables humans to ascend to him. I will turn now to the second question concerning the theological basis for the pleading — and still pleading[28] — Christ.

III. The Christological Basis for the Pleading Christ Motif

It is clear that Chrysostom could scarcely have preached Christ's pleading and συγκατάβασις if he had lived in Alexandria and been trained in Alexandrinian theology. A Christ who is pleading in συγκατάβασις, who is weak for the weak, as well as subordinates himself to the listener, is incompatible with the christology of, say, the Alexandrinian theologian Cyril. In Cyril's christology, Christ's human and divine natures are inexplicably and ontologically coexistent. In Beyschlag's summary, "the eternal, pre-existent Son of God has come so graphically in Jesus of Nazareth, that Christ's humanity is inherent essentially — even physically — in the divine Logos."[29] To be sure, Cyril would have recognized the συγκατάβασις of God in Jesus the Nazarene. But Chrysostom portrays the heavenly exalted Christ who in his human nature is still weak and pleading. This would be unthinkable in Cyrillian christology, which in Beyschlag's view runs the risk of denying the anthropological aspect of the two natures in contrast to Christ's deity.[30]

But Chrysostom was from Antioch and was instructed in Antiochean theology. Therefore, he began with the idea of the divine Christ as *being* man rather than with God *becoming* man.[31] Intellectually, he would have distinguished between the human and divine natures of Christ, but in his discussion, it was the biblical Christ whom he encountered, the inexplicable miracle by which God inhabits the virgin-born son of David. It is this Christ that Chrysostom recognizes by faith and introduces to his audience.

Portions of Chrysostom's portrait of Christ in the sixteenth homily refer specifically to Christ's divine nature: "God gave up his Son, but you will not so

27. Adv. haer. praef V. . . . γεγονότι τοῦτο ὅπερ ἐσμέν, ἵνα ἡμᾶς εἶναι καταρτίσῃ ἐκεῖνο ὅπερ ἐστὶν αὐτός.

28. Rom. h. 16 (15),6 (PG 60,548). Cf. Brändle (1979), pp. 235-38.

29. *Grundriß der Dogmengeschichte II, Gott und Mensch,* Part 1, *Das christologische Dogma* (Darmstadt, 1991), p. 75: "Nach dieser (sc. Cyrills) Auffassung ist der ewige, präexistente Gottessohn in der Gestalt Jesu derart 'anschaulich' geworden, daß das Menschsein in dem Subjekt der Logos-Gottheit geradezu 'physisch'-real inhäriert."

30. Cf. Beyschlag (n. 29), p. 76. ". . . während . . . die menschliche Existenz Jesu, und zwar auch als geist/leibliche Ganzheit, der Gottheit gegenüber keinen anthropologischen Selbststand besitzt."

31. See Beyschlag (n. 29), p. 76.

much as share your bread with him who was given up for you, who was slain for you. For your sake the Father did not spare him although he was indeed his Son (γνησίου ὄντος παιδός), but you disregard him though he is pining away from hunger."[32] In the following quote, Chrysostom even places Christ's completion of salvation (his death on the cross) next to the ever-present request: "He was given up for you, he was slain for you, he goes about in hunger for you; you need only give him what belongs to him, that you yourself may receive the gain, and still you do not give."[33] There is no difficulty here for the Antiochean exegete, because the unity of the two natures in the biblical Christ can be accepted by faith. If it is Christ who as a man with a free will is "adopted" into the fellowship of the Logos, and if it is he alone who brings salvation,[34] then it poses no contradiction for Chrysostom that this Christ is shown enticing and pleading with his people.

In the same concluding passage in which Chrysostom asserts the divinity of Jesus, he also refers to Christ's human nature: "Have you no regard for these (Christ's requests)? Then let (human) nature itself stir you. . . ."[35] It is without doubt for Chrysostom that the humanity and divinity of Christ are present in the unity of one person — which is apprehended by faith and ultimately confirmed by discipleship.[36]

In a certain sense, the synergistic problem is transcended for Chrysostom. For him, God has already done the most that could possibly be done.[37] "The one who saves the soul is the same one who makes the flesh obedient. It is easy to teach (the good); what is amazing is to show how to *do* it without difficulty." The following short anecdote helps Chrysostom to make his point. A fruit seller is being beaten. Christ saves her by claiming to be her son, even though he is actually the son of the King. In this story, Christ acts as the Son of God in human form, his intercession for the market woman can be assigned wholly in his humanity, but without violation of the unity of his person, so it is possible to accept by faith this ministry of a man who is God. Just as the synergistic problem did not exist for Christ himself,[38] it does not exist for us. For God, there is no greater joy than to live in human hearts, not even the joy of living in heaven.[39]

32. Rom. h. 16 (15),6 (PG 60,547).
33. Rom. h. 16 (15),6 (PG 60,547).
34. See Beyschlag (n. 29), p. 36.
35. Rom. h. 16 (15),6 (PG 60,547).
36. Chrysostom not only comprehends the distinction between Christ's humanity and divinity as a "christological reality" (Beyschlag, n. 29, p. 77), he also perceives the unity of Christ's person in Scripture without difficulty and applies it to the response that he wants to evoke in his hearers.
37. Cf. his exposition of Rom 8:3, h. 14 (13),5 (PG 60,514) et passim.
38. Cf. also Beyschlag (n. 29), p. 36, and n. 66.

That is why it is believable for people that their highest goal is to follow the human nature of Christ in his commitment to humanity. Trustworthy preaching!

IV. Preaching That Allows Free Acceptance

John Chrysostom's credible preaching maintains free choice. One of Chrysostom's most important concerns is that the human *autexousion* is not nullified.[40] This preaching with its Antiochean christology entreating us on behalf of Christ[41] calls the congregation to accept the truth and allows for that acceptance by respecting human free will. The humble Christ who sets himself as an example thus makes it possible for his listeners to follow their human nature in humility and not in arrogance as Christ demonstrated to them as a model.[42] The authority of the pleading is the same as the authority of the humble Christ. Both enable a discipleship that is free. Freedom, of course, was so important to the Greek John Chrysostom that he would not surrender it. His frequent handling of the theme also moved along the paths of popular stoic philosophy. He challenges his audience to abandon earthly passions, especially ambition[43] but also avarice, pride, and selfishness. Then, so he promises, "we will come to know freedom, a safe harbor and serene peace."[44] To the audience, these are familiar images. However, their power to persuade has been replaced by the humble, pleading Christ. The ethical demand alone will have no lasting impact even if it is reinforced by the most glorious reward. However much he uses these exhortations and promises, it is still Chrysostom's conviction that only a humble request will give people a real chance to grasp the truth of his demands.

39. Cf. concluding remarks to the 15th homily on Romans, in Rom. h. 15 (14),11 (PG 60,539).

40. Cf. Rom. h. 17 (16),8 (PG 60,559) (Rom 9:21).

41. Cf. 2 Cor 5:20 cited in Rom. h. 16 (15),3 (PG 60,544) (Rom 8:34).

42. Cf. the concluding remarks in the 21st homily on Romans, Rom. h. 21 (20),4 (PG 60,599-60,601).

43. Cf. especially the concluding remarks in the eighteenth homily on Romans.

44. PG 60,572.

PASTORAL/SERMONIC ESSAYS

Pastor Paul

Eugene H. Peterson

I am interested in Saint Paul's Letter to the Romans as a Holy Spirit source document for pastoral theology, a piece of writing that is a working demonstration of spiritual formation in the Christian community. My interest is piqued by living in an age in which the work of much of the church's leadership is neither pastoral nor theological. The pastoral dimensions of the church's leadership are badly eroded by technologizing and managerial influences. The theological dimensions of the church's leadership have been marginalized by therapeutic and marketing preoccupations. The gospel work of giving leadership to the community of the Christian faithful has been alienated from its source. Among leaders, at least, the rationalist mind has taken over in the schools, and the functionalist attitude has prevailed in churches to the extent that pastoral theology, as such, is barely recognizable. Rationalism and functionalism, both of them reductive, have left pastoral theology thin and anemic.

Paul, the church's first and most enduringly authoritative theologian, was a pastoral theologian. All his thinking and writing, his teaching and preaching in the service of God (i.e., his theology), was at the same time carried out in the service of a community of souls (i.e., it was pastoral).

Given the commanding eminence that Romans holds in the world as a theological document, it perhaps needs saying again that Romans is a letter written to Christians to help them live their lives Christianly; that is, it was totally pastoral. It is, as are all the documents comprised by our Scriptures, directed to living. There is nothing here that is merely intellectual. Paul's mind, one of the most vigorous intellects in the church's history, works entirely in the context of a congregation of souls, of men and women who find themselves called upon to repent and believe, obey and love, pray and forgive, in the sin-tangled disorder of family and culture, world and work.

The Letter to the Romans, our premier theological text, is best understood and put to use when it is read as pastoral theology.

* * *

Designating Paul as "pastor" may not be strictly accurate, at least in terms of contemporary usage of the word, for Paul was not resident among the Romans to whom he wrote; he was dealing with them from a distance, had never been to their city and walked its streets, hadn't been in their homes and eaten meals with them, and had no firsthand acquaintance with the conditions in which they did their work and raised their families. For most of us today, "pastor" connotes daily immersion in a worshiping and working community. Normally, the work of pastor is not generalized; it is specific to a particular community in a particular place. But if Paul was not on site in his work with the Roman Christians, he was intensely involved in helping them live the Christian life truly and well. Everything he wrote in his famous letter to them was in the service of *life,* of living immediately and believingly and obediently as disciples of Jesus Christ. Granted that Paul is a *thinking* theologian, he is simultaneously a *working* pastor: the Letter to the Romans is a major source document showing Paul thinking theologically as he goes about his pastoral work. There is little danger that the significance of Romans in establishing Paul as master theologian will be missed; he is one of "the giants in the land." But the way in which Romans shows Paul at work in the care of souls, Paul in his assigned work in the Christian community, is missed most of the time. It is missed by both pastors and scholars.

Pastors who on the one hand are pleased to sit at the feet of Paul the theologian more often than not sign up with the psychologists and management consultants for expert counsel when it comes to going about their daily work in the kingdom. This is understandable, for caring for souls is honored and demanding work; those who give their lives to it need all the help they can get. But without theology, caring for souls can easily transgress into manipulating or seducing selves, and "the last state of that man is worse than the first."

And scholars for whom Paul is the patron saint of the learned life frequently minimize the way in which Paul used his mind in the immediate service of God and souls, preferring thus to work in settings protected against interruption. Theological and exegetical study is honored and demanding work, but abstracted from the actual conditions of community and congregation it easily loses connection with the God who loves the world and gave himself for it. Having a mind, a glory we hold in common with the angels, is grand. Cultivating the life of the intellect is essential to the sanity of the Church of Christ. But the use of the mind can as easily lead us into pride as into truth. This happens when it severs itself from the pastoral.

I want to identify four elements in Paul's writing of Romans that contribute to his formative influence in pastoral theology: his submission to Scripture, his embrace of mystery, his use of language, and his sense of community.

I. Scripture

It becomes clear early on in the reading of Romans that Paul is not an independent thinker figuring things out on his own. Nor is he a speculative thinker playing with ideas, searching for some ultimate truth. His thinking is subordinated to all that God has revealed of himself and his purposes in Holy Scripture. Scripture for Paul was the Hebrew Bible, what we now designate as the Old Testament. At the time of his writing to the Romans, Paul's intellect is entirely harnessed to Scripture.

"Arrogant" is the accusation often directed against the professional intellectual — prideful reveling in the powers of mind. It is an accusation easy both to understand and substantiate. Men and women of conspicuous mental prowess easily acquire a sense of superiority over the less well endowed. That sense of superiority has a way of developing into an attitude of prideful condescension. The assumption that underlies the sin is that the ability to think is the distinctive glory of the human and therefore the more we think well the better humans we become. Our humanity is evaluated in terms of our minds: a man who writes excellent books is superior to an illiterate migrant worker picking fruit; a woman who manages the financial affairs of a large corporation is worth far more than the woman who cleans the toilets in a public washroom.

But Paul, one of the most competent minds in history, shows none of that intellectual hubris. And the reason is that all his mental processes are subdued and submissive to what has been handed to him by revelation in Scripture. He is not using his mind to figure things out; he is not using his mind to acquire the kind of knowledge that is power; he is not using his mind to probe the frontiers of thinking, conquering ignorance and setting himself up as a master of minds.

Not that he is incapable of rigorous reasoning. The grammatical accuracy of frequently used logical connectives such as *hina* and *hoti, hōste,* and *oun* are evidence of a keen mind disciplined to the standards of language developed by Greek and Roman intellectuals. The careful employment of verbal moods and voices displays his skill at nuance and modulation in conveying meaning. There can be no doubt that Paul *thinks* well. But he is not using his mind as an adventurer, as a conqueror, as a master — he uses his considerable powers of mind to enter into what has already been made known, what "God has revealed through faith for faith" (1:17).

The words of the scriptural revelation are the means by which Paul thinks. It is an embarrassment to some that Paul does not exegete Scripture according to modern standards, but he is no less an exegete for all that. Paul did not use his mind in isolation from his life — Paul's relation to the scriptures was not as a student finding out what was there but as a disciple living the text. Paul, gifted with a fine intellect, had a well-trained mind and had acquired a comprehensive knowledge of the scriptures. He spent the first part of his life as a Pharisee, using the scriptures zealously but wrongly; he spent the second part of his life as a Christian, living these same scriptures just as zealously but very differently. The difference between his life as a Pharisee and a Christian was not in his intellectual ability nor in his knowledge of Scripture but in his relation to the scriptures: as a Pharisee he *used* the scriptures; as a Christian he *submitted* to them.

It is in his relation to Holy Scripture that we see a primary characteristic of his work as a pastoral theologian: the scriptures were not so much something to use, as the text that furnished his vocabulary, shaped his imagination, and formed his life. The texts he cites are not set out merely as proofs in an argument; they are vast presences, suggesting the immense horizons within which he writes.

There are 65 quotations laced through his letter, cited from 16 of the 39 OT books available to him. Isaiah (with 18 citations) and Psalms (with 13) are his favorites, but he ranges widely, covering most of the territory from Genesis to Malachi.

But it is not only that he quotes, he *inhabits* the story, he gives the impression of being on familiar terms with everything written by his prophet ancestors, totally at ease in this richly expansive narrative of God's Word. The scriptures have become for him "all autobiographical" (Alexander Whyte's phrase). For instance, he puts the imagery of the Genesis creation to fresh but very different uses first in chapter 1 as he writes of culpable sin ("they exchanged the truth about God," 1:25) and later in chapter 8 as he writes of unavoidable suffering (". . . the whole creation has been groaning in travail . . . ," 8:22). Adam and Abraham, Sarah and Rebecca, Moses and Elijah are alive in his imagination. But he doesn't use his mind to invent plausible emotional and human interest details to elaborate the story; he discerns the action and purposes and presence of God in these lives and retells the story of salvation for his readers with his ancestors alive and present in it. We see this in various ways. For example, in the process of arguing the equal status of Jews and Gentiles as sinners before God (at 3:10-18), he pulls six strands of scriptural text out of their contexts in the Psalms and Isaiah and weaves them into a brilliant prophetic poem, as masterful a piece of rhetorical art as we are likely to come across (Ps 14:1-2; Ps 5:9; Ps 140:3; Ps 10:7; Isa 59:7-8; Ps 36:1). And he does it without violating or distorting the meaning of any of the six. There is a sense in which nothing in Scripture is ever "out of context" for Paul. He is so at home in the entire country of Scripture that he has an intuitive sense of what fits and where. He has not used his intellect to rearrange or correct or improve upon what he has been given; he enters it as a guest and receives with gratitude everything set before him, trusting the Host to see to his needs.

II. Mystery

Another aspect of pastoral theology embedded in Paul's Romans is his extravagant embrace of mystery. Paul is comfortable with mystery, he delights in mystery, he accepts mystery. His celebrated and joyous outburst at 11:33-36 is characteristic:

> O the depth of the riches and wisdom and knowledge of God! How unsearchable are his judgments and how inscrutable his ways!
>
> "For who has known the mind of the Lord,
> or who has been his counselor?" (Isa 40:13-14)
>
> "Or who has given a gift to him
> that he might be repaid?" (Job 35:7; 41:11)
>
> For from him and through him and to him are all things. To him be glory forever. Amen.

It is significant that this reverent but exuberant stance before the God who cannot be figured out or diagrammed, comes in the context of some of Paul's most vigorous reasoning (chapters 9–11). Mystery, for Paul, is not what is left over after we have done our best to reason things out on our own; it is inherent in the very nature of God and his works.

His personally expressed delight in the mystery of God's ways in verses 33 and 36 sandwiches lines from Job and Isaiah that likewise give witness to the "more" that we consistently encounter in God — more than we ever expected, more than we can ever grasp, more than we are capable of explaining. But the "more" is not some secret that is kept hidden from us, teasing our curiosity; it is not esoterica from which common people are excluded but to which privileged adepts are admitted.

Mystery, in other words, is not a fancy or spiritual word for ignorance that we can conquer by more knowledge; nor does it designate a secrecy that we can penetrate by painstaking search. A few sentences previous to his famous exclamation Paul is explicit on this point: "I do not want you to be ignorant of this mystery . . ." (11:25 NIV). Ignorance and mystery are not synonyms. Secrecy and mystery are not synonyms. Paul's subject is "the revelation of the mystery which was kept secret for long ages but is now disclosed . . ." (16:25-26).

There is a kind of mind, too common among us, that is impatient of mystery. Mystery, these minds assume, is what pastors and theologians are paid to get rid of. They assume, and not without evidence, that what we don't know is a breeding ground for superstition and uncertainty. If we don't have a clear and concise outline of what we must know, how can we think straight about God? And if we don't know the lay of the land, the problems that we face in our daily lives, how can we devise an effective plan or set workable goals? The task of the human mind is to *know;* if it doesn't know something it seeks to find it out.

The ability of the intellect to move into the unknown and make it known, to penetrate areas of ignorance and map reality, is, of course, formidable. This kind of aggressive intellectual work has primarily been associated with science; its results, always impressive, fairly stagger the imagination in our modern world. Robert Frost once likened the modern acceleration of results acquired by the scientific, ignorance-conquering mind to a hundred-yard dash followed by a pole vault. So it is understandable that the modern mind accustomed to seeing the tangled undergrowth of "mystery" cleared out by the "knowledge" bulldozers would retain little appreciation for the kind of mystery that Job and Isaiah and Paul speak of, a mystery that deepens as our knowledge increases.

But the conception of mystery as a quality of the Unknown has never satisfied the deepest insights of the human spirit. Children and poets, lovers and priests have, in Jaroslav Pelikan's words, "repeatedly gone on to recognize the mysterious quality of the Known."[1]

The mystery to which Paul gives witness is not the mystery of a darkness that must be dispelled but the mystery of light that may be entered. God and his operations cannot be reduced to what we are capable of knowing and explaining and reproducing. It takes considerable humility to embrace this mystery, for in the presence of mystery we are not in a position to control anything, to predict or manage, to pose as authorities, to, as we say, "master the subject."

Gabriel Marcel distinguished between approaching life as a problem and entering it as a mystery. If we deal with life as a problem we reduce it to what we can do something about; we are concerned with figuring out and fixing. We become myopic, managers and mechanics of what is immediately before us, with

1. Pelikan, *The Christian Intellectual* (London: Collins, 1966), p. 70.

no peripheral vision and no horizons. We miss most of life. But if we approach life as a mystery, we are forever coming upon meanings that exceed our definitions, energy and resources unguessed in our calculations. "Mystery is not the absence of meaning, but the presence of more meaning than we can comprehend."[2]

Paul's Romans deals with plenty of problems, problems both of behavior and thinking, as every pastoral theologian must. But the Letter is not "about" problems. It is about God and God's ways, which can only be approached rightly as mystery — the "more" that keeps surprising us with fresh light and grace. This "more," this mystery, is never used by Paul as an excuse to quit thinking and is never invoked as a diversion from doing what needs to be done for God. Rather, it draws Paul (and us) into ever more vigorous thinking and energetic obedience. It is a thinking that doesn't dispel mystery but deepens it. "Glory," the light of God that exceeds our capacity to take it all in, is the usual word in our scriptures to mark this mystery; it is a word that Paul uses easily and often: "to him be glory forever" (11:36 and often elsewhere).

III. Language

The way Paul uses language, in particular his employment of metaphor, is another element in the formation of a pastoral theology. Language is primary in gospel work. This comes as no surprise since language is primary in the making of the gospel itself: "The word is near you, on your lips and in your heart . . ." (10:8). And Jesus, of course, is *the* Word. All words are derivative from the Word, whether adoringly or blasphemously, whether in the service of God's truth or the devil's lies. Language, one of the defining characteristics of being human, is integral to the way God reveals and works. It follows that the *way* we use language, not simply *that* we use it, is significant.

Charles Williams noted that Paul produced ". . . practically a new vocabulary. To call him a poet would be perhaps improper (besides ignoring the minor but important fact that he wrote in prose). But he used words as poets do; he regenerated them."[3] Conspicuous in this crafting of words "as poets do" is his use of metaphor. This feature in Paul's use of language requires comment, for it is a major element in filling out his identity as a pastoral theologian.

The use of metaphor is not a precise use of language; in fact it is quite the opposite; a metaphor, instead of pinning down meaning, lets it loose. The met-

2. Denis Covington, *Salvation on Sand Mountain: Snake-handling and Redemption in Southern Appalachia* (New York: Addison-Wesley, 1995), pp. 203-4.

3. *The Descent of the Dove* (New York: Living Age Books, 1953), p. 8.

aphor does not so much define or label as it expands, forcing the mind into participating action. To use "rock" as a metaphor for God, as in "The LORD is my rock" (Ps 18:1), a common practice in our scriptures, does not define God. The statement taken literally is absurd. What it does is force the mind into action to find meaning at another level, "engaging the imagination in a cognitive and affective exploration of the subject in and through relationships that seem strange but, in fact, are more illuminating than literal predication."[4]

Paul, no doubt, acquired both his linguistic taste for metaphor and his skill in using it from the Hebrew scriptures, where it is used extensively. In doing so he established metaphor at the center of pastoral theology. If the language used in pastoral work diverges too far from this center, it inevitably wanders into a desert of definition and explanation.

One of the features of metaphor is its accessibility — metaphors come from common sensory experience. If, because of Romans' formidable reputation as a theological document, we suppose that we need a heavy dictionary to find our way through Paul's sentences, an actual reading of the text is a happy surprise. Paul has embraced the language of metaphor (and its sister metonymy) that comes out of the same world that we all grow up in and have lived in all our lives. One consequence of this accessibility by means of metaphor is that the same sentences on which scholars write learned books are also read and understood by truck drivers and waitresses in conversation over coffee. This kind of language doesn't just inform our minds, although it certainly does that; it enlists us in a believing/obeying participation. We cannot be passive before a metaphor, we have to imagine and enter into it. Paul's down-to-earth metaphorical speech occurs in virtually every paragraph. A cursory sampling: reap some harvest (1:13); written on their hearts (2:15); throat is an open grave (3:13); sins are covered (4:7); love has been poured into our hearts (5:5); death reigned through that one man (5:17); old self was crucified (6:6); wages of sin (6:23); sold under sin (7:14); creation has been groaning in travail (8:22); wild olive shoot (11:17); grafted (11:24); living sacrifice (12:1); heap burning coals on his head (12:20); armor of light (13:12); another man's foundation (15:20); crush Satan under your feet (16:20).

There are both theologians and pastors who like things tidy and neat, without loose ends and devoid of ambiguity. Ivory tower intellectuals and rubber-hits-the-road pragmatists like things organized and orderly and under control, whether by a system of thought or a management plan. But our first pastoral theologian was innocent of "systematics." He used words not to define but to evoke. He was not interested in containing and preserving all of God's truth

4. Sandra M. Schneiders, *The Revelatory Text* (New York: Harper San Francisco, 1991), p. 31.

in his language, protecting it from contamination and then serving it up for examination, like a specimen in a laboratory. Paul did not use the language that way; he didn't take sentences apart, trying to pry the truth out of them. He did not "murder to dissect" (Wordsworth).

Paul treats the language as a living energy field. Words are not tight containers of "meaning" but evocations of discourse, proliferating nuance and implication. He doesn't develop a special and disciplined jargon for the sake of being precise about God; he takes the language of common discourse, which is always redolent of metaphor — common things and common actions — and uses it freely, at ease with the ambiguities that are necessarily inherent in it. And in using language this way he sets the style for language in pastoral theology.

IV. Community

A fourth element in the Romans letter that makes it seminal for pastoral theology is a passionate concern for community. The concern pervades the letter, providing a comprehensive context of personal relationship. Pastoral theology, as Paul lives and writes it, is relational — persons are involved as persons-in-relationship.

This is signaled on the opening page of the letter as Paul addresses the Roman congregation as "all God's beloved in Rome" (1:7), expresses his personal feeling toward them in the phrase "I long to see you" (1:11), and notes how he has often looked forward to being with them "in order that I may reap some harvest among you" (1:13). This is not theology-in-general — it is personally written to a specific people living in a particular place. Even though Paul has not yet been to Rome he knows the names of many of the people who live and worship there; before the letter ends we will read some of their names (chapter 16).

But it is easy to lose touch with this personal context when Paul launches the main body of his text at 1:16, for at this point the rich interpersonal context apparently recedes into the shadows as large theological truths blaze up. But only apparently, for Paul's concern, while expressed in terms that refer to categories (Jew and Gentile) rather than individual persons, still has to do with the formation of community, the "communion" of saints. Paul finds himself dealing with Jews who feel superior to Gentiles and Gentiles who feel superior to Israel. But Paul refuses to be pastor to a divided congregation. Their spiritual formation requires that they live in open communion with one another.

In chapters 1–8 Paul deals with Jews, the insiders to the historic revelation of God in Israel and Jesus, who are using their ethnic distinction as a mark of privilege, setting themselves off as superior to the Gentiles. Paul argues vigorously and relentlessly that there is no difference, "no distinction" (3:22). All of Paul's biggest theological guns are brought out to demolish Jewish assumptions of advantage over the Gentile, Jewish attitudes of condescension to the Gentile. The theological arguments are so brilliantly worked out, have become so fundamental to the entire Christian world of thought, and have such far-reaching implications that it is easy to overlook the obvious: the theology is being put to use in the Romans letter entirely in the immediate service of establishing and nurturing a Christian community, a congregation free from class distinctions.

In chapters 9–11 the tables are turned: "Now I am speaking to you Gentiles . . ." (11:13). Gentiles are addressed, warning them against looking down on or excluding Israel. Gentiles, finding themselves included as insiders in God's ways of grace and salvation, could easily assume a place of privilege that has just been taken away from the Jews and now in their turn look down on or exclude Jews, reversing the process of discrimination. In chapters 1–8 Jews are prevented from excluding Gentiles by insisting that they, the Jews, are sinners to the same degree as the Gentiles; in chapters 9–11 Gentiles are prevented from excluding Jews because they are only in by virtue of a miracle, God's miracle of "grafting" them into the salvation tree. Paul's image of the wild olive branch being grafted into the cultivated olive tree, the Gentiles finding themselves "in" only by God's action and grace, is set alongside the parallel image of the natural branch (the Jews) who have been broken off; they can be put back in again (". . . for God has the power to graft them in again," 11:23). Gentiles do not hold a position of privilege because of their miraculous status; Jews will also get in by means of miracle.

Paul's argument is different, but its effect is the same. The sin argument ("all have sinned," 3:23) directed to the Jews in chapters 1–8 is matched by the miracle argument ("life from the dead," 11:15) in chapters 9–11. There can be no categories in the Christian community that sort the members into first class and second class: we are all first class sinners; we are all miraculously "grafted" into God's olive tree.

There can be no community where there is no mutuality. Privilege is a breeding ground for pride. And once pride is given class sanction it corrupts every person. Class designation of any sort (Jew/Gentile, capitalist/worker, white/colored, rich/poor, young/old, literate/illiterate) is death on community. The frightening thing is that the moment we get our identity from a classification, we lose awareness of the other as a person and the gospel of Jesus is sabotaged at an unconscious level.

At chapter 12, having gotten everyone thinking truly about one another, their minds scrubbed clean of distorting class assumptions, Paul addresses a community, a congregation of Jews and Gentiles of all sorts, and instructs them in life together. They are now standing on level ground, Jews and Gentiles alongside one another as peers, brothers and sisters in the same family, their self-identities restructured by Paul's powerful arguments and images. There is neither motive nor excuse now for Jew to push Gentile into the background or for Gentile to elbow Jew to the sidelines. In these final chapters of his letter (12–16), Paul addresses them in common, instructing them in the ways of community ("I appeal to you therefore, *brethren* . . . ," 12:1) and brings the letter to a conclusion in a flourish of personal names, 35 of them, Jews and Gentiles mixed together with no racial or religious distinction.

Paul addresses them not as discrete individuals nor as a generic class — they are a community, a community that can only be achieved and understood theologically, that is, in terms of what God has done in Christ through the Spirit, and only dealt with pastorally, that is, as persons-in-relationship. Pastoral theology is not interested in abstract truths on the one hand nor private individual instances on the other, but in the formation of community by the Holy Spirit in Christ.

* * *

I have farmer friends who have told me of their experience with herbicides and pesticides during their younger years. Agents of government agricultural laboratories and salesmen from chemical companies came to them with impressive studies and statistics urging them to make their fields more productive and efficient by using powerful chemicals to get rid of devouring insects and destructive disease.

Impressed by the combination of expertise and enthusiasm they did it. The results were wonderful: production increased remarkably. For a while. It took a few years to realize that the chemicals were killing a lot more than the bad bugs and malign diseases. Soon the fields were sterile and could only be kept productive by the lavish application of fertilizers. The soil was no longer a living organism. Along the way awareness gradually grew among the people who were buying the grains and vegetables and fruits from these fields and making meals of them, an awareness that the nourishing vitamins they were putting on their plates were laced with lethal poisons. That is when the movement back toward "organic" began — finding ways to grow food without killing the soil in which it is grown and the people who eat it.

Every time I hear these stories — and I've heard and read a lot of them by now — I think of my own field of pastoral theology. The "herbicides and pesticides" that promised to revolutionize the work of spiritual leadership are rationalism and functionalism — they promised to banish ignorance and error in our biblical and theological thinking and to get rid of the inefficiency and waste in the way we conduct our community and institutional lives. And they did, in fact, deliver on what they promised — made us far more knowledgeable about God and the scriptures, made us efficient in the management of religion. But at a terrible cost: theology that is less and less interested in God-with-us; pastoral work that deals less and less with persons-in-relationship.

When pastor and theology get separated from their biblical sources and then through specialization separated from each other, everybody loses. Paul in Romans offers a substantial impetus to the recovery of an organic biblical pastoral theology: Paul submissive to Holy Scripture, open to divine mystery, alive to metaphoric language, and insistent on the conditions of community.

"The Full Blessing of Christ" (Romans 15:29): A Sermon

R. Paul Stevens

> I know that when I come to you, I will come in the full measure of the blessing of Christ. (Rom 15:29)

Gordon Fee is one of the few people on earth that could lecture on exegetical method or textual criticism and have people respond to an altar call! So it seems entirely appropriate that my friend, brother, and colleague should be honored with a sermon. That is how he teaches. Even when separated by two glass walls from his large class in the chapel, I can hear him preaching. Passionately. Luminously. A mind on fire. A heart bringing every thought captive to the obedience of Christ. But his passion is not simply self-generated enthusiasm; it is born of the truth of the gospel whose servant he is. It is this passion for the gospel in the life of the apostle Paul that we are invited to contemplate at the end of chapter 15 of Romans.

But why this text in particular? — Paul's hope of arriving in Rome in the "full measure of the blessing of Christ" after having visited Jerusalem (15:25)? Is there a timeless word of God in Paul's off-the-cuff statement in A.D. 57 writing to the Romans from Corinth explaining why he wants to take a two-thousand-mile detour to Jerusalem instead of going directly to Rome? Why does he associate "the *full* blessing of Christ" with his travels and arrival in Rome? Is there a *second* blessing? A *third?* Why must Paul go *first* to Jerusalem in order to have this full blessing? Is the "full blessing" somehow related to the completion of his mission in the eastern regions of the empire, since Paul wanted to complete the "harvest among the other Gentiles" (1:13; 15:19-23) before having the Romans "assist" (15:24) him on his way to Spain? And, since this text speaks to us, how can we enter into the blessing of Christ more fully? These are some of the questions that the text tosses up for us.

I. Orthopathy

All of these questions and observations must be placed in tension with what distresses me in Western Christianity — a passionlessness that is spiritual sloth. In many theological colleges people are progressively inoculated against passionate Christianity by constantly handling the *outside* of holy things. Quenched passion. Consumer churchgoers pay religious professionals to entertain them, and the people evaluate sermons as though they were at a country livestock auction, failing to be grasped by the passionate privilege and duty of the whole people of God. Titillated passion. Suffering as we are from information overload, we continue to wolf down our dinners while the nightly news describes this or that massacre. Seared passion.

Orthopathy is a term coined by Richard Mouw, though it is based on the thought of the Jewish theologian Abraham Heschel. "Ortho" means straight or right, and "pathy" means passion. The cultivation of the heart — a more holistic way of knowing — is the very thing our postmodern culture desperately seeks. The biblical response to this postmodern challenge is not to abandon reason but to allow God to evangelize our hearts as well as our heads, so we care for what God cares for (Mic 6:8). What can be done, therefore, to recover our spiritual passion?

The vignette from Paul's travel plans that we are contemplating becomes an aperture through which we can grasp and be grasped by the central passion of being Christian. Paul, time and time again, puts his inner life at our disposal, not to parade his secrets before spiritual voyeurs observing him in his weakness, but so we will look *through* him like a Kodachrome transparency and see a fraction of the image of Christ (2 Cor 3:18). With considerable vulnerability and Holy Spirit boldness Paul invites us to imitate him (1 Cor 11:1). Even Paul's travel plans here and in Corinth (2 Cor 1:12-24) contain God-soaked inspiration in such mundane geographical notes as the three places he must visit: Rome, Spain (Rom 15:28), and Jerusalem (15:25). In connection with these three he believes he will come to Rome in the full measure of the blessing of Christ. As we explore what was going on in Paul's heart as he prepared to go to Rome, Spain, and Jerusalem, our personal stories are taken into the metastory of Christ's passion to bless all the nations, which of course includes ourselves.

II. Rome: A Passion for the Gospel of God

Some manuscripts of Romans 15:29 include the words "the fullness of the blessing *of the gospel* of Christ" (KJV). But even if the phrase "of the gospel" was not present in the original document, there is no doubt that the letter to the Romans from beginning to end is a gospel document. Paul claims in the introduction to be "set apart for the gospel *(euangelion)* of God" (1:1). The English word "gospel" is related to the old English "godspel," which means a good tale (hence, good news). Similarly, the Greek word for "blessing" *(eulogia)* in our text of 15:29 simply means "good word." We can say, therefore, that to have the blessing of Christ is to have Christ speak a good and gracious word to us. This Christ does supremely well, not least through the special medium of Paul's letter to the Romans.

Probably Paul has several things in mind in writing this letter. But one thing we know: in writing this letter he has explained "the gospel of God," especially as it relates to Jews and Gentiles in Christ together. We also know that for him the message of the gospel is no mere academic matter. It is head, heart, and hand. Paul has been apprehended by Christ. He has been justified by the grace of Christ, thereby released to serve God voluntarily and passionately in a way he never did, nor could, as a law-keeper. The full blessing of Christ is the inworking and outworking of this glorious gospel of justification: it is the inscape and outscape of a person undergoing transformation (2 Cor 3:18; Rom 6:4).

Justification is that act of God whereby sinners (both religious and irreligious), though deserving of God's wrath, are offered full pardon, acceptance, adoption into God's family, and power in the Holy Spirit to live a new life. We have this solely and simply on the grounds of the death of Jesus and obtain this through faith in Jesus Christ and not on grounds of worth or achievement (Rom 4:3, 9, 22-23; Gal 3:6; Jas 2:23). Through God's gospel, Paul (and all other gospeled people) experience a *double exchange:* our sin is placed on Christ and dealt with finally on the cross; Christ's righteousness is imputed to the believer (2 Cor 5:21). In this the "righteousness of God is revealed, a righteousness that is by faith from first to last" (Rom 1:17). In this matter Jews and Gentiles are on the same footing — both the circumcised and the uncircumcised.

Justification gives freedom from guilt and self-criticism, acceptance with God and power to live a new life. Luther said the doctrine of justification is the doctrine of a standing or falling church. Where it is preached people are liberated, grow, and thrive; where it is not preached there is self-doubt, depression, guilt, and the impossible burden of religious obligation. Paul never tired of preaching and expounding this gospel because it is "the blessing of Christ." He felt obligated both to Greeks and non-Greeks, both to the wise and foolish.

"That is why," he says, "I am eager to preach the gospel also to you who are at Rome" (1:15). Rome is the established church, but the established church also needs the gospel of God.

Have we got beyond the gospel? No longer preach it? Hardly believe it? Have we been reduced to a religion of performance and spiritual workaholism in church and college? Right passion is not "worked up" by religious enthusiasm or ecclesiastical activism; it is inspired — more like an artesian well than a fence. We are inundated as we hear and do the gospel. Luther described the qualifications of a theologian this way: "living, or rather dying and being damned, make a theologian, not understanding, reading or speculating." By following in the footsteps of the Master, undergoing the torment of the cross, of death and hell, true theology and the knowledge of God come about.

The Roman believers and all Paul's readers need this God-speech and the spiritual discipline it implies. But because of the revelatory word embodied in the gospel, Paul must go to Spain — the church yet to be born.

III. Spain: A Passion for the Mission of God

Reaching out to Spain, the "backwaters" of the Roman Empire, was a holy passion for Paul. "It has always been my ambition to preach the gospel where Christ was not known" (15:20). Spain was one of the last frontiers. But "the need is the call" is not Paul's motivation. This spiritual heresy drives multitudes of believers to fill every vacancy, and thereby to reduce God's will to simply seeking the "open doors." Not so for Paul; for him it was a mission passion born not in circumstances but in the heart of God.

Theologically, mission is not a human activity undertaken out of obligation to the great commission, or even simple gratitude. It is God's own going forth. Centuries ago, reflecting on the Trinity, Augustine said that God is Lover, Beloved, and Love itself. But there is more. God is Sender, Sent, and Sending. Thus in the High Priestly prayer Jesus prayed, "As you sent me into the world, I have sent them into the world" (Jn 17:18; cf. 20:21). Mission is our inclusion into the ecstatic life of God — the outgoingness of God, the passion of God to bless the world. The church does not *have* a mission, as one of its many activities to which specially called and unusually gifted people dedicate themselves, and in which special interest groups support those who become involved in mission as their proxies. The church *is* mission. It exists in the sending of God, of our ecstatic God. The whole *laos* of God is missionary. If we are not "beside ourselves" in mission we are not being truly ourselves. The church exists in mission as fire exists in burning, by reaching new fuel. The God who is Lover, Beloved, and Love cannot keep to himself. God is Sender, Sent, and Sending. So too are the people of God.

Paul was not motivated by the need of the Gentile world; he was motivated by a "heavenly vision" (Acts 26:19). Thus, when Paul speaks of his mission to the Gentiles, of which Spain is symbolic, he uses the language of worship. Paul is a *leitourgos* (15:16; cf. Heb 8:2), a sanctuary minister. But his sanctuary was a Roman boat, a Philippian jail, the Ephesian Hall of Tyrannus, a Thessalonian home, and (possibly) one of the Spanish synagogues. Paul's proclamation of the gospel is a priestly duty, a *hierourgounta* (15:16). Paul serves the gospel as a priest ministering the things of God and building a bridge between God and humankind. But far from being a sacerdotal minister, Paul engages in his priestly duties with jeans on, working night and day with his tent-making awl. Finally, Paul speaks of his Gentile converts as an offering *(prosphora)* acceptable to God sanctified by the Holy Spirit (15:16). What he offers to God is not a sacrificial lamb or even religious bread but the *people* in their down-to-earthness, people he has loved into the Kingdom through the gospel.

Years ago George MacLeod of the Iona Community wrote:

> I simply argue that the cross be raised again at the center of the market place as well as on the steeple of the church. I am recovering the claim that Jesus was not crucified in a cathedral between two candles, but on a cross between two thieves; on the town garbage heap; on a cross-roads so cosmopolitan that they had to write his title in Hebrew and Latin and in Greek . . . ; at the kind of place where cynics talk smut, and thieves curse, and soldiers gamble. Because that is where he died and that is what he died about. And that is where churchmen should be and what churchmen should be about.[1]

In the same way Paul says in Romans 12:1 that our priestly and spiritual service is the offering of our bodily lives to God. Priesthood is not now a matter of sanctuary, sacerdotalism, and sacrifice but of serving God and God's purposes in the nitty-gritty everydayness of life in the world, not a matter of sacred times and sacred places but ordinary time and ordinary places, not now a matter of designated and ordained missioners but the whole people of God — which is God's missionary people seeded and folded into the world as seed and yeast. Every church of two hundred members has two hundred missionaries penetrating neighborhoods, offices, factories, workshops, and schools, into all the powers and places, seven days a week.

Of course, this way of speaking of mission as worship is not new. In fact, it is sometimes noted that the glory of God is the prime motive of mission. Therefore, so it is argued, mission is an act of worship, a way of honoring and

1. George MacLeod, *Only One Way Left: Church Prospect* (Glasgow: The Iona Community, 1956), p. 38.

giving worth to God. But there is more to it than that. Mission is worship precisely because it is God's own out-working, out-living, out-loving. Mission is worship because God is beside himself, so to speak. Evidence of God at work is not Paul's own deeds but the signs and miracles through the power of the Spirit (15:19). It is God's work from first to last.

Spain symbolizes a passion for the mission of God. One cannot have the "full blessing of Christ" without sharing Christ's determination to bless all the nations. For that reason, as Jonah discovered, the first mission of God is to reach the heart of the missionary so that God's servant will know the wideness of God's mercy. And, as Jonah discovered, God plunges us into the world through our daily work and our multiplexed service not only to "reach the lost" but so that we also will be missionized by God in the context of the very people we are sent to missionize.

Why then must Paul go to Jerusalem? And why this diversion from the crucial work of planting self-propagating, self-supporting churches everywhere, especially in the unreached West? Why Jerusalem — the church of Paul's Jewish roots?

IV. Jerusalem: A Passion for the Unity of the People of God

I am struck by the fact that Paul's prayer in 15:31 that he be delivered from the unbelievers in Judea seems to have been answered negatively. When he arrived in Jerusalem a riot ensued. They arrested him. When a plot on his life was discovered they shipped him to another prison, and when he finally arrived in Rome, after appealing to Caesar, he did so in chains. Not surprisingly there are those who have insisted that Paul was out of the will of God in spending so much effort in raising relief funds among the Gentile churches (1 Cor 16:1-4; 2 Cor 8-9; 12:14-18) and taking these funds personally to the financially strapped saints in Jerusalem.

Even his own friends and companions questioned his motives. When Paul arrived at Tyre, Luke and the other disciples . . . urged Paul "through the Spirit" not to go to Jerusalem (Acts 21:4). At Caesarea a prophet named Agabus came from Judea, tied Paul's hands and feet with Paul's belt, and said, "The Holy Spirit says, 'In this way the Jews of Jerusalem will bind the owner of this belt and will hand him over to the Gentiles'" (21:10-11). Paul's companions pleaded with him not to go but in the end sighed, "The Lord's will be done" (which is exactly what Paul thought he was doing). Upon arrival in Jerusalem Paul agreed to accommodate the Jews by undergoing a purification rite which inadvertently led to a riot, Paul's arrest, a lengthy imprisonment in Caesarea, and his ultimate arrival in Rome as a prisoner of Rome *and* Christ.

So we ask, Did Paul *really* come to Rome in the full measure of the blessing of Christ?

When making his travel plans for going to Rome Paul prayerfully submitted his aspirations to "God's will" (15:32), not wishing to force a matter in which he had received no revelatory word. But in the matter of going to Jerusalem Paul does not use the language of "if it is the Lord's will." Was he sincerely wrong? Can we do the right thing for wrong motives, or the wrong thing with right motives, and still obtain the blessing of God? Was that the case with Paul? But there is another perspective on the story.

Paul did have in the earliest days of his apostleship an apostolic command to remember the poor (Gal 2:10). Paul must have seen this as a glorious opportunity to embody his mission of unity. As has often been noted, the single most important theme in Romans is the equality and unity of Jews and Gentiles. For Paul the gospel is inclusive. Receiving the gospel led to a God-initiated miracle — the new humanity of God (Eph 2:15) in which Jews do not become Gentiles, or Gentiles become Jews; rather, both get incorporated into a rich diverse unity that is enriched by the contribution of each. Jews and Gentiles are interdependent. This is the mystery of God's purposes that inspires the longest doxology in Romans (11:33-36). The same point is made in the heart of the passage under consideration: If "the Gentiles have shared in the Jews' spiritual blessings, they owe it to the Jews to share with them their material blessings" (Rom 15:27). It is only after Paul "has completed this task" that he is sure he will come to Rome "in the full blessing of Christ" (15:29).

Wherever Paul went he built a bridge of unity between Jews and Gentiles, symbolized by this love-gift. Indeed, it is not too much to say that this bridge-building dominated Paul's sense of mission. He was an ecumenical missionary. Unity is not the means to the end, the precondition for God's people getting God's work done on earth. Unity *is* the end. It is the goal (cf. Eph 4:11-16) since God's mission is ultimately to build community on earth under the headship of Christ. That glorious unifying mission will be completed when Christ comes again through the final reunification and transfiguration of all creation and "makes all things new" (Rev 21:5). The filling (Rom 15:13) for which Paul prays is not an individual "fill-fulment," but joy, peace, and hope in the Holy Spirit (15:13) experienced *together.* The "all things" to be given to God (according to the doxology of 11:36) surely includes the unity of Jews and Gentiles — and all kinds of formerly alienated peoples — in Christ together: rich and poor, people of various skin colors, the religious and nonreligious, the Third World Christian and the First World Christian.

Yes, some prophets warned Paul "in the Spirit." But the Spirit graciously warned Paul once more to count the cost (cf. Acts 20:23). To his apprehensive friends Paul countered, "I am ready not only to be bound, but also to die in Jerusalem for the name of the Lord Jesus" (21:13). He was shuffled from prison to prison but never confesses, "I was out of the will of God in going to Jerusalem." In a sense, his prayer that he may be rescued from the unbelievers in Judea (Rom 15:31) was answered positively. He was three times rescued from lynching (Acts 21:30ff.; 22:22ff.; 23:10), once from flogging (22:25ff.), and once from a plot to kill him (23:12ff.). So we need not doubt Paul's motives, the Spirit's leading, or God's protection.

If Rome represents *one faith* and Spain represents *one mission,* Jerusalem stands for the *one people.* If the gospel is God-speech, the mission is God-work and the people of God is God-life. Unity in the church, like unity in the One God, is not fusion, merging, and homogeneity. It is not "mashed potato" unity. Rather it is Trinitarian unity: communion without union, dependence without codependence, unity without uniformity. The fourth-century Cappadocian fathers called this "perichoretic" unity, a term which suggests interpenetration, dwelling in one another, without losing identity or personhood.

It is because of "the blessing of Christ" that Paul must make the long journey to Jerusalem; and it because of the same "blessing" that we must journey to our neighbor and be ecumenical missionaries. We can only be in Christ together. The Bible knows nothing of solitary religion, nothing of denominational isolationism, nothing of monocultural Christianity, nothing of mashed potato unity.

All too often cross-cultural work is a one-way street — serving, saving, and giving. We go (wrongly) into the world as patrons. In our missionary strategy there is all too often little of Paul's vision of "equality" (2 Cor 8:14) applied to relations between the developing world and the first world. Little grasp of the truth that the "sending" church is also a receiving church, that the rich cannot be saved without the poor, or Gentiles without Jews. There is meager appreciation for the fact that the missionary should also be missionized, little appreciation for the celebration of diversity in Paul's 1 Corinthians 12. Instead we are urged to "grow" churches in fast-track ways so as to become one ethnic entity, one economic group, and thus pride ourselves on quantitative growth — a growth that is not by biblical standards growth at all (Eph 4:1-16)! Instead, such settings can easily become a "you-all" club, where Christ is hardly confessed since they would gather anyway. In such settings, where is the "blessing"?

We must ask, therefore: What is it really like to have the full blessing of Christ? It is to be constantly evangelized by the *euangelion* of God (that is precisely why Paul wrote to Rome). It is to be included in the mission of God, so giving ourselves away in service of the world (that is why Paul wanted to go to Spain). It is to discover God's perichoretic unity in the fellowship of the most unlikely saints without whom we cannot be truly in Christ (that is why Paul must go to Jerusalem).

And how do we get this orthopathic passion? We are not convinced by arguments about it; no, we are converted to it. This kind of "conversion" happens repeatedly as we hear and do God-speech, God-work, and God-life. So Paul concludes the letter with a prayer that includes the gospel, the missionary proclamation of the gospel, and the mysterious unity of Jews and Gentiles in Christ: "Now to him who is able to establish you by my gospel and the proclamation of Jesus Christ, according to the revelation of the mystery hidden for long ages past . . . so that all nations might believe and obey him — to the only wise God be glory forever through Jesus Christ! Amen" (16:25-27). Whoever truly says "Amen" to that prayer will know the "full blessing of Christ."

Select List of Publications by Gordon D. Fee

I. Books (Authored)

Papyrus Bodmer II (P^{66}): Its Textual Relationships and Scribal Characteristics (Studies and Documents 34; Salt Lake City: University of Utah Press, 1968), 152 pp.

Corinthians: A Study Guide (Brussels: International Correspondence Inst., 1979), 268 pp.

How to Read the Bible for All Its Worth: A Guide to Understanding the Bible, with Douglas Stuart (Grand Rapids: Zondervan, 1982), 232 pp. [Translated into Spanish, French, Portuguese, Polish, Chinese, Korean, Thai, Indonesian, Croatian, Swedish, German, Russian] (Second edition; Grand Rapids: Zondervan, 1993), 265 pp.

New Testament Exegesis: A Handbook for Students and Pastors (Philadelphia: Westminster Press, 1983), 154 pp. [Translated into Spanish, Korean] (Second, revised edition; Louisville: Westminster/John Knox Press, 1993), 194 pp.

1 and 2 Timothy and Titus: A Good News Commentary (San Francisco: Harper & Row, 1984), 262 pp.

1 and 2 Timothy, Titus (New International Biblical Commentary; Peabody, MA: Hendrickson Publishers, 1988), 332 pp. [a revised edition set to the NIV].

Commentary on the First Epistle to the Corinthians (New International Commentary on the NT; Grand Rapids: Eerdmans, 1987), 880 pp. [translated into Spanish; Eerdmans, 1994].

Gospel and Spirit: Issues in New Testament Hermeneutics (Peabody, MA: Hendrickson, 1991), 143 pp.
The Text of the Fourth Gospel in the Writings of Origen, with Bart D. Ehrman and Michael Holmes (NTGF 3; Atlanta: Scholars, 1992), 499 pp.
Studies in the Theory and Method of New Testament Textual Criticism, with Eldon J. Epp (Studies and Documents 45: Grand Rapids: Eerdmans, 1993), 414 pp.
God's Empowering Presence: The Holy Spirit in the Letters of Paul (Peabody, MA: Hendrickson, 1994), 967 pp.
Paul's Letter to the Philippians (New International Commentary on the NT; Grand Rapids: Eerdmans, 1995), 528 pp.
Paul, the Spirit, and the People of God (Peabody: Hendrickson, 1996), 208 pp.

II. Books (Edited)

New Testament Textual Criticism: Its Significance for Exegesis: Essays in Honour of Bruce M. Metzger (Oxford University Press, 1981), 444 pp. (with Eldon J. Epp)

Series: The New Testament in the Greek Fathers

1. Bart D. Ehrman, *Didymus the Blind and the Text of the Gospels* (Atlanta: Scholars Press, 1986), 288 pp.
2. James A. Brooks, *The New Testament Text of Gregory of Nyssa* (Atlanta: Scholars Press, 1991), 267 pp.

Series: The New International Commentary on the New Testament

1. Douglas Moo, *The Epistle to the Romans* (Grand Rapids: Eerdmans, 1996), 1012 pp.
2. Paul Barnett, *The Second Epistle to the Corinthians* (1997), 662 pp.
3. Joel B. Green, *The Gospel of Luke* (1997), 928 pp.
4. Robert H. Mounce, *The Book of Revelation* (rev. ed., 1997), 439 pp.

III. Journal Articles

"Corrections of Papyrus Bodmer II and the Nestle Greek Testament," *Journal of Biblical Literature* 84 (1965) 66-72.

"The Corrections of Papyrus Bodmer II and Early Textual Transmission," *Novum Testamentum* 7 (1965) 247-57.

"Codex Sinaiticus in the Gospel of John: A Contribution to Methodology in Establishing Textual Relationships," *New Testament Studies* 15 (1968/69) 23-44.

"The Text of John in *The Jerusalem Bible:* A Critique of the Use of Patristic Citations in New Testament Textual Criticism," *Journal of Biblical Literature* 90 (1971) 163-73.

"The Text of John in Origen and Cyril of Alexandria: A Contribution to Methodology in the Recovery and Analysis of Patristic Citations," *Biblica* 52 (1971) 357-94.

"The Use of the Definite Article with Personal Names in the Gospel of John," *New Testament Studies* 17 (1970/71) 168-83.

"Some Dissenting Notes on 7Q5 = Mark 6:52-53," *Journal of Biblical Literature* 92 (1973) 109-12.

"The *Lemma* of Origen's Commentary on John, Book X: An Independent Witness to the Egyptian Textual Tradition?" *New Testament Studies* 20 (1973/74) 78-81.

"II Corinthians vi.14: vii.1 and Food Offered to Idols," *New Testament Studies* 23 (1976/77) 140-61.

"Once More: John 7:37-39," *The Expository Times* 89 (1977/78)116-18.

"Modern Textual Criticism and the Revival of the *Textus Receptus*," *Journal of the Evangelical Theological Society* 21 (1978) 19-34.

"Modern Textual Criticism and the Majority Text: A Rejoinder," *Journal of the Evangelical Theological Society* 21 (1978) 157-60.

"χάρις in II Corinthians i.15: Apostolic Parousia and Paul-Corinth Chronology," *New Testament Studies* 24 (1977/78) 533-38.

"A Critique of W. N. Pickering's *The Identity of the New Testament Text*," *Westminster Theological Journal* 41 (1978/79) 397-423.

"The Majority Text and the Original Text of the New Testament," *The Bible Translator* 31 (1980) 107-18.

"A Text-Critical Look at the Synoptic Problem," *Novum Testamentum* 22 (1980) 12-28.

"εἰδωλόθυτα Once Again: An Interpretation of 1 Corinthians 8–10," *Biblica* 61 (1980) 172-97.

"The Text of John and Mark in the Writings of Chrysostom," *New Testament Studies* 26 (1979/80) 525-47.

"1 Corinthians 7:1 in the NIV," *Journal of the Evangelical Theological Society* 23 (1980) 307-14.
"Tongues: Least of the Gifts? Some Exegetical Observations on 1 Corinthians 12–14," *Pneuma* 2 (1980) 3-14.
"On the Inauthenticity of John 5:3b, 4," *The Evangelical Quarterly* 54 (1982) 207-18.
"Origen's Text of the New Testament and the Text of Egypt," *New Testament Studies* 28 (1982) 348-64.
"Baptism in the Holy Spirit: The Issue of Separability and Subsequence," *Pneuma* 7 (1985) 87-99.
"Reflections on Church Order in the Pastoral Epistles, with Further Reflection on the Hermeneutics of *ad hoc* Documents," *Journal of the Evangelical Theological Society* 28 (1985) 141-51.
"L'organisation de l'Eglise dans les Épîtres pastorales. Quelle herméneutique pour de écrits de circonstance?" *Hokhma* 36 (1987) 1-20 [transl. of previous item].
"John 14:8-17" [an "Expository Article"], *Interpretation* 43 (1989) 170-74.
"Laos and Leadership under the New Covenant," *Crux* 25 (1989)3-13. [Reprinted in *With Heart, Mind, and Strength, The Best of Crux — 1979-1989* (ed. D. M. Lewis; Langley, B.C.: Credo, 1990) 171-92].
"Reflections on Commentary Writing," *Theology Today* 46 (1990) 387-92.
"Issues in Evangelical Hermeneutics: Hermeneutics and the Nature of Scripture," *Crux* 26 (1990) 21-26.
"Women in Ministry: The Meaning of 1 Timothy 2:8-15 in Light of the Purpose of 1 Timothy," *Journal of the Christian Brethren Research Fellowship* 122 (August 1990) 11-18.
"Issues in Evangelical Hermeneutics, Part II: The Crucial Issue: Authorial Intentionality: A Proposal regarding New Testament Imperatives," *Crux* 26/3 (1990) 35-42.
"Issues in Evangelical Hermeneutics, Part III: The Great Watershed: Intentionality and Particularity/Eternality: 1 Timothy 2:8-15 as a Test Case," *Crux* 26/4 (1990) 31-37.
"Issues in Evangelical Hermeneutics, Part IV: Hermeneutics, Exegesis and the Role of Tradition," *Crux* 27/1 (1991) 12-20.
"On Being a Trinitarian Christian," *Crux* 28/2 (1992) 2-5.
"Philippians 2:5-11: Hymn or Exalted Pauline Prose?" *Bulletin for Biblical Research* 2 (1992) 29-46.
"The Bishop and the Bible," *Crux* 29/4 (1993) 34-39.
"Freedom and the Life of Obedience (Galatians 5:1-6:18)," *Review and Expositor* 91/2 (1994) 201-17.
"Toward a Pauline Theology of Glossolalia," *Crux* 31/1 (1995) 22-31.

"Exegesis and Spirituality: Reflections on Completing the Exegetical Circle," *Crux* 31/4 (1995) 29-35.

"*God's Empowering Presence:* A Response to Eduard Schweizer," *Journal of Pentecostal Theology* 8 (1996) 23-30.

"To What End Exegesis? Reflections on Exegesis and Spirituality in Philippians 4:10-20," *Bulletin for Biblical Research* 8 (1998) 75-88.

IV. Articles in Works of Composite Authorship

"P^{75}, P^{66}, and Origen: The Myth of Early Textual Recension in Alexandria," in *New Dimensions in New Testament Study* (ed. R. N. Longenecker and M. C. Tenney; Grand Rapids: Zondervan, 1974) 19-45.

In *The Zondervan Pictorial Encyclopedia of the Bible* (ed. M. C. Tenney; Grand Rapids: Zondervan, 1975):
"Doctrine," II, 151-52;
"Priest in the New Testament," IV, 849-52;
"Self-Righteousness," V, 336-37.

"The Genre of New Testament Literature and Biblical Hermeneutics," in *Interpreting the Word of God,* Festschrift in Honor of Steven Barabas (ed. M. Inch and S. Schultz; Chicago: Moody Press, 1976) 105-27.

"Rigorous or Reasoned Eclecticism: Which?" in *Studies in New Testament Language and Text: Essays in Honour of George D. Kilpatrick on the Occasion of His Sixty-fifth Birthday* (ed. J. K. Elliott; Leiden: Brill, 1976) 174-97.

"Hermeneutics and Historical Precedent: A Major Problem in Pentecostal Hermeneutics," in *Perspectives on the New Pentecostalism* (ed. R. P. Spittler; Grand Rapids: Baker, 1976) 118-32.

"The Textual Criticism of the New Testament," in *Biblical Criticism: Historical, Literary and Textual* (Contemporary Evangelical Perspectives; Grand Rapids: Zondervan, 1978) 127-55; *idem,* "The Textual Criticism of the New Testament," in *The Expositor's Bible Commentary* (ed. F. E. Gaebelein; Grand Rapids: Zondervan, 1979) I.419-33.

"Modern Textual Criticism and the Synoptic Problem," in *J. J. Griesbach: Synoptic and Text-Critical Studies 1776-1976* (ed. B. Orchard and T. R. W. Longstaff; SNTSMS 34; Cambridge: University Press, 1978) 154-69.

"Hermeneutics and Common Sense: An Exploratory Essay on the Hermeneutics of the Epistles," in *Inerrancy and Common Sense* (ed. J. R. Michaels and R. R. Nicole; Grand Rapids: Baker, 1980) 161-86.

"'One Thing is Needful'? Luke 10:42," in *New Testament Textual Criticism, Its Significance for Exegesis: Essays in Honour of Bruce M. Metzger* (ed. E. J. Epp and G. D. Fee; Oxford: University Press, 1981) 61-75.

"New Testament Quotations in Patristic Authors," in *Harper's Bible Dictionary* (ed. P. J. Achtemeier; San Francisco: Harper, 1985) 701-3.

"Pauline Literature," *Dictionary of Pentecostal and Charismatic Movements* (ed. S. M. Burgess and G. B. McGee; Grand Rapids: Zondervan, 1988) 665-83.

"Toward a Theology of 1 Corinthians," *Society of Biblical Literature 1989 Seminar Papers* (ed. David J. Lull; Atlanta: Scholars Press, 1989) 265-281.

"Textual Criticism," in *Encyclopedia of Early Christianity* (ed. Everett Ferguson; New York: Garland Publishing, 1990) 886-87.

"The Kingdom of God and the Church's Global Mission," in *Called and Empowered: Pentecostal Perspectives on Global Mission* (eds. Murray W. Dempster, Byron D. Klaus, and Douglas Petersen; Peabody MA: Hendrickson, 1991) 7-21.

"Textual Criticism," in *Dictionary of Jesus and the Gospels* (eds. J. B. Green, S. McKnight, and I. H. Marshall; Downers Grove: InterVarsity, 1992) 827-31.

"On the Text and Meaning of Jn 20,30-31," in *The Four Gospels 1992: Festschrift Frans Neirynck* (eds. F. Van Segbroeck, C. M. Tuckett, B. Van Belle, and J. Verheyden; Leuven: University Press, 1992) III.2193-2205.

"The Use of Greek Patristic Citations in New Testament Textual Criticism: The State of the Question," in *Aufstieg und Niedergang der römischen Welt* II.26.1 (eds. H. Temporini and W. Haase; Berlin: Walter de Gruyter, 1992) 246-65.

"On Text and Commentary on 1 and 2 Thessalonians," *Society of Biblical Literature 1992 Seminary Papers* (ed. Eugene H. Lovering, Jr.; Atlanta: Scholars Press, 1992) 165-183.

"Some Reflections on Pauline Spirituality," in *Alive to God: Studies in Spirituality Presented to James Houston* (ed. J. I. Packer and Loren Wilkinson; Downers Grove: InterVarsity, 1992) 96-107.

"Textual-Exegetical Observations on 1 Corinthians 1:2, 2:1, and 2:10," in *Scribes and Scripture: New Testament Essays in Honor of J. Harold Greenlee* (ed. David Alan Black; Winona Lake IN: Eisenbrauns, 1992) 1-15.

"Hermeneutics Today: A Prescriptive View," in *The Vision Continues: Essays Marking the Centennial of Gordon-Conwell Theological Seminary* (ed. Garth M. Rosell; South Hamilton, MA: Gordon-Conwell, 1992) 115-27.

"Gifts of the Spirit," in *Dictionary of Paul and His Letters* (ed. G. F. Hawthorne, R. P. Martin, and D. Reid; Downers Grove: InterVarsity, 1993) 339-47.

"Toward a Theology of 1 Corinthians," in *Pauline Theology, Volume II, 1 & 2 Corinthians* (ed. D. M. Hay; Minneapolis: Fortress, 1993) 37-58.

"Some Exegetical and Theological Reflections on Ephesians 4.30 and Pauline Pneumatology," in *Spirit and Renewal: Essays in Honor of J. Rodman Williams* (JPTS 5; Sheffield: Academic Press, 1994) 129-44.

"Christology and Pneumatology in Romans 8:9-11 and Elsewhere: Some Reflections on Paul as a Trinitarian," in *Jesus of Nazareth, Lord and Christ: Essays on the Historical Jesus and New Testament Christology* (I. H. Marshall *Festschrift;* ed. J. B. Green and M. Turner; Grand Rapids: Eerdmans, 1994) 312-31.

"*Pneuma* and Eschatology in 2 Thessalonians 2.1-2: A Proposal about 'Testing the Prophets' and the Purpose of 2 Thessalonians," in *To Tell the Mystery: Essays on New Testament Eschatology in Honor of Robert H. Gundry* (ed. T. E. Schmidt and M. Silva; JSNTSS 100; Sheffield: JSOT Press, 1994) 196-215.

"'Another Gospel Which You did not Embrace': 2 Corinthians 11.4 and the Theology of 1 and 2 Corinthians," in *Gospel in Paul: Studies on Corinthians, Galatians and Romans for Richard Longenecker* (ed. L. Ann Jervis and Peter Richardson; JSNTSS 108; Sheffield: Academic Press, 1994) 111-33.

"The Use of the Greek Fathers for New Testament Textual Criticism," in *The Text of the New Testament in Contemporary Research: Essays on the* Status Quaestionis. *A Volume in Honor of Bruce M. Metzger* (ed. Bart D. Ehrman and Michael W. Holmes; SD 46; Grand Rapids: Eerdmans, 1995) 191-207.

"History as Context for Interpretation," in *The Act of Bible Reading* (ed. Elmer Dyck; Downers Grove: InterVarsity Press, 1996) 10-32.

"Toward a Pauline Theology of Glossolalia," in *Pentecostalism in Context: Essays in Honor of William W. Menzies* (ed. Wonsuk Ma and Robert P. Menzies; JPTS 11; Sheffield Academic Press, 1997) 24-37.

"Paul's Conversion as Key to His Understanding of the Spirit," in *The Road from Damascus: The Impact of Paul's Conversion on His Life, Thought, and Ministry* (ed. Richard N. Longenecker; Grand Rapids: Eerdmans, 1997) 166-83.

"Toward a Theology of 2 Timothy: From a Pauline Perspective," in *Society of Biblical Literature 1997 Seminar Papers* (Atlanta: Scholars Press, 1997) 732-49.

V. Other Articles and Pamphlets

"A Plea for Accuracy," *Pulpit* (July, 1961) 3-5.

"The Place of Negative Preaching," *Pulpit* (September, 1961) 8-10.

"Worldliness, A Word Study," *Pulpit* (January, 1962) 11-13.

"The Cross in Christian Experience," *The Pentecostal Evangel* (April 15, 1962) 4-5; repr. October 21, 1979, pp. 14-15.

"The Christian Doctrine of the Body," *Pulpit* (July, 1962) 4-6.

"The Text of the New Testament and Modern Translations," *Christianity Today* 17 (June 22, 1973) 6-11.

"The Way God Handles Rebels," *Advance* (October, 1974), 12-13; repr. as "The Content of Revelation," *Insight* 23 (Fall, 1976) 2-4.

"Critical Loyalty: An Essay," *Agora* (Fall, 1977) 10-11.

"Some Reflections on a Current Disease, Part I: The Cult of Prosperity," *Agora* 2:4 (1979) 12-16.

"The 'Gospel' of Prosperity: An Alien Gospel," *The Pentecostal Evangel* (June 24, 1979) 4-8.

"Some Reflections on a Current Disease, Part 2: The 'Gospel of Perfect Health," *Agora* 3:1/2 (1979) 12-18.

The Disease of the Wealth and Health Gospels (Costa Mesa, CA: God's Word for Today, 1980), 22 pp. [repr. Beverly, MA: Frontline Publishing, 1985; Regent College, 1996].

"The New Testament View of Wealth and Possessions," *New Oxford Review* 48 (May, 1981) 8-11.

"Criticism and Faith: An Enduring Tension," *Catalyst* 9:4 (April, 1983) 1-3.

"Current Trends in New Testament Studies," *Christianity Today* 27 (September 16, 1983) 52.

Images of the Church (Messiah College Occasional Papers 8; Grantham, PA: Messiah College, 1984), 29 pp.

"How to Make Sense Out of the Bible," *Equipping the Saints* 3/1 (1989) 7-11.

"The Myth of Ordination," *On Being (the Servant's Servant)* 19 (7 August 1992) 4-9 [condensed version of chap. 8 of *Gospel and Spirit*].

"Response to Roger Stronstad's 'The Biblical Precedent for Historical Precedent,'" *Paraclete* 27/3 (1993) 11-14.

"Testing the Prophets: A Pauline View," *Streams of Shiloh* 1/4 (1994) 235-39.

Anden och Ordet: förhållandet mellan spiritualitet och exegetik (Örebro Missionsskolas Skriftserie Nr 11; Örebro Missionskola, 1995), 25 pp.

11858343R0019

Made in the USA
Lexington, KY
05 November 2011